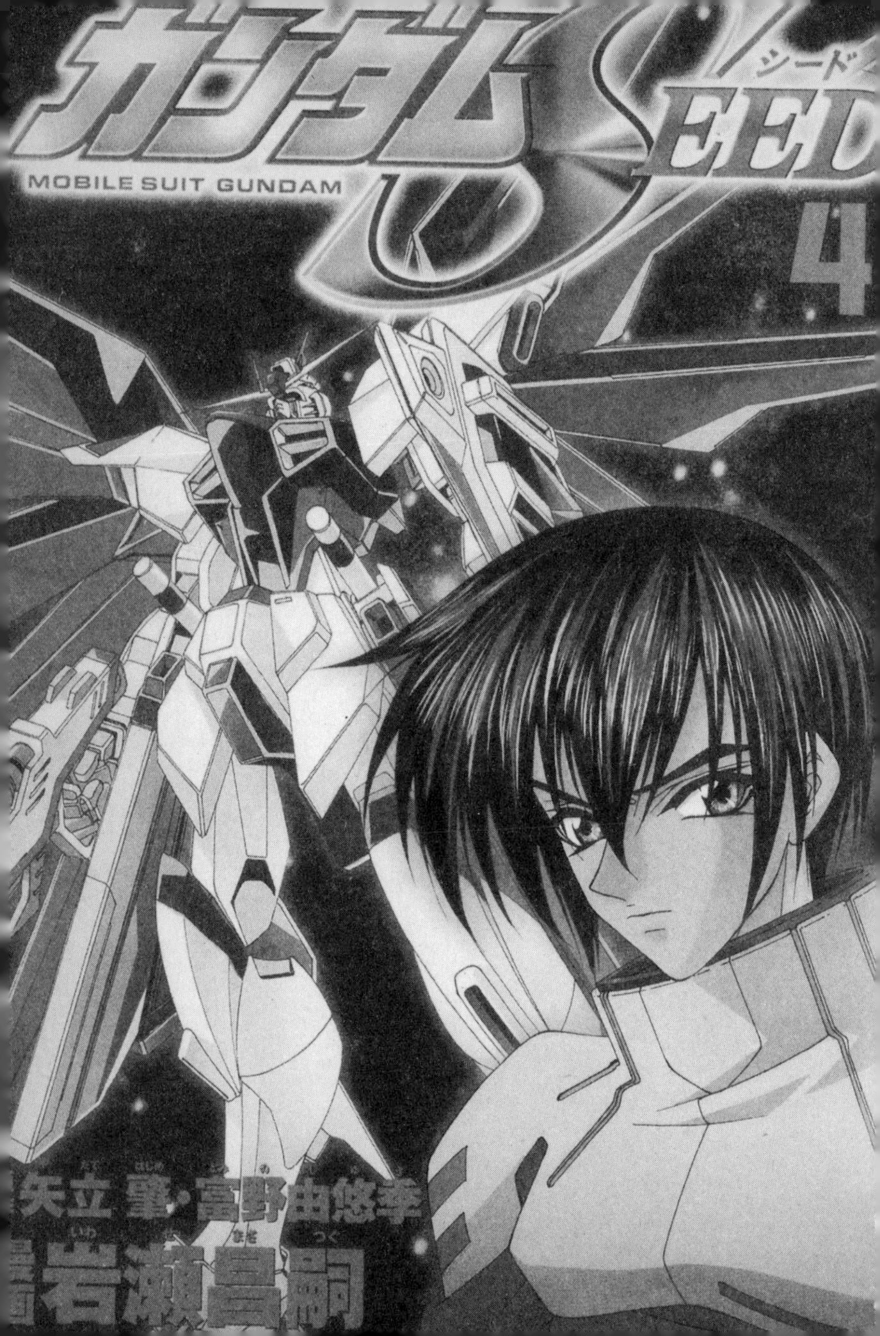
ガンダム
シード
SEED
MOBILE SUIT GUNDAM
4
矢立肇・富野由悠季
岩瀬昌嗣

MOBILE SUIT GUNDAM SEED

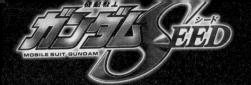

# THE STORY SO FAR

THE CREW OF THE ARCHANGEL MAKES A CRASH LANDING INTO AFRICA'S LIBYAN DESERT—ZAFT TERRITORY. THERE THEY ENCOUNTER GENERAL WALTFIELD, ALSO KNOWN AS THE "DESERT TIGER." THE ARCHANGEL CREW JOINS FORCES WITH THE LOCAL RESISTANCE TO DEFEAT THE "DESERT TIGER" AND HIS ARMY. THE ARCHANGEL THEN HEADS TOWARD THE INDIAN OCEAN, BUT THEY ARE ATTACKED ALONG THE WAY BY ZAFT'S UNDERWATER FLEET. DURING THE BATTLE, CAGALLI GOES MISSING AND ENDS UP STRANDED ON A DESERTED ISLAND. THERE SHE FINDS ATHRUN, WHOSE SHIP WAS ALSO SHOT DOWN. ALTHOUGH ATHRUN AND CAGALLI ARE ENEMIES, THEY DEVELOP A BOND BEFORE THEY EACH GO THEIR SEPARATE WAYS. THE ARCHANGEL, AFTER FACING A FIERCE ATTACK FROM ATHRUN'S ARMY, MANAGES TO REACH AUBE TERRITORY. KIRA AGREES TO HELP THE MORGENROETE CORPORATION DEVELOP ITS NEW TECHNOLOGY IN EXCHANGE FOR REPAIRING THE ARCHANGEL AND PROVIDING SUPPLIES.

AT MORGENROETE, KIRA UNEXPECTEDLY RUNS INTO ATHRUN, WHO IS GATHERING RESEARCH UNDERCOVER. KIRA AND ATHRUN SHARE AN AWKWARD MOMENT, BUT REVEAL THE STRONG FEELINGS OF FRIENDSHIP THEY HAVE FOR ONE ANOTHER. AFTER REPAIRS ARE MADE, THE ARCHANGEL HEADS FOR ALASKA WHERE IT IS AMBUSHED BY ATHRUN'S ARMY. A BITTER BATTLE ENSUES. TOLLE IS SHOT DOWN WHILE TRYING TO PROTECT KIRA, AND NICOL IS KILLED WHILE DEFENDING ATHRUN. KIRA AND ATHRUN, BOTH OVERCOME WITH SADNESS, ENGAGE IN A FIERCE ONE-ON-ONE BATTLE. ATHRUN ATTACHES GUNDAM AEGIS TO KIRA'S GUNDAM UNIT AND PROGRAMS AEGIS TO SELF-DESTRUCT. ATHRUN ABANDONS SHIP AS GUNDAM STRIKE EXPLODES IN A BALL OF FIRE. DID KIRA SURVIVE?

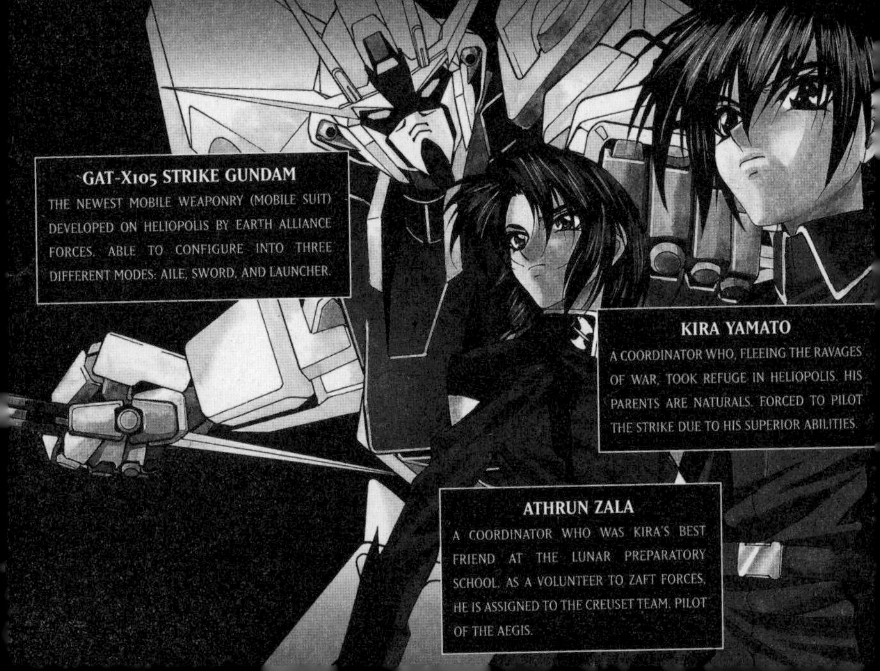

**GAT-X105 STRIKE GUNDAM**

THE NEWEST MOBILE WEAPONRY (MOBILE SUIT) DEVELOPED ON HELIOPOLIS BY EARTH ALLIANCE FORCES. ABLE TO CONFIGURE INTO THREE DIFFERENT MODES: AILE, SWORD, AND LAUNCHER.

**KIRA YAMATO**

A COORDINATOR WHO, FLEEING THE RAVAGES OF WAR, TOOK REFUGE IN HELIOPOLIS. HIS PARENTS ARE NATURALS. FORCED TO PILOT THE STRIKE DUE TO HIS SUPERIOR ABILITIES.

**ATHRUN ZALA**

A COORDINATOR WHO WAS KIRA'S BEST FRIEND AT THE LUNAR PREPARATORY SCHOOL. AS A VOLUNTEER TO ZAFT FORCES, HE IS ASSIGNED TO THE CREUSET TEAM, PILOT OF THE AEGIS.

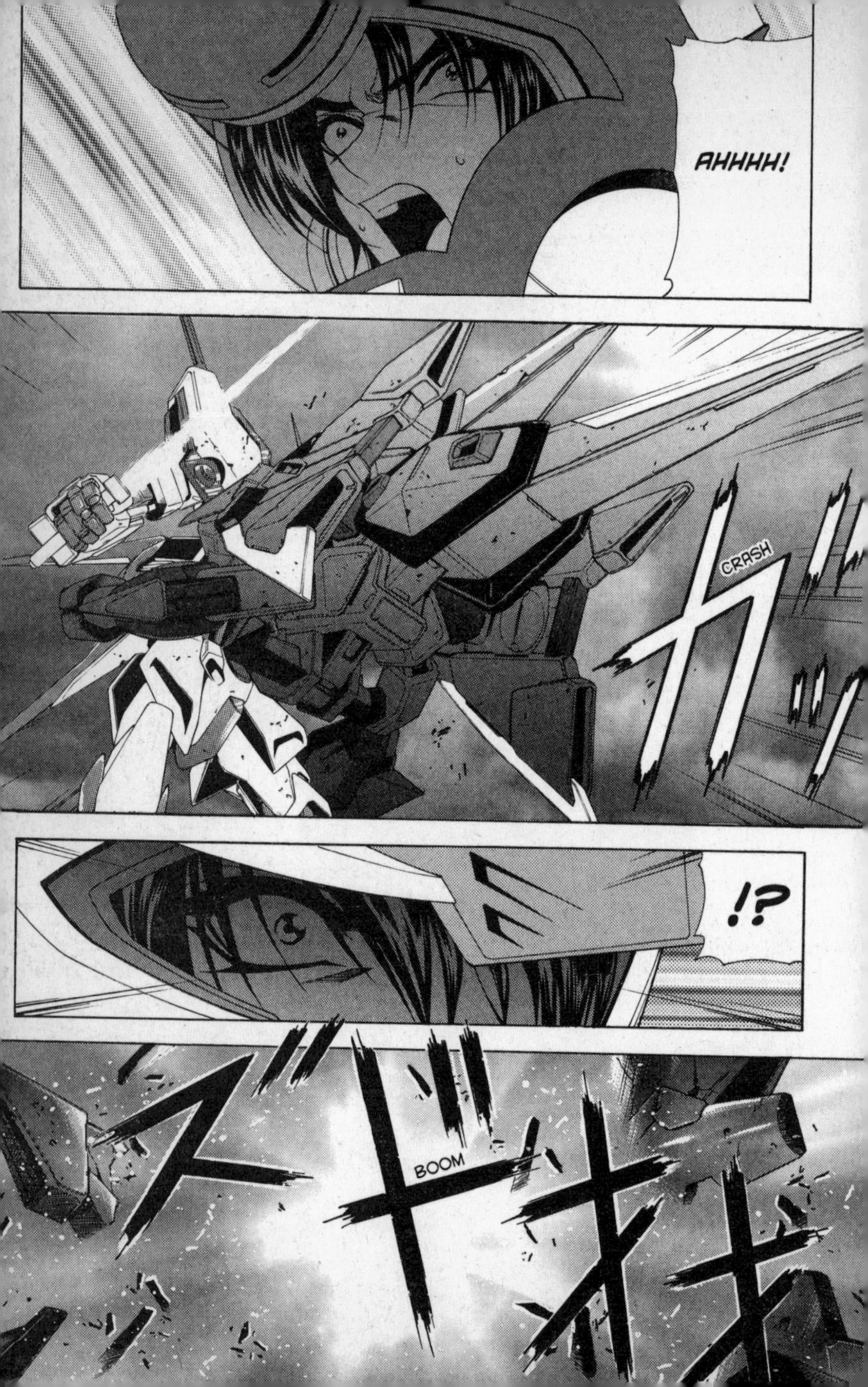
AHHHH!
CRASH
!?
BOOM

# PHASE-16 THE WAILING SKY

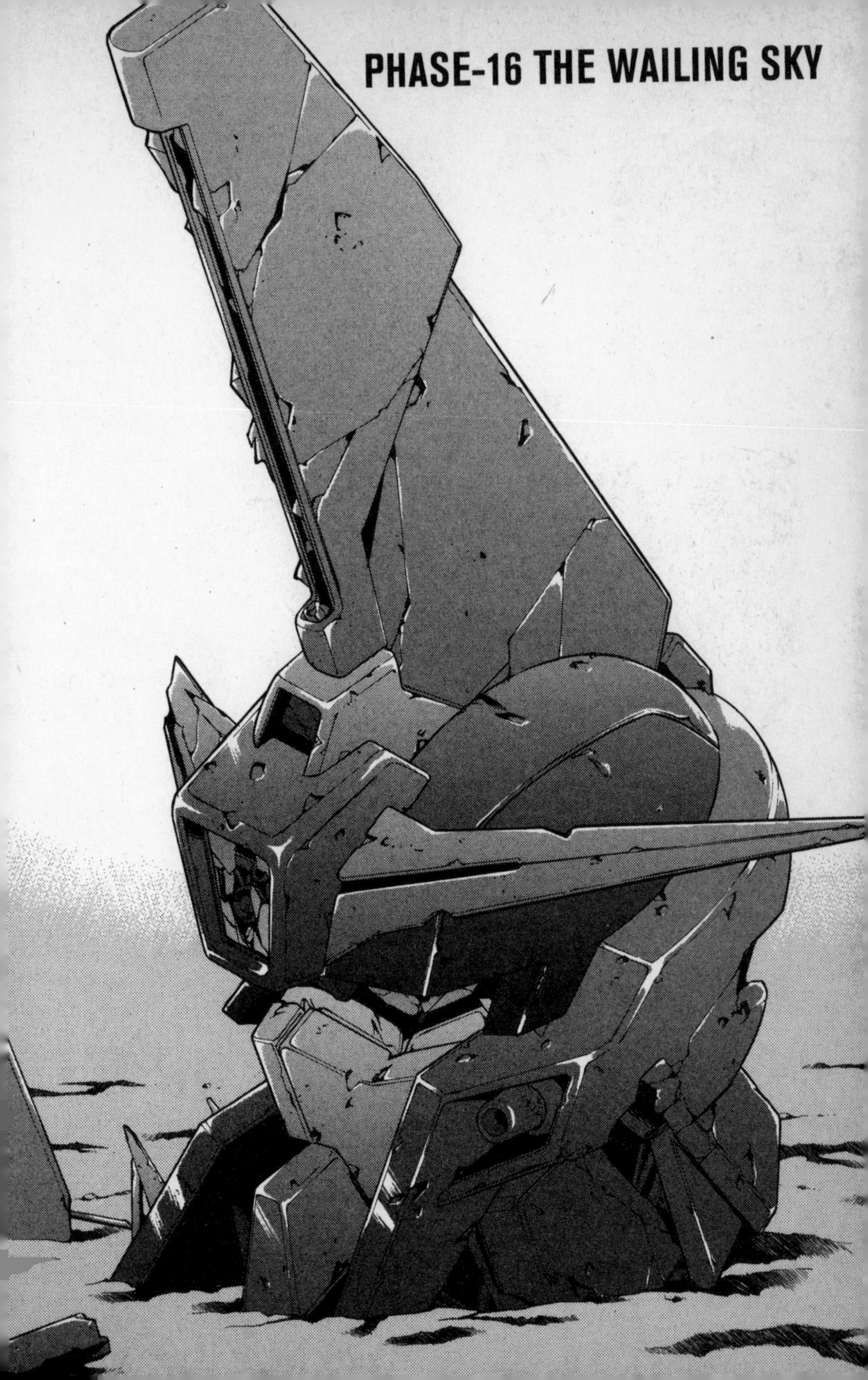

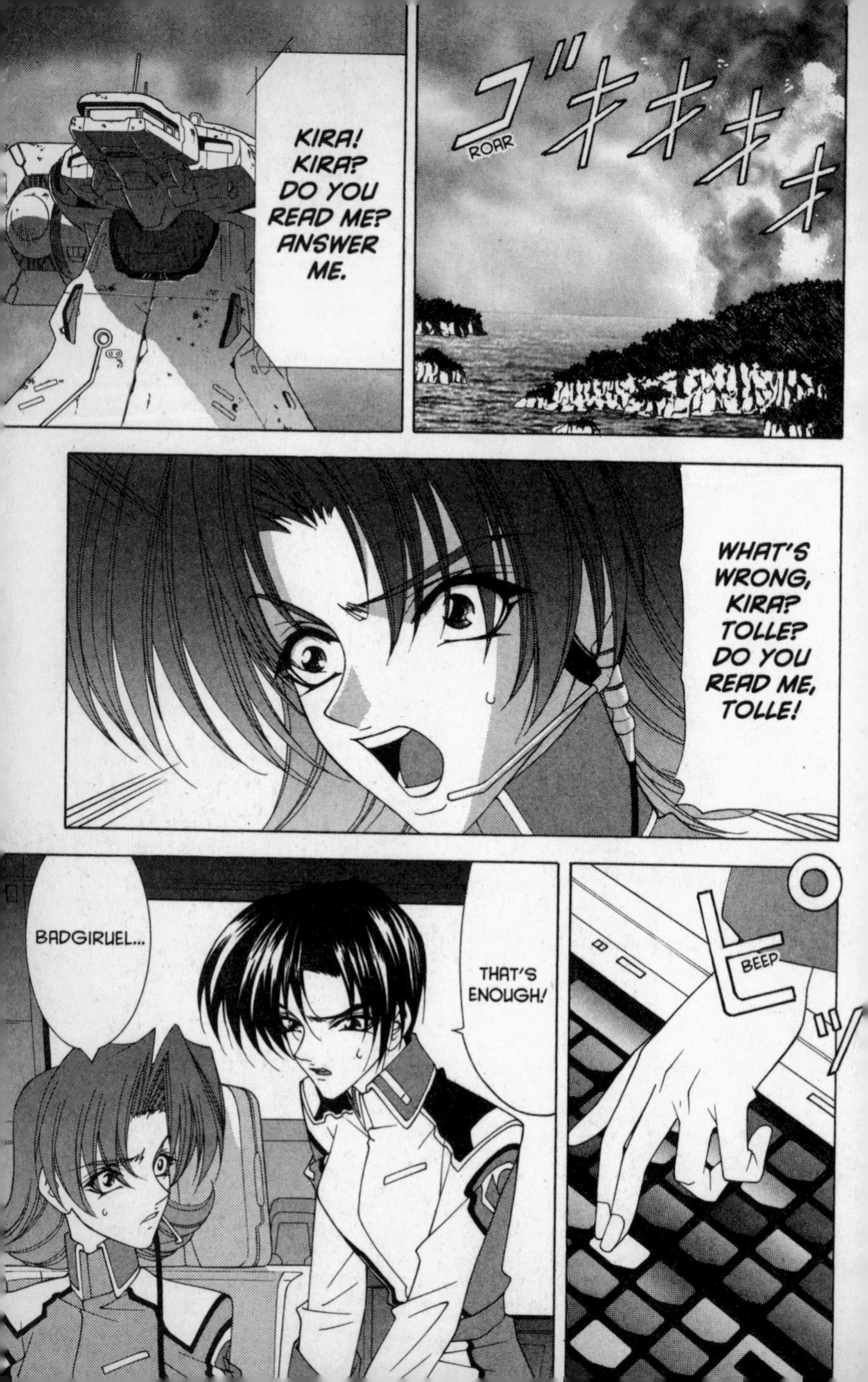
ゴオオオオ
ROAR
KIRA! KIRA? DO YOU READ ME? ANSWER ME.
WHAT'S WRONG, KIRA? TOLLE? DO YOU READ ME, TOLLE!
ピッ
BEEP
THAT'S ENOUGH!
BADGIRUEL...

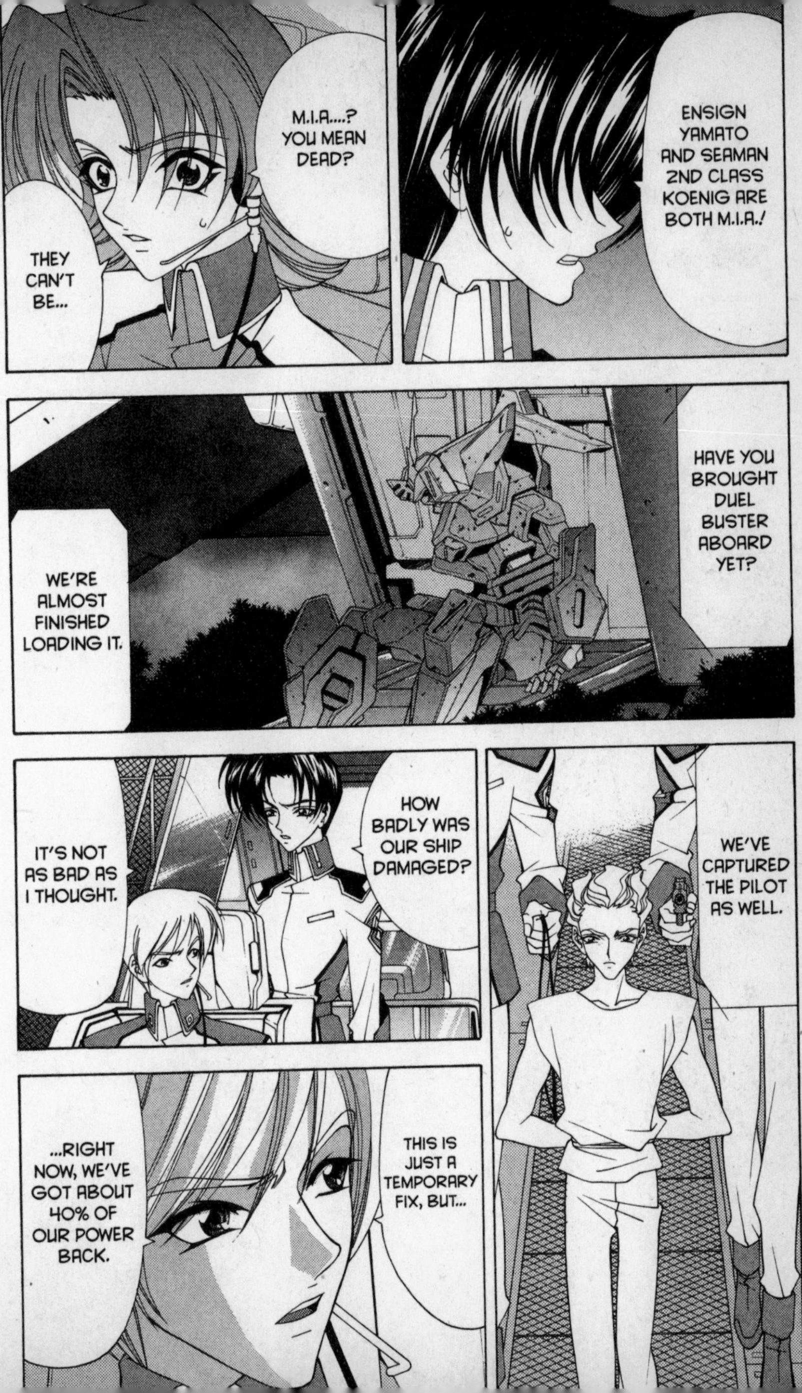
ENSIGN YAMATO AND SEAMAN 2ND CLASS KOENIG ARE BOTH M.I.A.!
M.I.A....? YOU MEAN DEAD?
THEY CAN'T BE...
HAVE YOU BROUGHT DUEL BUSTER ABOARD YET?
WE'RE ALMOST FINISHED LOADING IT.
WE'VE CAPTURED THE PILOT AS WELL.
HOW BADLY WAS OUR SHIP DAMAGED?
IT'S NOT AS BAD AS I THOUGHT.
THIS IS JUST A TEMPORARY FIX, BUT...
...RIGHT NOW, WE'VE GOT ABOUT 40% OF OUR POWER BACK.

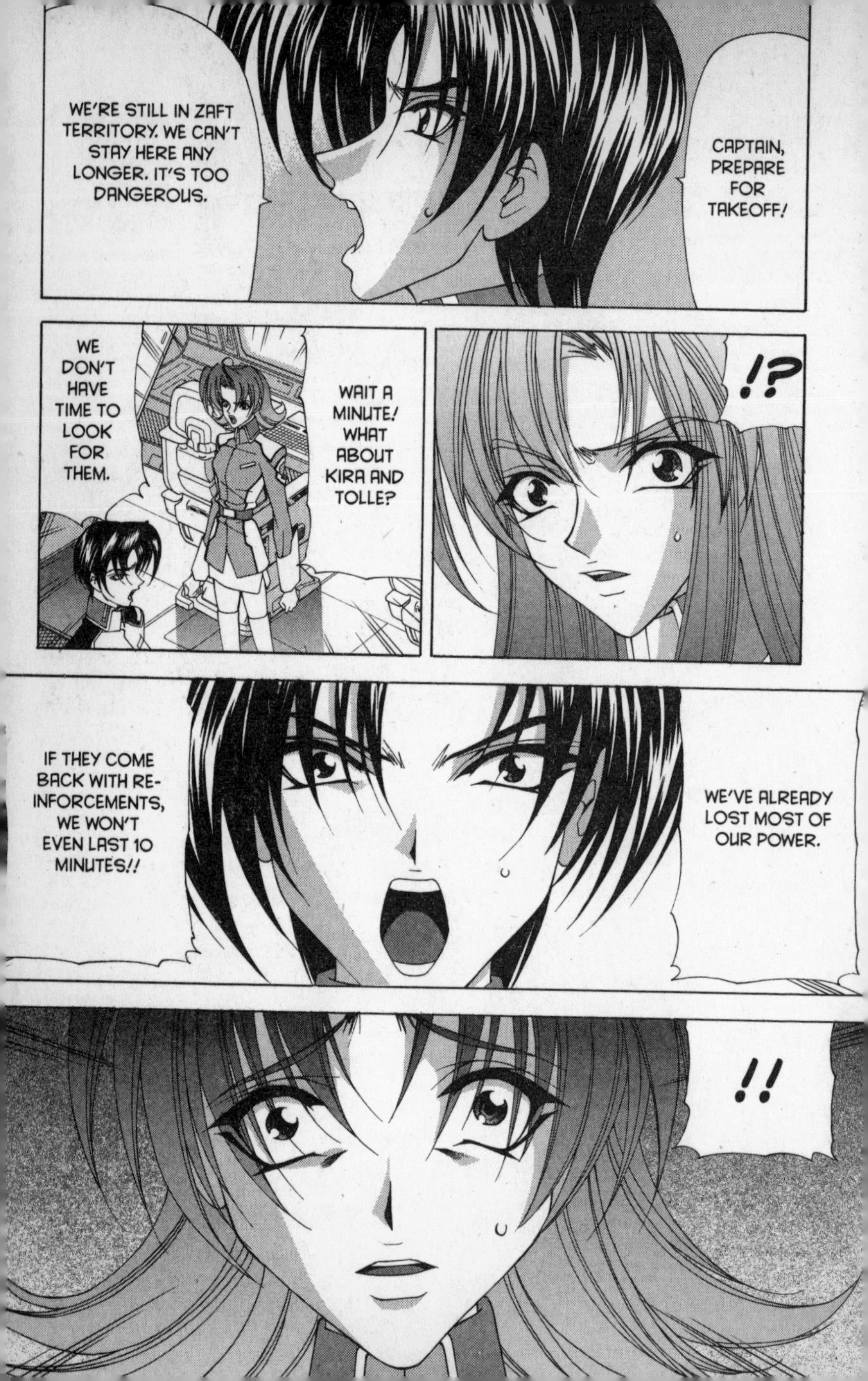
CAPTAIN, PREPARE FOR TAKEOFF!
WE'RE STILL IN ZAFT TERRITORY. WE CAN'T STAY HERE ANY LONGER. IT'S TOO DANGEROUS.
!?
WAIT A MINUTE! WHAT ABOUT KIRA AND TOLLE?
WE DON'T HAVE TIME TO LOOK FOR THEM.
WE'VE ALREADY LOST MOST OF OUR POWER.
IF THEY COME BACK WITH RE-INFORCEMENTS, WE WON'T EVEN LAST 10 MINUTES!!
!!

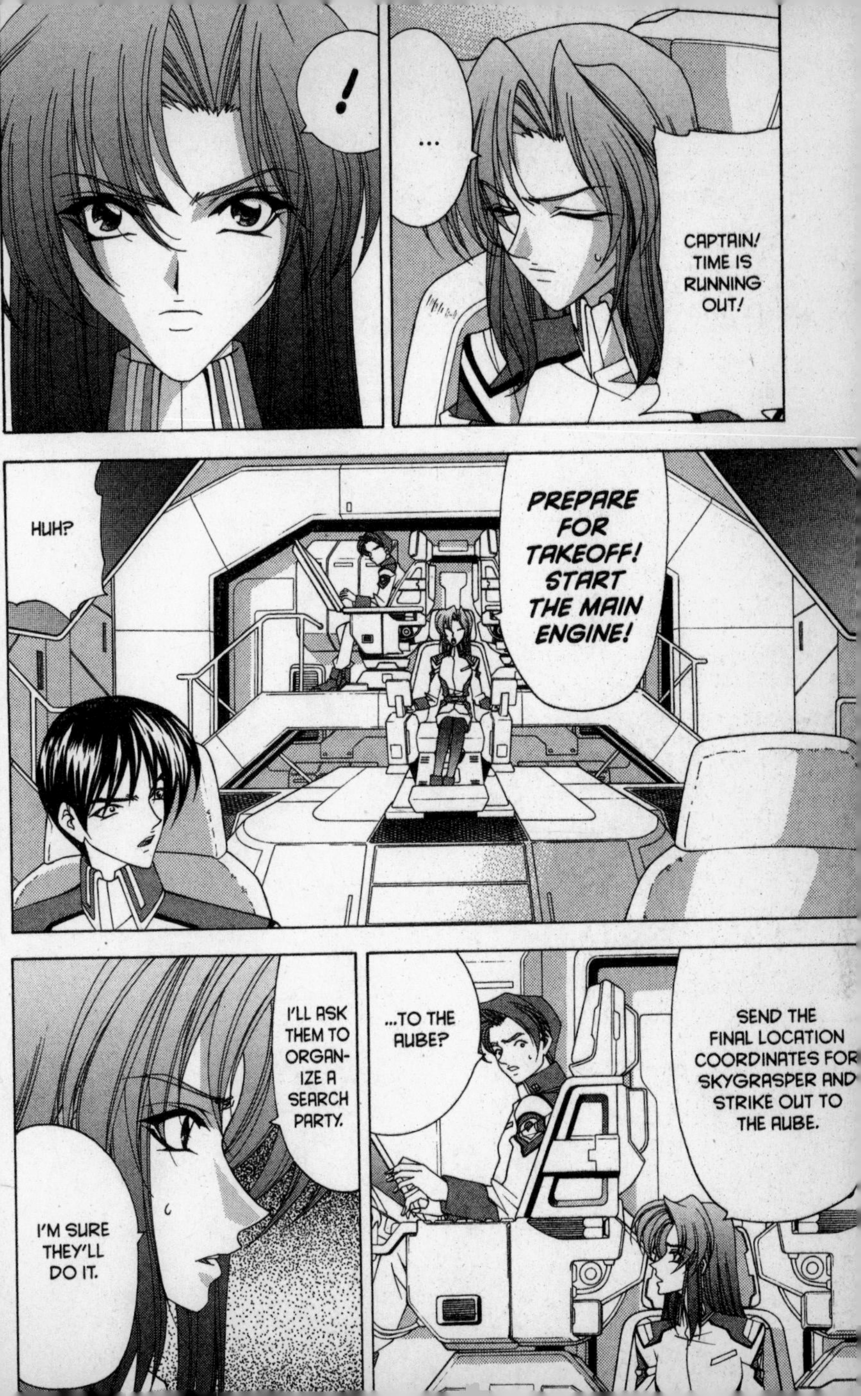
CAPTAIN! TIME IS RUNNING OUT!
...
!
PREPARE FOR TAKEOFF! START THE MAIN ENGINE!
HUH?
SEND THE FINAL LOCATION COORDINATES FOR SKYGRASPER AND STRIKE OUT TO THE AUBE.
...TO THE AUBE?
I'LL ASK THEM TO ORGAN-IZE A SEARCH PARTY.
I'M SURE THEY'LL DO IT.

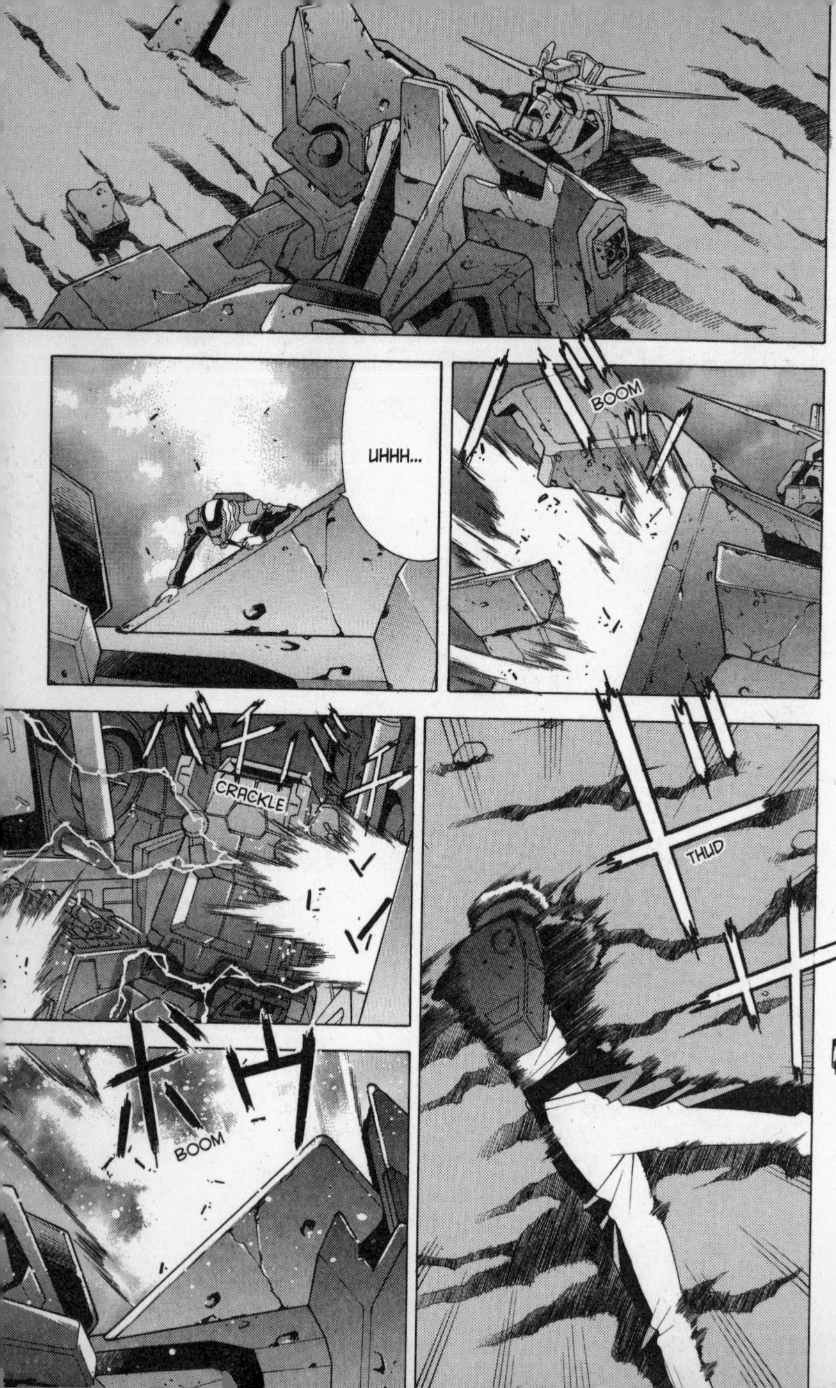
BOOM
UHHH...
THUD
CRACKLE
BOOM

ROAR

WHERE'S THE ARCH-ANGEL...?

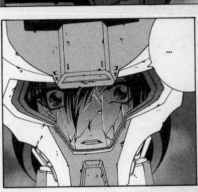
...

SMASH

OUCH!!

STING

DRIP

DRIP

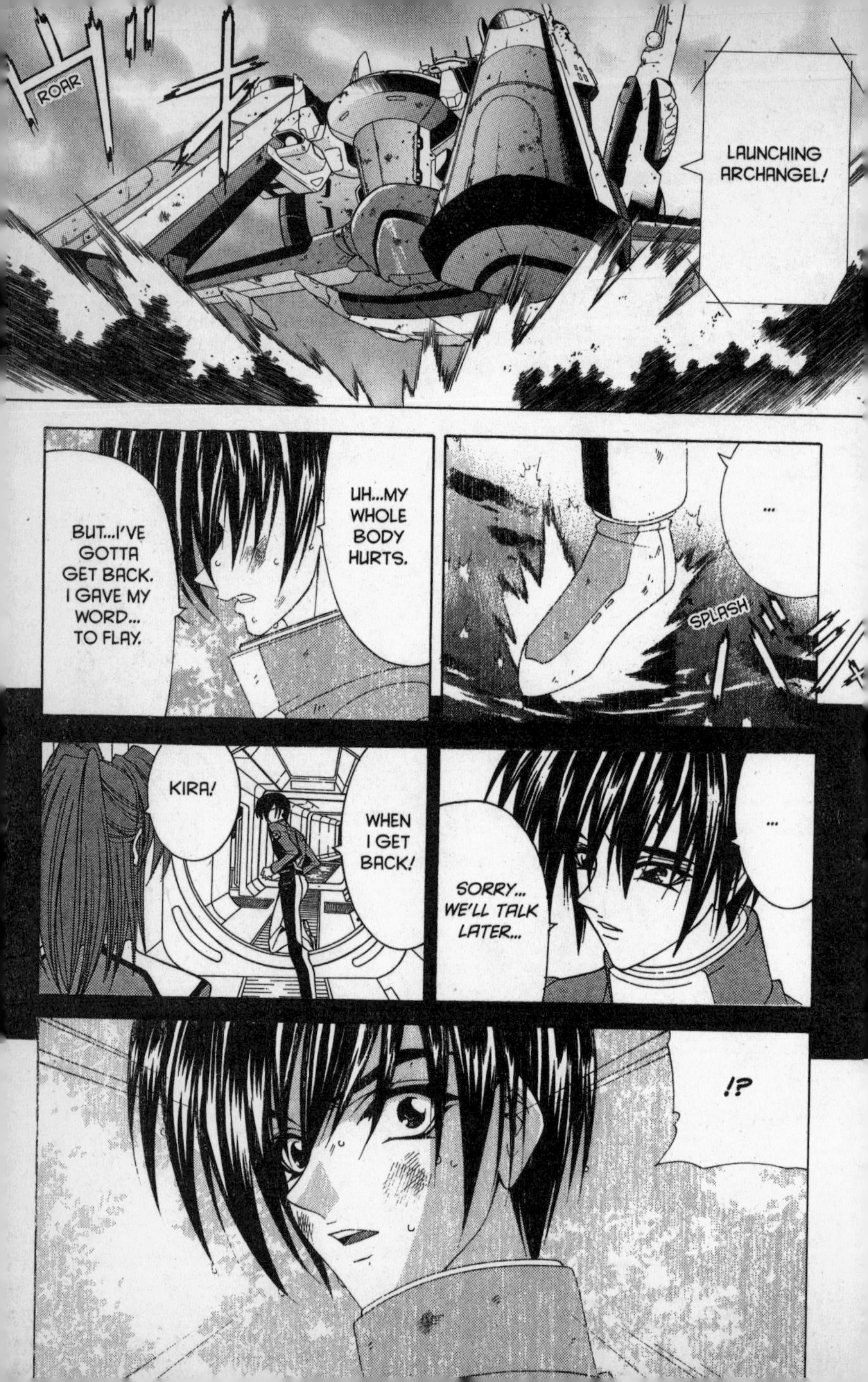
LAUNCHING ARCHANGEL!
ROAR
...
SPLASH
UH...MY WHOLE BODY HURTS.
BUT...I'VE GOTTA GET BACK. I GAVE MY WORD... TO FLAY.
...
SORRY... WE'LL TALK LATER...
WHEN I GET BACK!
KIRA!
!?

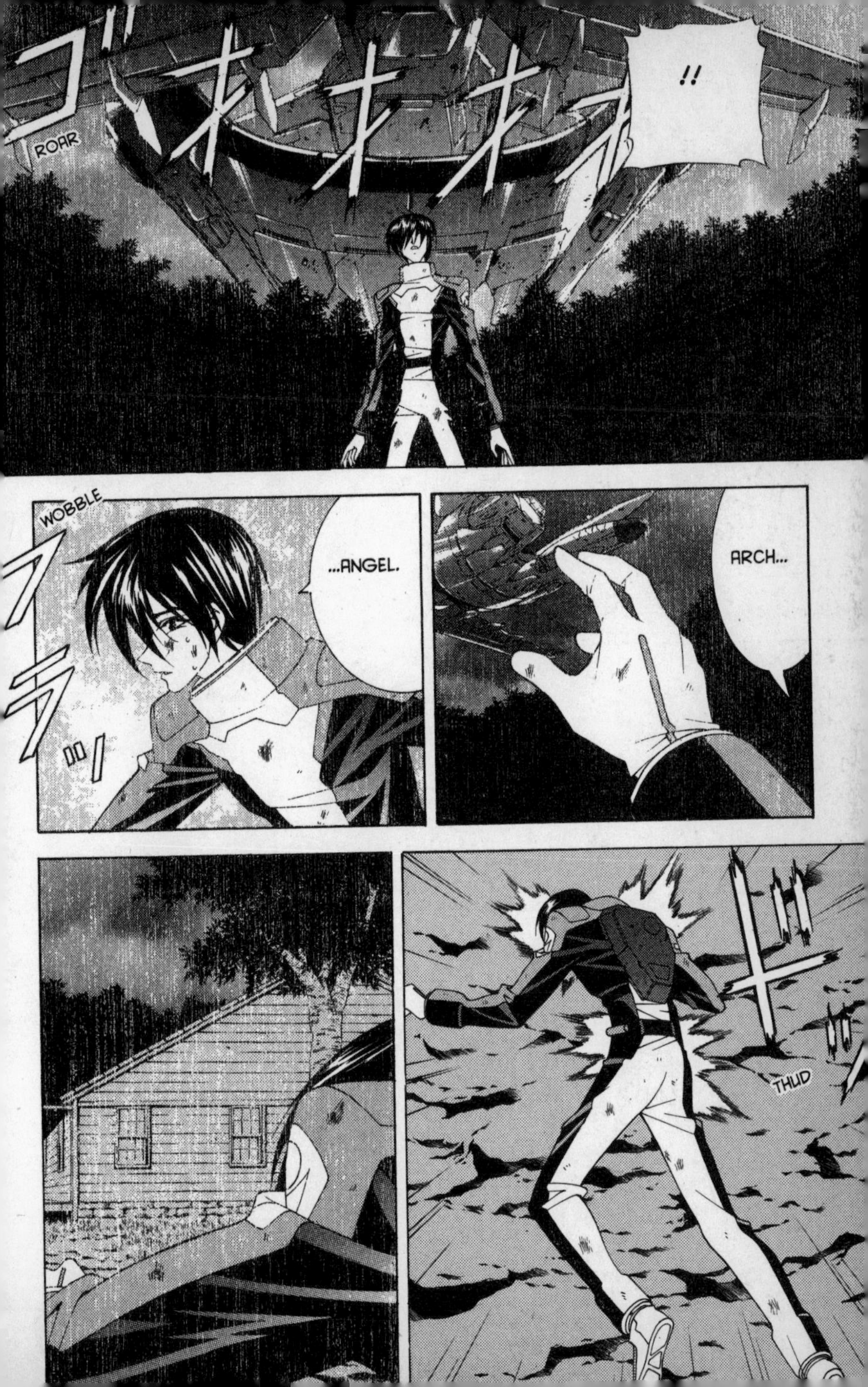
ROAR
!!
ARCH...
WOBBLE
...ANGEL.
THUD

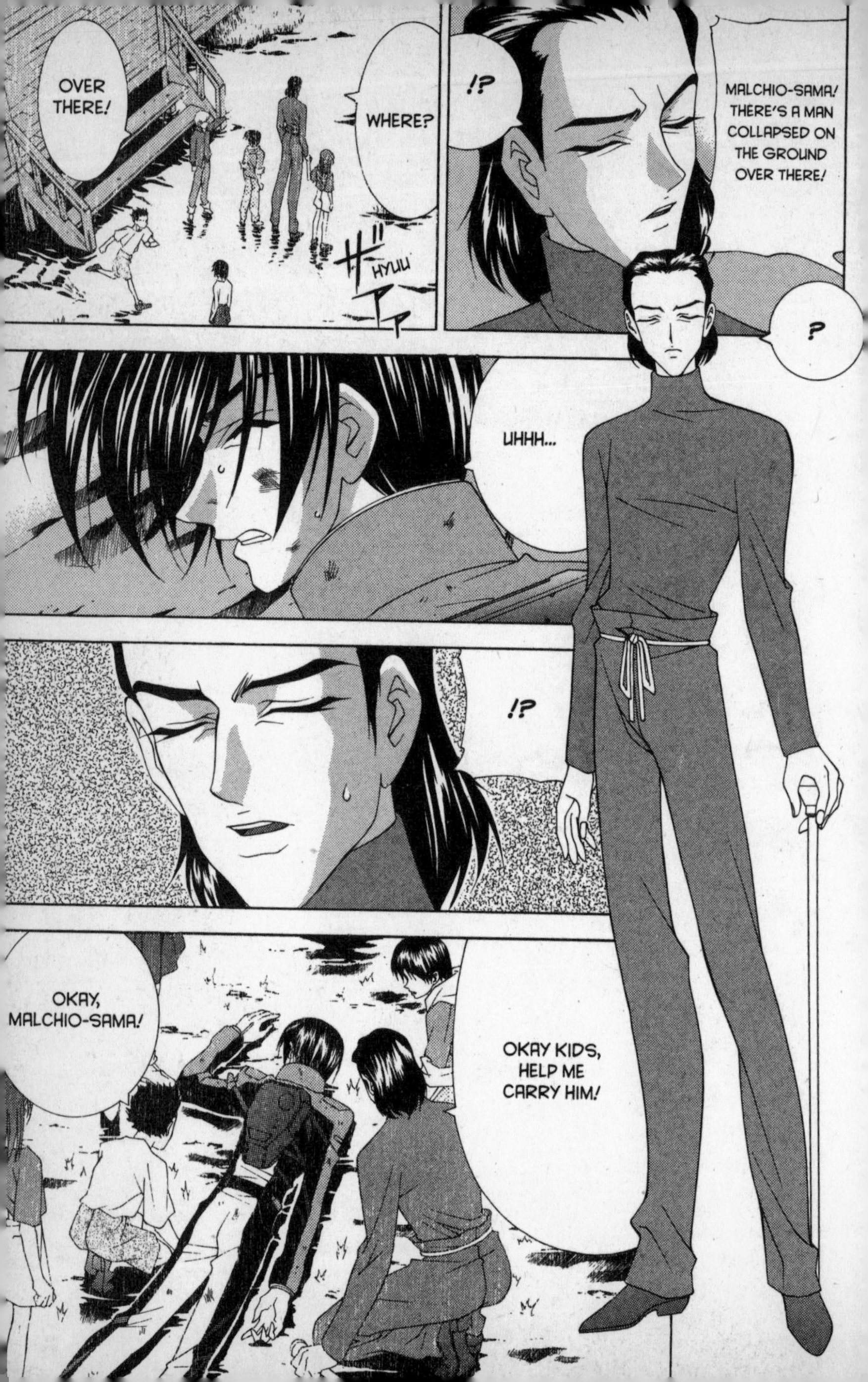
MALCHIO-SAMA! THERE'S A MAN COLLAPSED ON THE GROUND OVER THERE!
!?
WHERE?
OVER THERE!
HYUU
?
UHHH...
!?
OKAY KIDS, HELP ME CARRY HIM!
OKAY, MALCHIO-SAMA!

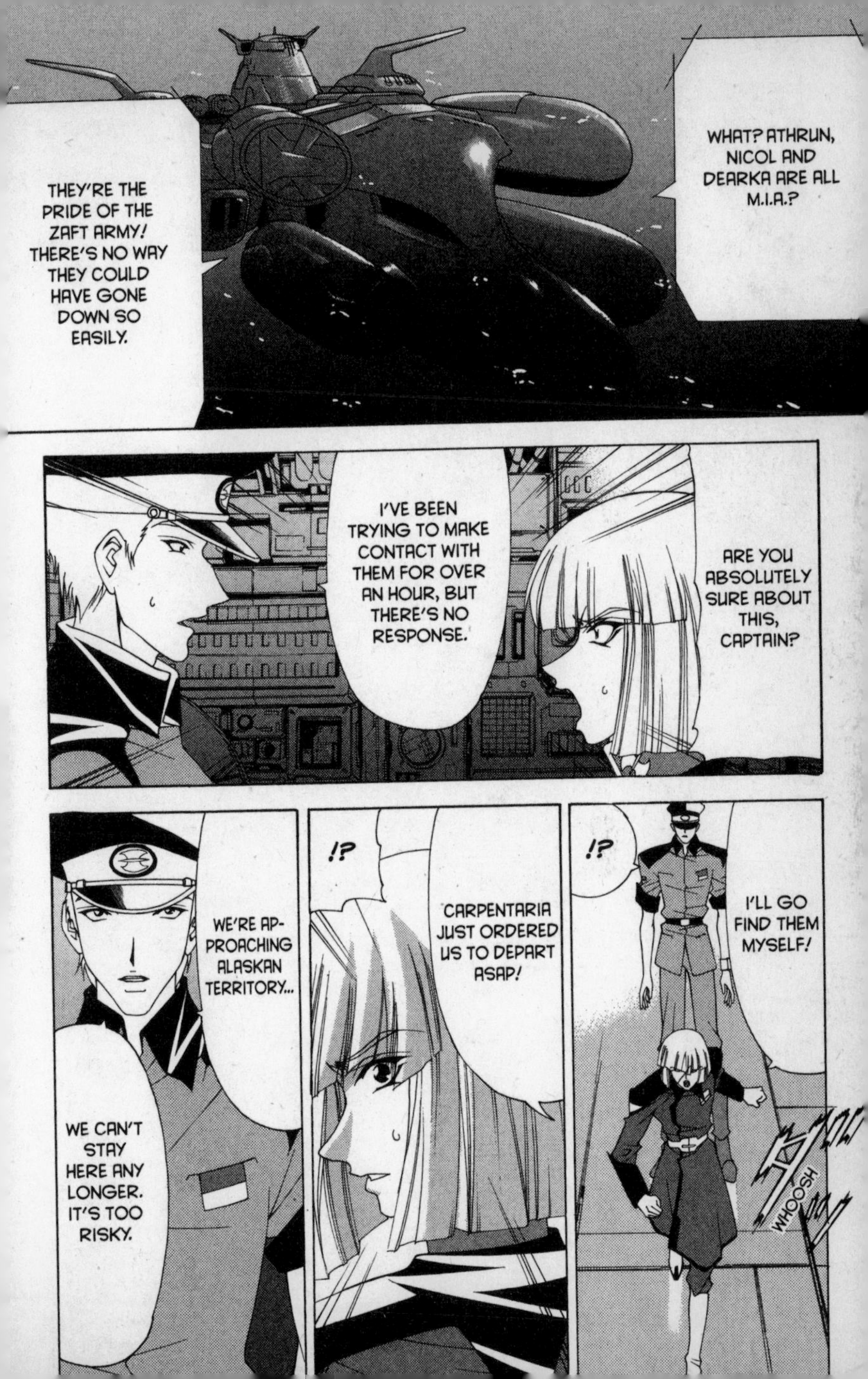
WHAT? ATHRUN, NICOL AND DEARKA ARE ALL M.I.A.?
THEY'RE THE PRIDE OF THE ZAFT ARMY! THERE'S NO WAY THEY COULD HAVE GONE DOWN SO EASILY.
ARE YOU ABSOLUTELY SURE ABOUT THIS, CAPTAIN?
I'VE BEEN TRYING TO MAKE CONTACT WITH THEM FOR OVER AN HOUR, BUT THERE'S NO RESPONSE.
!?
I'LL GO FIND THEM MYSELF!
WHOOSH
!?
CARPENTARIA JUST ORDERED US TO DEPART ASAP!
WE'RE AP- PROACHING ALASKAN TERRITORY...
WE CAN'T STAY HERE ANY LONGER. IT'S TOO RISKY.

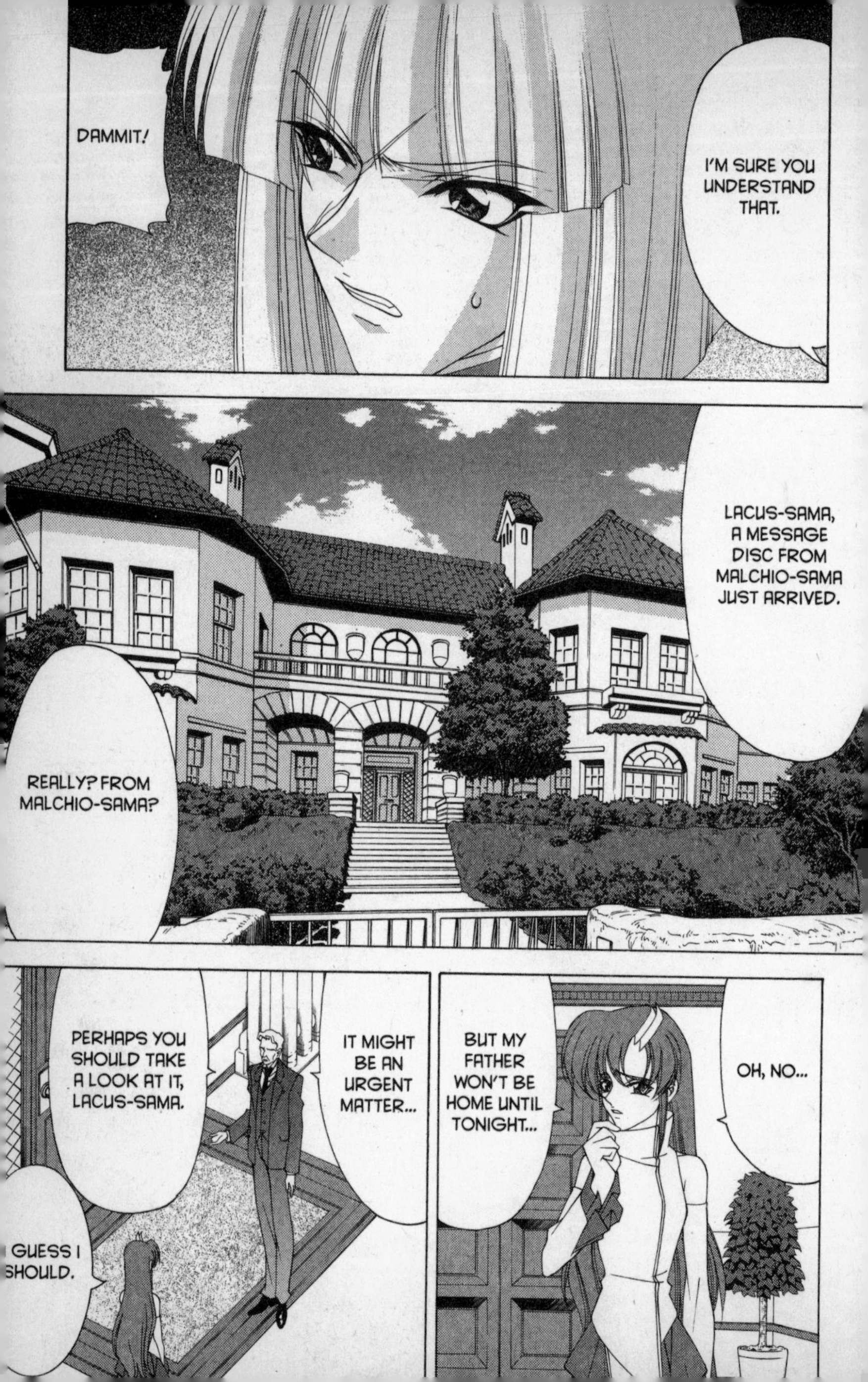
I'M SURE YOU UNDERSTAND THAT.
DAMMIT!
LACUS-SAMA, A MESSAGE DISC FROM MALCHIO-SAMA JUST ARRIVED.
REALLY? FROM MALCHIO-SAMA?
OH, NO...
BUT MY FATHER WON'T BE HOME UNTIL TONIGHT...
IT MIGHT BE AN URGENT MATTER...
PERHAPS YOU SHOULD TAKE A LOOK AT IT, LACUS-SAMA.
I GUESS I SHOULD.

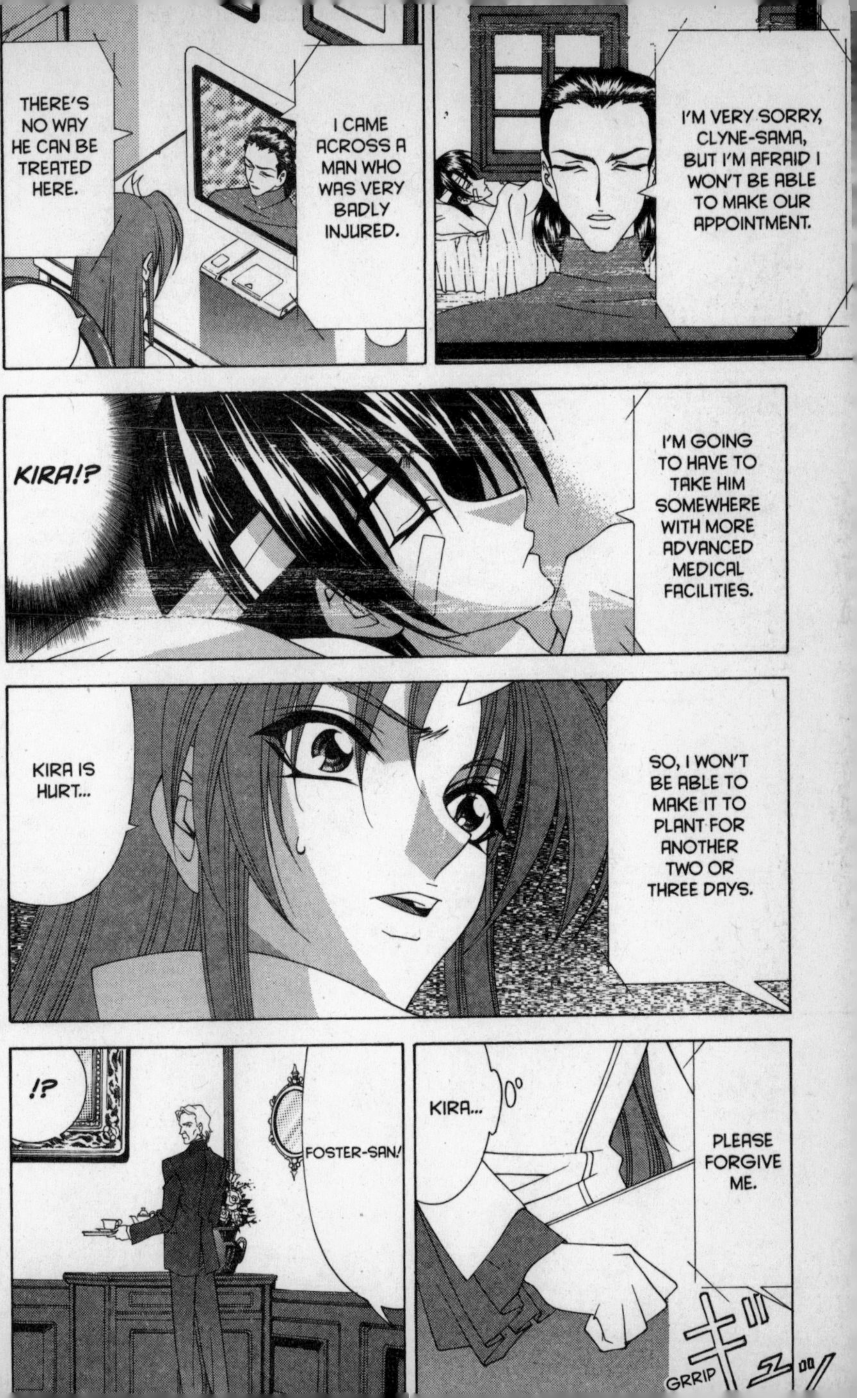
I'M VERY SORRY, CLYNE-SAMA, BUT I'M AFRAID I WON'T BE ABLE TO MAKE OUR APPOINTMENT.
I CAME ACROSS A MAN WHO WAS VERY BADLY INJURED.
THERE'S NO WAY HE CAN BE TREATED HERE.
I'M GOING TO HAVE TO TAKE HIM SOMEWHERE WITH MORE ADVANCED MEDICAL FACILITIES.
KIRA!?
SO, I WON'T BE ABLE TO MAKE IT TO PLANT FOR ANOTHER TWO OR THREE DAYS.
KIRA IS HURT...
PLEASE FORGIVE ME.
KIRA...
GRRIP
FOSTER-SAN!
!?

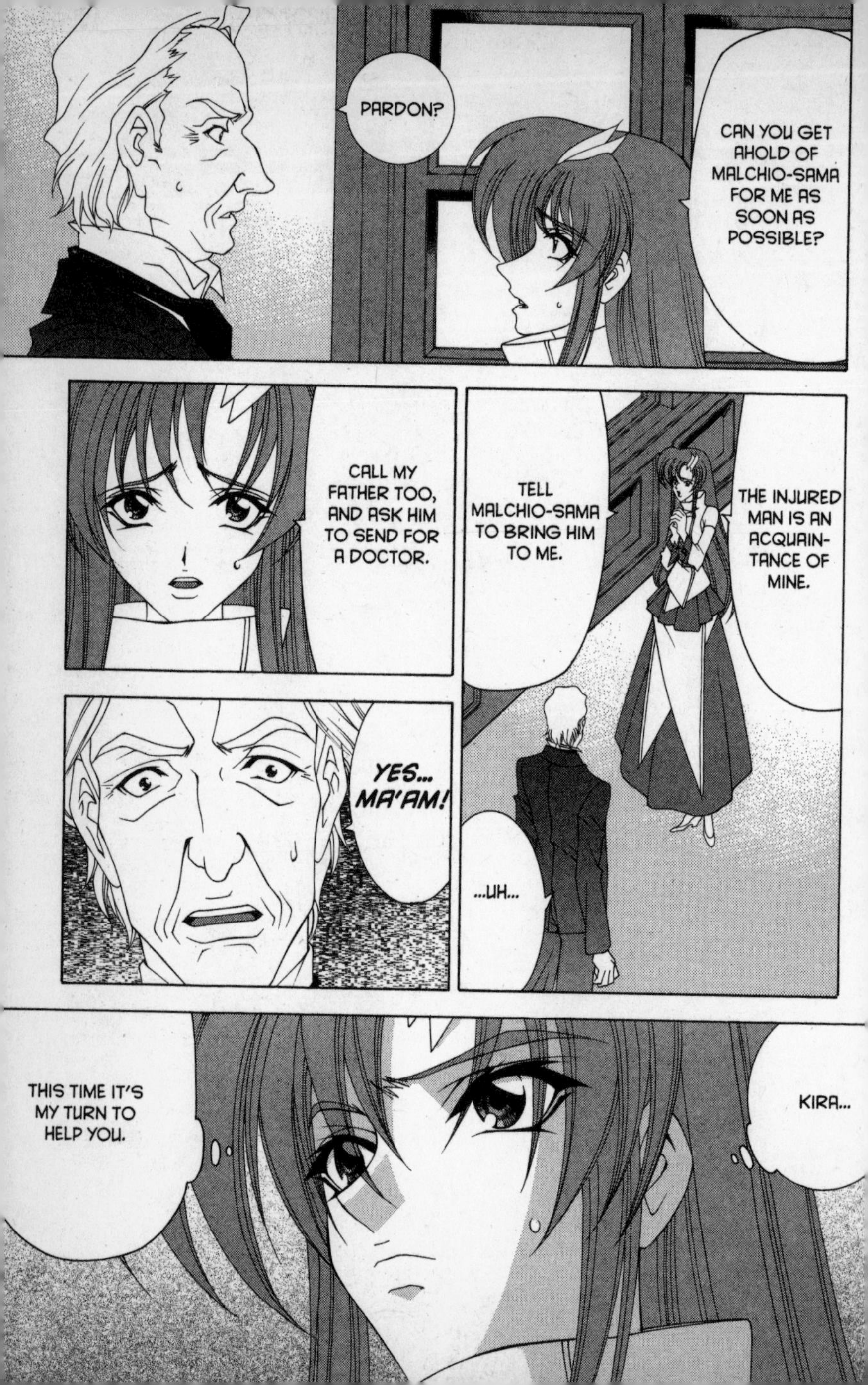
CAN YOU GET AHOLD OF MALCHIO-SAMA FOR ME AS SOON AS POSSIBLE?
PARDON?
THE INJURED MAN IS AN ACQUAIN-TANCE OF MINE.
TELL MALCHIO-SAMA TO BRING HIM TO ME.
...UH...
CALL MY FATHER TOO, AND ASK HIM TO SEND FOR A DOCTOR.
YES... MA'AM!
KIRA...
THIS TIME IT'S MY TURN TO HELP YOU.

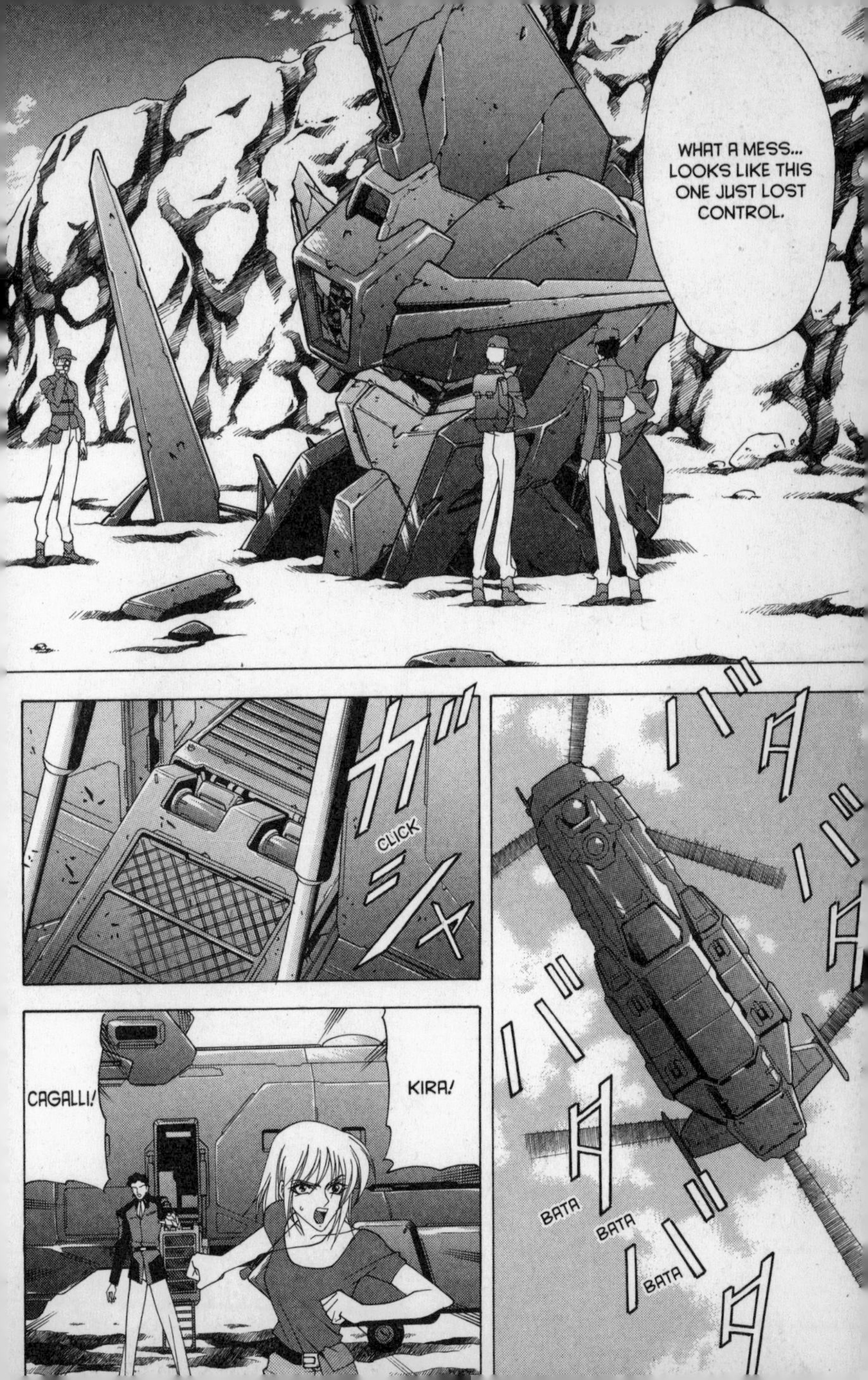
WHAT A MESS... LOOKS LIKE THIS ONE JUST LOST CONTROL.
BATA
BATA
BATA
CLICK
KIRA!
CAGALLI!

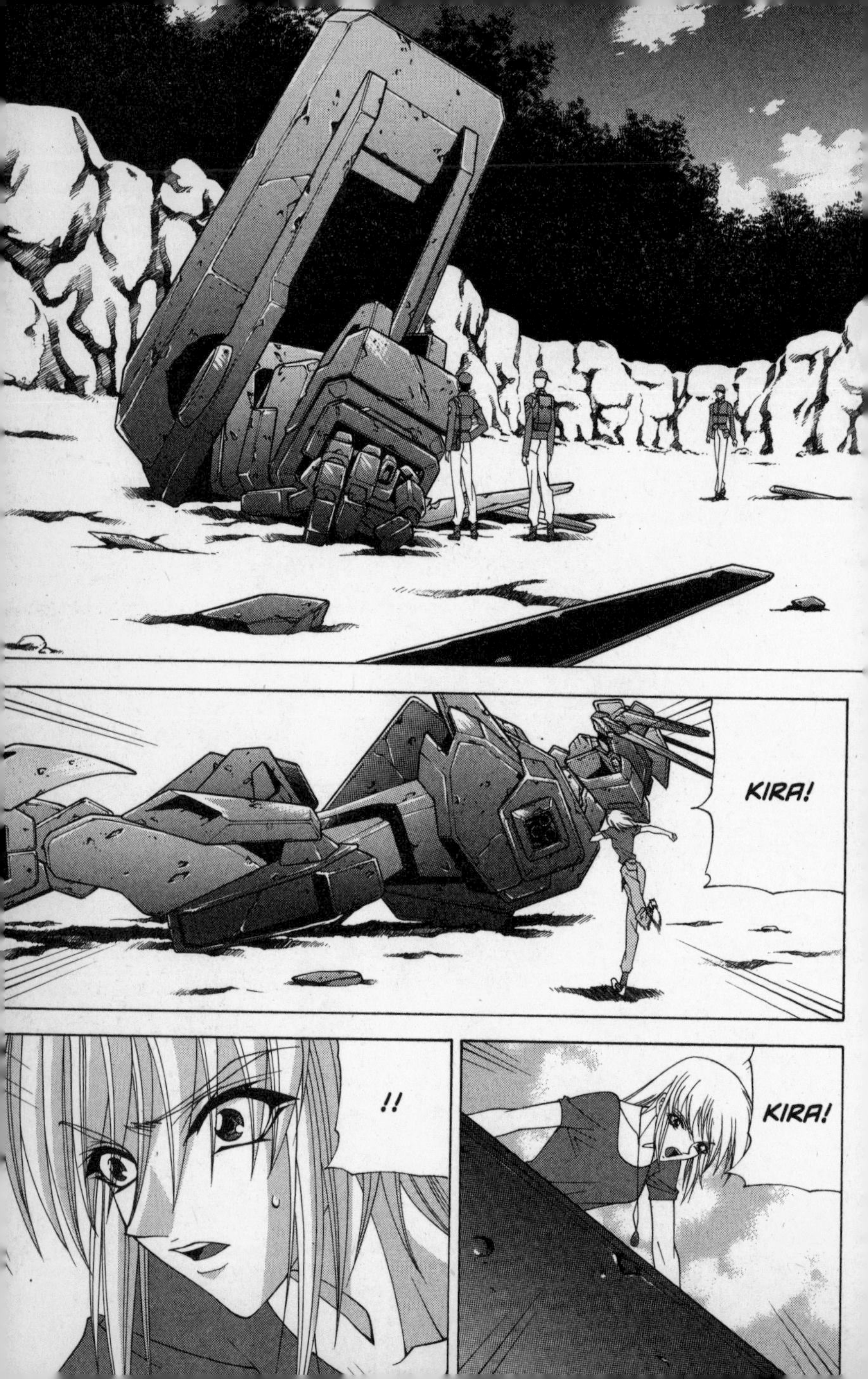
KIRA!
KIRA!
!!

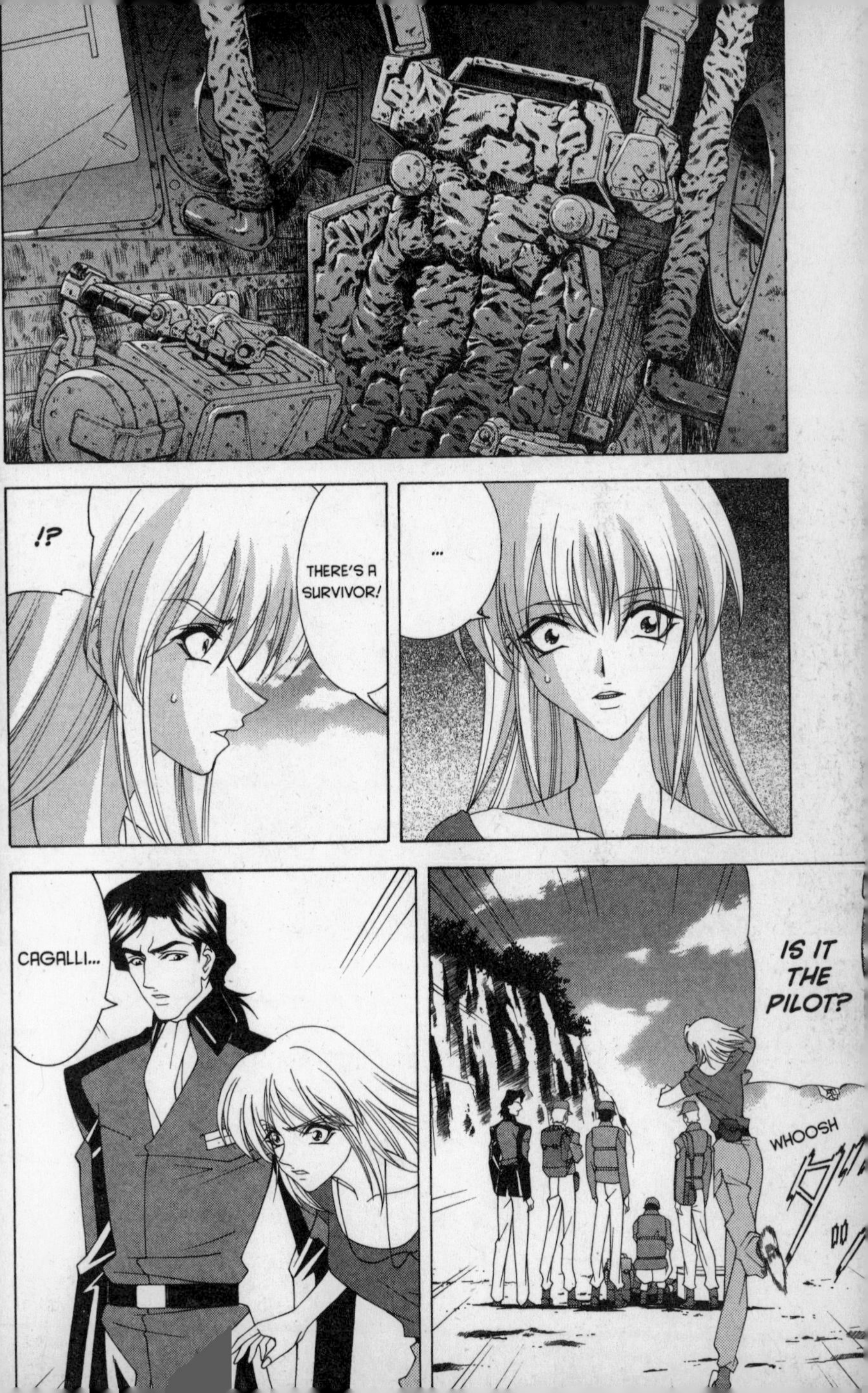
...
THERE'S A SURVIVOR!
!?
IS IT THE PILOT?
WHOOSH
CAGALLI...

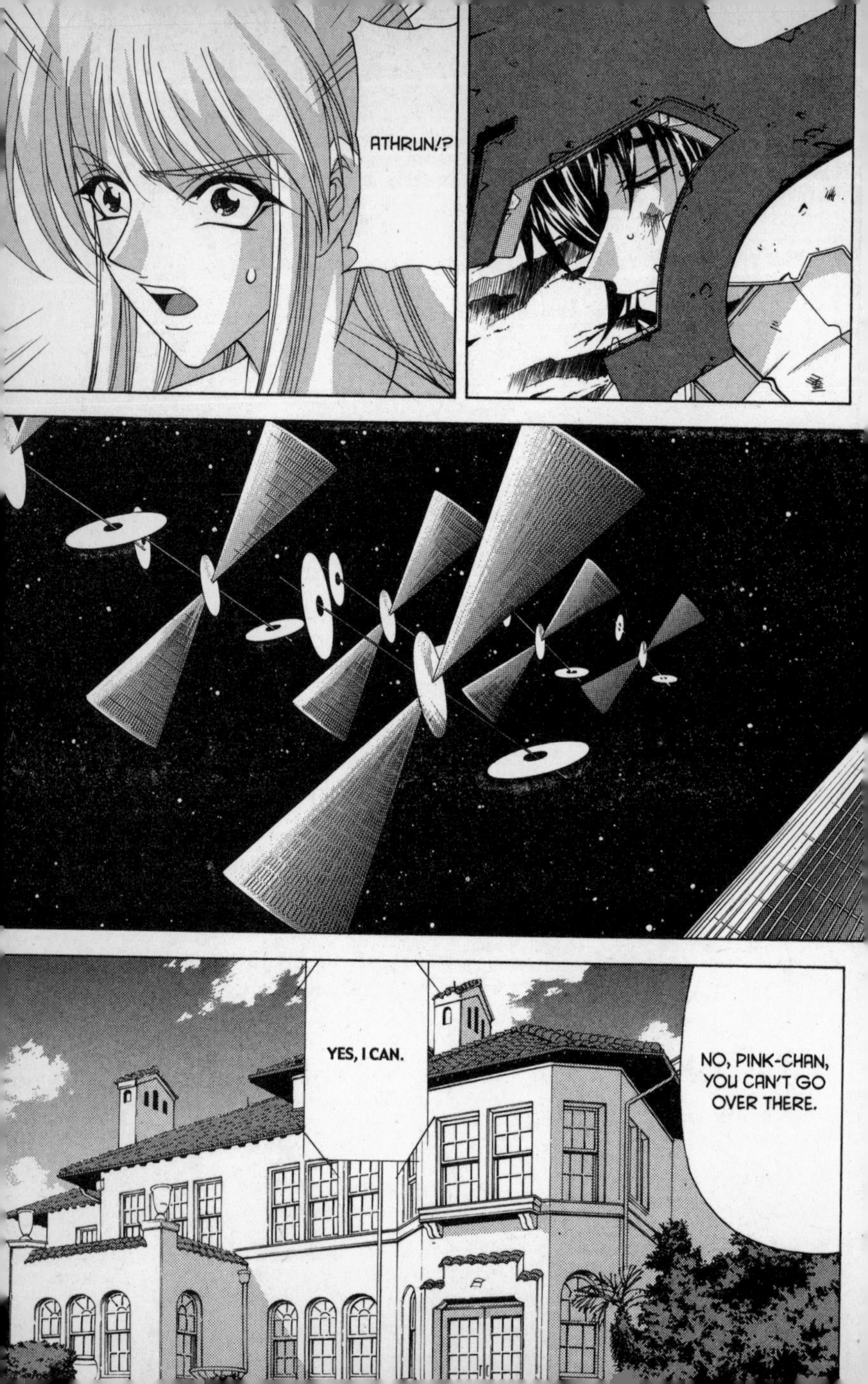
ATHRUN!?
NO, PINK-CHAN, YOU CAN'T GO OVER THERE.
YES, I CAN.

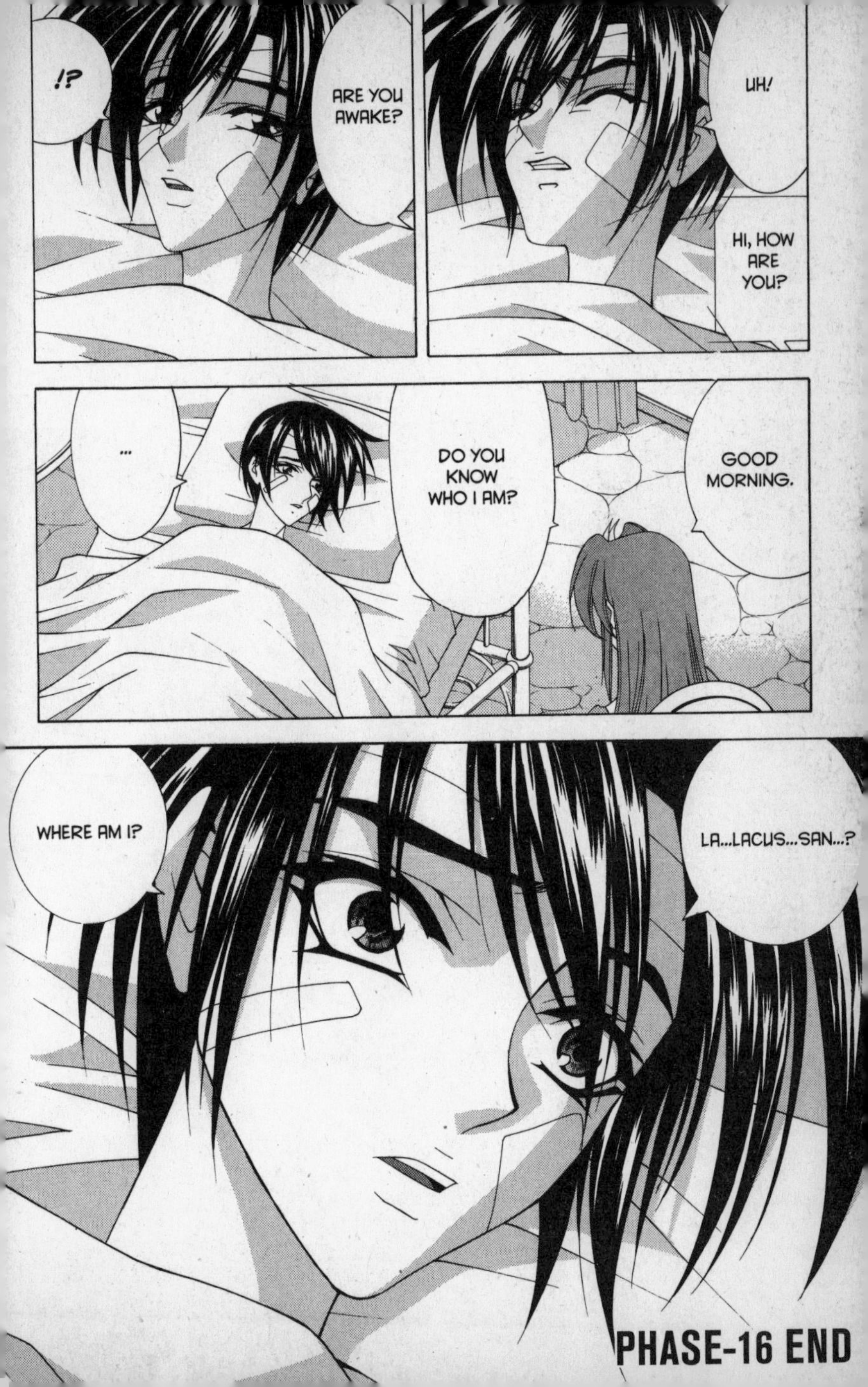
UH!
HI, HOW ARE YOU?
ARE YOU AWAKE?
!?
GOOD MORNING.
DO YOU KNOW WHO I AM?
...
LA...LACUS...SAN...?
WHERE AM I?
PHASE-16 END

# PHASE-17 THE MEETING PLACE

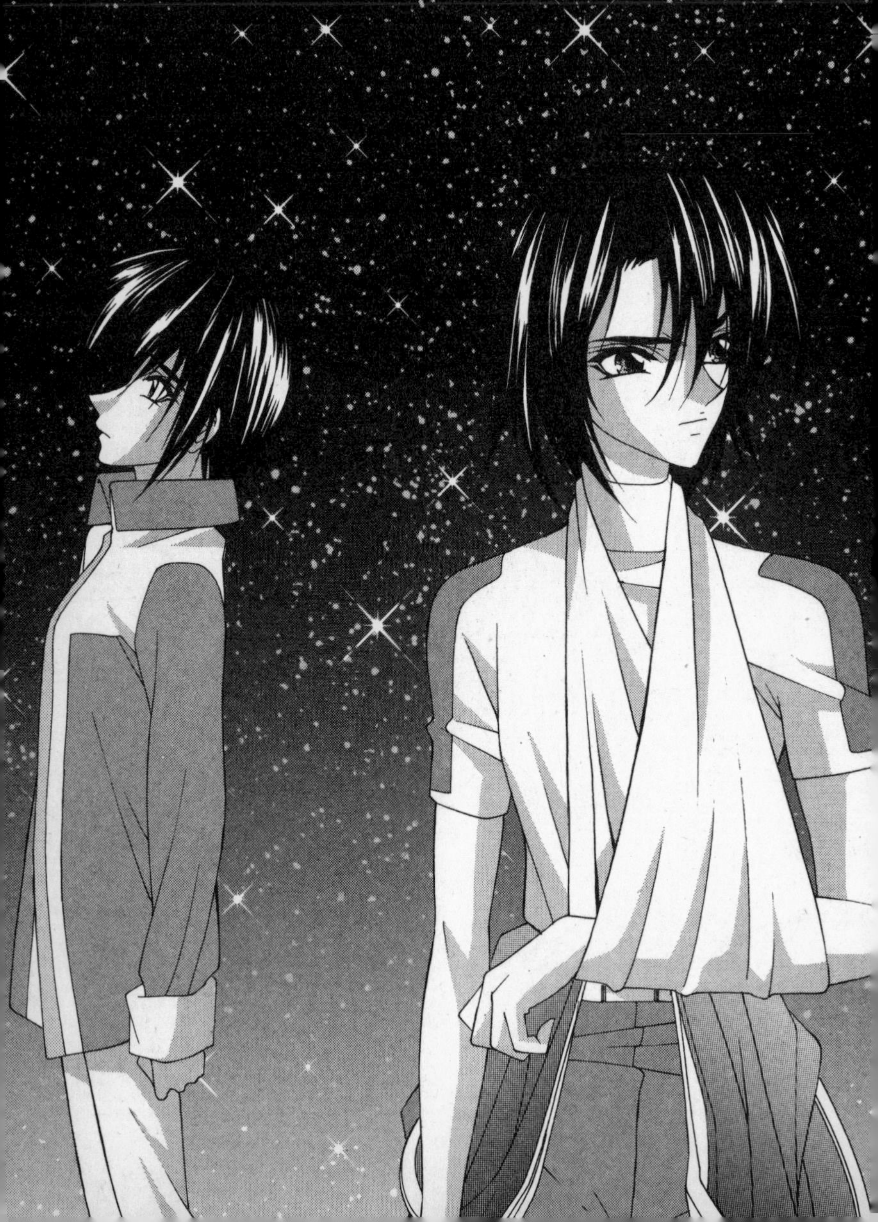

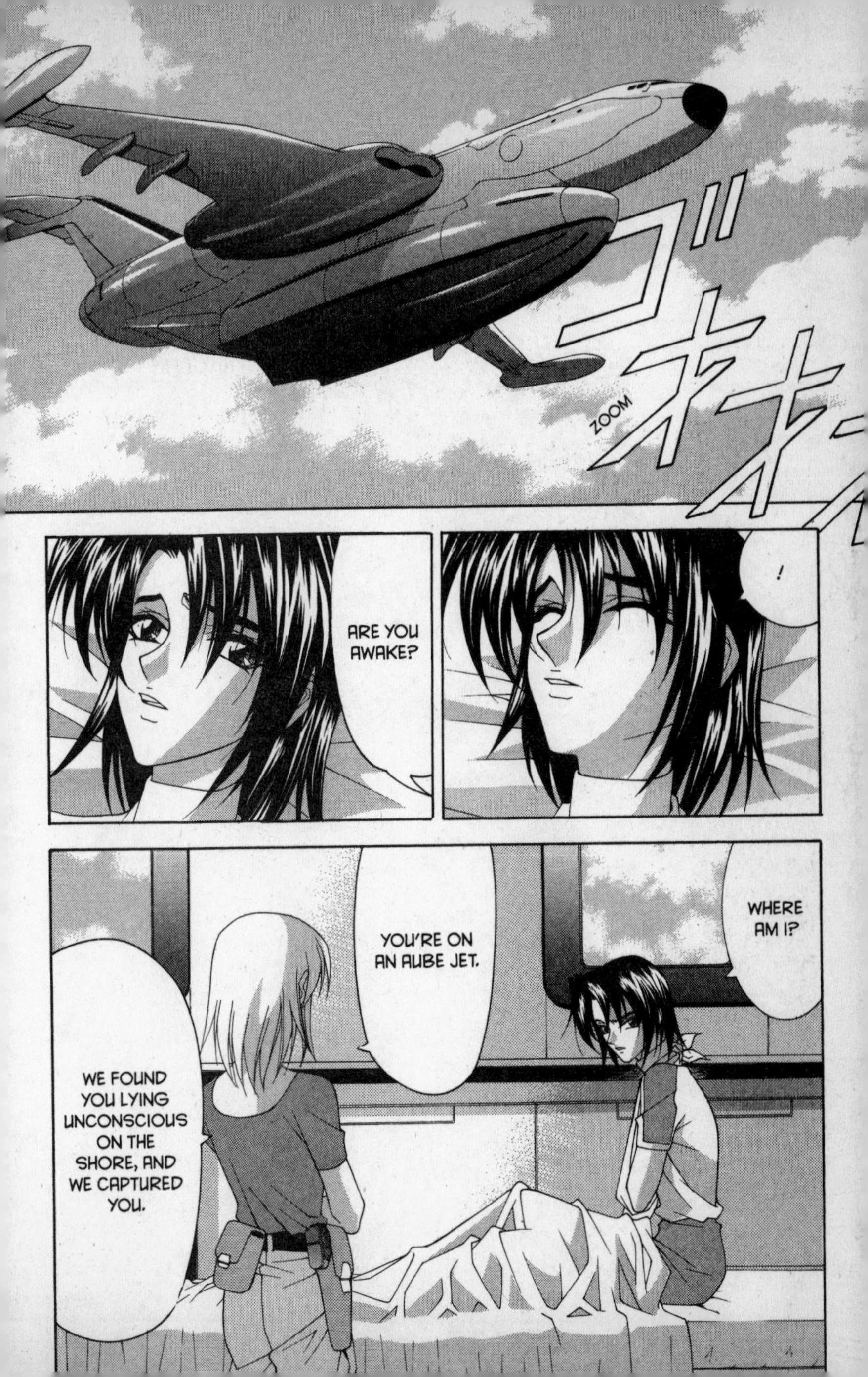
ZOOM
!
ARE YOU AWAKE?
WHERE AM I?
YOU'RE ON AN AUBE JET.
WE FOUND YOU LYING UNCONSCIOUS ON THE SHORE, AND WE CAPTURED YOU.

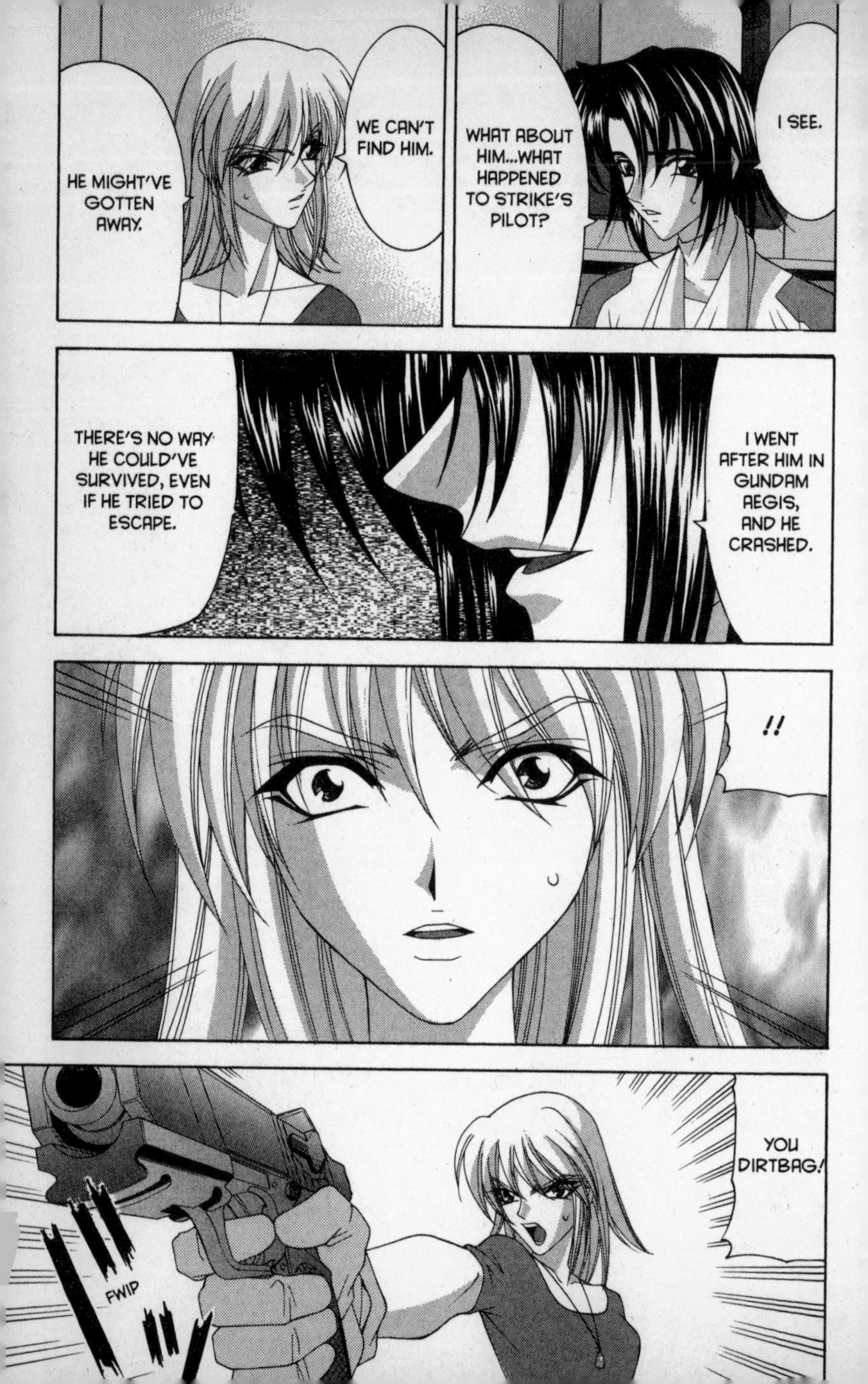
I SEE.
WHAT ABOUT HIM...WHAT HAPPENED TO STRIKE'S PILOT?
WE CAN'T FIND HIM.
HE MIGHT'VE GOTTEN AWAY.
I WENT AFTER HIM IN GUNDAM AEGIS, AND HE CRASHED.
THERE'S NO WAY HE COULD'VE SURVIVED, EVEN IF HE TRIED TO ESCAPE.
!!
YOU DIRTBAG!
FWIP

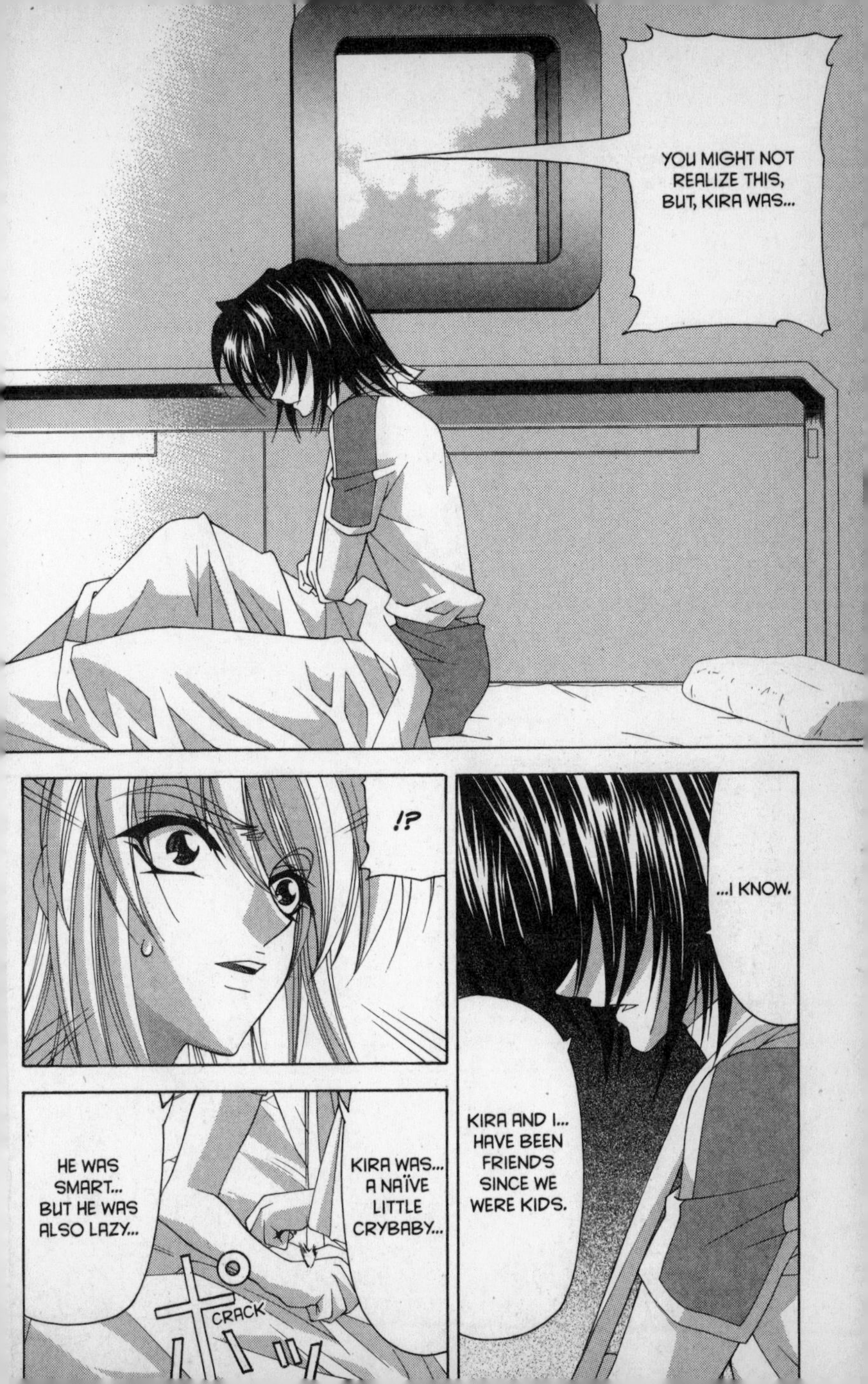
YOU MIGHT NOT REALIZE THIS, BUT, KIRA WAS...
...I KNOW.
KIRA AND I... HAVE BEEN FRIENDS SINCE WE WERE KIDS.
!?
KIRA WAS... A NAÏVE LITTLE CRYBABY...
HE WAS SMART... BUT HE WAS ALSO LAZY...
CRACK

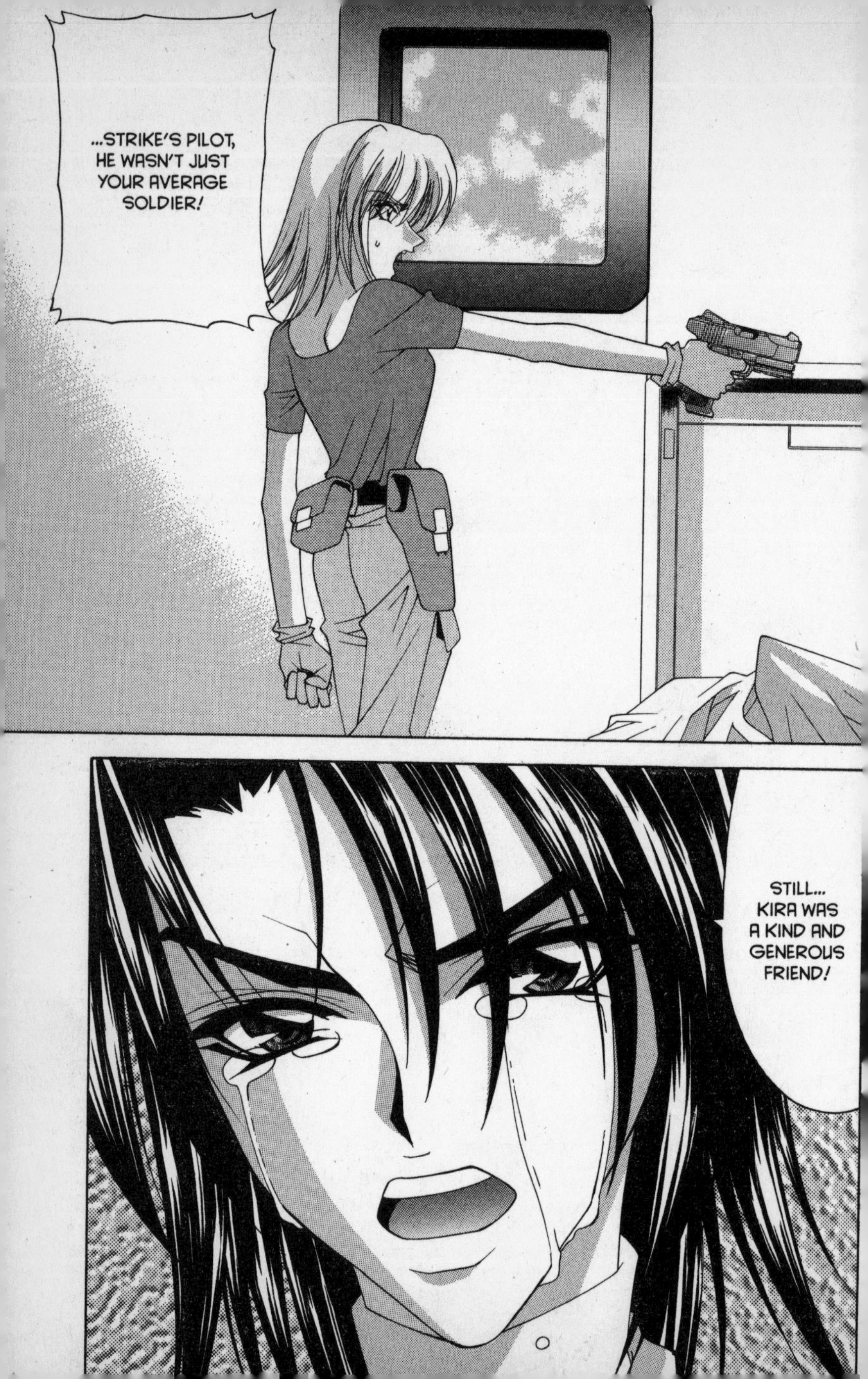
...STRIKE'S PILOT, HE WASN'T JUST YOUR AVERAGE SOLDIER!
STILL... KIRA WAS A KIND AND GENEROUS FRIEND!

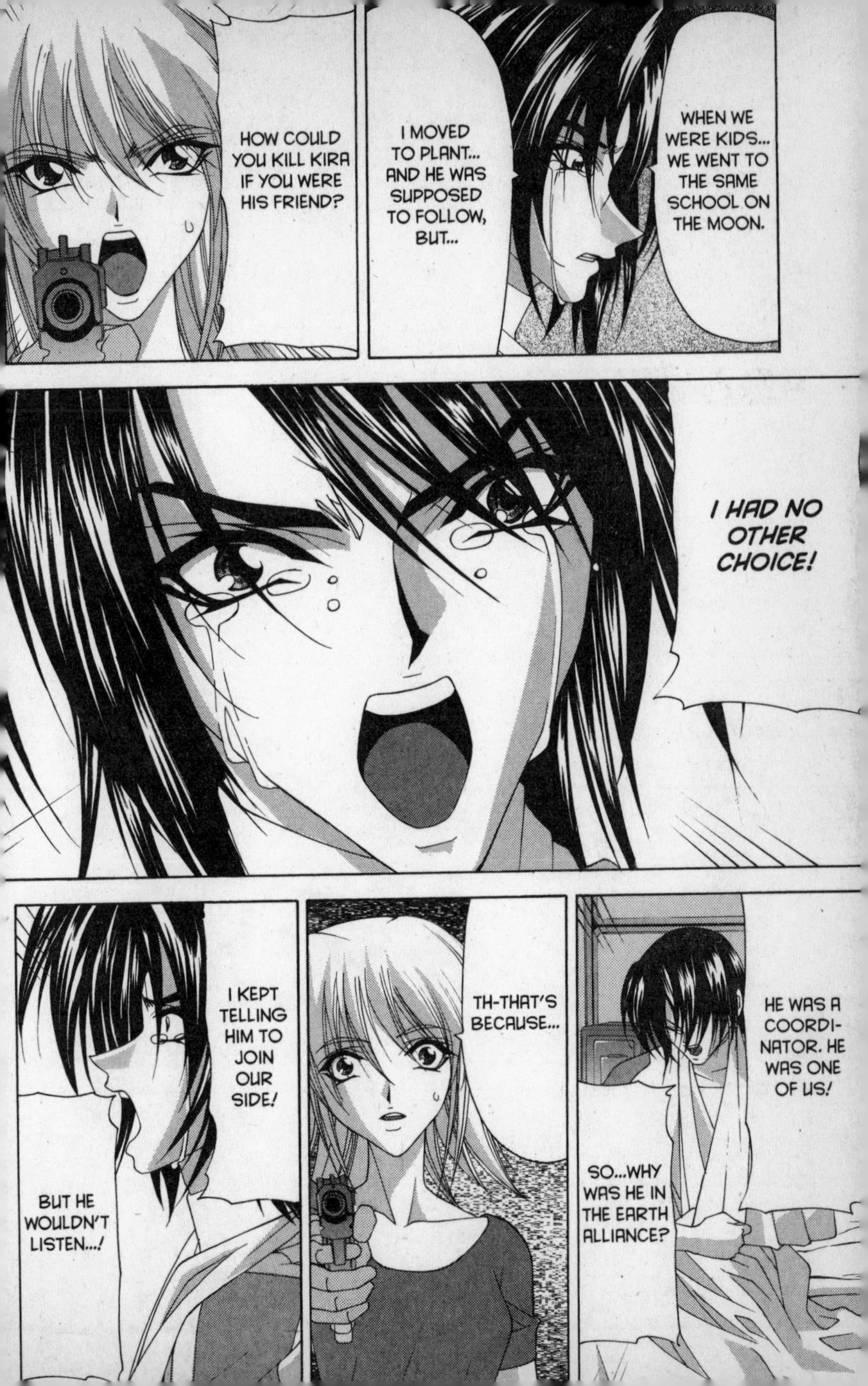
WHEN WE WERE KIDS... WE WENT TO THE SAME SCHOOL ON THE MOON.
I MOVED TO PLANT... AND HE WAS SUPPOSED TO FOLLOW, BUT...
HOW COULD YOU KILL KIRA IF YOU WERE HIS FRIEND?
I HAD NO OTHER CHOICE!
HE WAS A COORDI-NATOR. HE WAS ONE OF US!
SO...WHY WAS HE IN THE EARTH ALLIANCE?
TH-THAT'S BECAUSE...
I KEPT TELLING HIM TO JOIN OUR SIDE!
BUT HE WOULDN'T LISTEN...!

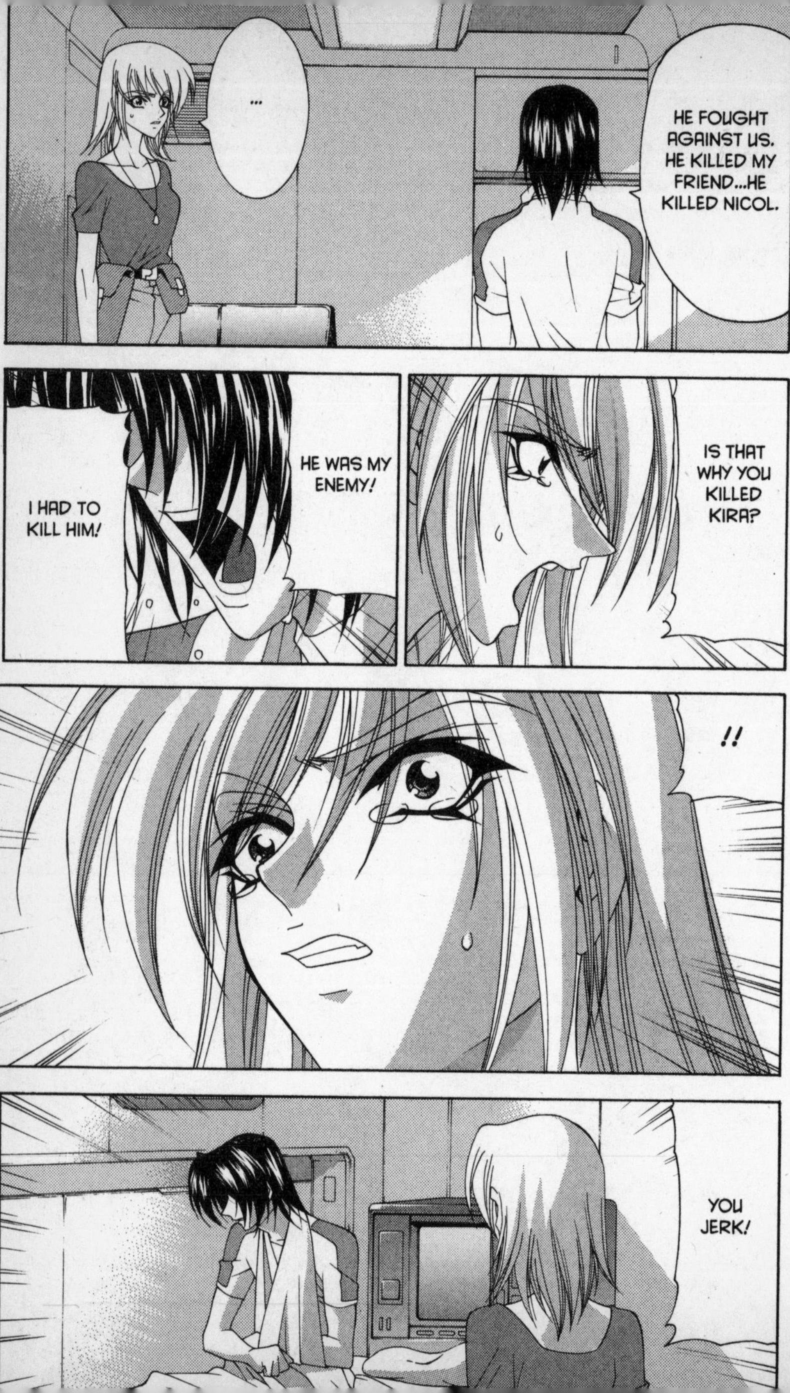
HE FOUGHT AGAINST US. HE KILLED MY FRIEND...HE KILLED NICOL.
...
IS THAT WHY YOU KILLED KIRA?
HE WAS MY ENEMY!
I HAD TO KILL HIM!
!!
YOU JERK!

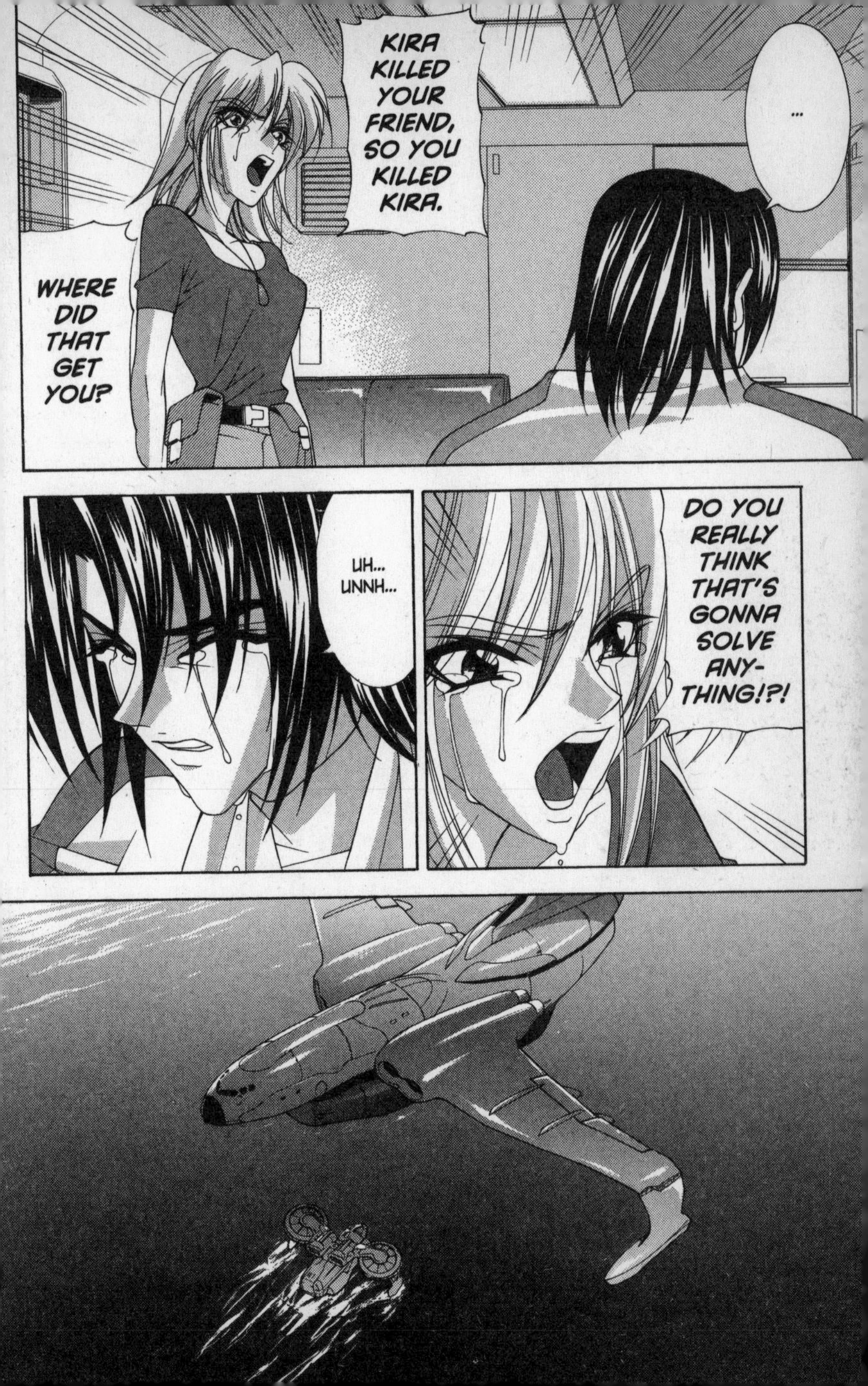
...
KIRA KILLED YOUR FRIEND, SO YOU KILLED KIRA.
WHERE DID THAT GET YOU?
DO YOU REALLY THINK THAT'S GONNA SOLVE ANY-THING!?!
UH... UNNH...

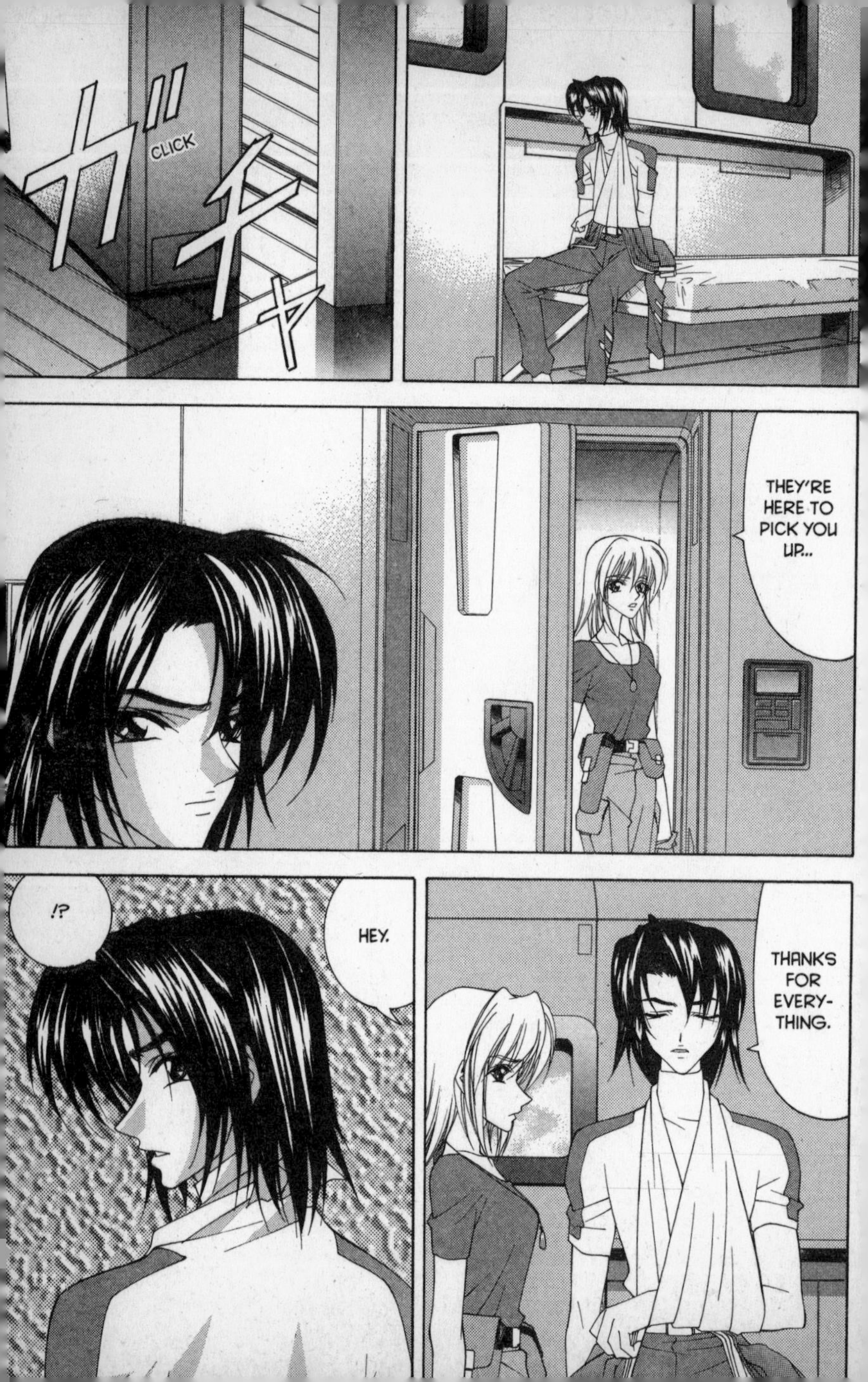
ガチャ
CLICK
THEY'RE HERE TO PICK YOU UP...
THANKS FOR EVERY-THING.
HEY.
!?

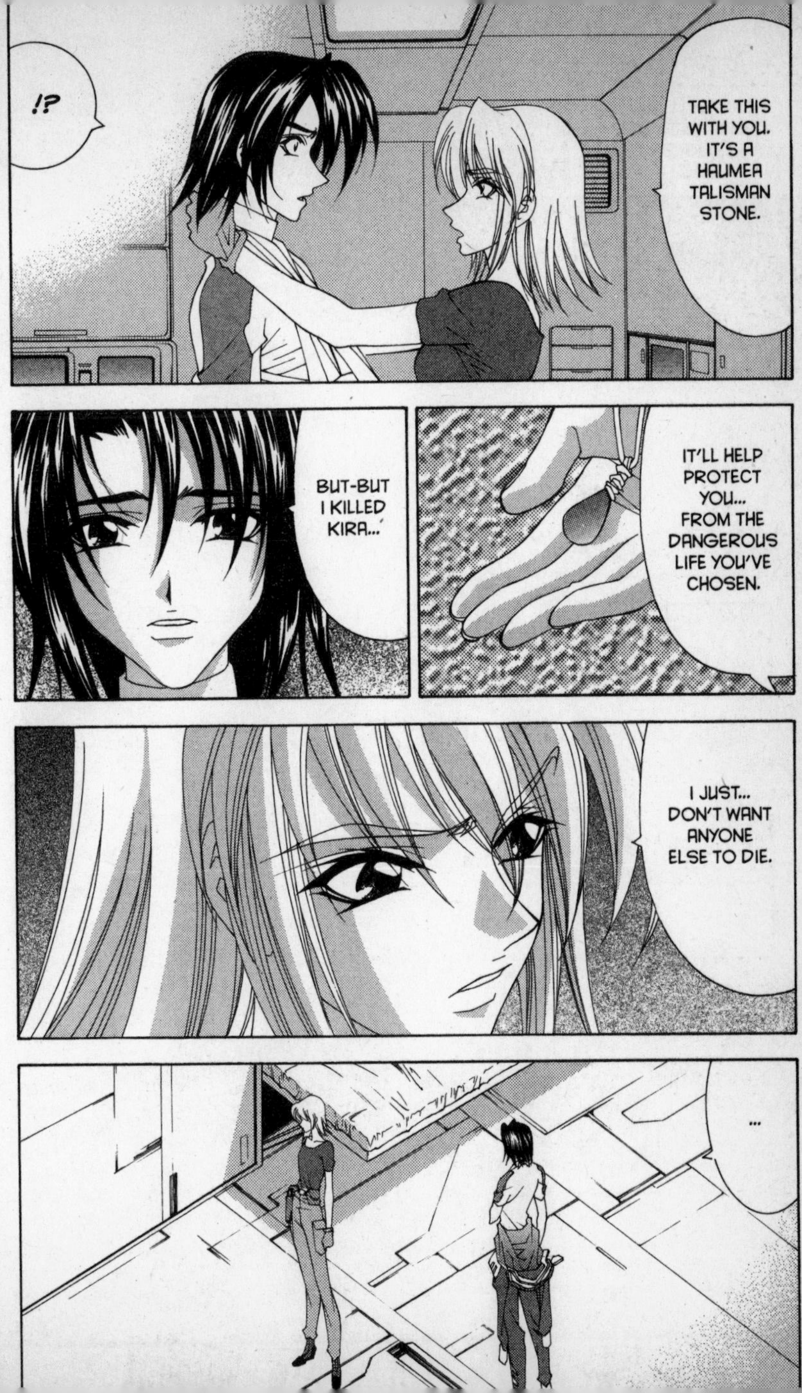
TAKE THIS WITH YOU. IT'S A HAUMEA TALISMAN STONE.
!?
IT'LL HELP PROTECT YOU... FROM THE DANGEROUS LIFE YOU'VE CHOSEN.
BUT-BUT I KILLED KIRA...
I JUST... DON'T WANT ANYONE ELSE TO DIE.
...

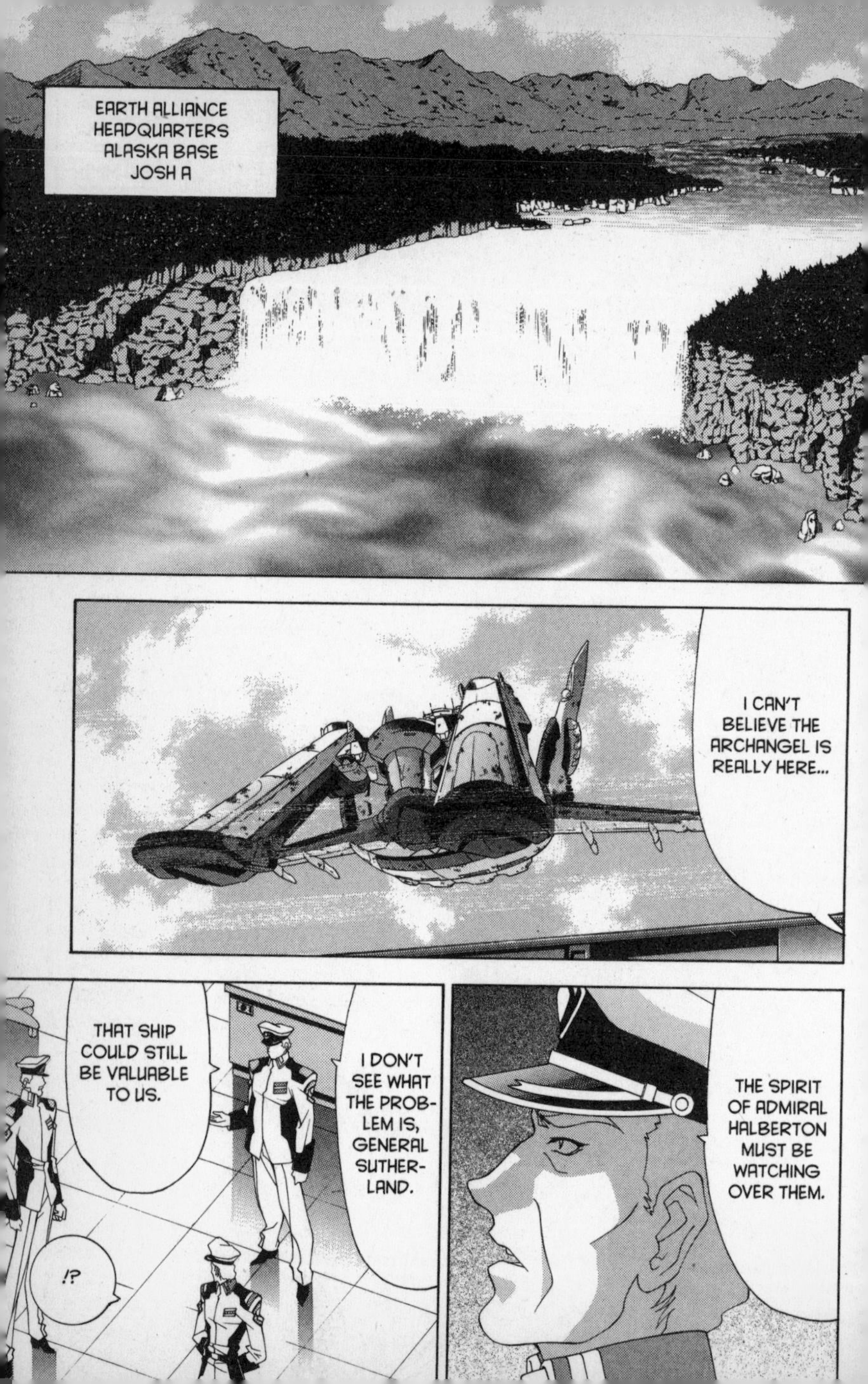
EARTH ALLIANCE HEADQUARTERS ALASKA BASE JOSH A
I CAN'T BELIEVE THE ARCHANGEL IS REALLY HERE...
THE SPIRIT OF ADMIRAL HALBERTON MUST BE WATCHING OVER THEM.
I DON'T SEE WHAT THE PROB-LEM IS, GENERAL SUTHER-LAND.
THAT SHIP COULD STILL BE VALUABLE TO US.
!?

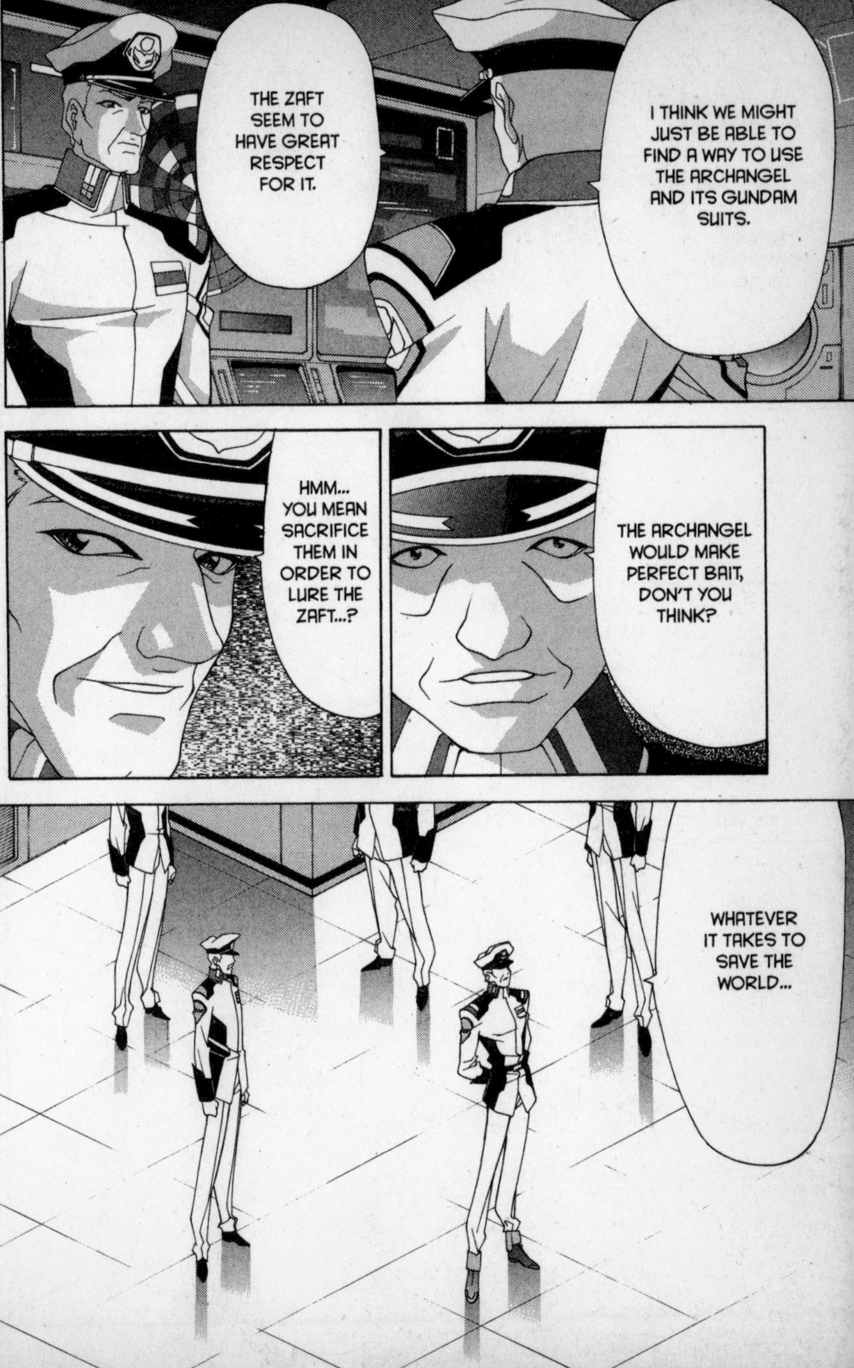
I THINK WE MIGHT JUST BE ABLE TO FIND A WAY TO USE THE ARCHANGEL AND ITS GUNDAM SUITS.
THE ZAFT SEEM TO HAVE GREAT RESPECT FOR IT.
THE ARCHANGEL WOULD MAKE PERFECT BAIT, DON'T YOU THINK?
HMM... YOU MEAN SACRIFICE THEM IN ORDER TO LURE THE ZAFT...?
WHATEVER IT TAKES TO SAVE THE WORLD...

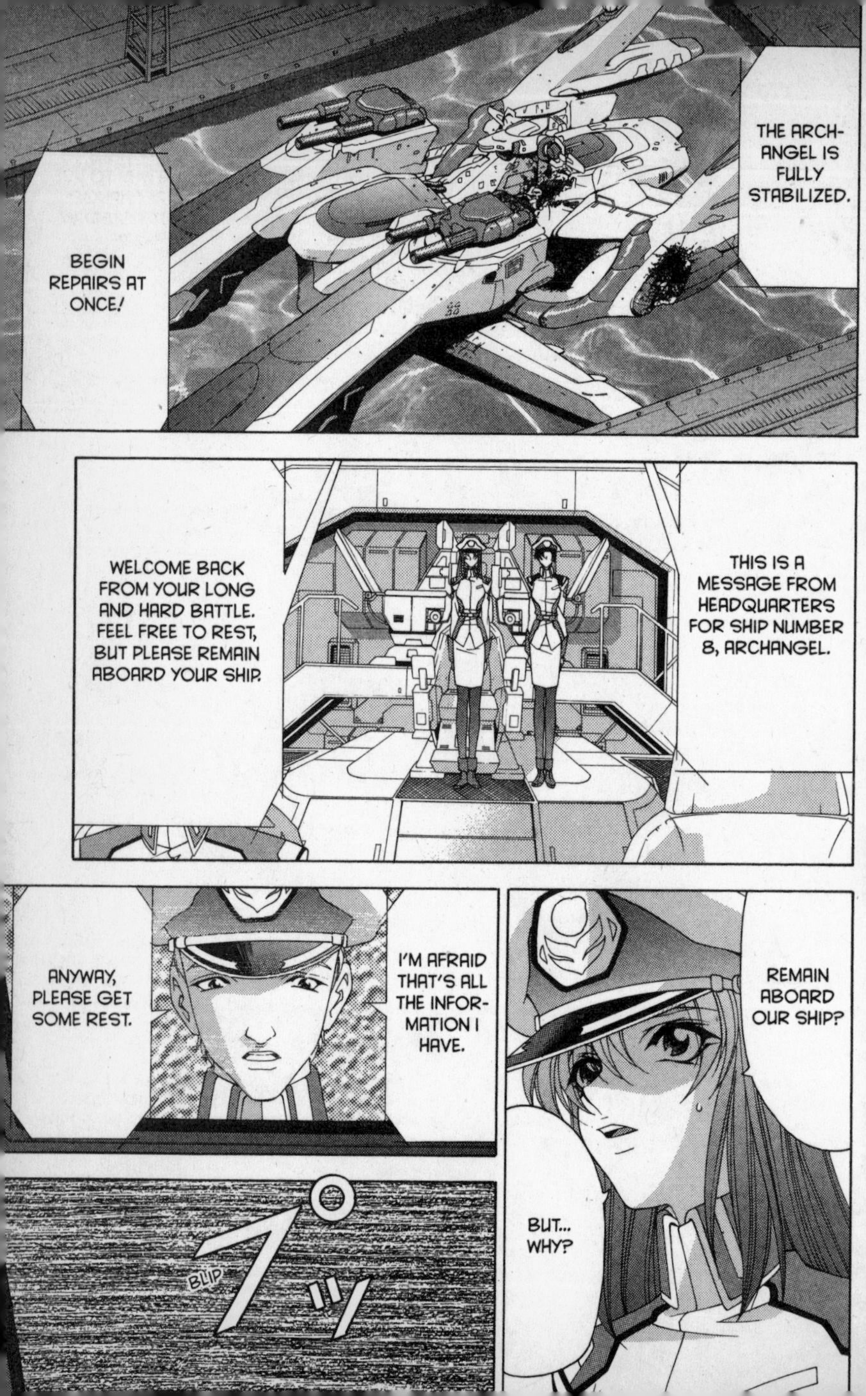
THE ARCH-ANGEL IS FULLY STABILIZED.
BEGIN REPAIRS AT ONCE!
THIS IS A MESSAGE FROM HEADQUARTERS FOR SHIP NUMBER 8, ARCHANGEL.
WELCOME BACK FROM YOUR LONG AND HARD BATTLE. FEEL FREE TO REST, BUT PLEASE REMAIN ABOARD YOUR SHIP.
REMAIN ABOARD OUR SHIP?
BUT... WHY?
I'M AFRAID THAT'S ALL THE INFOR-MATION I HAVE.
ANYWAY, PLEASE GET SOME REST.
BLIP

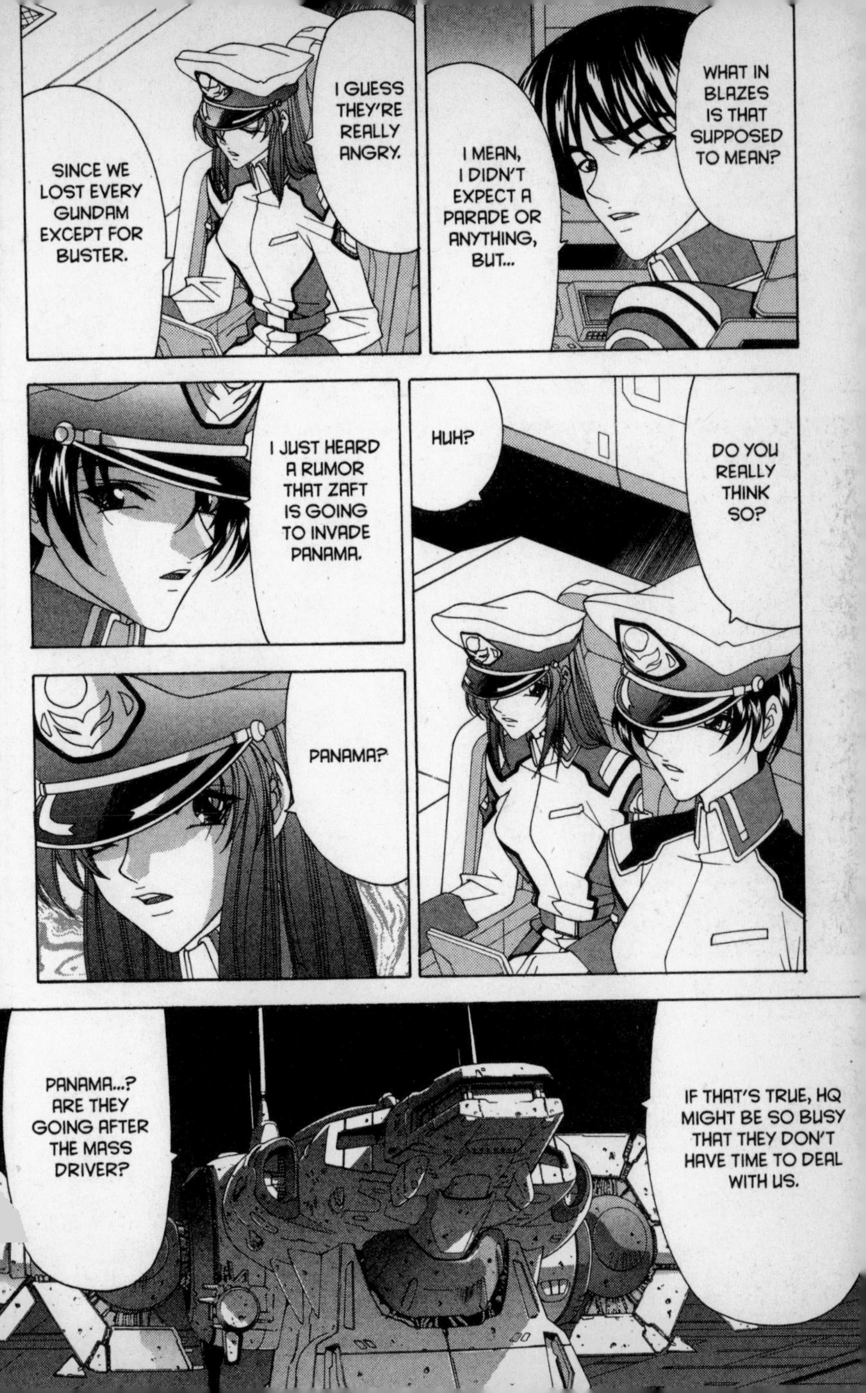
WHAT IN BLAZES IS THAT SUPPOSED TO MEAN?
I MEAN, I DIDN'T EXPECT A PARADE OR ANYTHING, BUT...
I GUESS THEY'RE REALLY ANGRY.
SINCE WE LOST EVERY GUNDAM EXCEPT FOR BUSTER.
DO YOU REALLY THINK SO?
HUH?
I JUST HEARD A RUMOR THAT ZAFT IS GOING TO INVADE PANAMA.
PANAMA?
IF THAT'S TRUE, HQ MIGHT BE SO BUSY THAT THEY DON'T HAVE TIME TO DEAL WITH US.
PANAMA...? ARE THEY GOING AFTER THE MASS DRIVER?

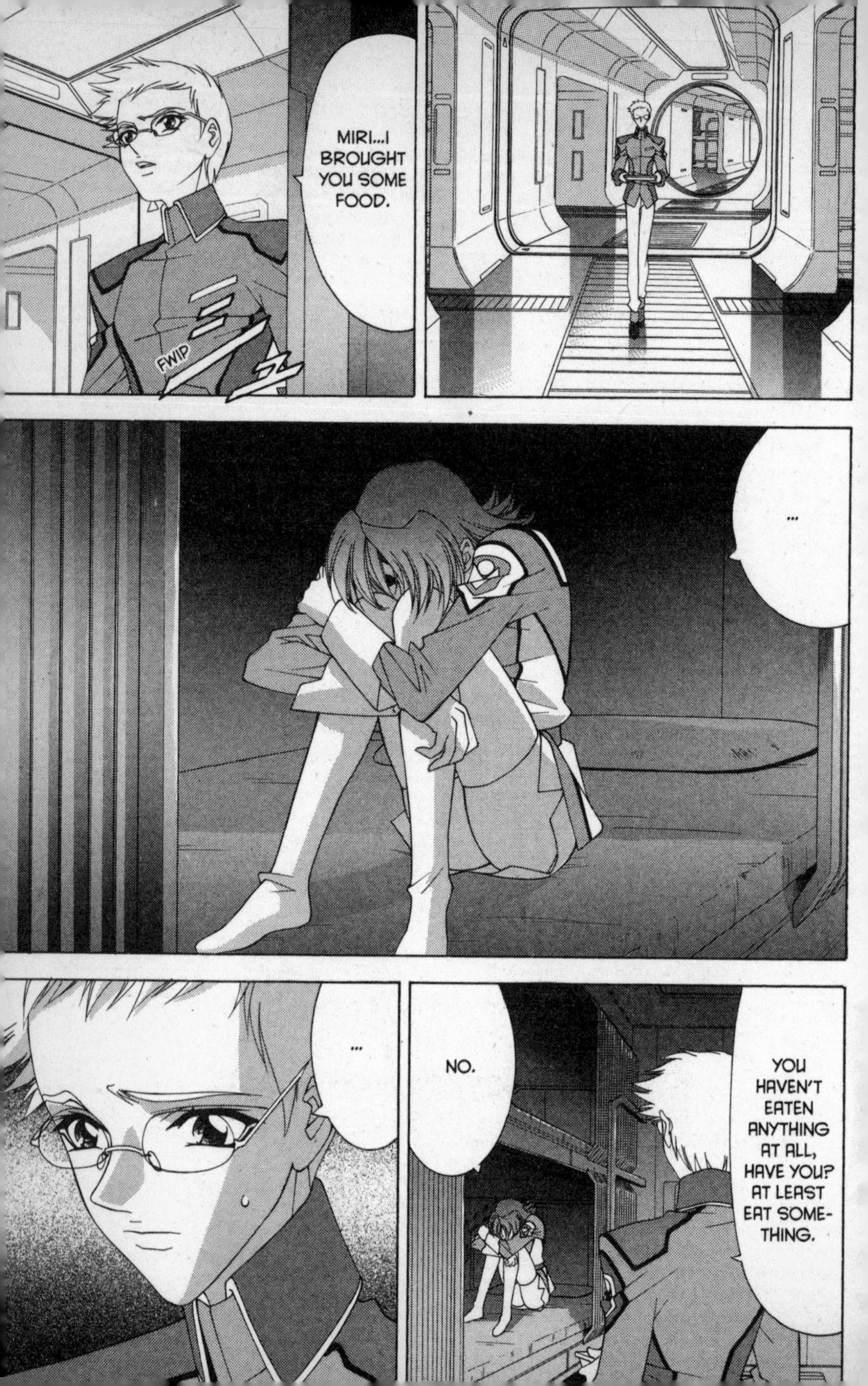
MIRI...I BROUGHT YOU SOME FOOD.
FWIP
...
YOU HAVEN'T EATEN ANYTHING AT ALL, HAVE YOU? AT LEAST EAT SOME-THING.
NO.
...

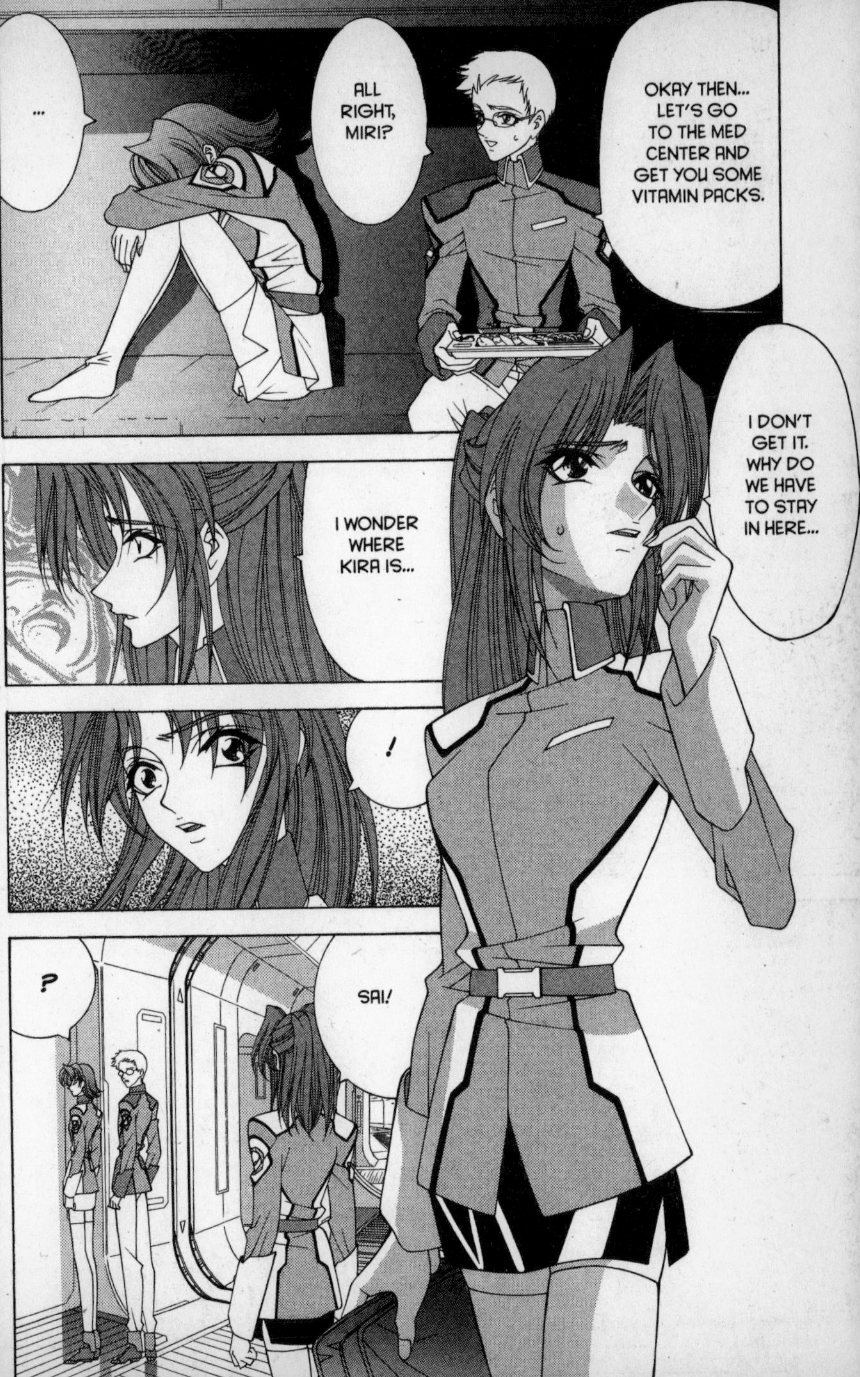
OKAY THEN... LET'S GO TO THE MED CENTER AND GET YOU SOME VITAMIN PACKS.
ALL RIGHT, MIRI?
...
I DON'T GET IT. WHY DO WE HAVE TO STAY IN HERE...
I WONDER WHERE KIRA IS...
!
SAI!
?

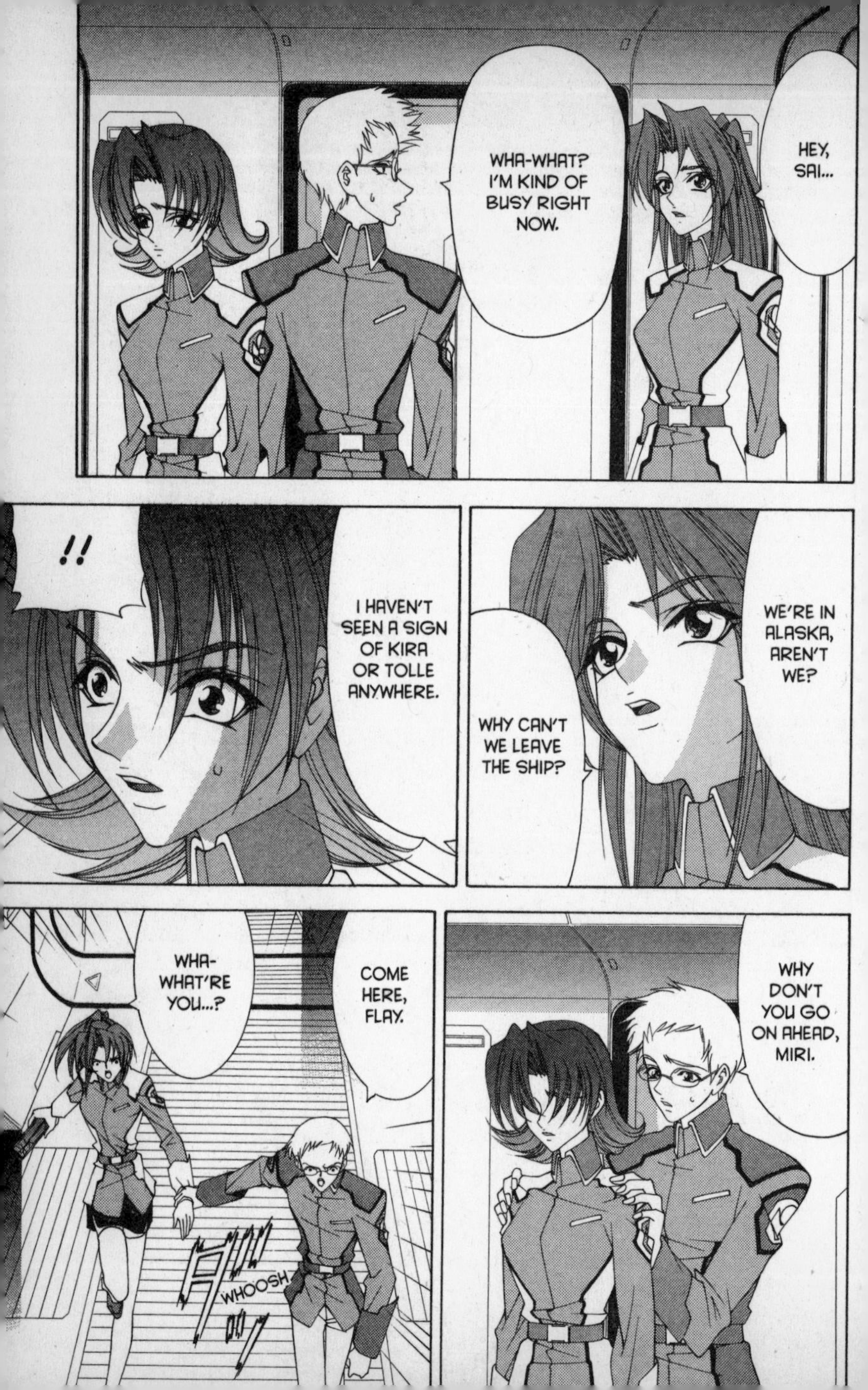
HEY, SAI...
WHA-WHAT? I'M KIND OF BUSY RIGHT NOW.
WE'RE IN ALASKA, AREN'T WE?
WHY CAN'T WE LEAVE THE SHIP?
I HAVEN'T SEEN A SIGN OF KIRA OR TOLLE ANYWHERE.
!!
WHY DON'T YOU GO ON AHEAD, MIRI.
COME HERE, FLAY.
WHA-WHAT'RE YOU...?
WHOOSH

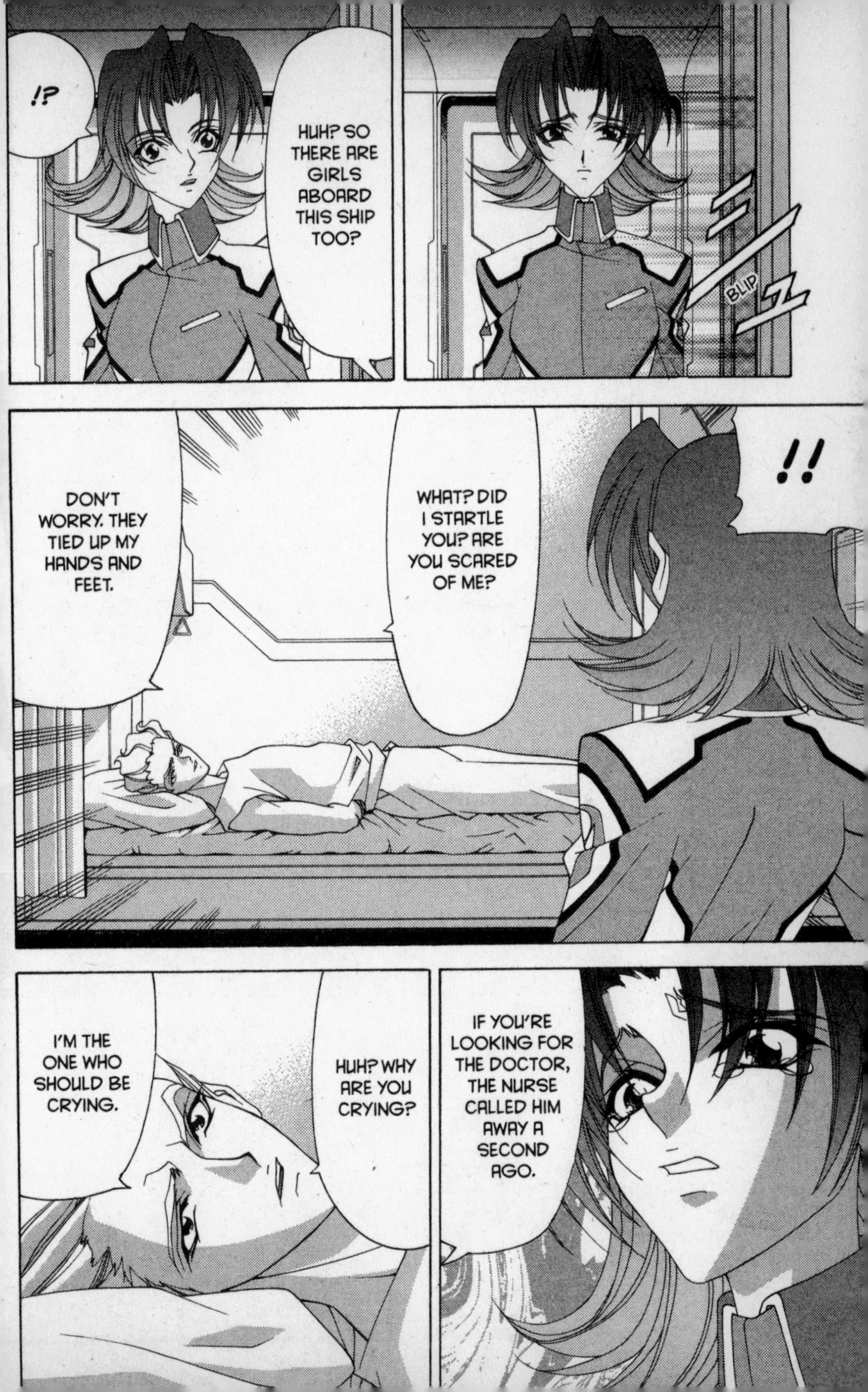
BLIP
HUH? SO THERE ARE GIRLS ABOARD THIS SHIP TOO?
!?
!!
WHAT? DID I STARTLE YOU? ARE YOU SCARED OF ME?
DON'T WORRY. THEY TIED UP MY HANDS AND FEET.
IF YOU'RE LOOKING FOR THE DOCTOR, THE NURSE CALLED HIM AWAY A SECOND AGO.
HUH? WHY ARE YOU CRYING?
I'M THE ONE WHO SHOULD BE CRYING.

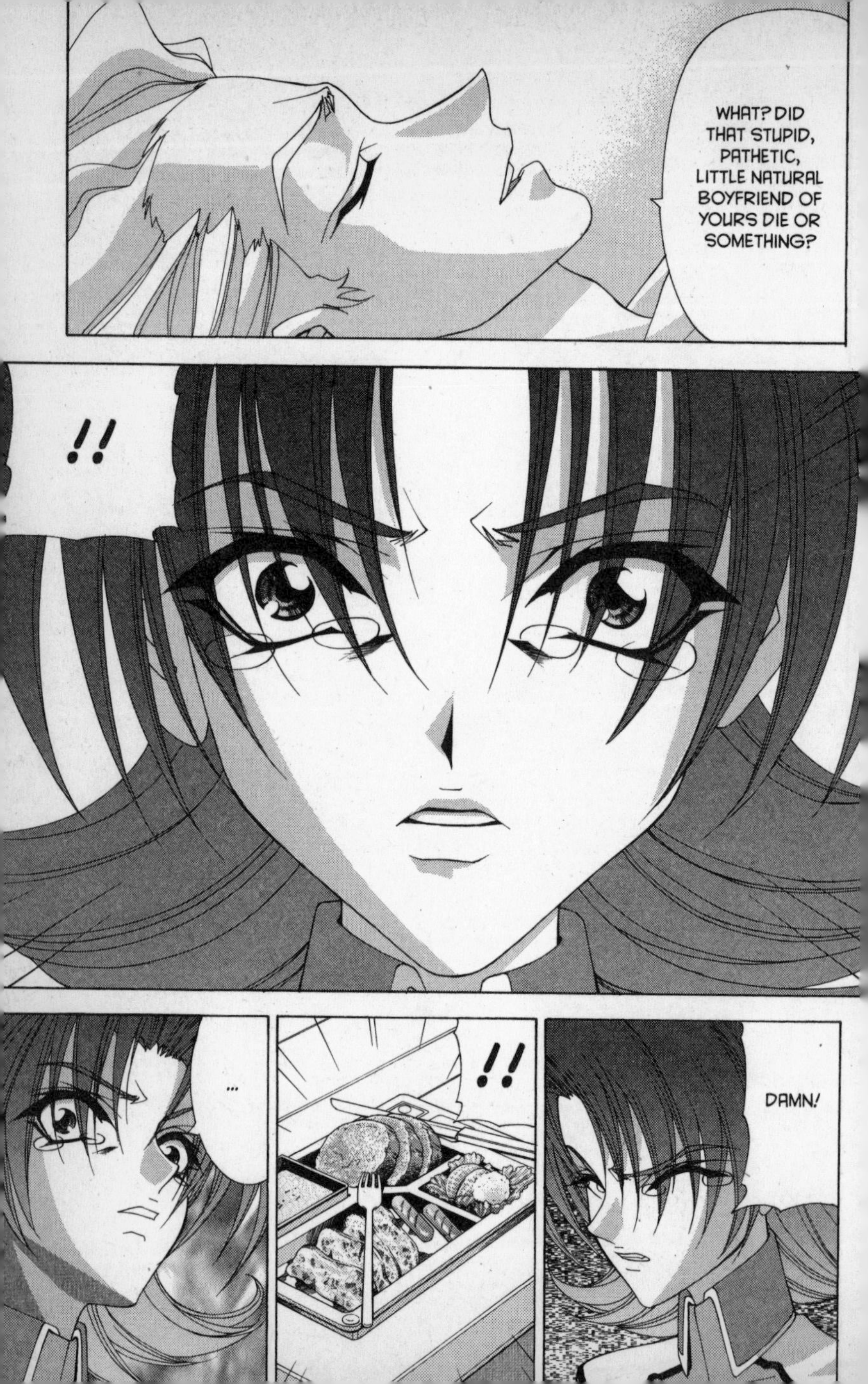
WHAT? DID THAT STUPID, PATHETIC, LITTLE NATURAL BOYFRIEND OF YOURS DIE OR SOMETHING?
!!
DAMN!
!!
...

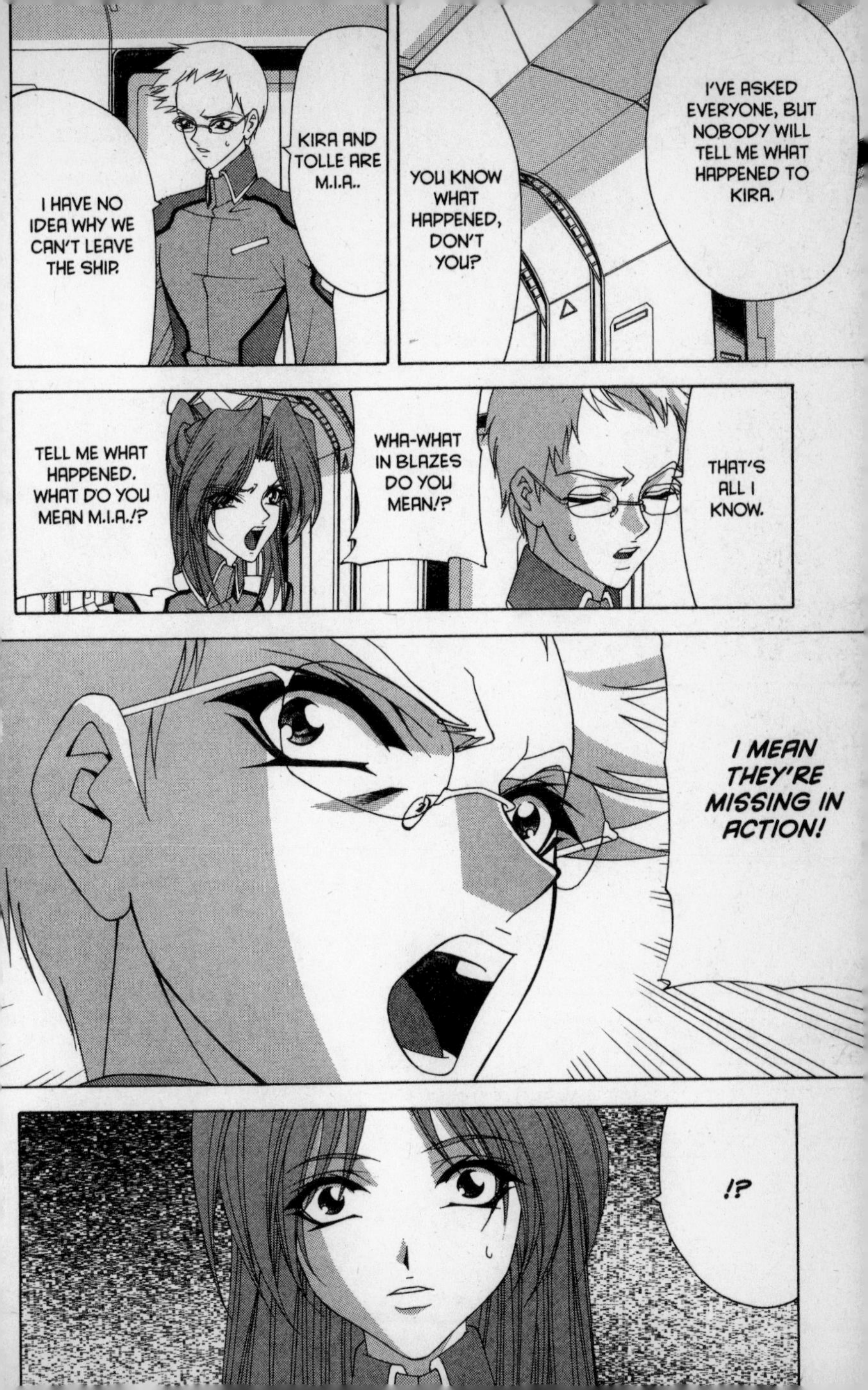
I'VE ASKED EVERYONE, BUT NOBODY WILL TELL ME WHAT HAPPENED TO KIRA.
YOU KNOW WHAT HAPPENED, DON'T YOU?
KIRA AND TOLLE ARE M.I.A..
I HAVE NO IDEA WHY WE CAN'T LEAVE THE SHIP.
THAT'S ALL I KNOW.
WHA-WHAT IN BLAZES DO YOU MEAN!?
TELL ME WHAT HAPPENED. WHAT DO YOU MEAN M.I.A.!?
I MEAN THEY'RE MISSING IN ACTION!
!?

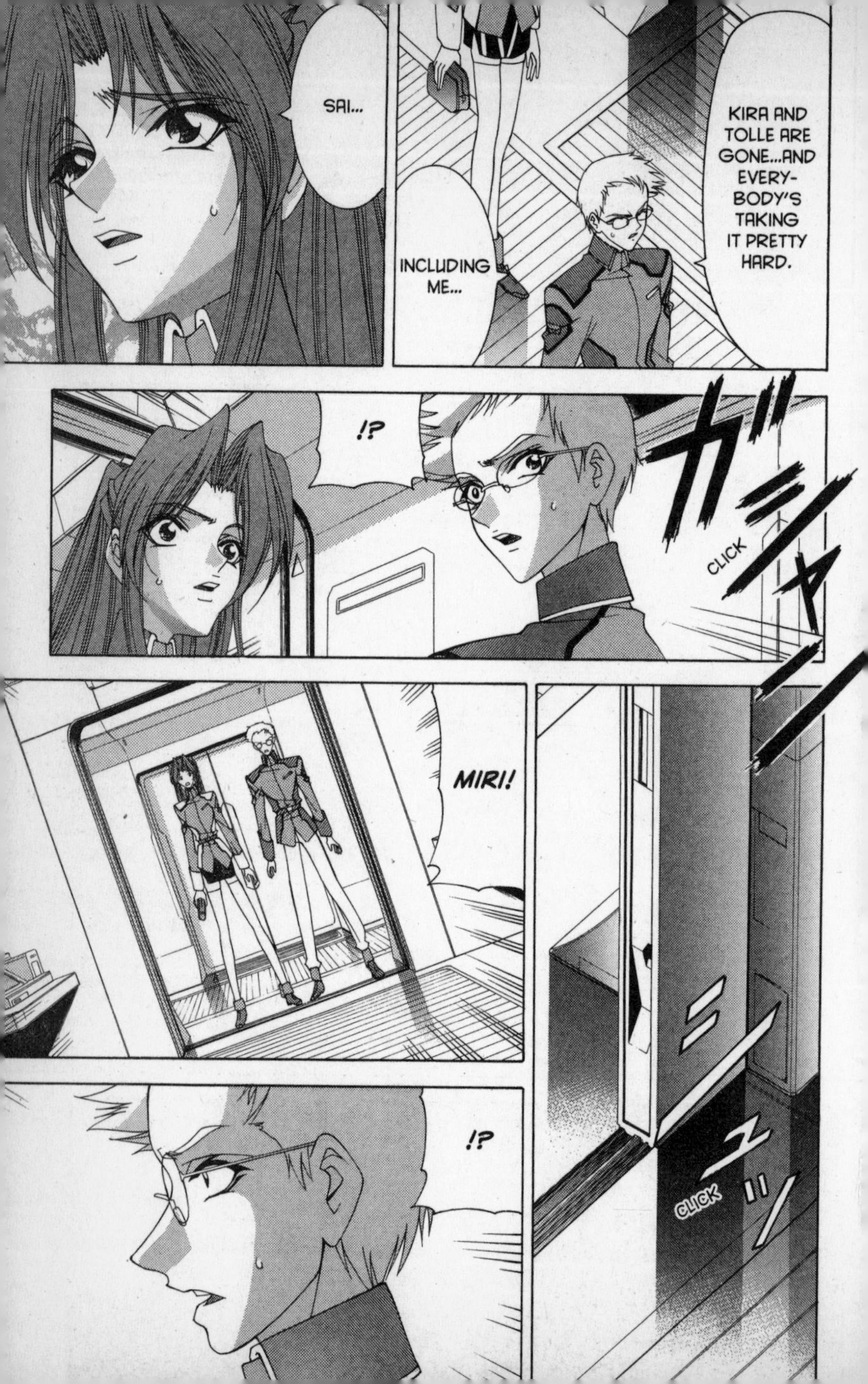
KIRA AND TOLLE ARE GONE...AND EVERY-BODY'S TAKING IT PRETTY HARD.
INCLUDING ME...
SAI...
!?
CLICK
CLICK
MIRI!
!?

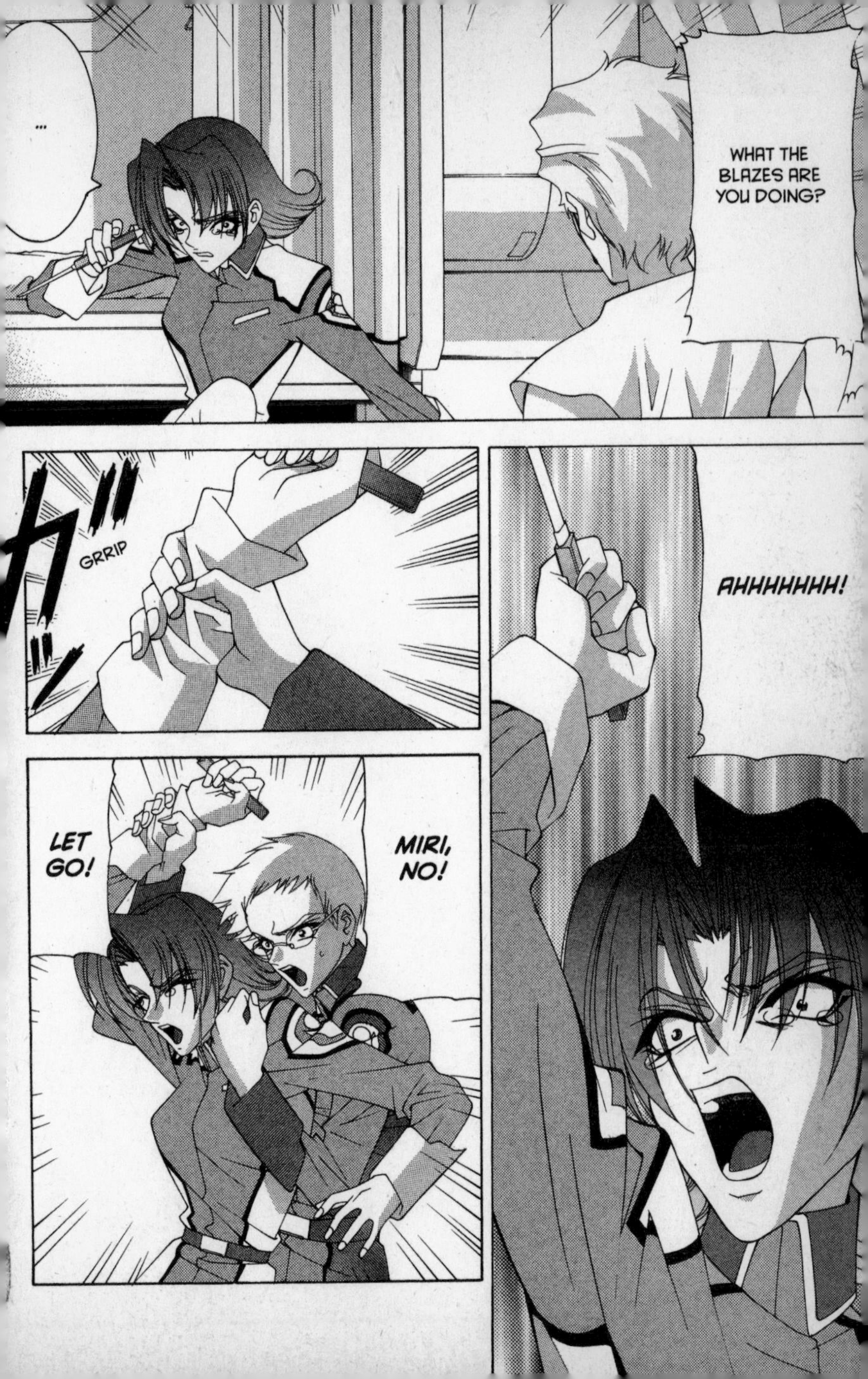
WHAT THE BLAZES ARE YOU DOING?
...
AHHHHHHH!
GRRIP
MIRI, NO!
LET GO!

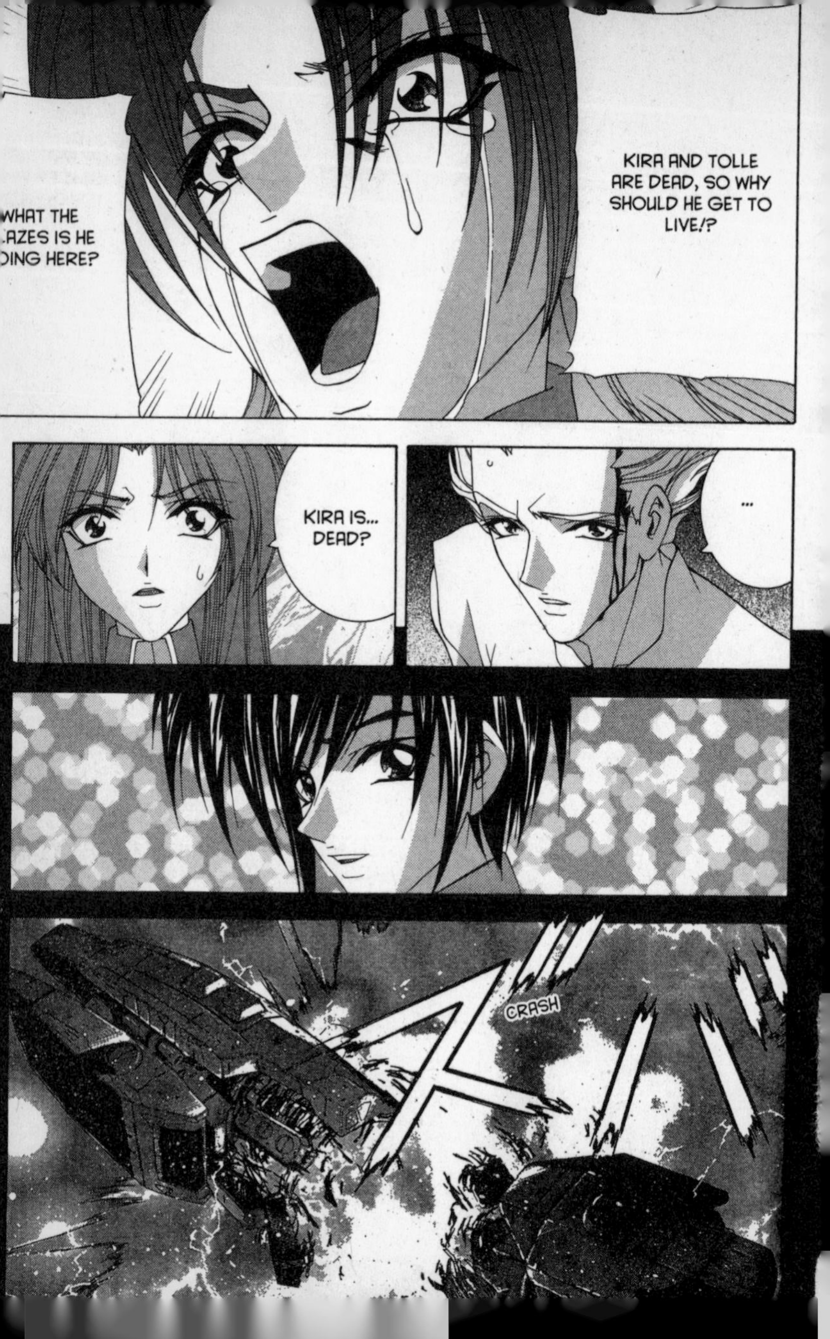
KIRA AND TOLLE ARE DEAD, SO WHY SHOULD HE GET TO LIVE!?
WHAT THE AZES IS HE DING HERE?
...
KIRA IS... DEAD?
CRASH

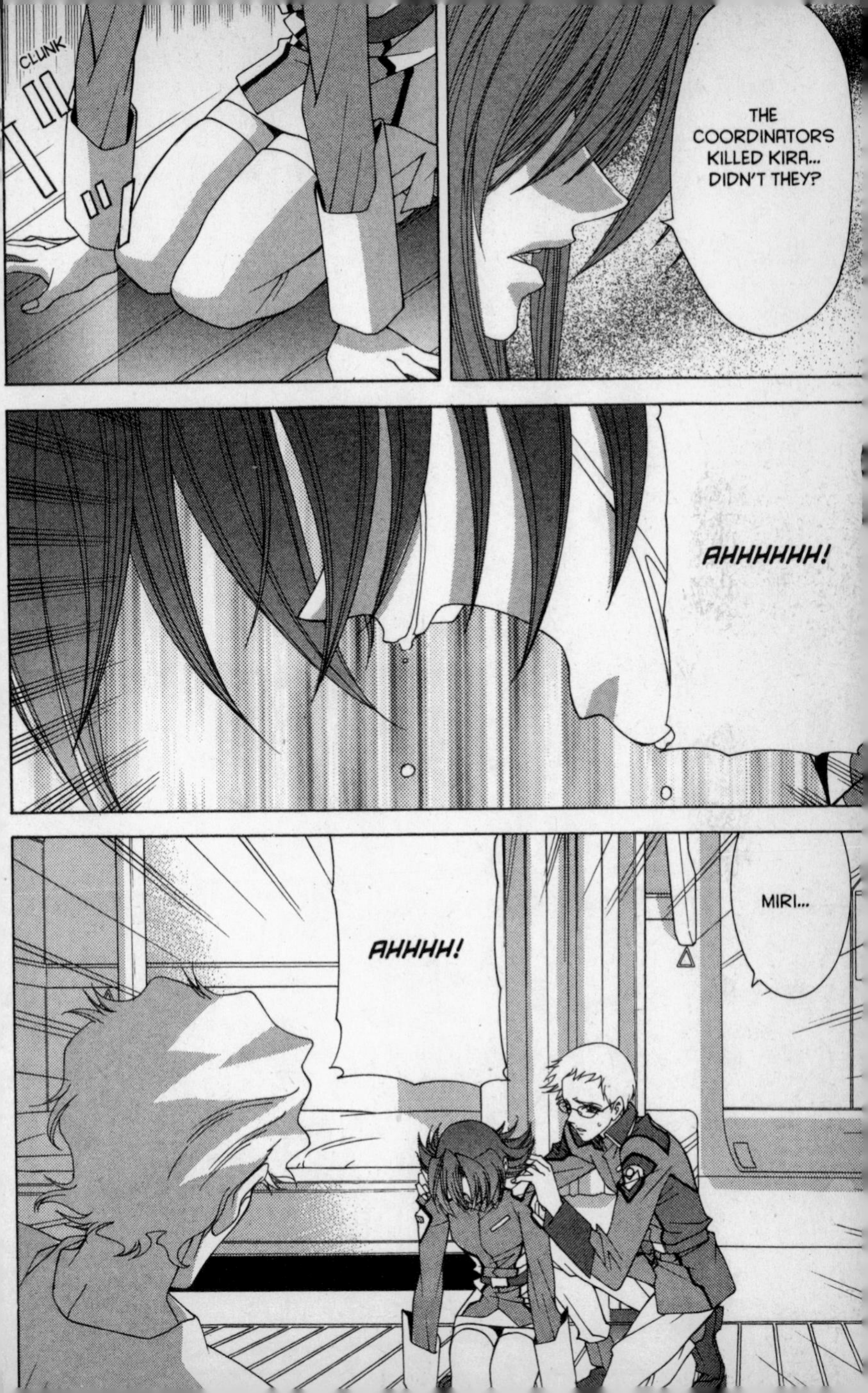
THE COORDINATORS KILLED KIRA... DIDN'T THEY?
CLUNK
AHHHHHH!
MIRI...
AHHHH!

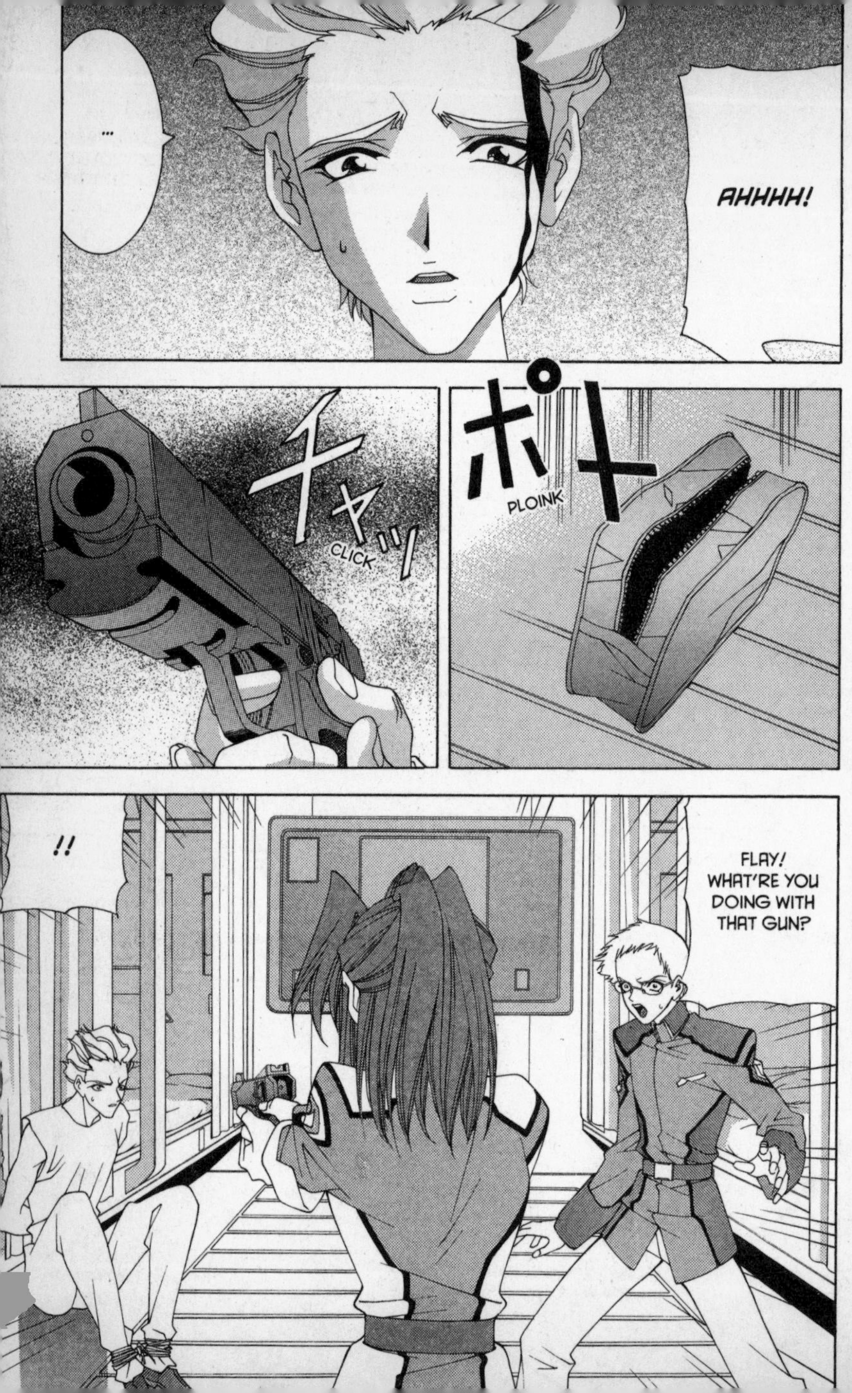
AHHHH!
...
ポイ
PLOINK
チャッ
CLICK
FLAY! WHAT'RE YOU DOING WITH THAT GUN?
!!

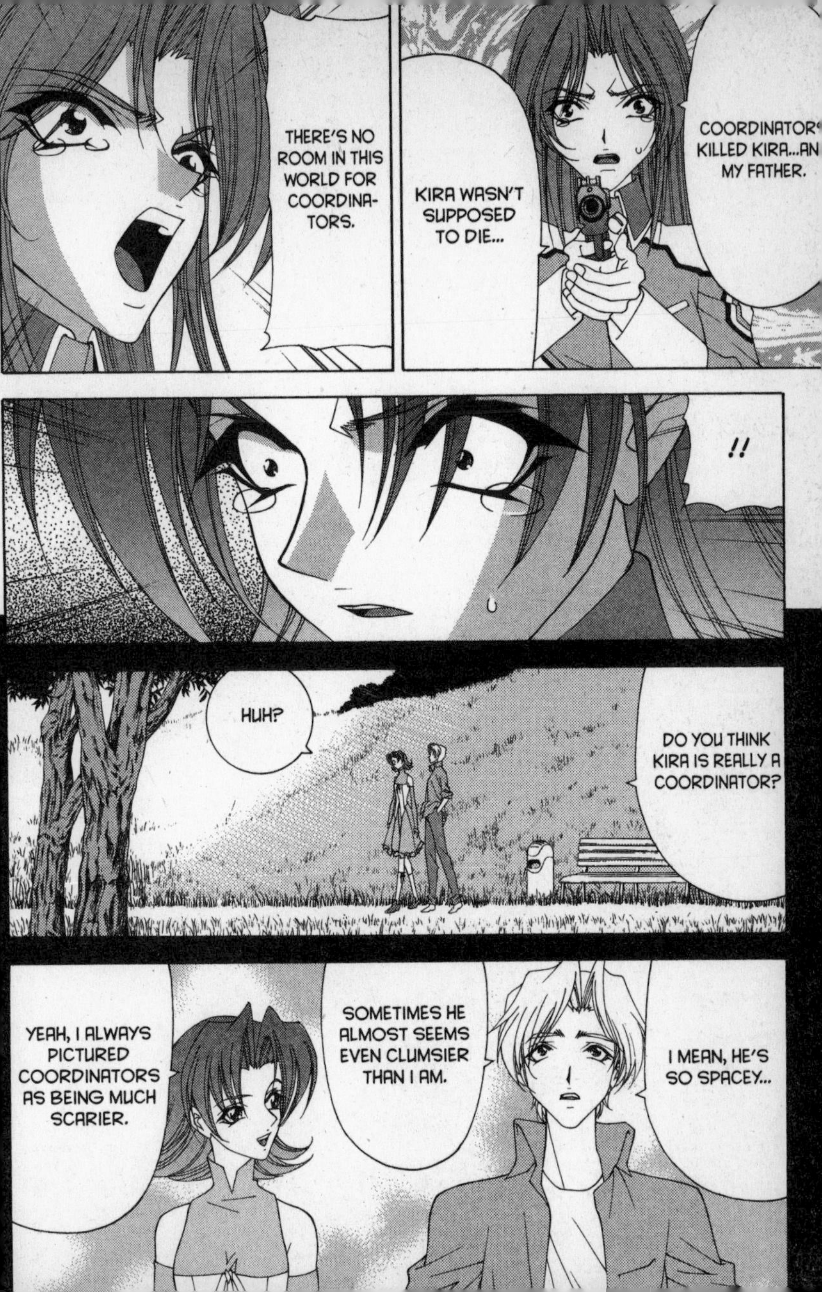
COORDINATOR KILLED KIRA...AN MY FATHER.
KIRA WASN'T SUPPOSED TO DIE...
THERE'S NO ROOM IN THIS WORLD FOR COORDINA-TORS.
!!
DO YOU THINK KIRA IS REALLY A COORDINATOR?
HUH?
I MEAN, HE'S SO SPACEY...
SOMETIMES HE ALMOST SEEMS EVEN CLUMSIER THAN I AM.
YEAH, I ALWAYS PICTURED COORDINATORS AS BEING MUCH SCARIER.

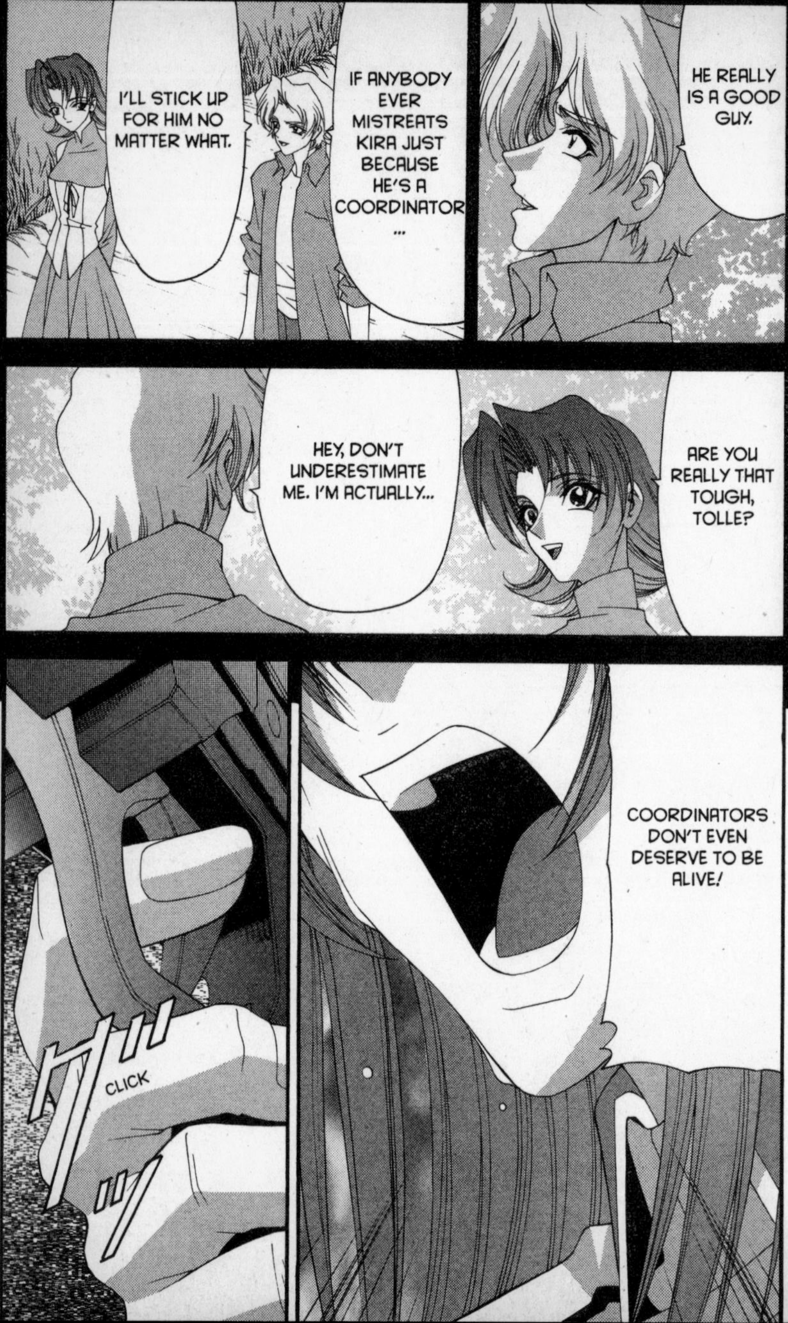
HE REALLY IS A GOOD GUY.
IF ANYBODY EVER MISTREATS KIRA JUST BECAUSE HE'S A COORDINATOR...
I'LL STICK UP FOR HIM NO MATTER WHAT.
ARE YOU REALLY THAT TOUGH, TOLLE?
HEY, DON'T UNDERESTIMATE ME. I'M ACTUALLY...
COORDINATORS DON'T EVEN DESERVE TO BE ALIVE!
CLICK

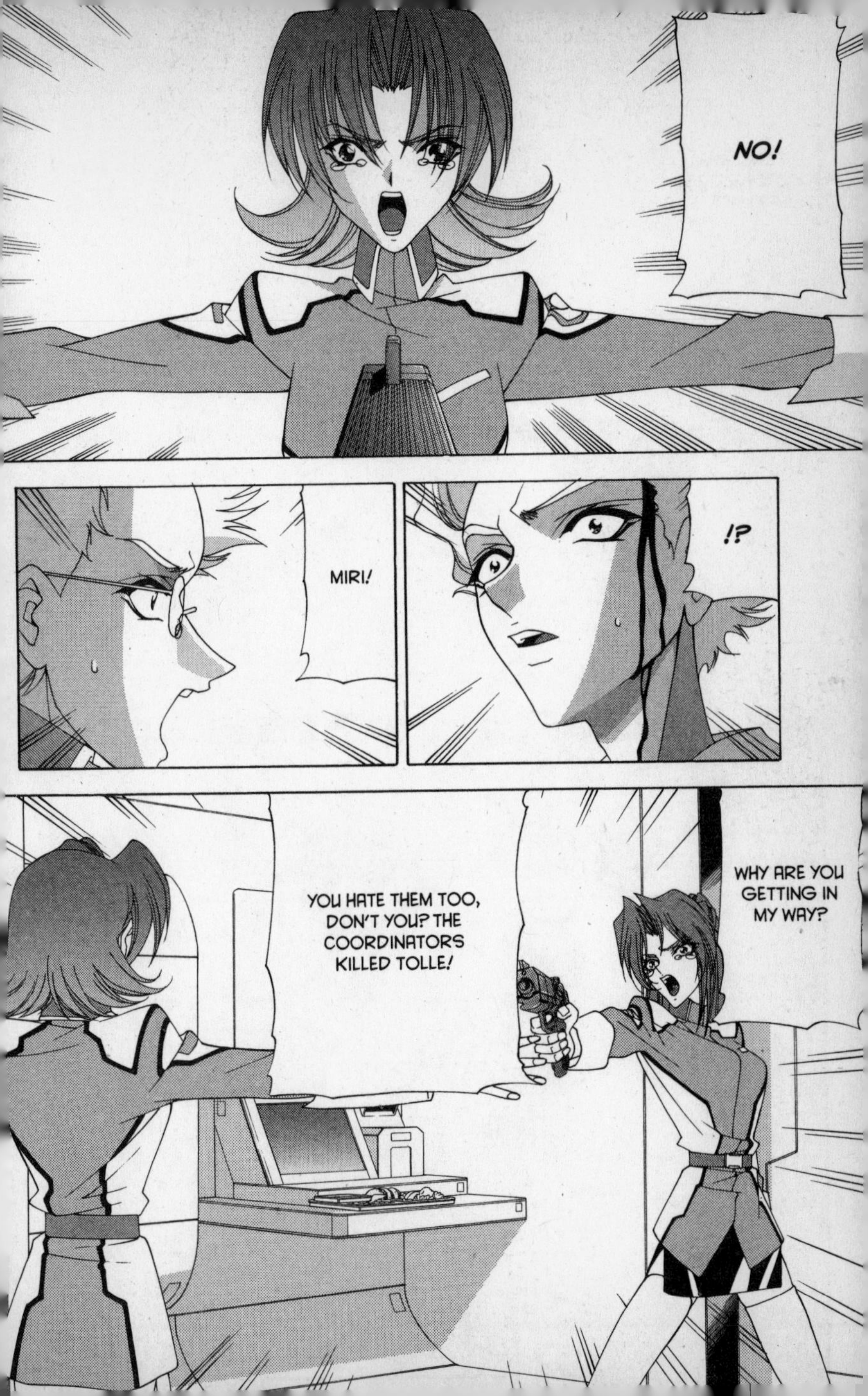
NO!
!?
MIRI!
WHY ARE YOU GETTING IN MY WAY?
YOU HATE THEM TOO, DON'T YOU? THE COORDINATORS KILLED TOLLE!

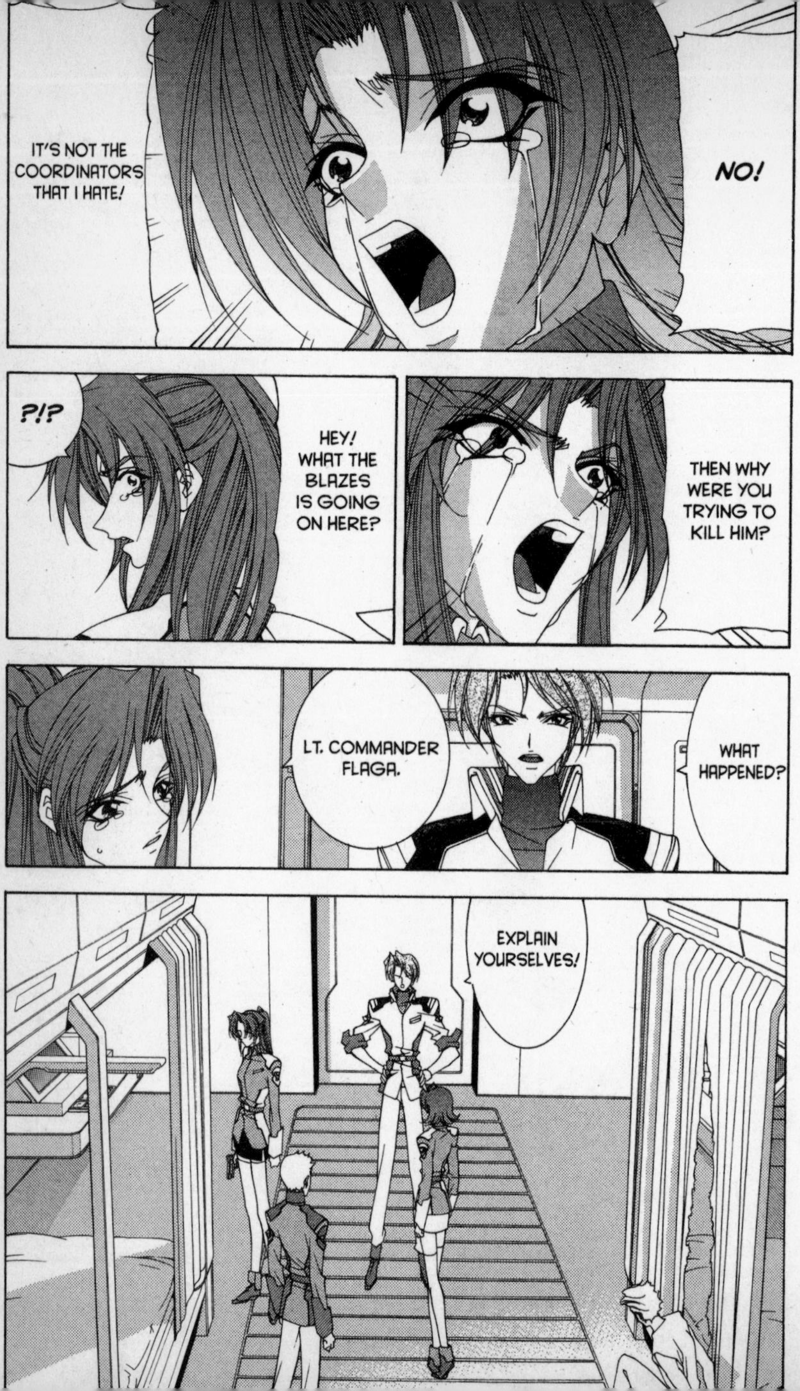
NO!
IT'S NOT THE COORDINATORS THAT I HATE!
THEN WHY WERE YOU TRYING TO KILL HIM?
HEY! WHAT THE BLAZES IS GOING ON HERE?
?!?
WHAT HAPPENED?
LT. COMMANDER FLAGA.
EXPLAIN YOURSELVES!

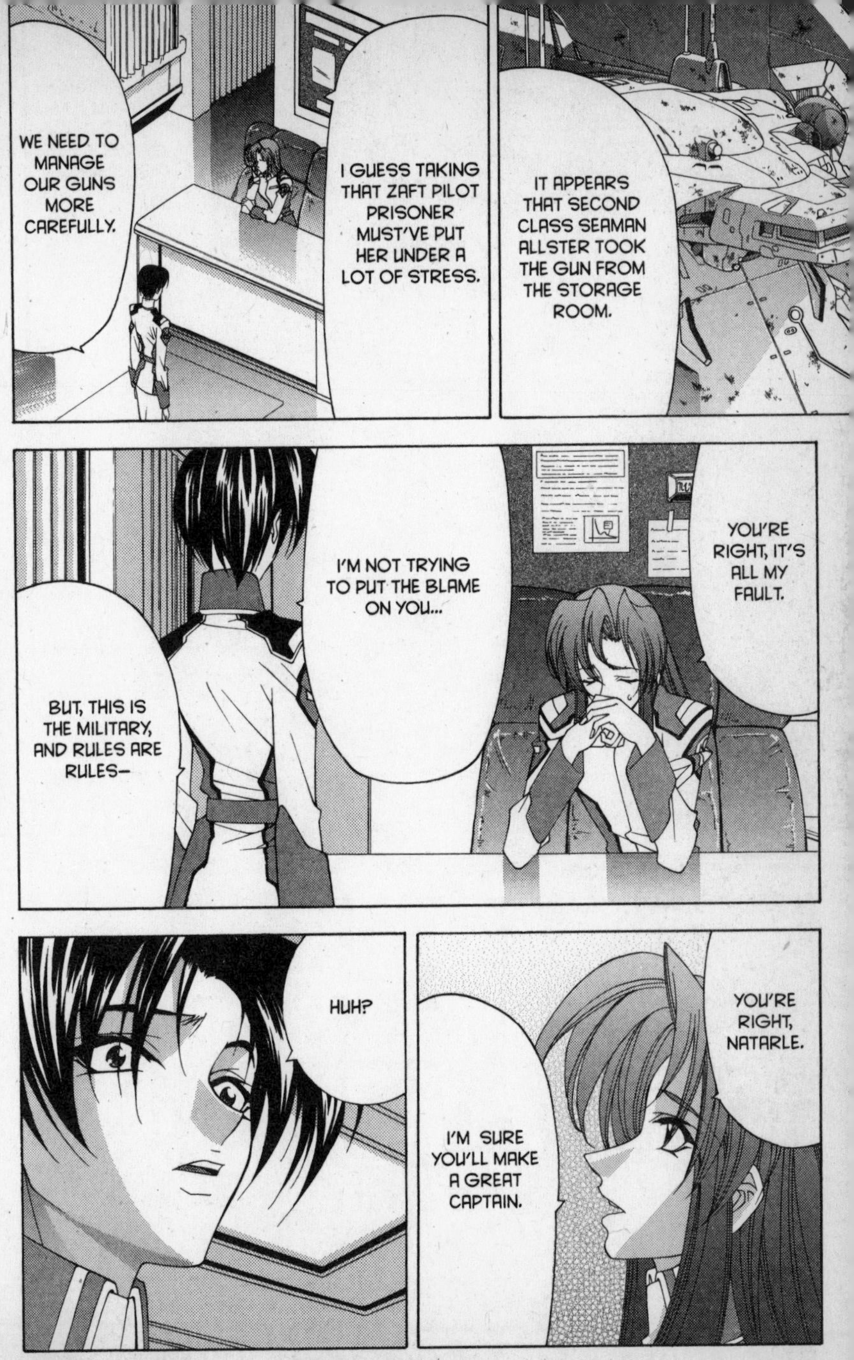
IT APPEARS THAT SECOND CLASS SEAMAN ALLSTER TOOK THE GUN FROM THE STORAGE ROOM.
I GUESS TAKING THAT ZAFT PILOT PRISONER MUST'VE PUT HER UNDER A LOT OF STRESS.
WE NEED TO MANAGE OUR GUNS MORE CAREFULLY.
YOU'RE RIGHT, IT'S ALL MY FAULT.
I'M NOT TRYING TO PUT THE BLAME ON YOU...
BUT, THIS IS THE MILITARY, AND RULES ARE RULES—
YOU'RE RIGHT, NATARLE.
I'M SURE YOU'LL MAKE A GREAT CAPTAIN.
HUH?

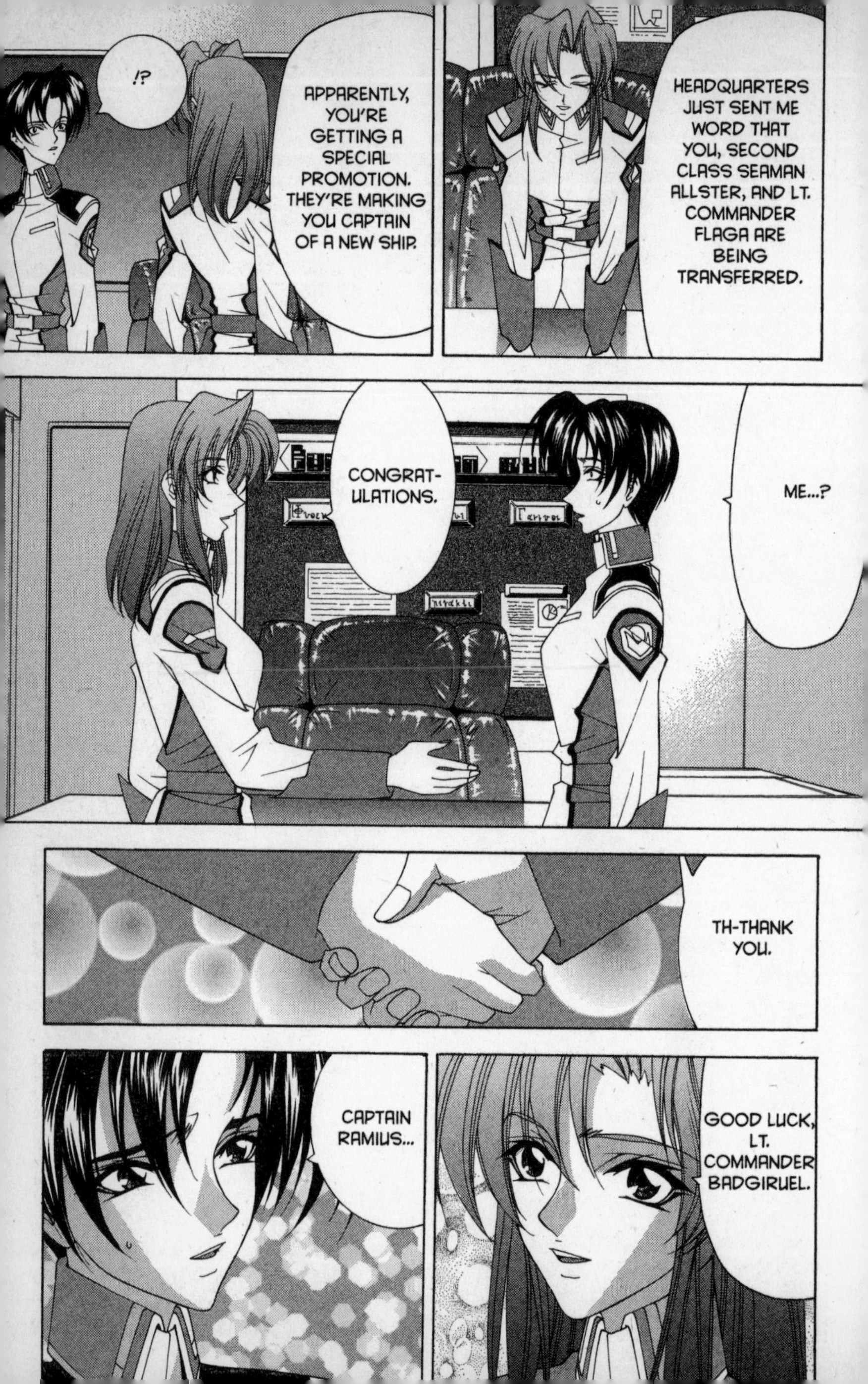
HEADQUARTERS JUST SENT ME WORD THAT YOU, SECOND CLASS SEAMAN ALLSTER, AND LT. COMMANDER FLAGA ARE BEING TRANSFERRED.
APPARENTLY, YOU'RE GETTING A SPECIAL PROMOTION. THEY'RE MAKING YOU CAPTAIN OF A NEW SHIP.
!?
ME...?
CONGRAT-ULATIONS.
TH-THANK YOU.
GOOD LUCK, LT. COMMANDER BADGIRUEL.
CAPTAIN RAMIUS...

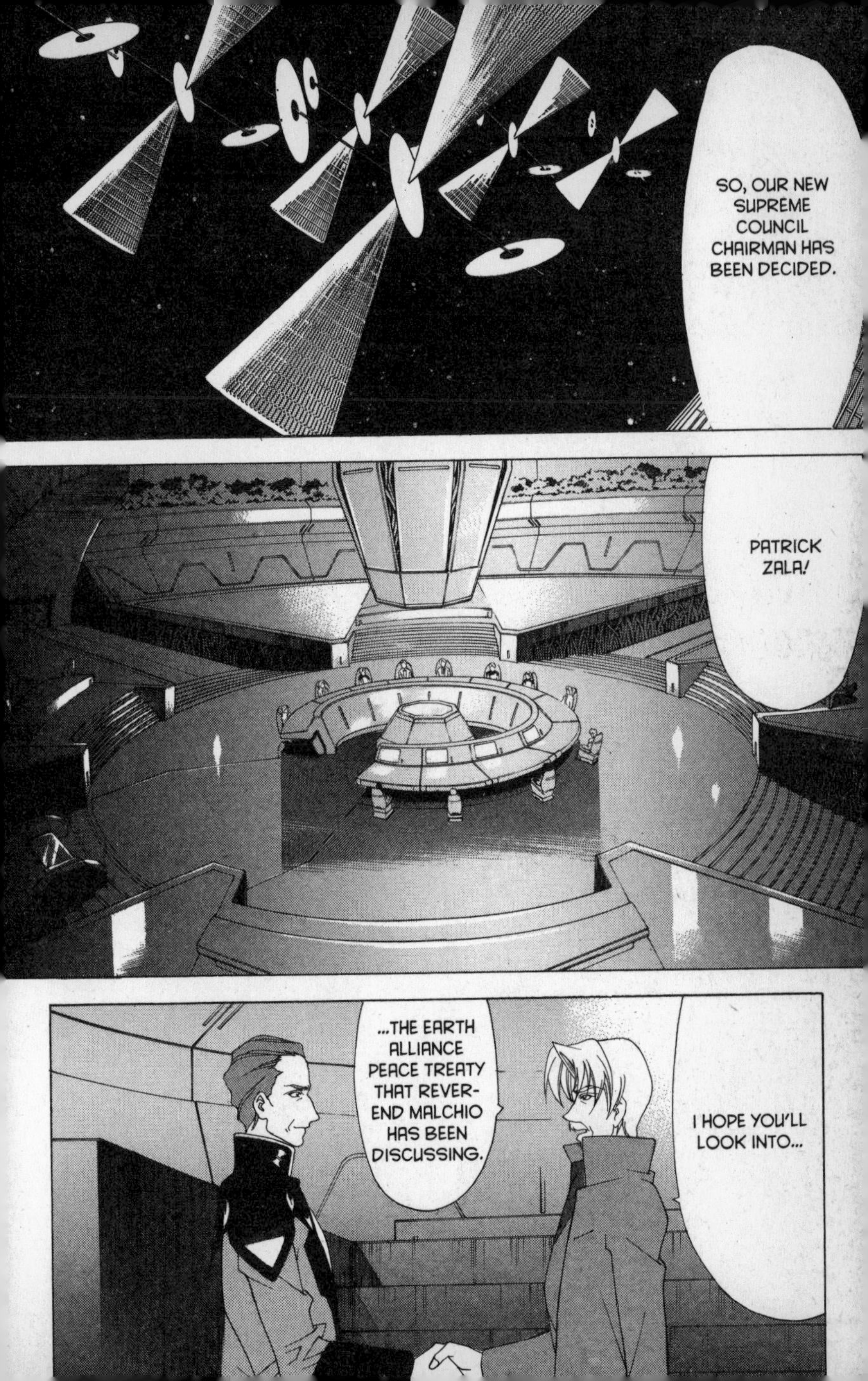
SO, OUR NEW SUPREME COUNCIL CHAIRMAN HAS BEEN DECIDED.
PATRICK ZALA!
I HOPE YOU'LL LOOK INTO...
...THE EARTH ALLIANCE PEACE TREATY THAT REVEREND MALCHIO HAS BEEN DISCUSSING.

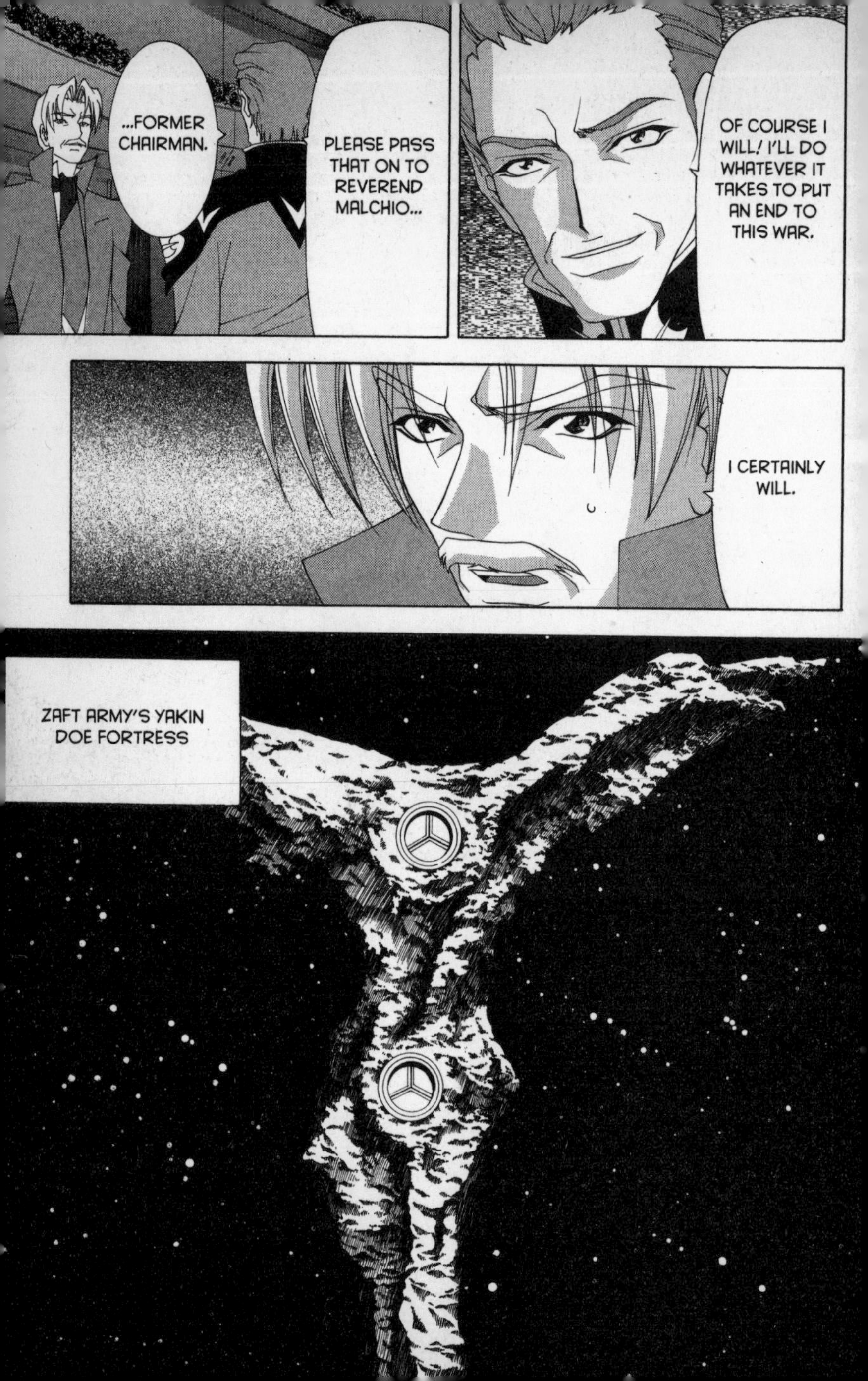
OF COURSE I WILL! I'LL DO WHATEVER IT TAKES TO PUT AN END TO THIS WAR.
PLEASE PASS THAT ON TO REVEREND MALCHIO...
...FORMER CHAIRMAN.
I CERTAINLY WILL.
ZAFT ARMY'S YAKIN DOE FORTRESS

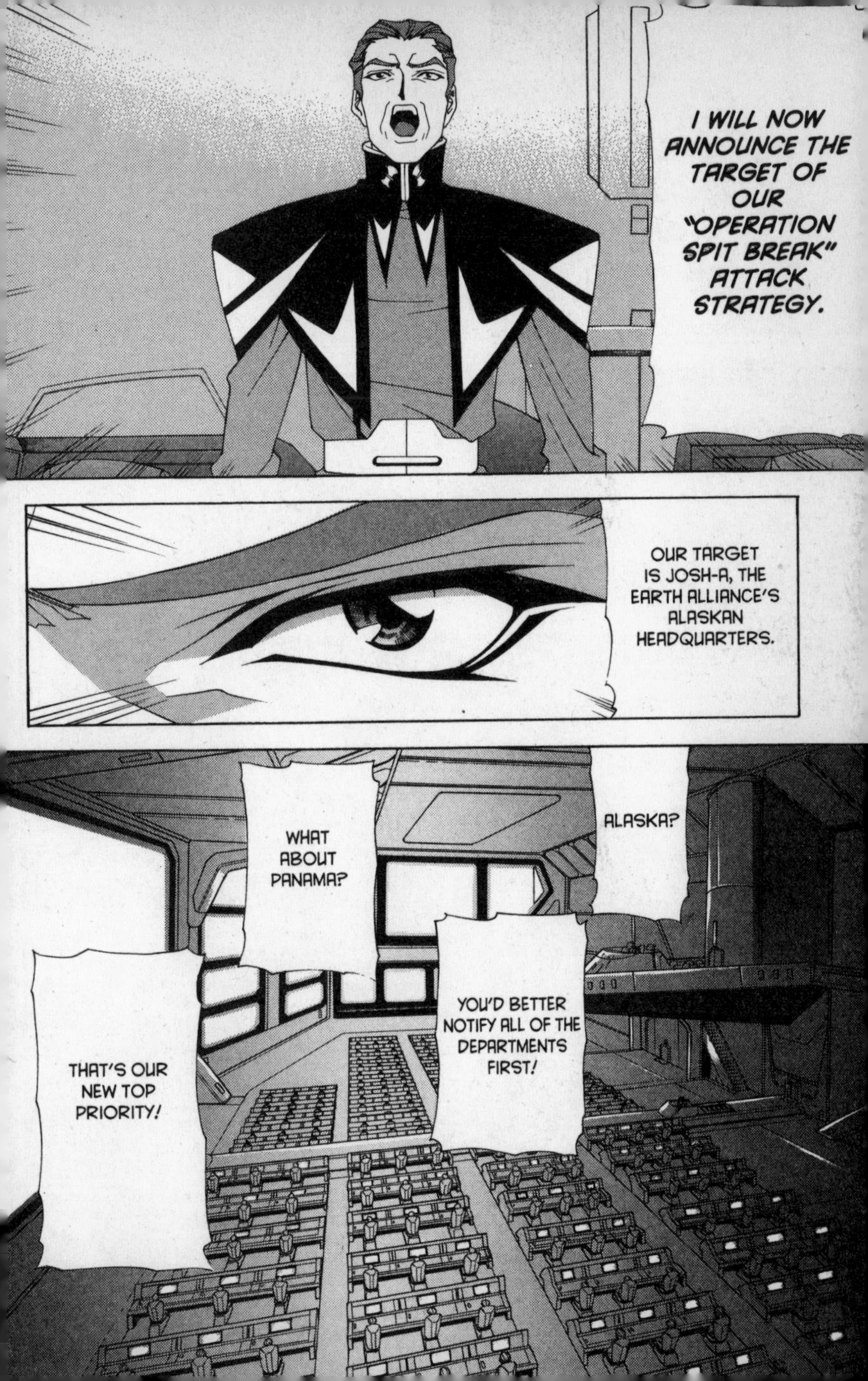
I WILL NOW ANNOUNCE THE TARGET OF OUR "OPERATION SPIT BREAK" ATTACK STRATEGY.
OUR TARGET IS JOSH-A, THE EARTH ALLIANCE'S ALASKAN HEADQUARTERS.
ALASKA?
WHAT ABOUT PANAMA?
YOU'D BETTER NOTIFY ALL OF THE DEPARTMENTS FIRST!
THAT'S OUR NEW TOP PRIORITY!

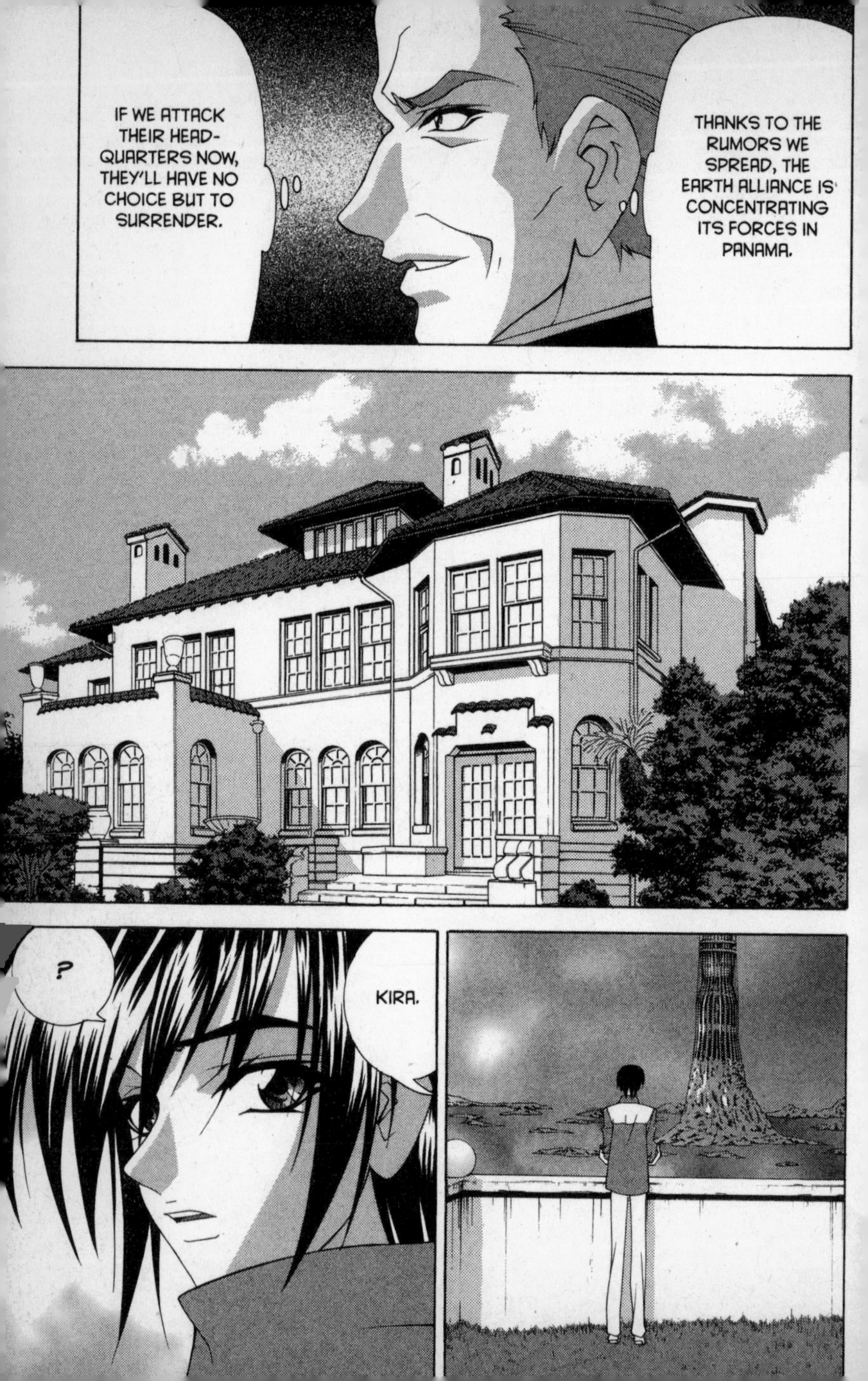
THANKS TO THE RUMORS WE SPREAD, THE EARTH ALLIANCE IS CONCENTRATING ITS FORCES IN PANAMA.
IF WE ATTACK THEIR HEAD-QUARTERS NOW, THEY'LL HAVE NO CHOICE BUT TO SURRENDER.
KIRA.
?

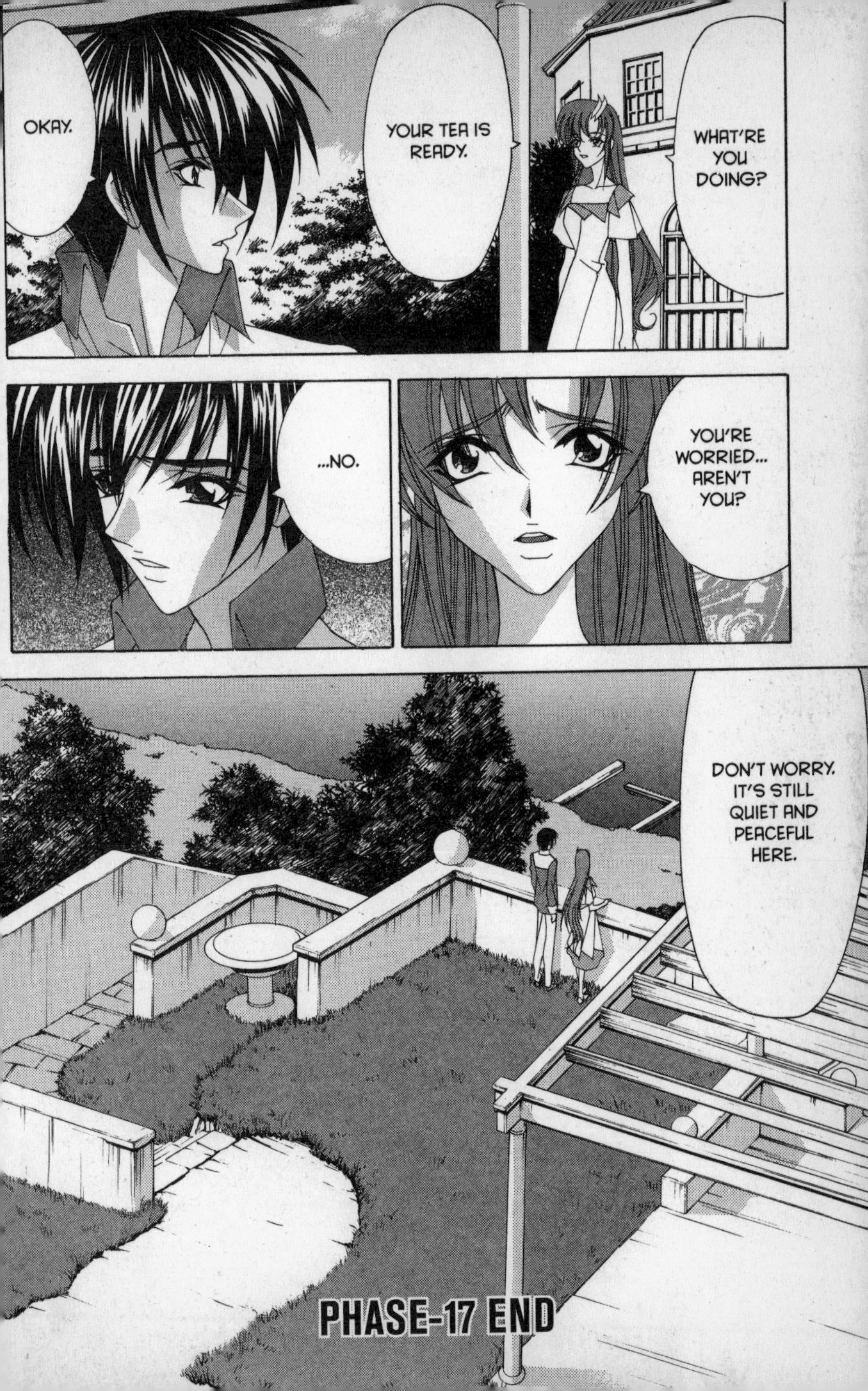
WHAT'RE YOU DOING?
YOUR TEA IS READY.
OKAY.
YOU'RE WORRIED... AREN'T YOU?
...NO.
DON'T WORRY. IT'S STILL QUIET AND PEACEFUL HERE.
PHASE-17 END

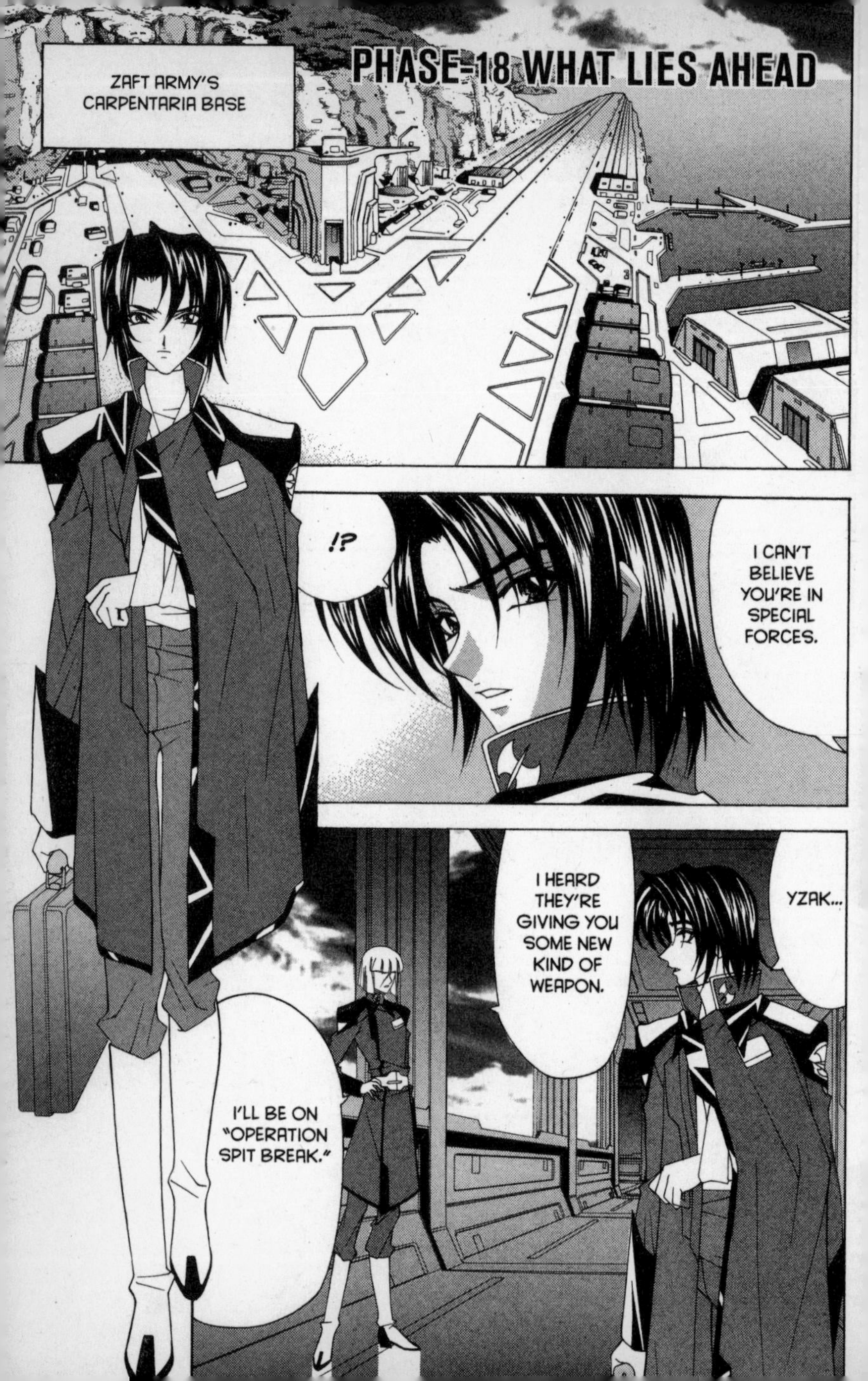
PHASE-18 WHAT LIES AHEAD
ZAFT ARMY'S CARPENTARIA BASE
I CAN'T BELIEVE YOU'RE IN SPECIAL FORCES.
!?
YZAK...
I HEARD THEY'RE GIVING YOU SOME NEW KIND OF WEAPON.
I'LL BE ON "OPERATION SPIT BREAK."

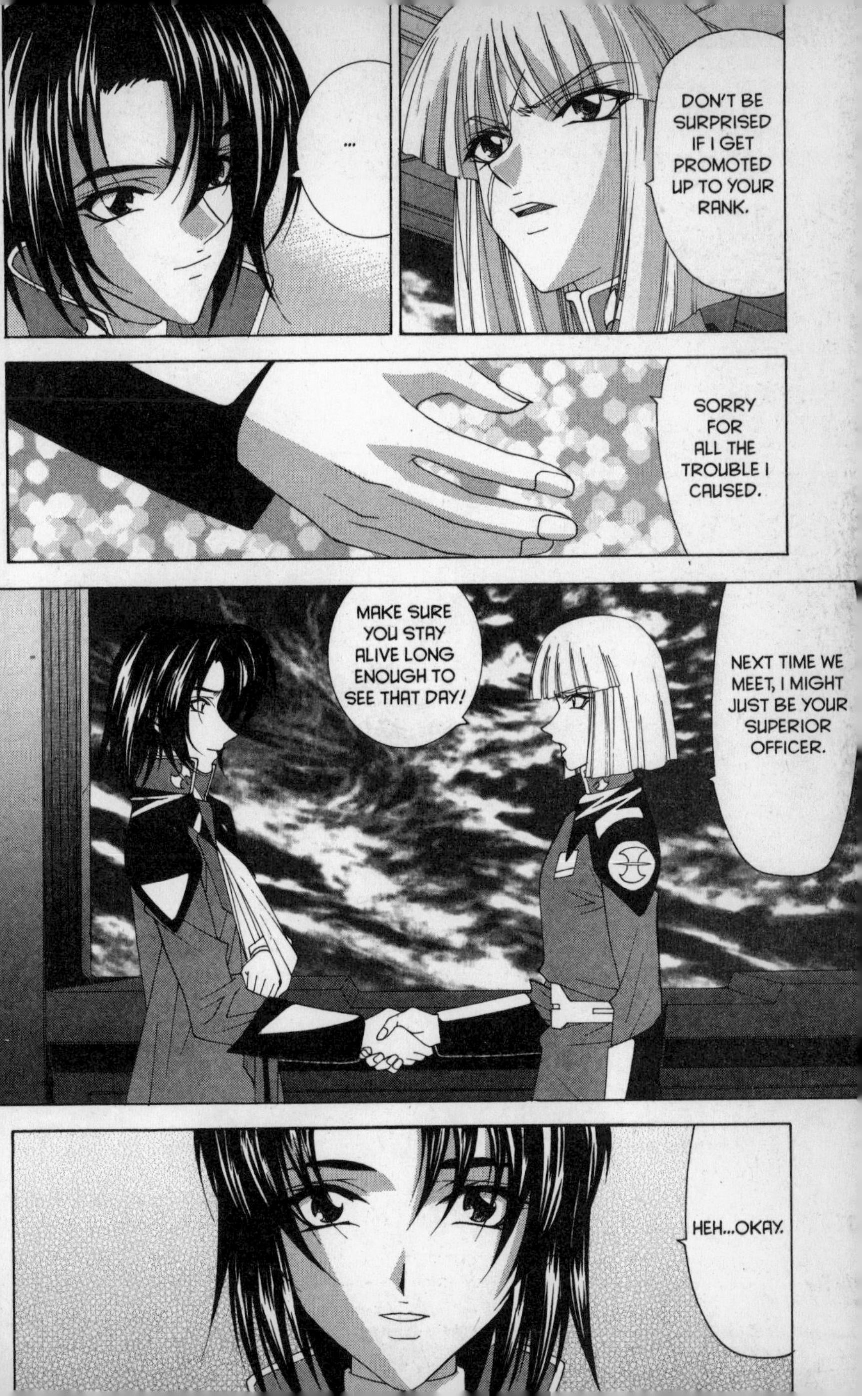
DON'T BE SURPRISED IF I GET PROMOTED UP TO YOUR RANK.
...
SORRY FOR ALL THE TROUBLE I CAUSED.
NEXT TIME WE MEET, I MIGHT JUST BE YOUR SUPERIOR OFFICER.
MAKE SURE YOU STAY ALIVE LONG ENOUGH TO SEE THAT DAY!
HEH...OKAY.

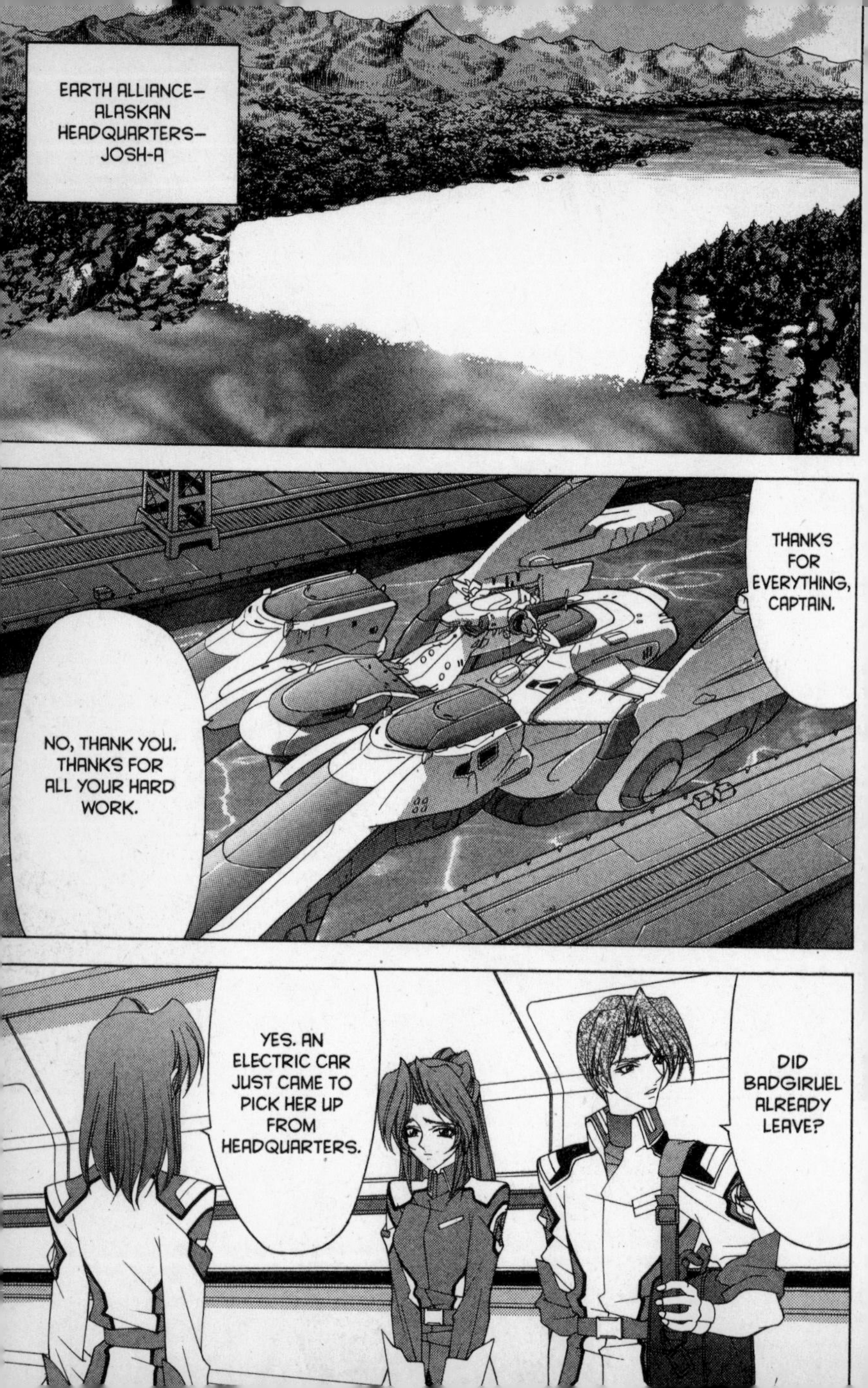
EARTH ALLIANCE—ALASKAN HEADQUARTERS—JOSH-A
THANKS FOR EVERYTHING, CAPTAIN.
NO, THANK YOU. THANKS FOR ALL YOUR HARD WORK.
DID BADGIRUEL ALREADY LEAVE?
YES. AN ELECTRIC CAR JUST CAME TO PICK HER UP FROM HEADQUARTERS.

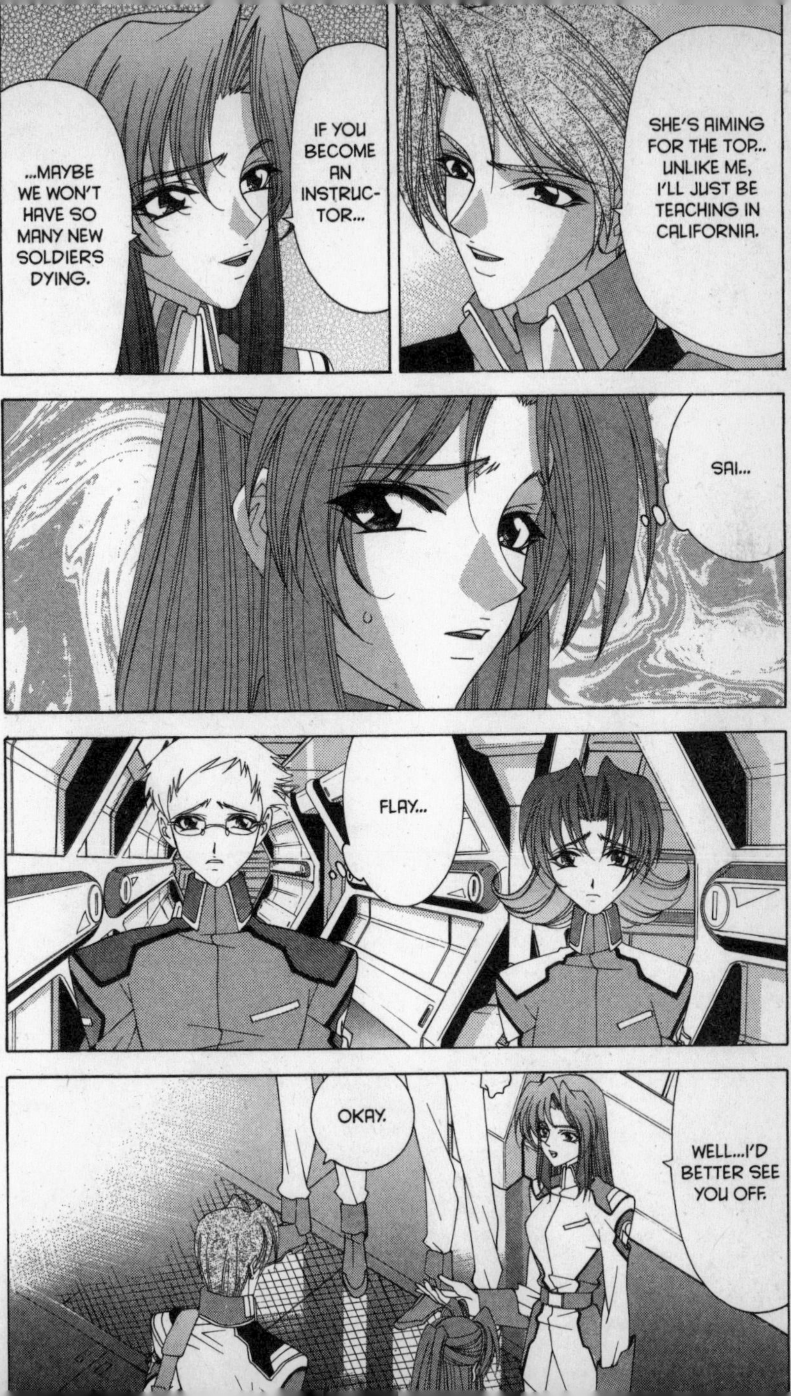
SHE'S AIMING FOR THE TOP... UNLIKE ME, I'LL JUST BE TEACHING IN CALIFORNIA.
IF YOU BECOME AN INSTRUCTOR...
...MAYBE WE WON'T HAVE SO MANY NEW SOLDIERS DYING.
SAI...
FLAY...
WELL...I'D BETTER SEE YOU OFF.
OKAY.

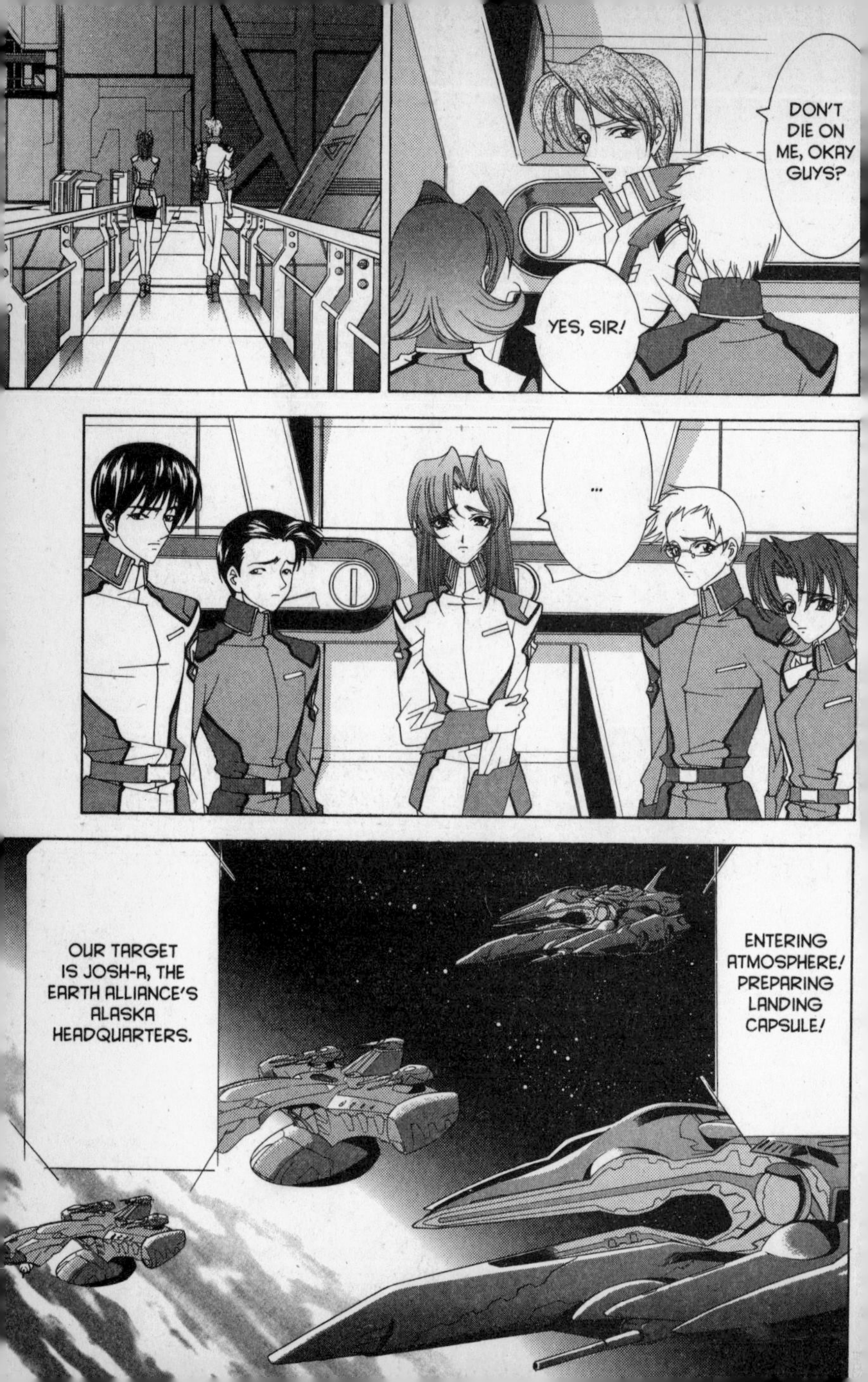
DON'T DIE ON ME, OKAY GUYS?
YES, SIR!
...
ENTERING ATMOSPHERE! PREPARING LANDING CAPSULE!
OUR TARGET IS JOSH-A, THE EARTH ALLIANCE'S ALASKA HEADQUARTERS.

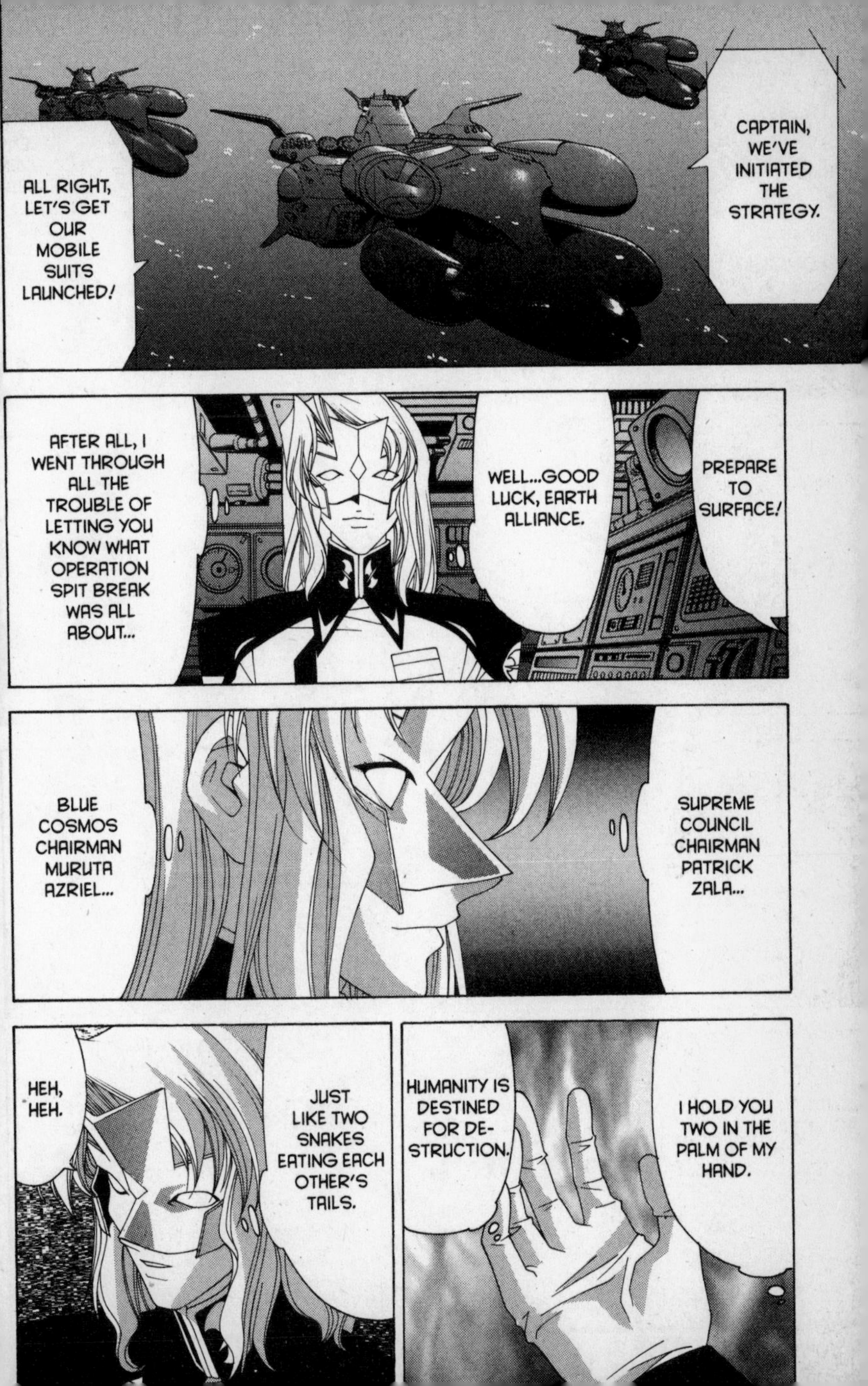
CAPTAIN, WE'VE INITIATED THE STRATEGY.
ALL RIGHT, LET'S GET OUR MOBILE SUITS LAUNCHED!
PREPARE TO SURFACE!
WELL...GOOD LUCK, EARTH ALLIANCE.
AFTER ALL, I WENT THROUGH ALL THE TROUBLE OF LETTING YOU KNOW WHAT OPERATION SPIT BREAK WAS ALL ABOUT...
SUPREME COUNCIL CHAIRMAN PATRICK ZALA...
BLUE COSMOS CHAIRMAN MURUTA AZRIEL...
I HOLD YOU TWO IN THE PALM OF MY HAND.
HUMANITY IS DESTINED FOR DE-STRUCTION.
JUST LIKE TWO SNAKES EATING EACH OTHER'S TAILS.
HEH, HEH.

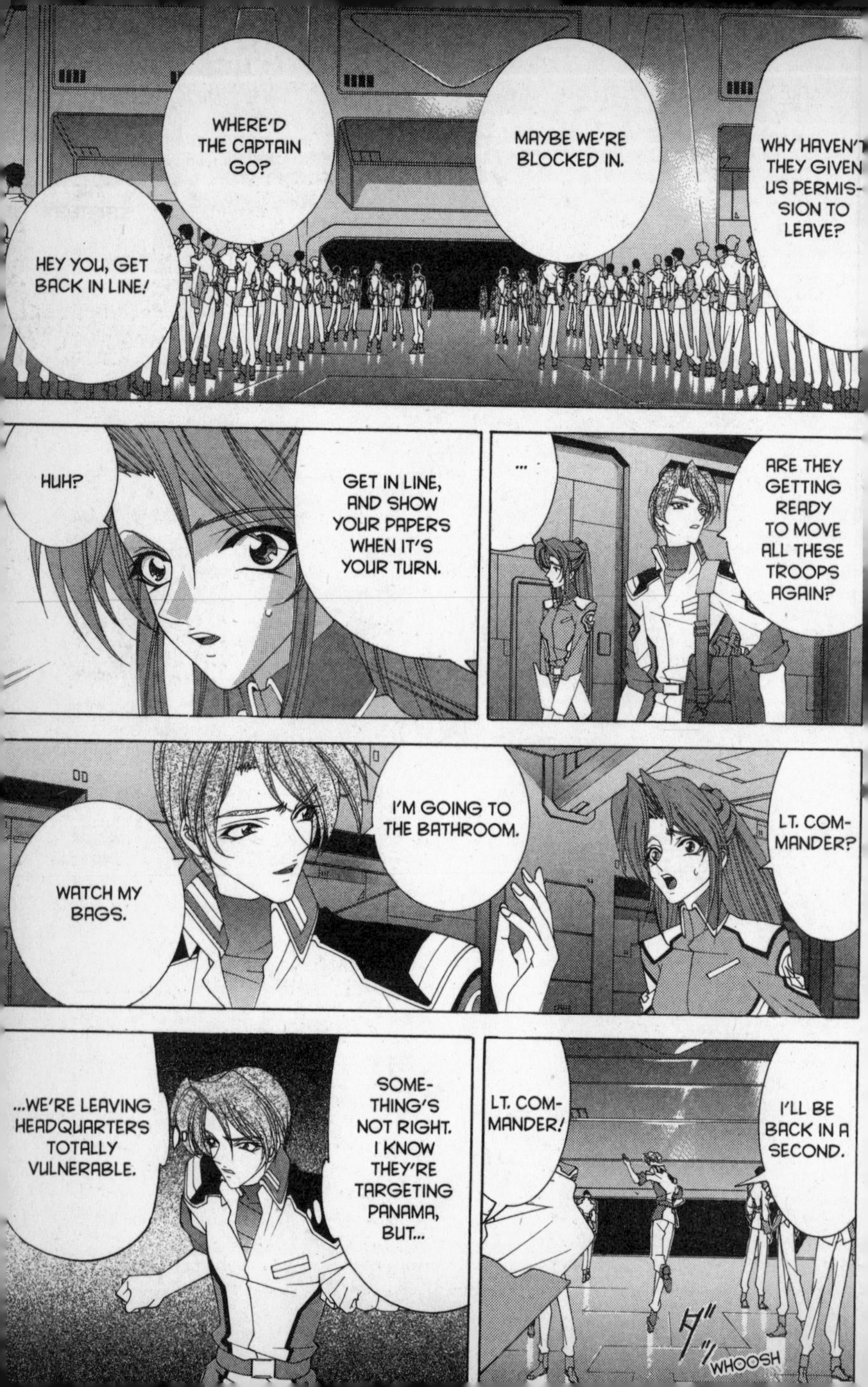
WHY HAVEN'T THEY GIVEN US PERMISSION TO LEAVE?
MAYBE WE'RE BLOCKED IN.
WHERE'D THE CAPTAIN GO?
HEY YOU, GET BACK IN LINE!
ARE THEY GETTING READY TO MOVE ALL THESE TROOPS AGAIN?
...
GET IN LINE, AND SHOW YOUR PAPERS WHEN IT'S YOUR TURN.
HUH?
LT. COMMANDER?
I'M GOING TO THE BATHROOM.
WATCH MY BAGS.
I'LL BE BACK IN A SECOND.
LT. COMMANDER!
WHOOSH
SOMETHING'S NOT RIGHT. I KNOW THEY'RE TARGETING PANAMA, BUT...
...WE'RE LEAVING HEADQUARTERS TOTALLY VULNERABLE.

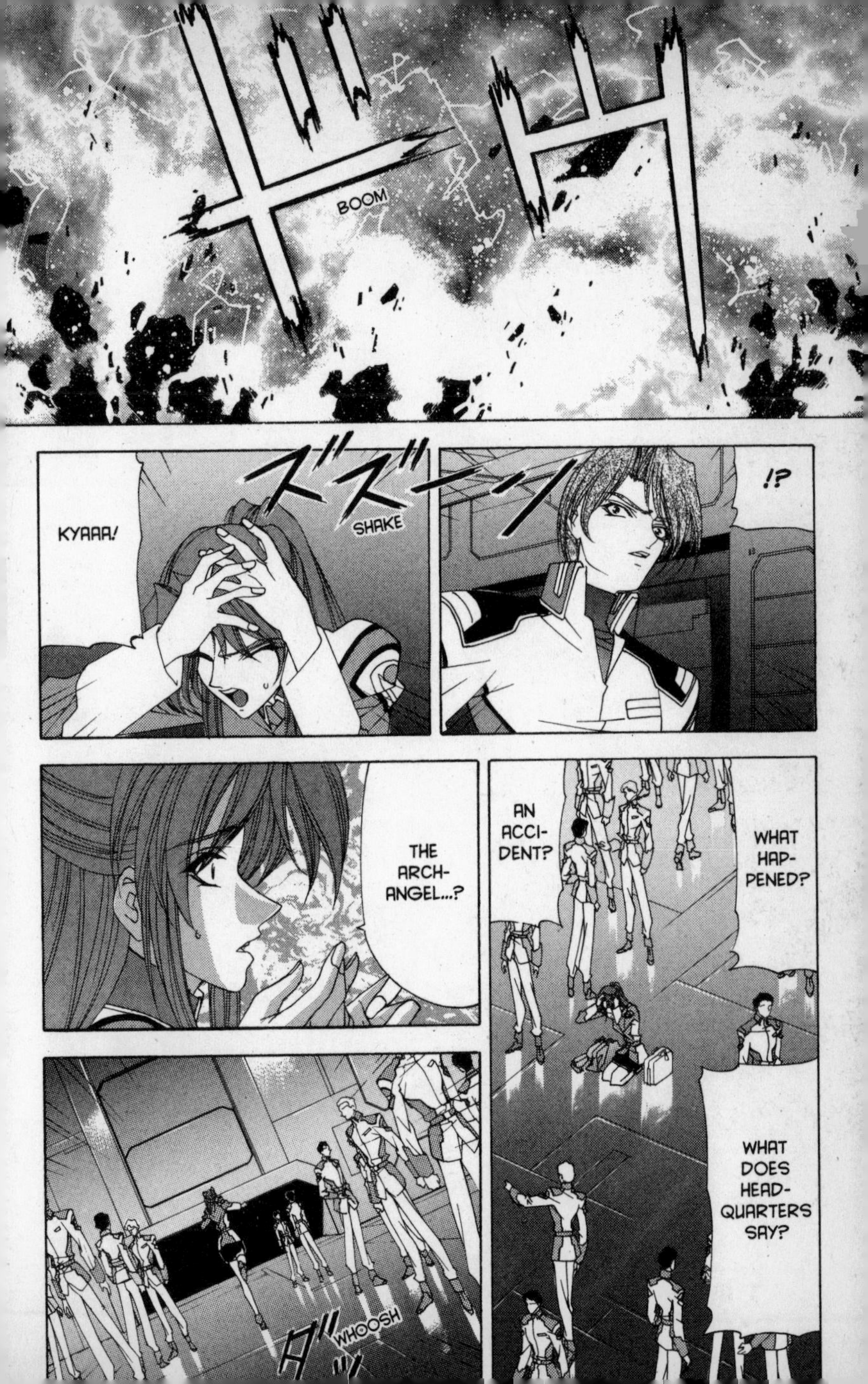
BOOM
!?
SHAKE
KYAAA!
WHAT HAP-PENED?
AN ACCI-DENT?
WHAT DOES HEAD-QUARTERS SAY?
THE ARCH-ANGEL...?
WHOOSH

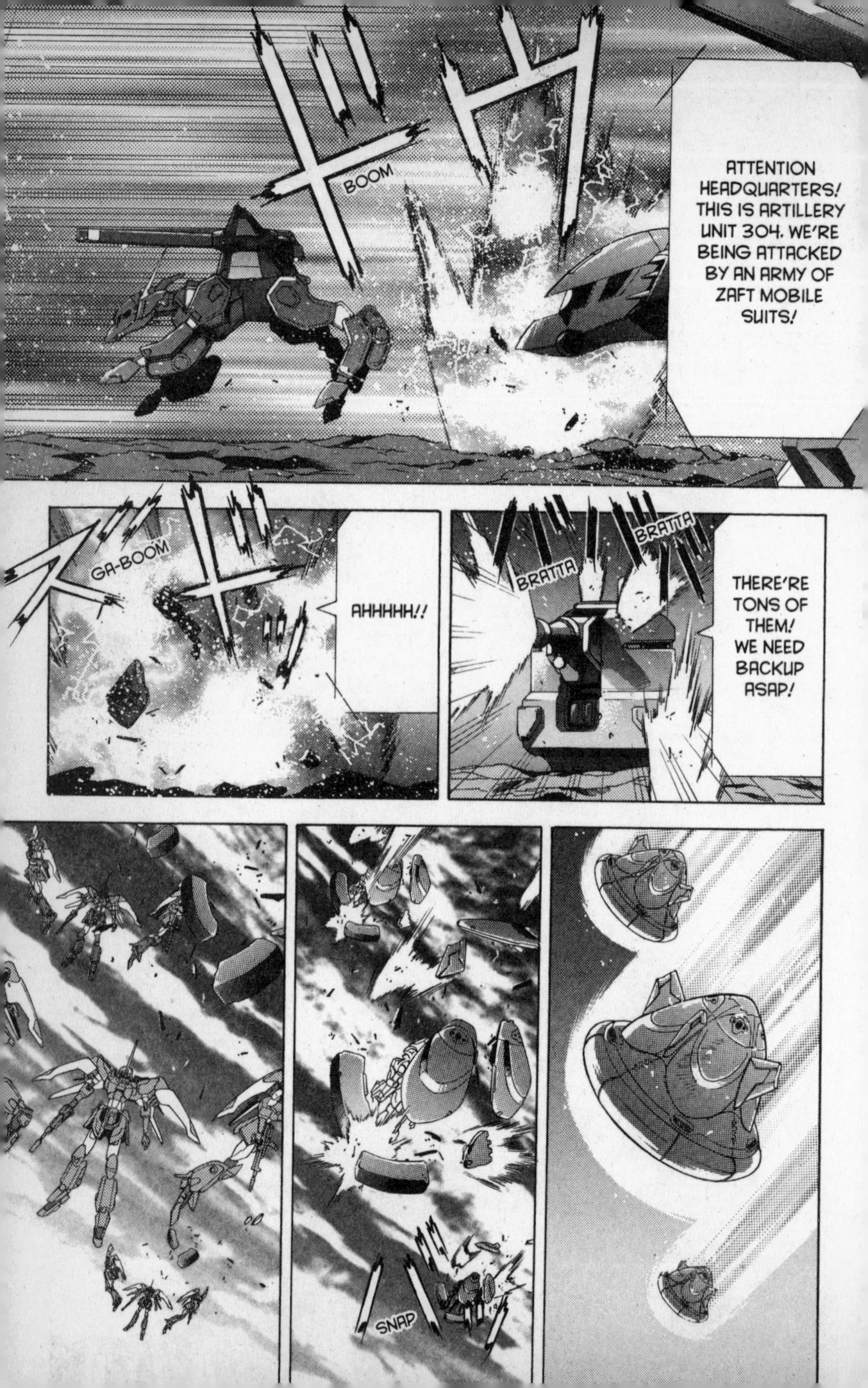
ATTENTION HEADQUARTERS! THIS IS ARTILLERY UNIT 304. WE'RE BEING ATTACKED BY AN ARMY OF ZAFT MOBILE SUITS!
BOOM
BRATTA
BRATTA
THERE'RE TONS OF THEM! WE NEED BACKUP ASAP!
AHHHHH!!
GA-BOOM
SNAP

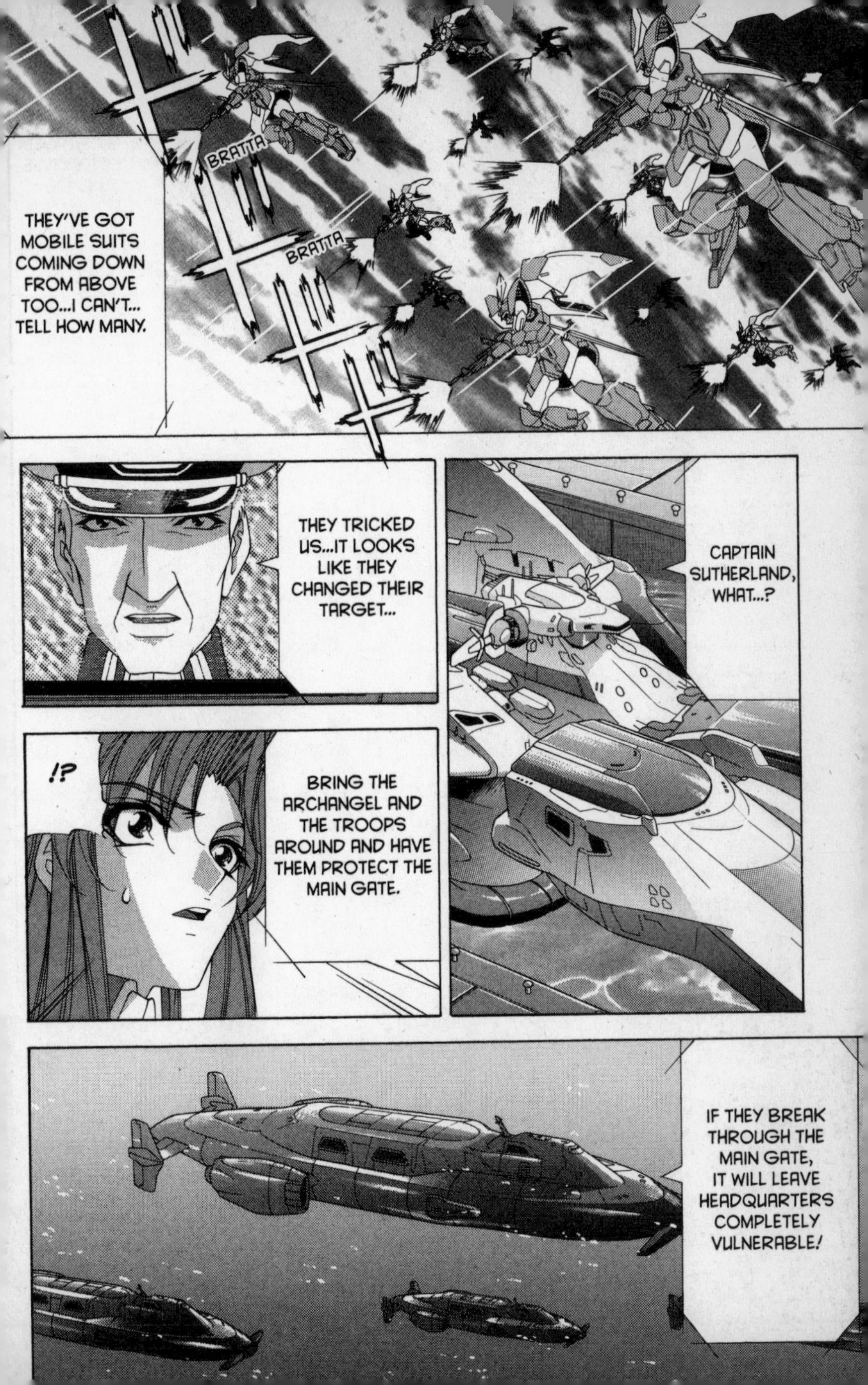

BRATTA
BRATTA
THEY'VE GOT MOBILE SUITS COMING DOWN FROM ABOVE TOO...I CAN'T... TELL HOW MANY.
CAPTAIN SUTHERLAND, WHAT...?
THEY TRICKED US...IT LOOKS LIKE THEY CHANGED THEIR TARGET...
!?
BRING THE ARCHANGEL AND THE TROOPS AROUND AND HAVE THEM PROTECT THE MAIN GATE.
IF THEY BREAK THROUGH THE MAIN GATE, IT WILL LEAVE HEADQUARTERS COMPLETELY VULNERABLE!

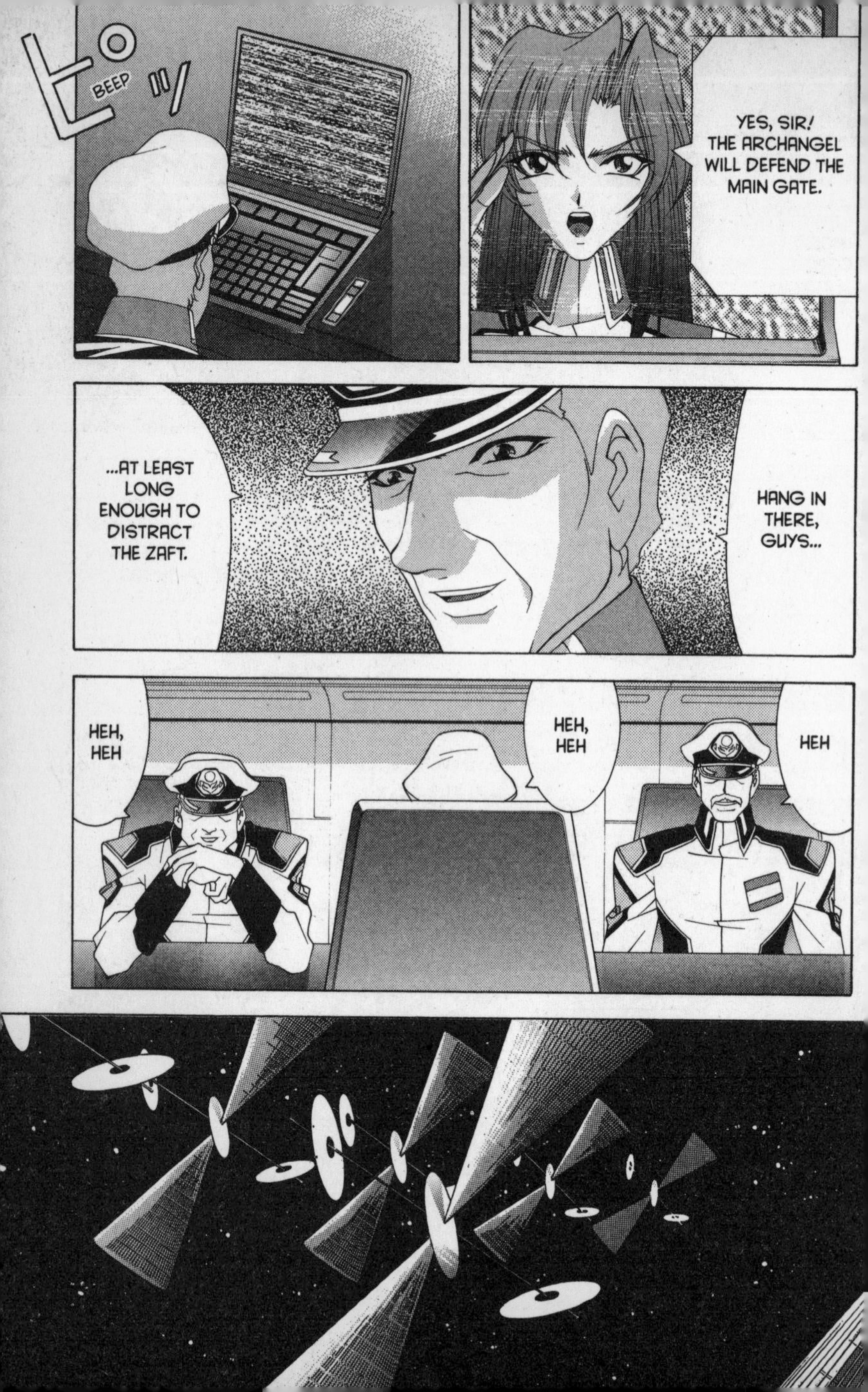
YES, SIR! THE ARCHANGEL WILL DEFEND THE MAIN GATE.
BEEP
HANG IN THERE, GUYS...
...AT LEAST LONG ENOUGH TO DISTRACT THE ZAFT.
HEH
HEH, HEH
HEH, HEH

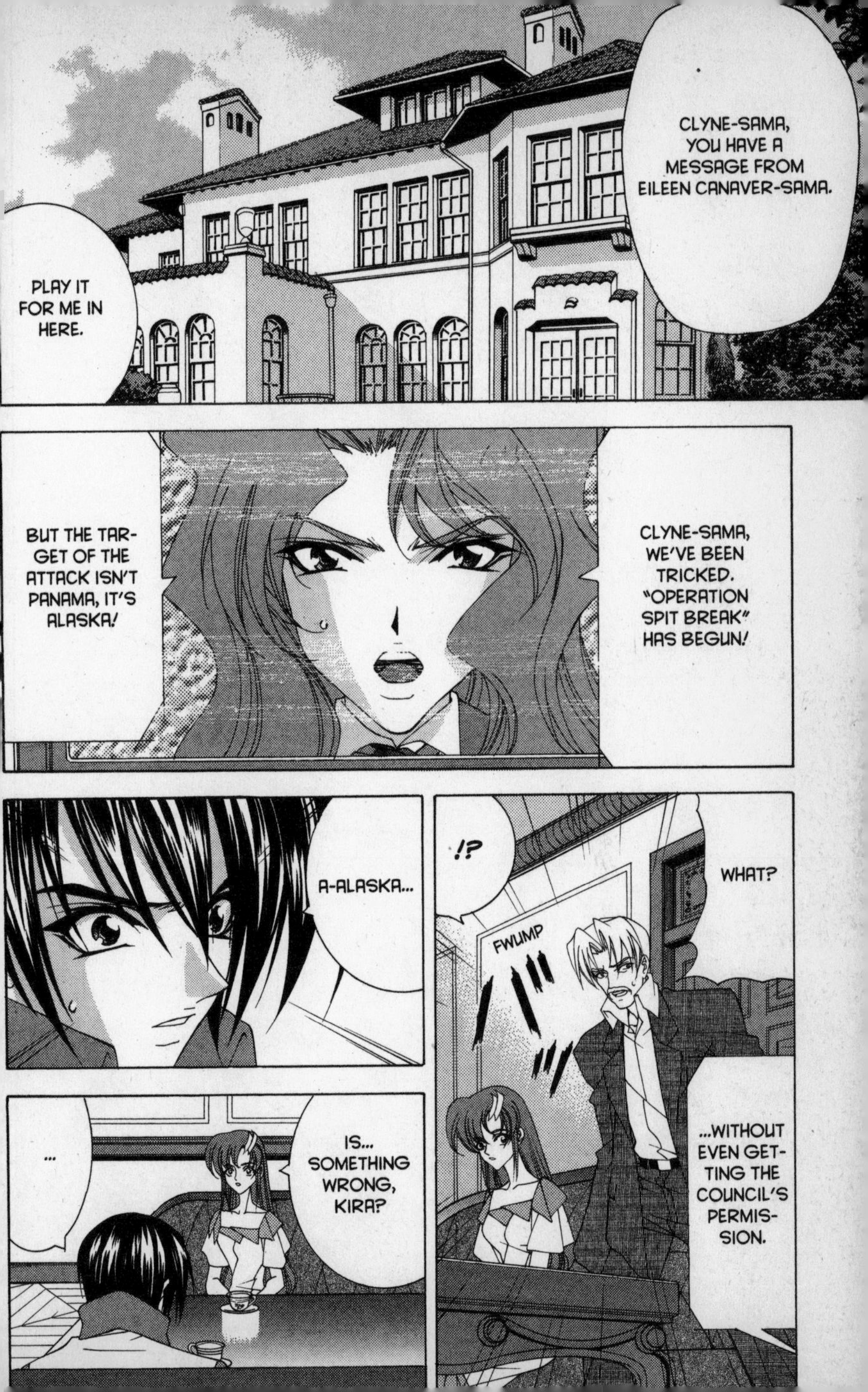
CLYNE-SAMA, YOU HAVE A MESSAGE FROM EILEEN CANAVER-SAMA.
PLAY IT FOR ME IN HERE.
CLYNE-SAMA, WE'VE BEEN TRICKED. "OPERATION SPIT BREAK" HAS BEGUN!
BUT THE TARGET OF THE ATTACK ISN'T PANAMA, IT'S ALASKA!
WHAT?
!?
FWUMP
...WITHOUT EVEN GETTING THE COUNCIL'S PERMISSION.
A-ALASKA...
IS... SOMETHING WRONG, KIRA?
...

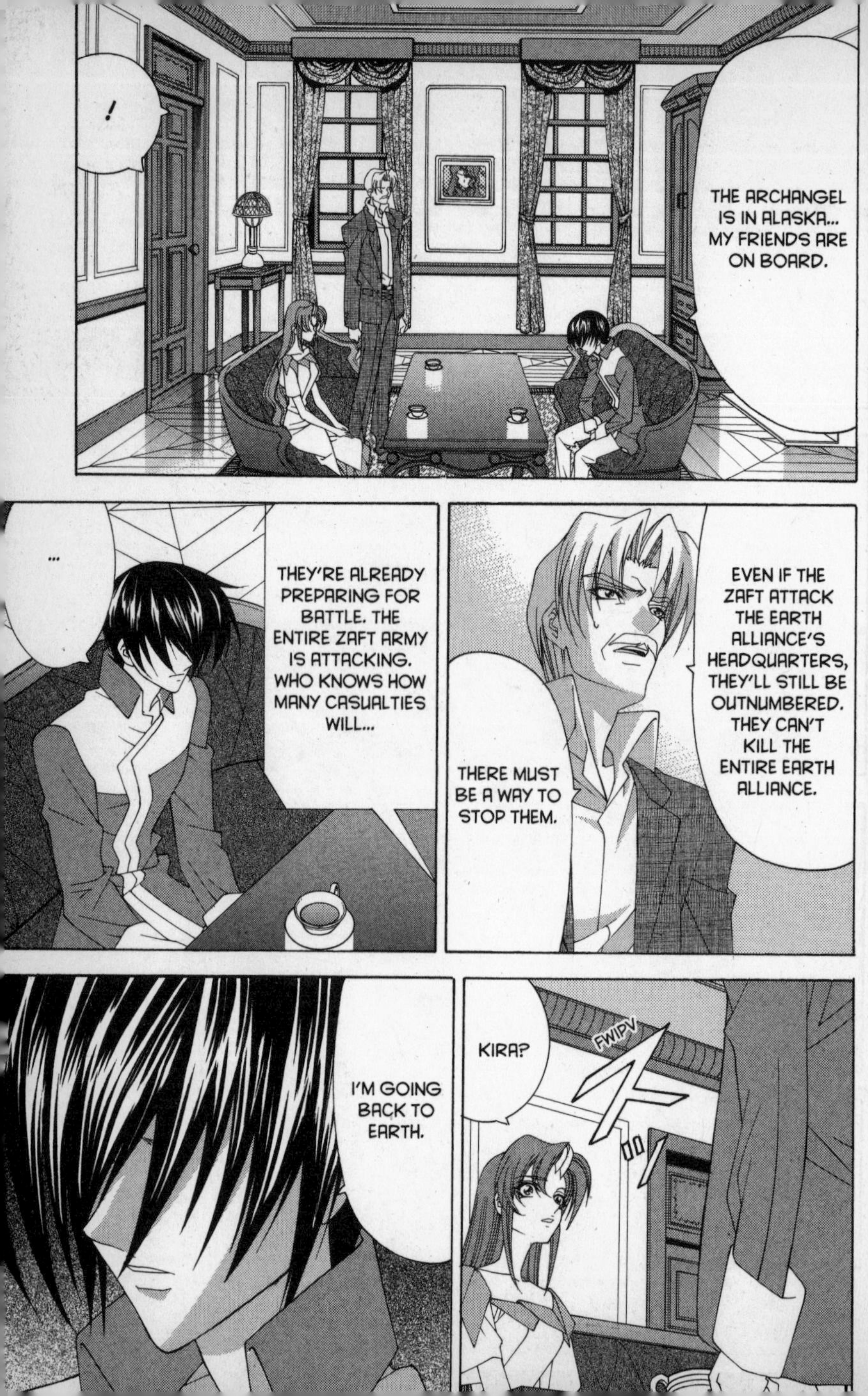
THE ARCHANGEL IS IN ALASKA... MY FRIENDS ARE ON BOARD.
!
EVEN IF THE ZAFT ATTACK THE EARTH ALLIANCE'S HEADQUARTERS, THEY'LL STILL BE OUTNUMBERED. THEY CAN'T KILL THE ENTIRE EARTH ALLIANCE.
THERE MUST BE A WAY TO STOP THEM.
THEY'RE ALREADY PREPARING FOR BATTLE. THE ENTIRE ZAFT ARMY IS ATTACKING. WHO KNOWS HOW MANY CASUALTIES WILL...
...
KIRA?
FWIPV
I'M GOING BACK TO EARTH.

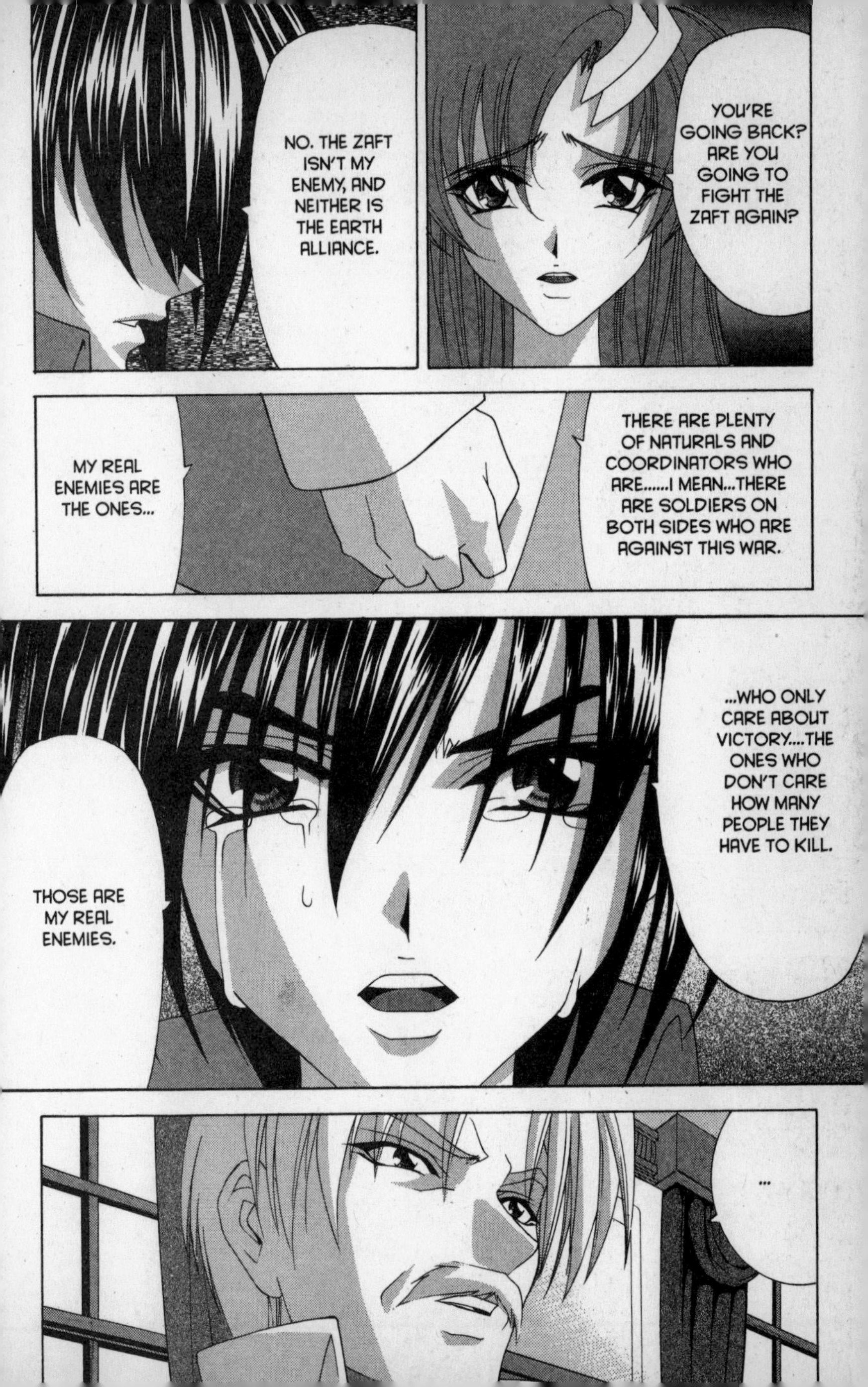
YOU'RE GOING BACK? ARE YOU GOING TO FIGHT THE ZAFT AGAIN?
NO. THE ZAFT ISN'T MY ENEMY, AND NEITHER IS THE EARTH ALLIANCE.
THERE ARE PLENTY OF NATURALS AND COORDINATORS WHO ARE......I MEAN...THERE ARE SOLDIERS ON BOTH SIDES WHO ARE AGAINST THIS WAR.
MY REAL ENEMIES ARE THE ONES...
...WHO ONLY CARE ABOUT VICTORY....THE ONES WHO DON'T CARE HOW MANY PEOPLE THEY HAVE TO KILL.
THOSE ARE MY REAL ENEMIES.
...

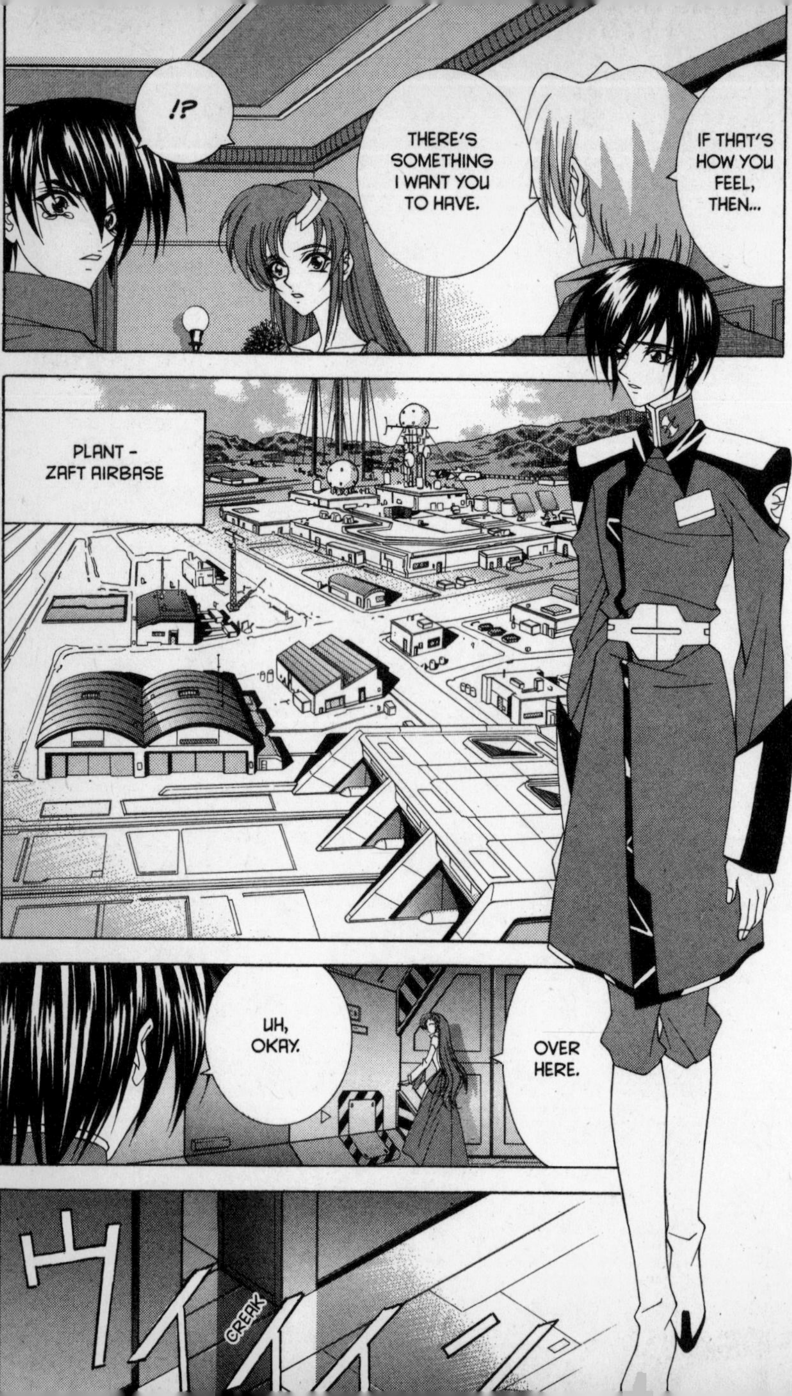
IF THAT'S HOW YOU FEEL, THEN...
THERE'S SOMETHING I WANT YOU TO HAVE.
!?
PLANT - ZAFT AIRBASE
OVER HERE.
UH, OKAY.
CREAK

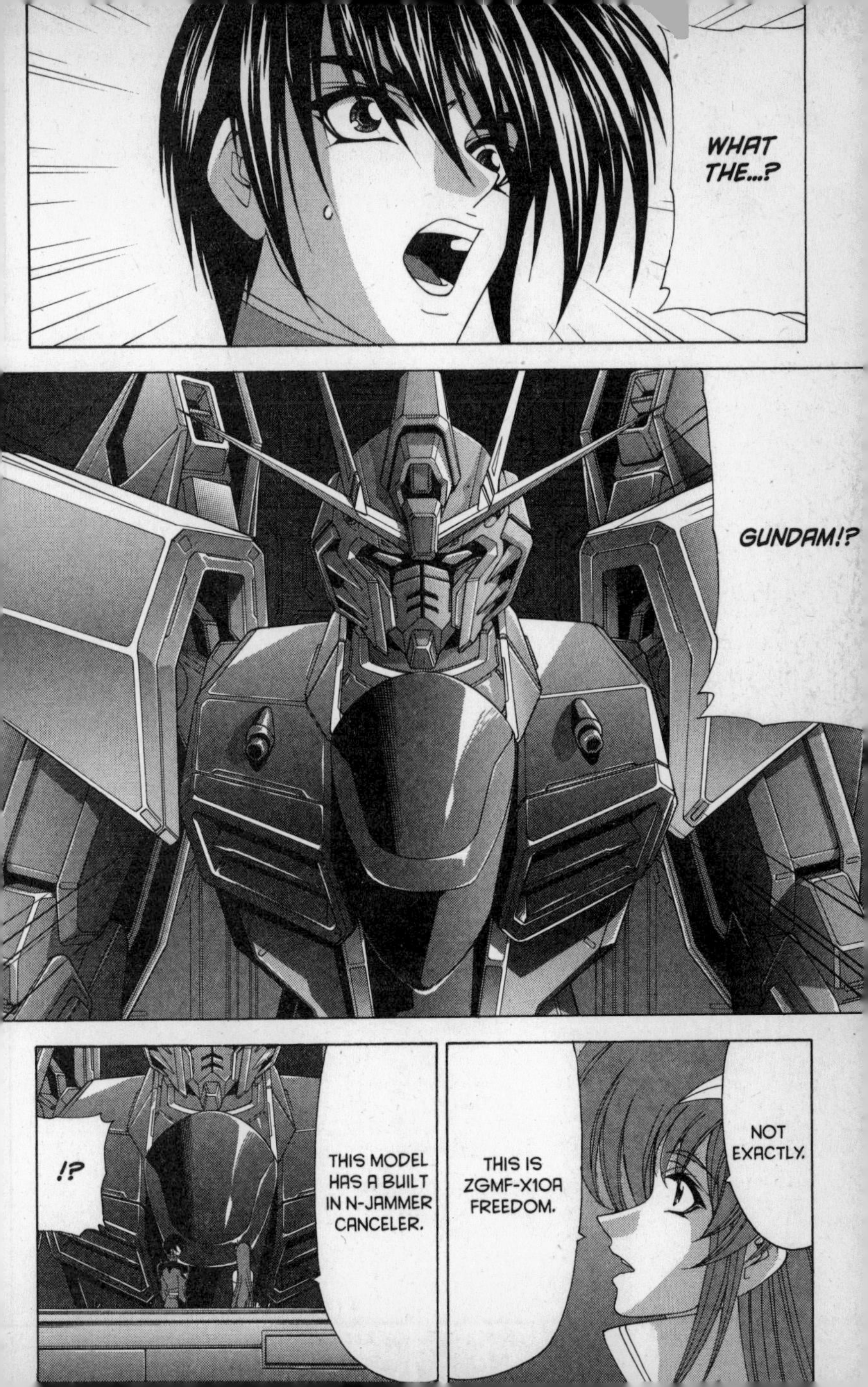
WHAT THE...?
GUNDAM!?
NOT EXACTLY.
THIS IS ZGMF-X10A FREEDOM.
THIS MODEL HAS A BUILT IN N-JAMMER CANCELER.
!?

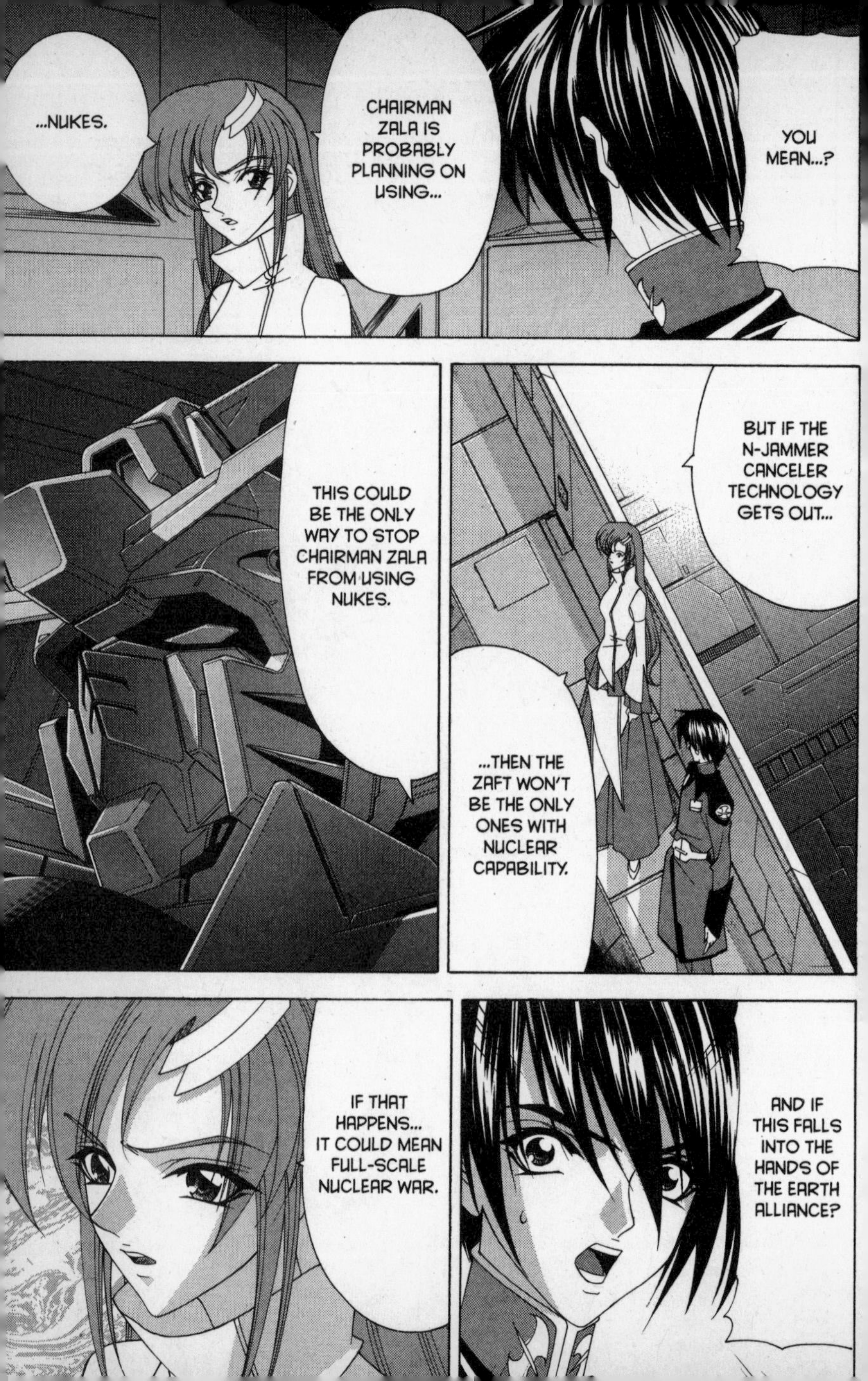
YOU MEAN...?
CHAIRMAN ZALA IS PROBABLY PLANNING ON USING...
...NUKES.
BUT IF THE N-JAMMER CANCELER TECHNOLOGY GETS OUT...
...THEN THE ZAFT WON'T BE THE ONLY ONES WITH NUCLEAR CAPABILITY.
THIS COULD BE THE ONLY WAY TO STOP CHAIRMAN ZALA FROM USING NUKES.
AND IF THIS FALLS INTO THE HANDS OF THE EARTH ALLIANCE?
IF THAT HAPPENS... IT COULD MEAN FULL-SCALE NUCLEAR WAR.

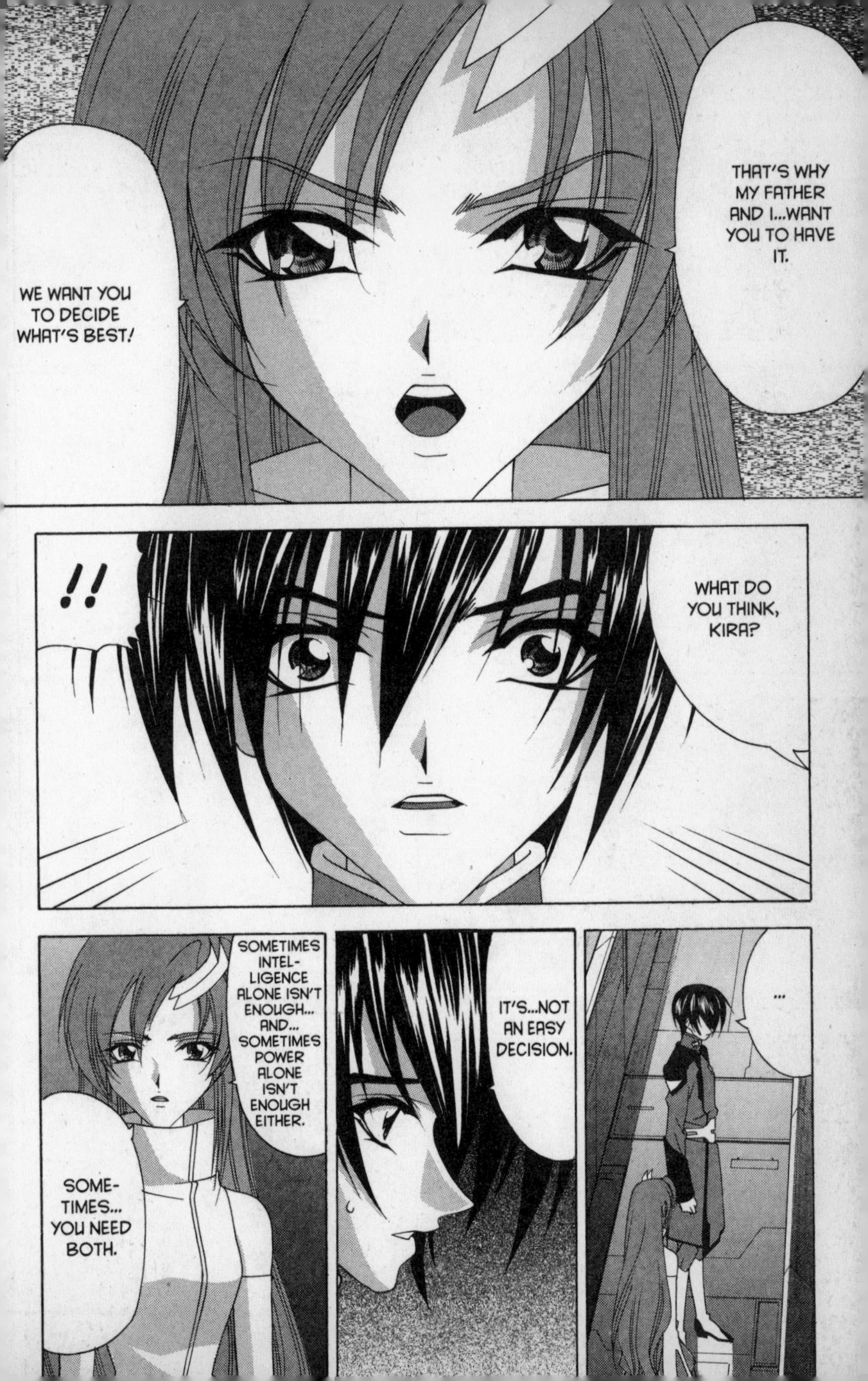
THAT'S WHY MY FATHER AND I...WANT YOU TO HAVE IT.
WE WANT YOU TO DECIDE WHAT'S BEST!
WHAT DO YOU THINK, KIRA?
!!
...
IT'S...NOT AN EASY DECISION.
SOMETIMES INTEL-LIGENCE ALONE ISN'T ENOUGH... AND... SOMETIMES POWER ALONE ISN'T ENOUGH EITHER.
SOME-TIMES... YOU NEED BOTH.

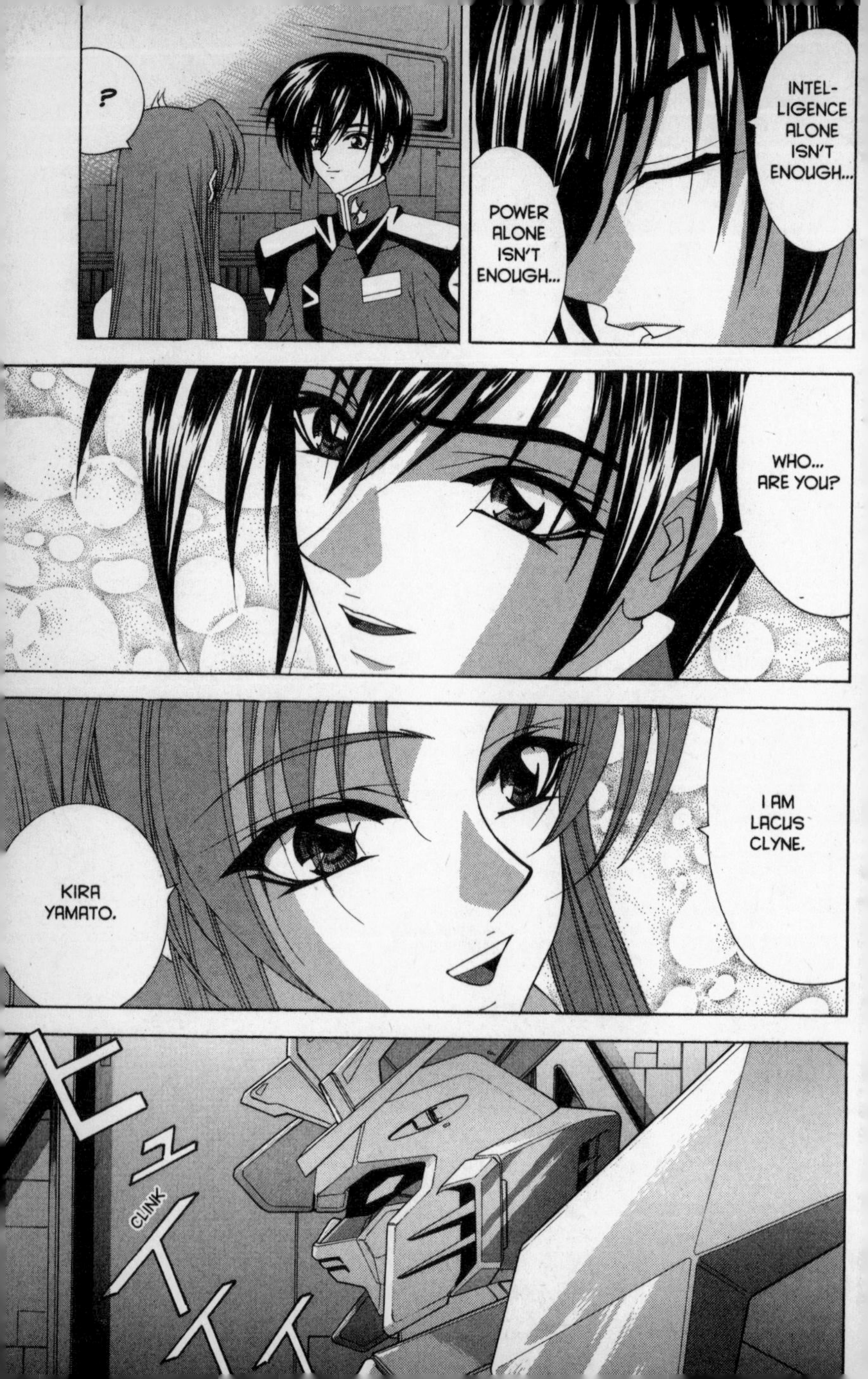
INTEL-LIGENCE ALONE ISN'T ENOUGH...
POWER ALONE ISN'T ENOUGH...
?
WHO... ARE YOU?
I AM LACUS CLYNE.
KIRA YAMATO.
ヒュイイイ
CLINK

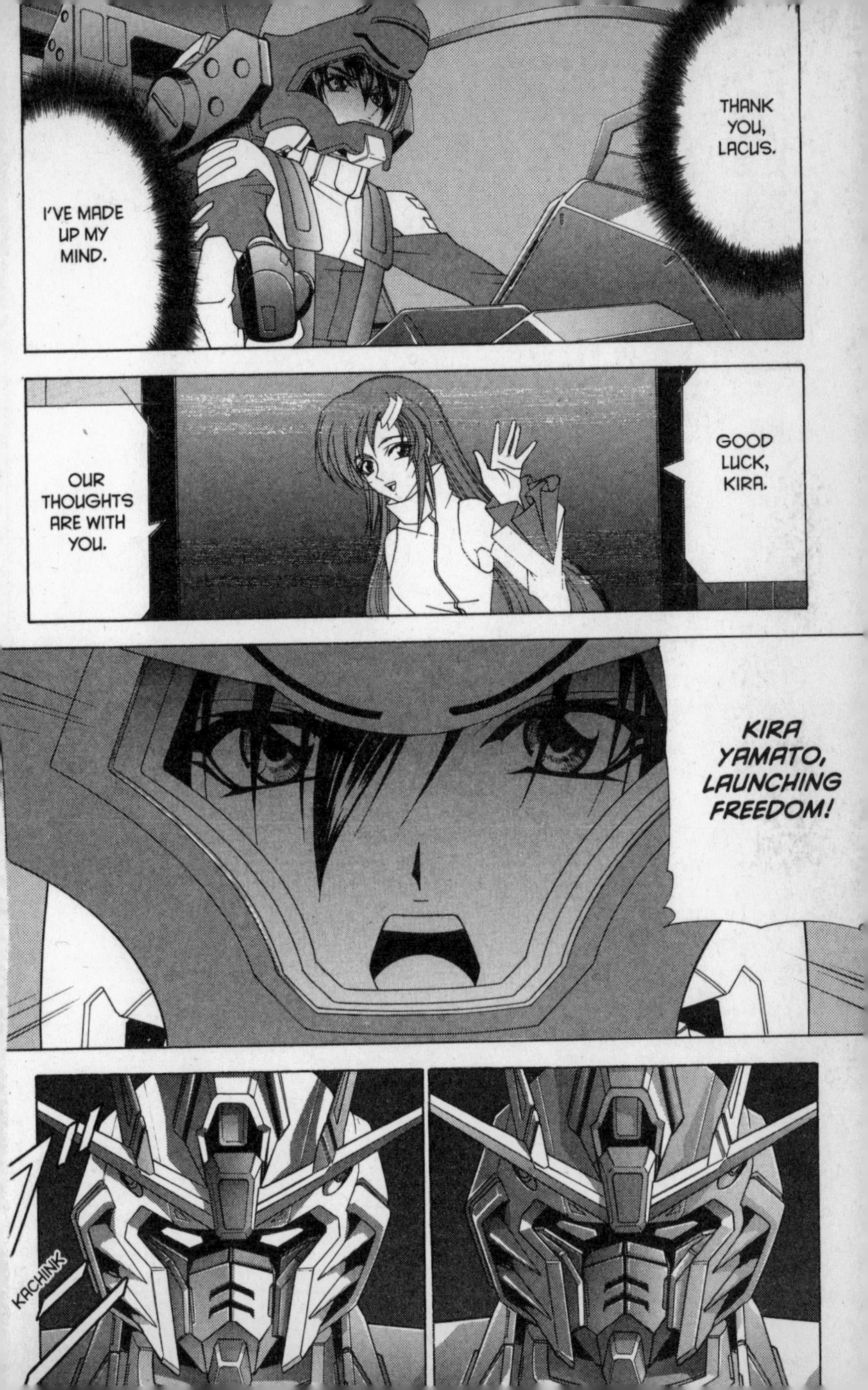
THANK YOU, LACUS.
I'VE MADE UP MY MIND.
GOOD LUCK, KIRA.
OUR THOUGHTS ARE WITH YOU.
KIRA YAMATO, LAUNCHING FREEDOM!
KACHINK

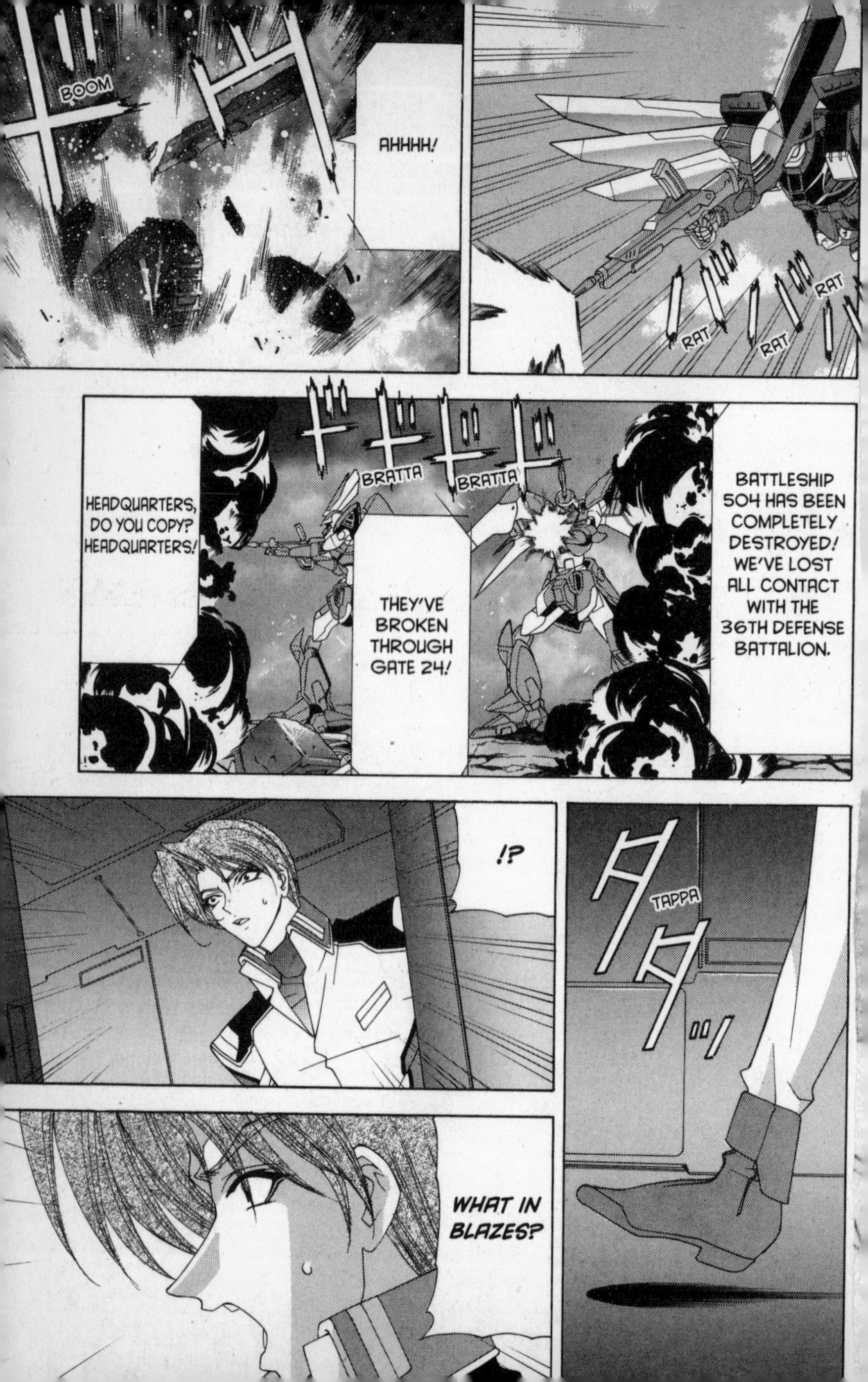
RAT
RAT
RAT
BOOM
AHHHH!
BATTLESHIP 504 HAS BEEN COMPLETELY DESTROYED! WE'VE LOST ALL CONTACT WITH THE 36TH DEFENSE BATTALION.
BRATTA
BRATTA
THEY'VE BROKEN THROUGH GATE 24!
HEADQUARTERS, DO YOU COPY? HEADQUARTERS!
TAPPA
!?
WHAT IN BLAZES?

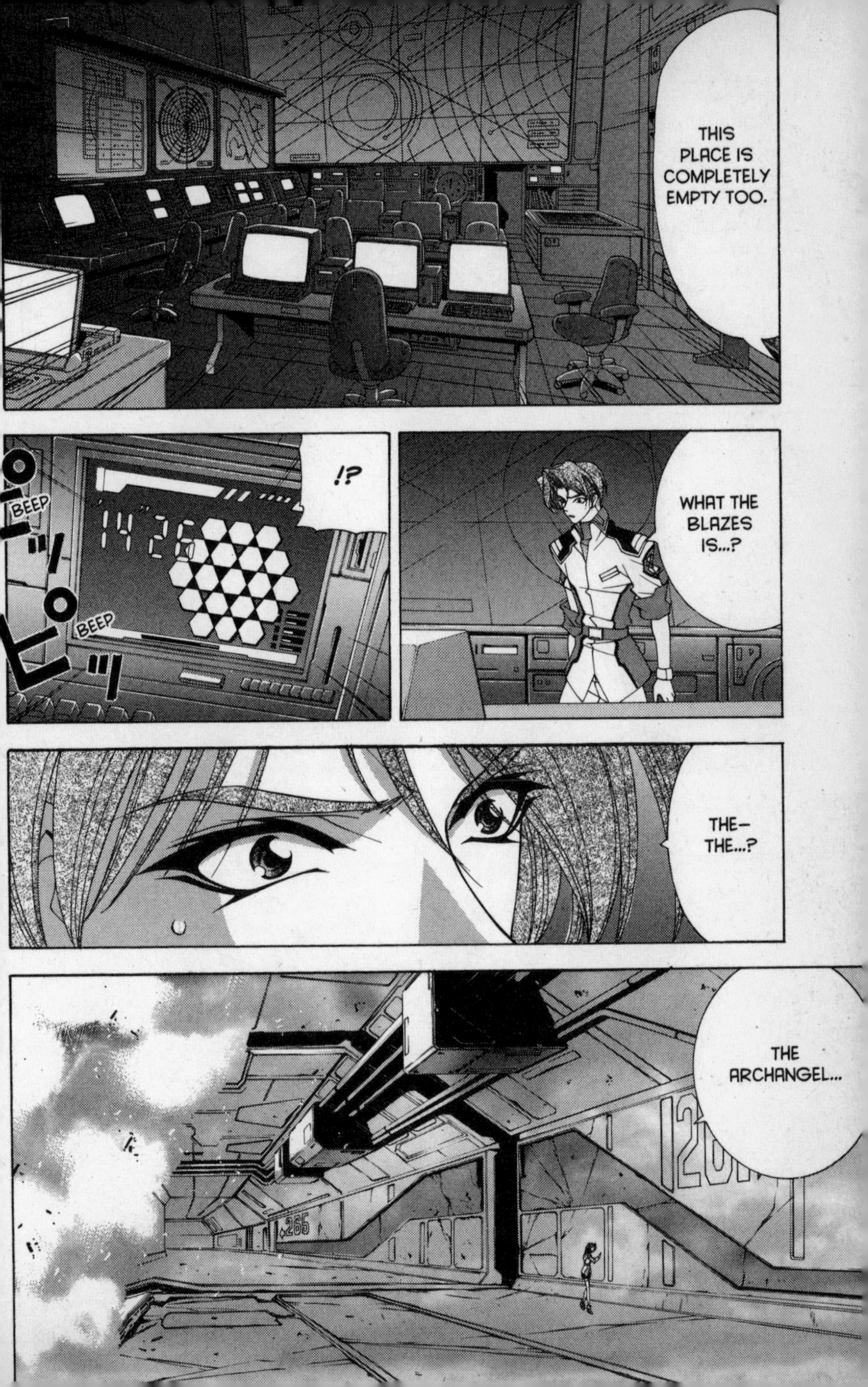
THIS PLACE IS COMPLETELY EMPTY TOO.
WHAT THE BLAZES IS...?
!?
BEEP
BEEP
THE— THE...?
THE ARCHANGEL...

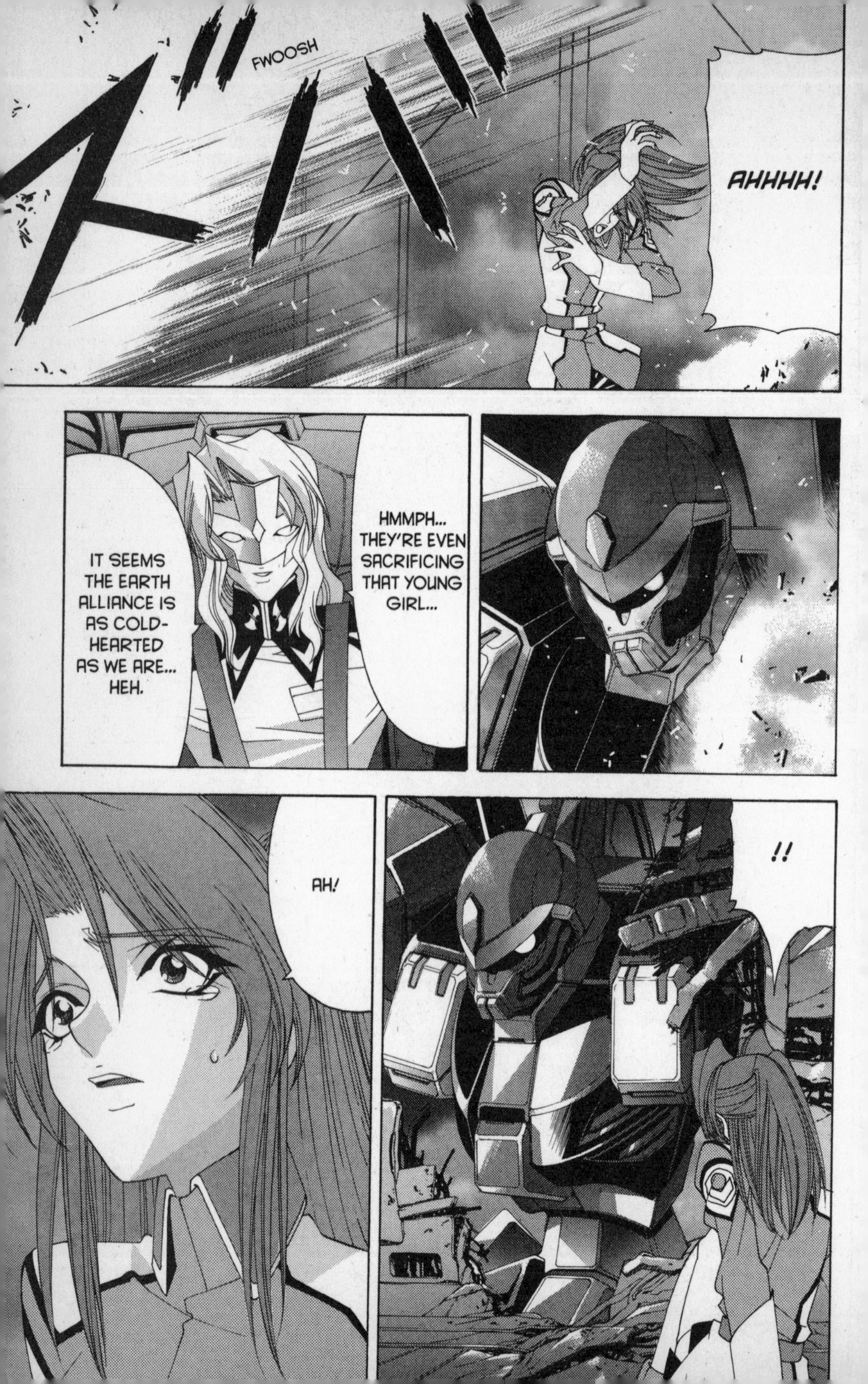
AHHHH!
FWOOSH
HMMPH... THEY'RE EVEN SACRIFICING THAT YOUNG GIRL...
IT SEEMS THE EARTH ALLIANCE IS AS COLD-HEARTED AS WE ARE... HEH.
!!
AH!

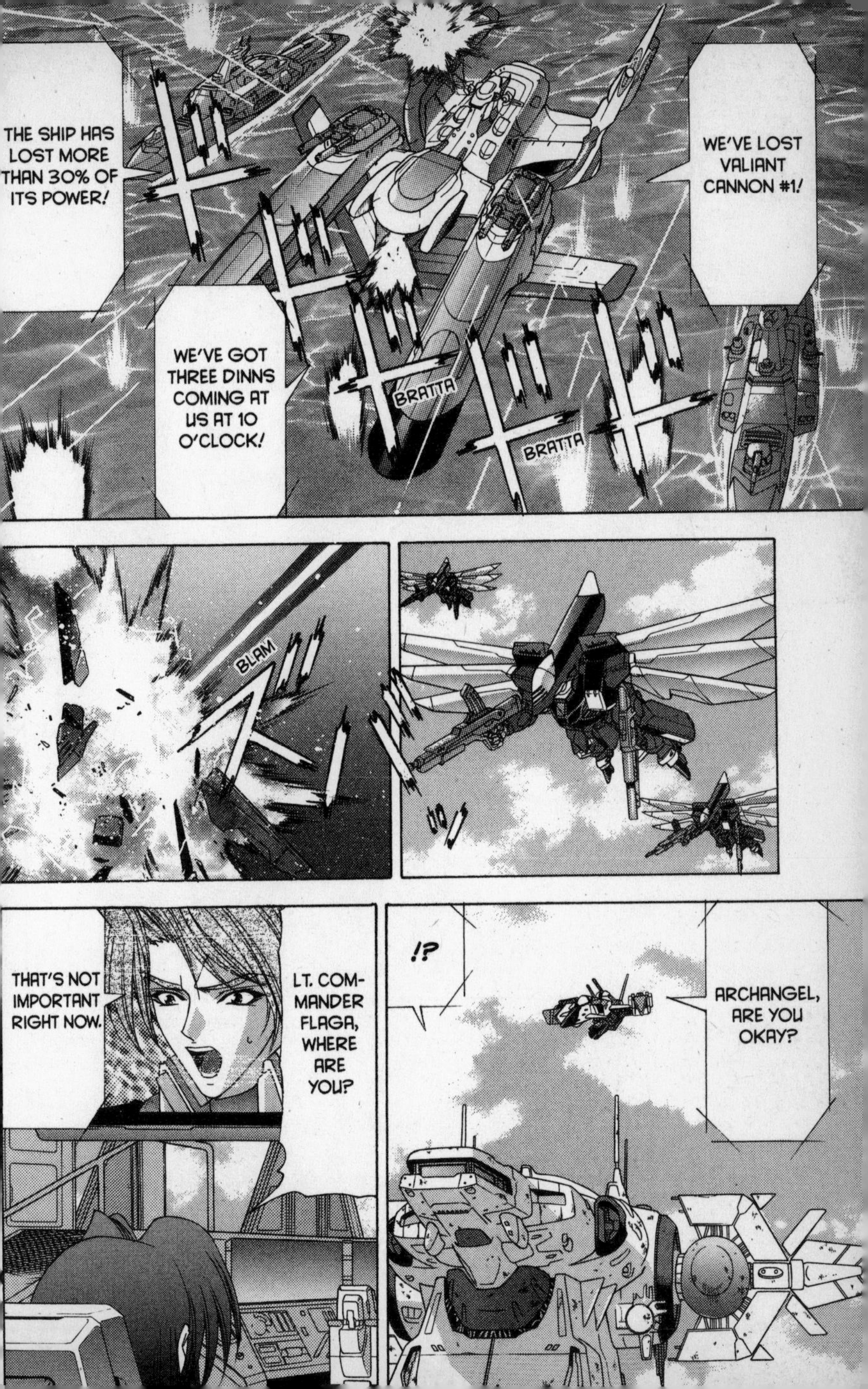
WE'VE LOST VALIANT CANNON #1!
THE SHIP HAS LOST MORE THAN 30% OF ITS POWER!
BRATTA
BRATTA
WE'VE GOT THREE DINNS COMING AT US AT 10 O'CLOCK!
BLAM
ARCHANGEL, ARE YOU OKAY?
!?
LT. COMMANDER FLAGA, WHERE ARE YOU?
THAT'S NOT IMPORTANT RIGHT NOW.

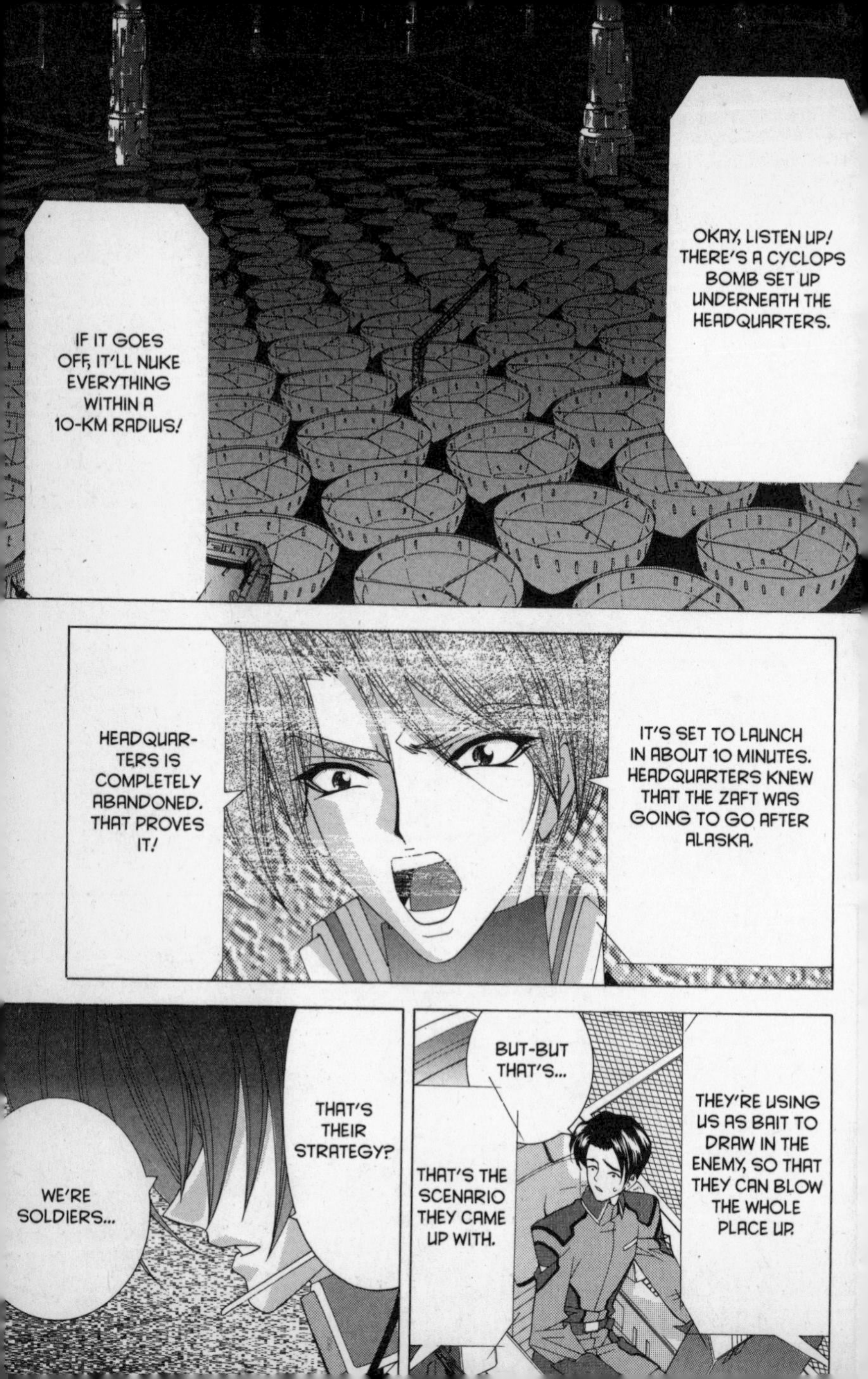
OKAY, LISTEN UP! THERE'S A CYCLOPS BOMB SET UP UNDERNEATH THE HEADQUARTERS.
IF IT GOES OFF, IT'LL NUKE EVERYTHING WITHIN A 10-KM RADIUS!
IT'S SET TO LAUNCH IN ABOUT 10 MINUTES. HEADQUARTERS KNEW THAT THE ZAFT WAS GOING TO GO AFTER ALASKA.
HEADQUAR-TERS IS COMPLETELY ABANDONED. THAT PROVES IT!
THEY'RE USING US AS BAIT TO DRAW IN THE ENEMY, SO THAT THEY CAN BLOW THE WHOLE PLACE UP.
BUT-BUT THAT'S...
THAT'S THE SCENARIO THEY CAME UP WITH.
THAT'S THEIR STRATEGY?
WE'RE SOLDIERS...

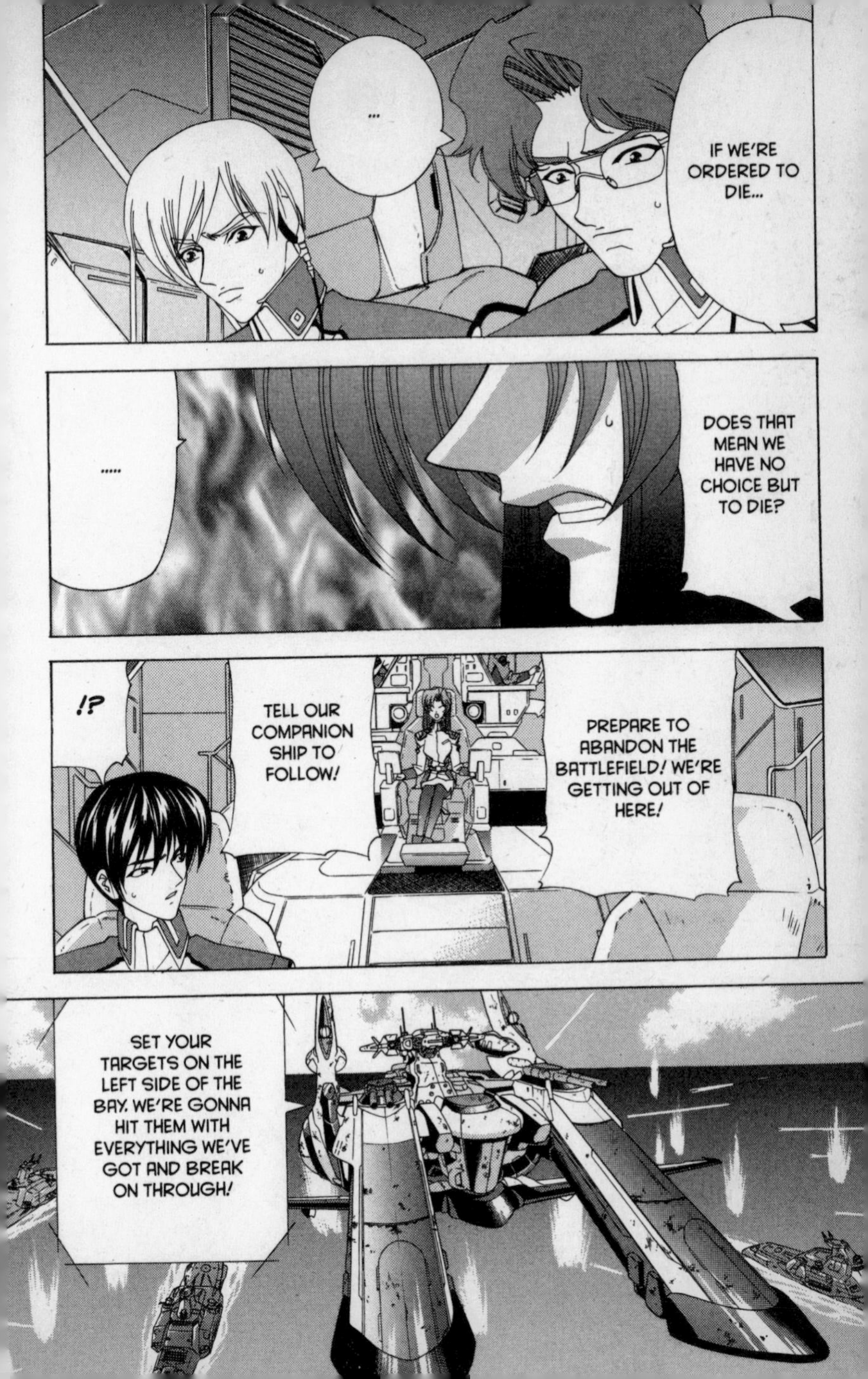
IF WE'RE ORDERED TO DIE...
...
DOES THAT MEAN WE HAVE NO CHOICE BUT TO DIE?
......
PREPARE TO ABANDON THE BATTLEFIELD! WE'RE GETTING OUT OF HERE!
TELL OUR COMPANION SHIP TO FOLLOW!
!?
SET YOUR TARGETS ON THE LEFT SIDE OF THE BAY. WE'RE GONNA HIT THEM WITH EVERYTHING WE'VE GOT AND BREAK ON THROUGH!

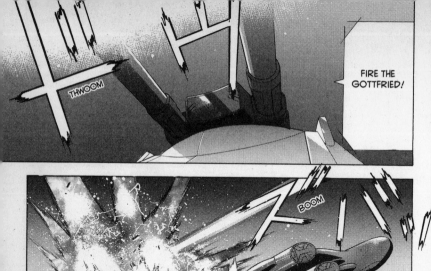

THWOOM

FIRE THE GOTTFRIED!

BOOM

!?

IT'S... X-102.

WE'VE GOT A MOBILE SUIT HITTING US WITH HEAVY FIRE!

HUH!?

IT'S GUNDAM DUEL!

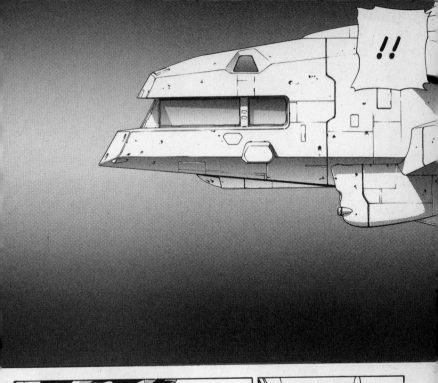

AHHHHH!

NO!

THIS IS FOR NICOL AND DEARKA!

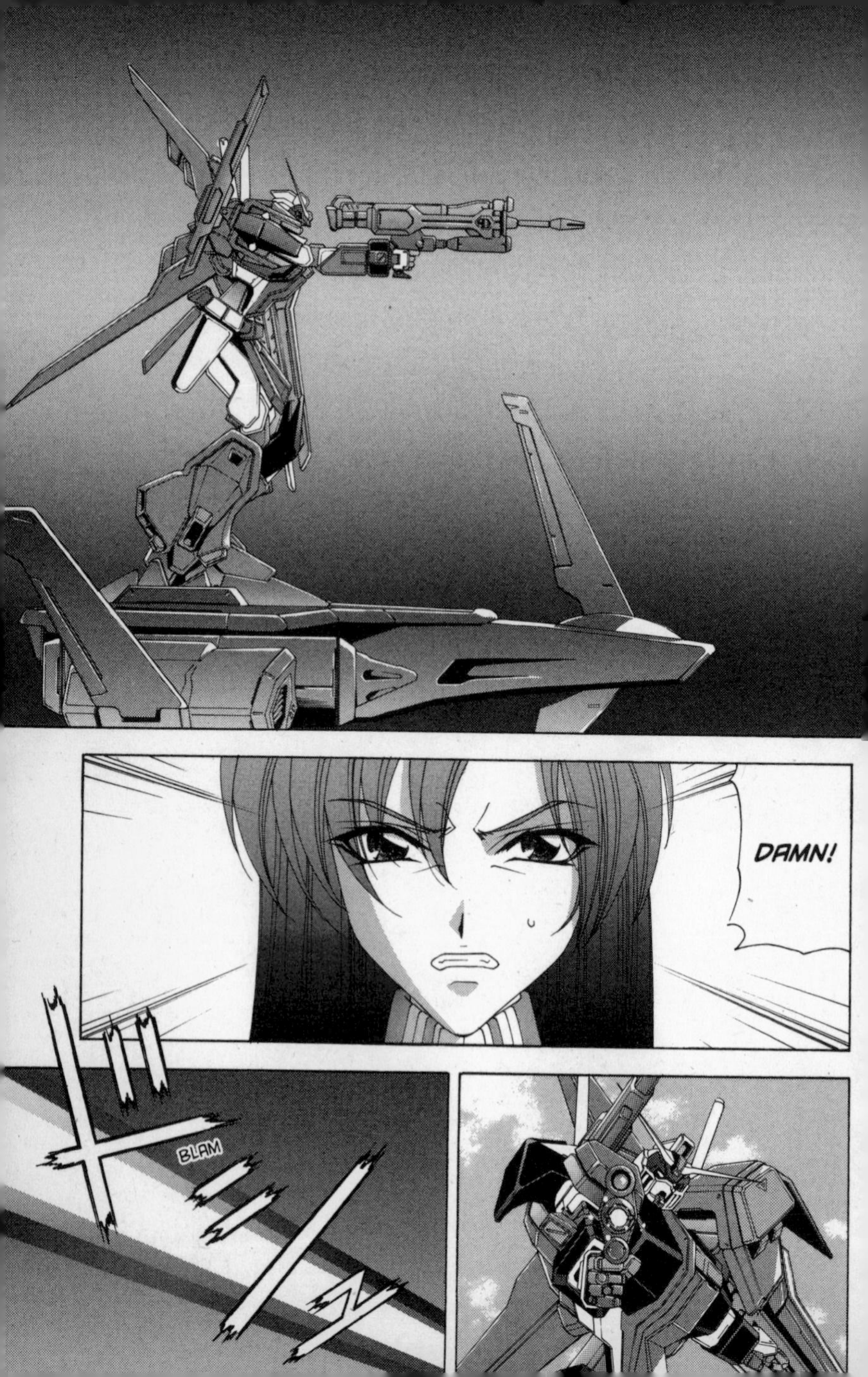
DAMN!
BLAM

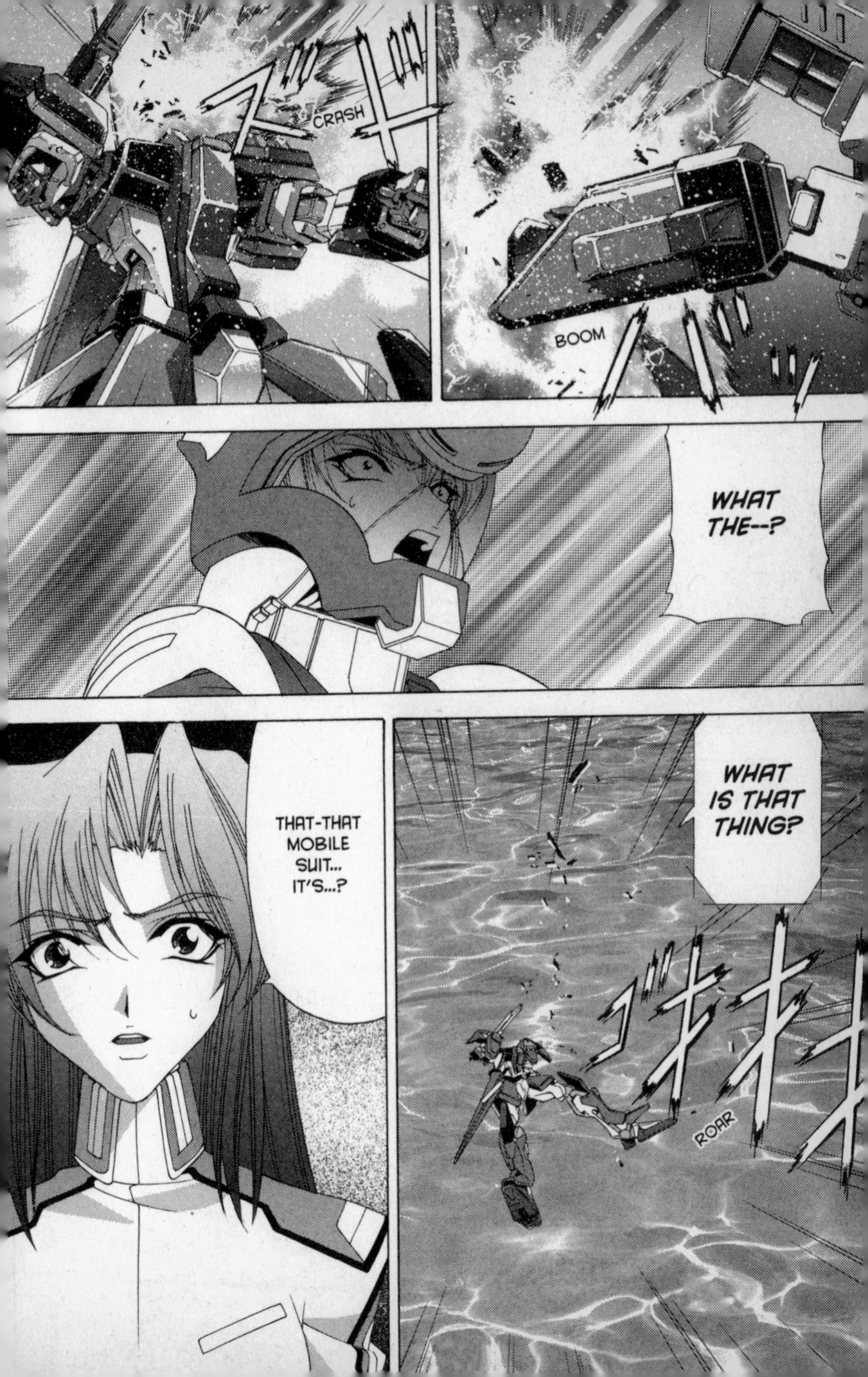
BOOM
CRASH
WHAT THE--?
WHAT IS THAT THING?
ROAR
THAT-THAT MOBILE SUIT... IT'S...?

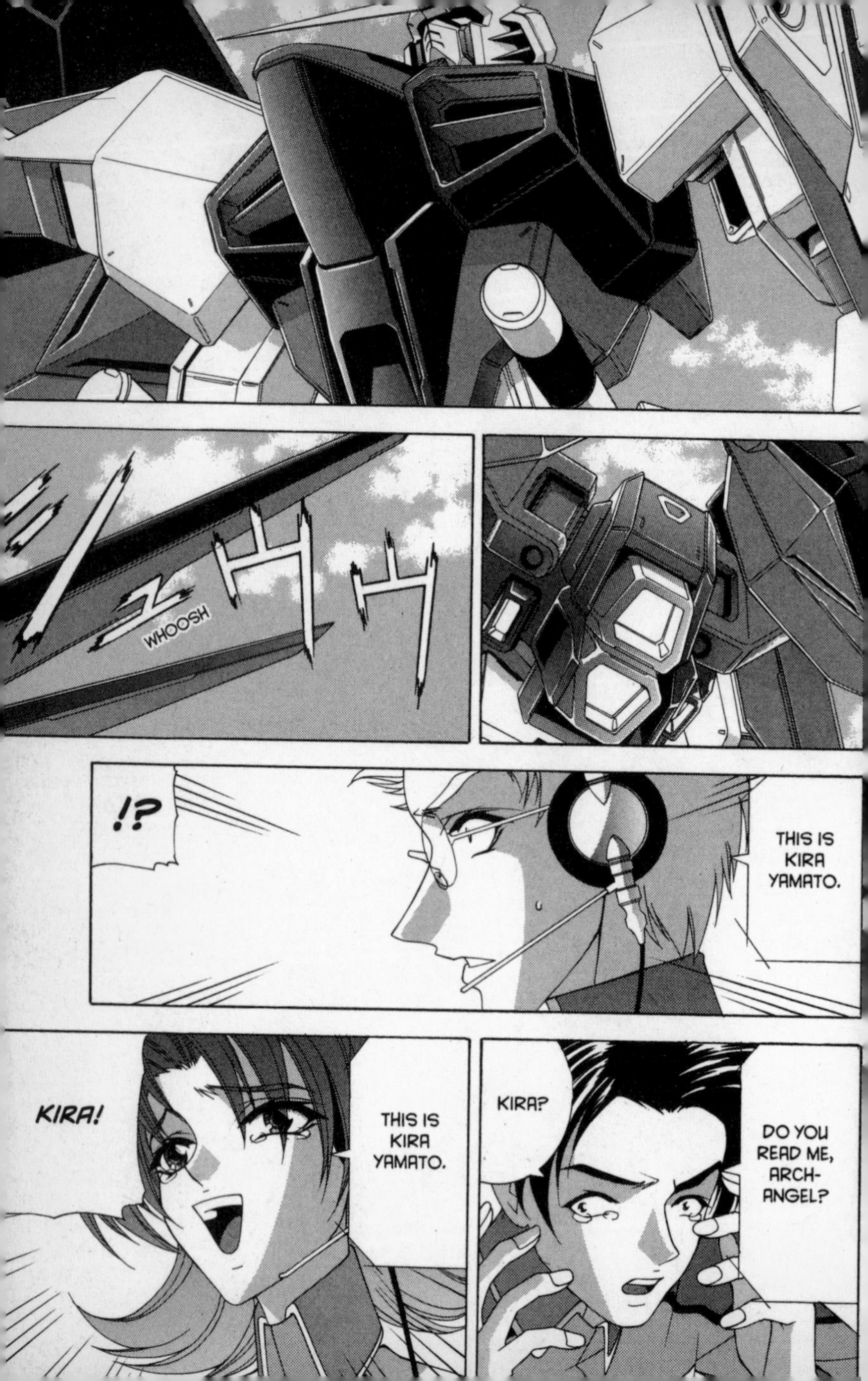
WHOOSH
THIS IS KIRA YAMATO.
!?
DO YOU READ ME, ARCH-ANGEL?
KIRA?
THIS IS KIRA YAMATO.
KIRA!

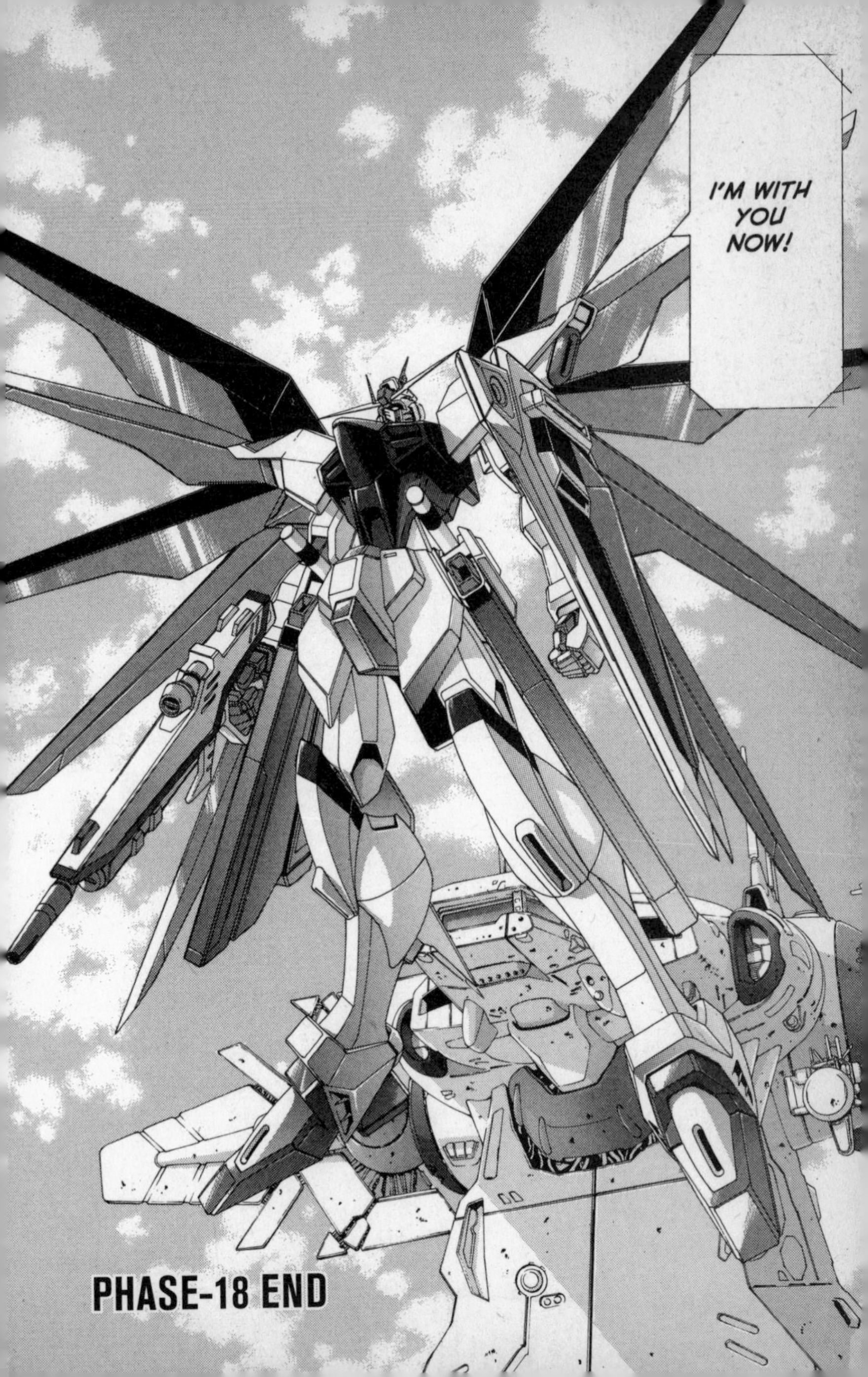
I'M WITH YOU NOW!
PHASE-18 END

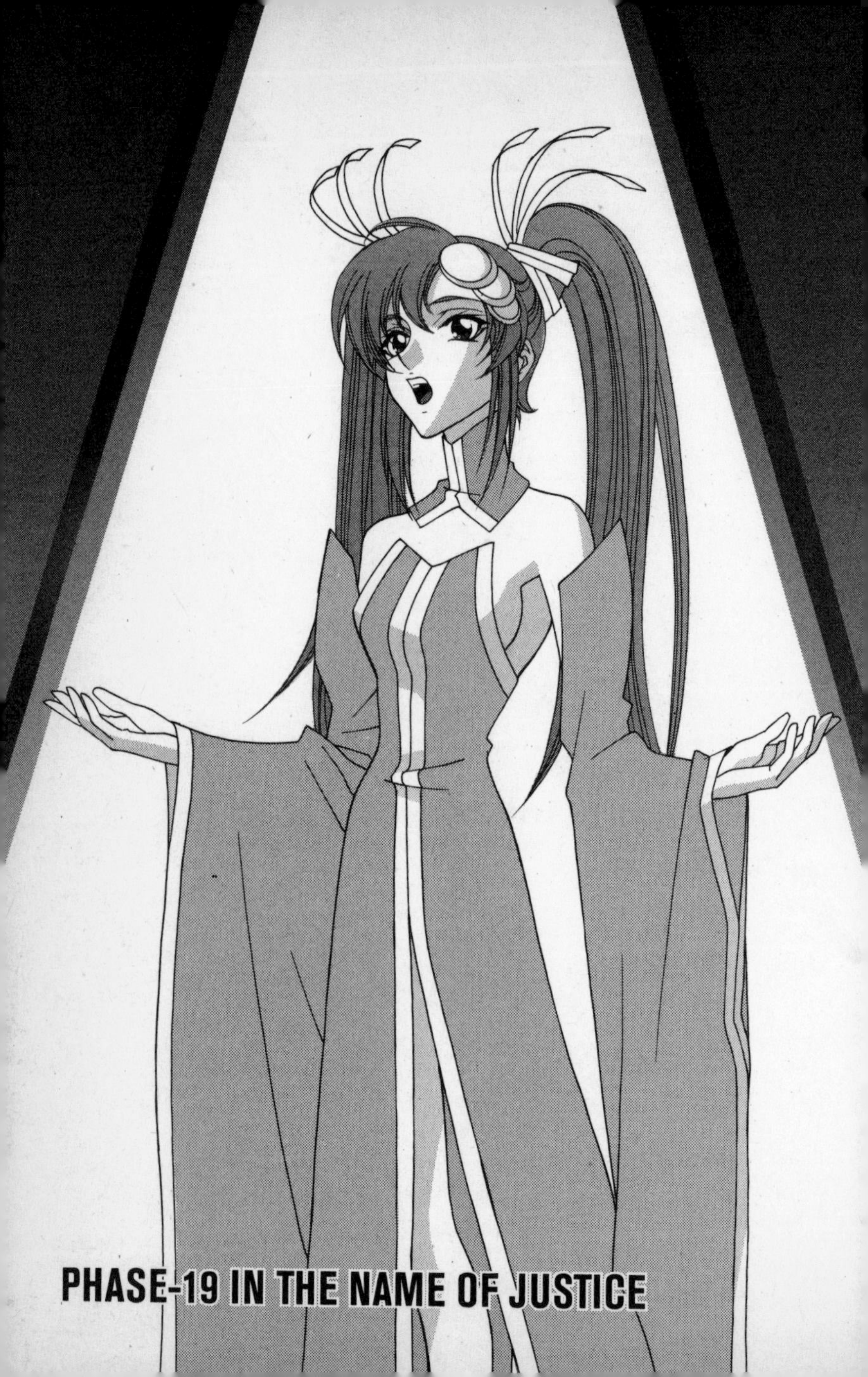

# PHASE-19 IN THE NAME OF JUSTICE

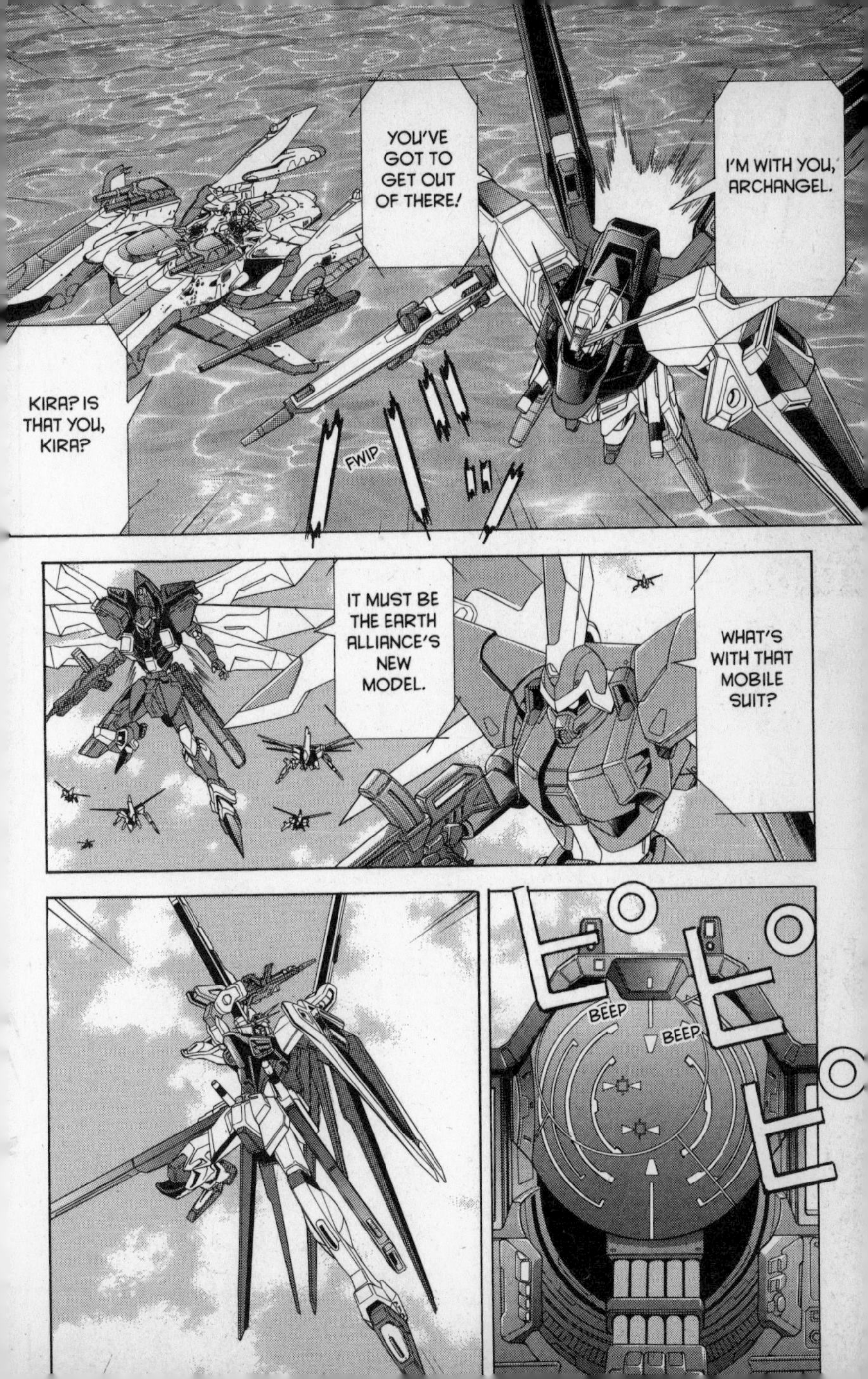
I'M WITH YOU, ARCHANGEL.
YOU'VE GOT TO GET OUT OF THERE!
KIRA? IS THAT YOU, KIRA?
FWIP
WHAT'S WITH THAT MOBILE SUIT?
IT MUST BE THE EARTH ALLIANCE'S NEW MODEL.
BEEP
BEEP

BLAM

AHHHH!

WHAT THE—?

FWAP

FWAP

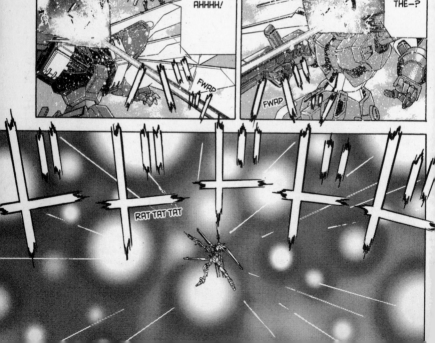

RAT TAT TAT

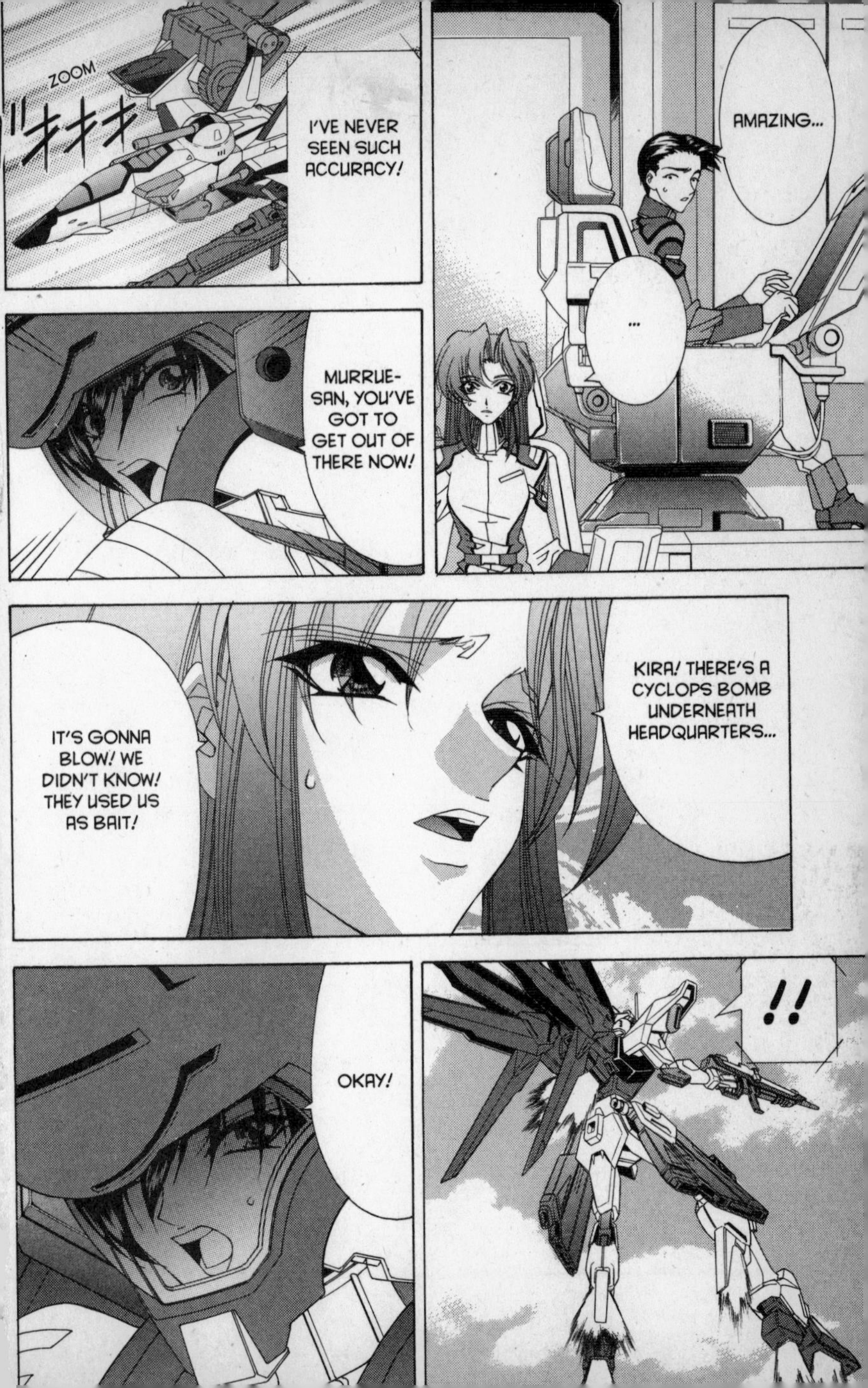

AMAZING...
...
I'VE NEVER SEEN SUCH ACCURACY!
ZOOM
MURRUE-SAN, YOU'VE GOT TO GET OUT OF THERE NOW!
KIRA! THERE'S A CYCLOPS BOMB UNDERNEATH HEADQUARTERS...
IT'S GONNA BLOW! WE DIDN'T KNOW! THEY USED US AS BAIT!
!!
OKAY!

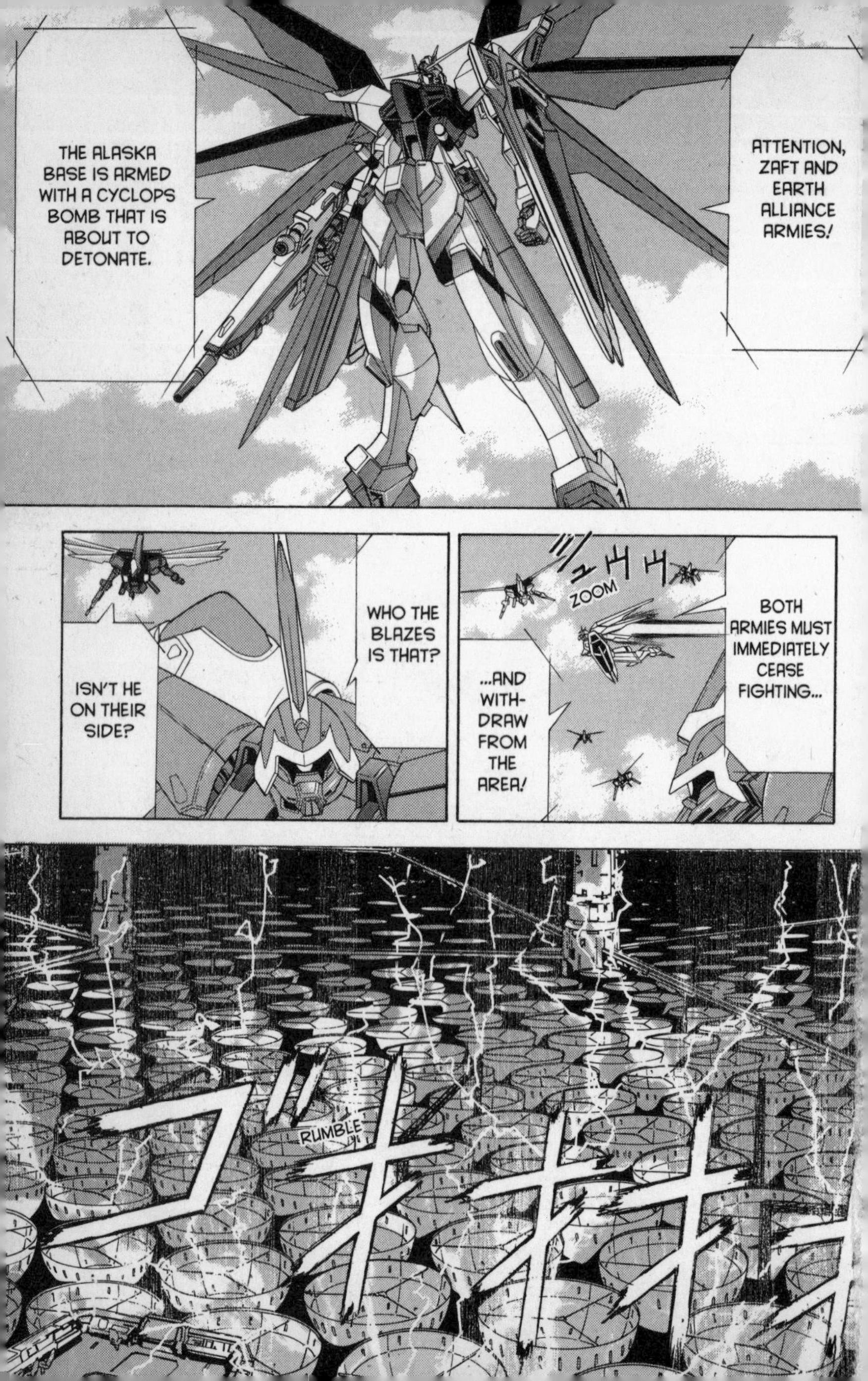
ATTENTION, ZAFT AND EARTH ALLIANCE ARMIES!
THE ALASKA BASE IS ARMED WITH A CYCLOPS BOMB THAT IS ABOUT TO DETONATE.
BOTH ARMIES MUST IMMEDIATELY CEASE FIGHTING...
ZOOM
...AND WITH-DRAW FROM THE AREA!
WHO THE BLAZES IS THAT?
ISN'T HE ON THEIR SIDE?
RUMBLE

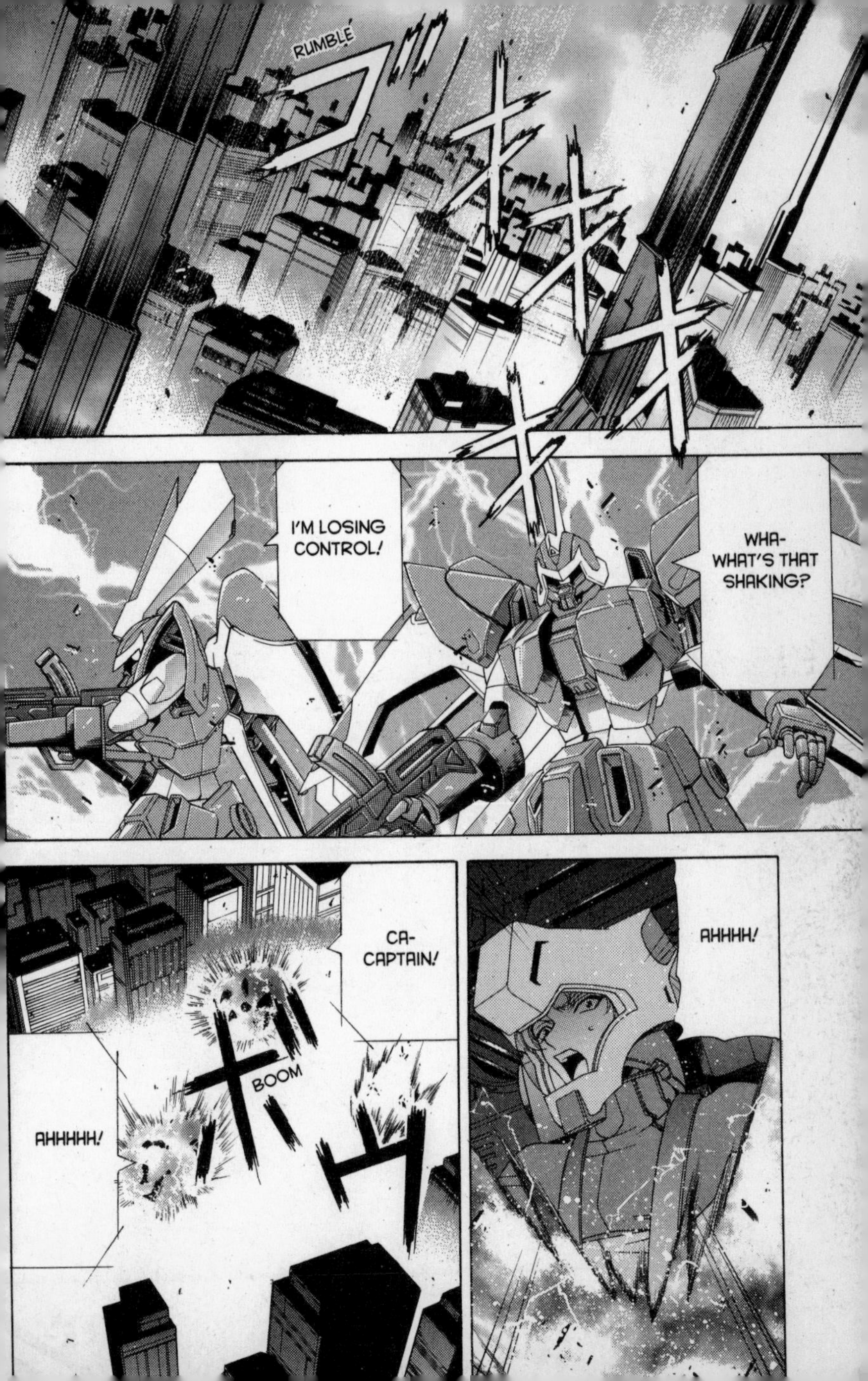
RUMBLE
WHA-
WHAT'S THAT
SHAKING?
I'M LOSING
CONTROL!
AHHHH!
CA-
CAPTAIN!
BOOM
AHHHHH!

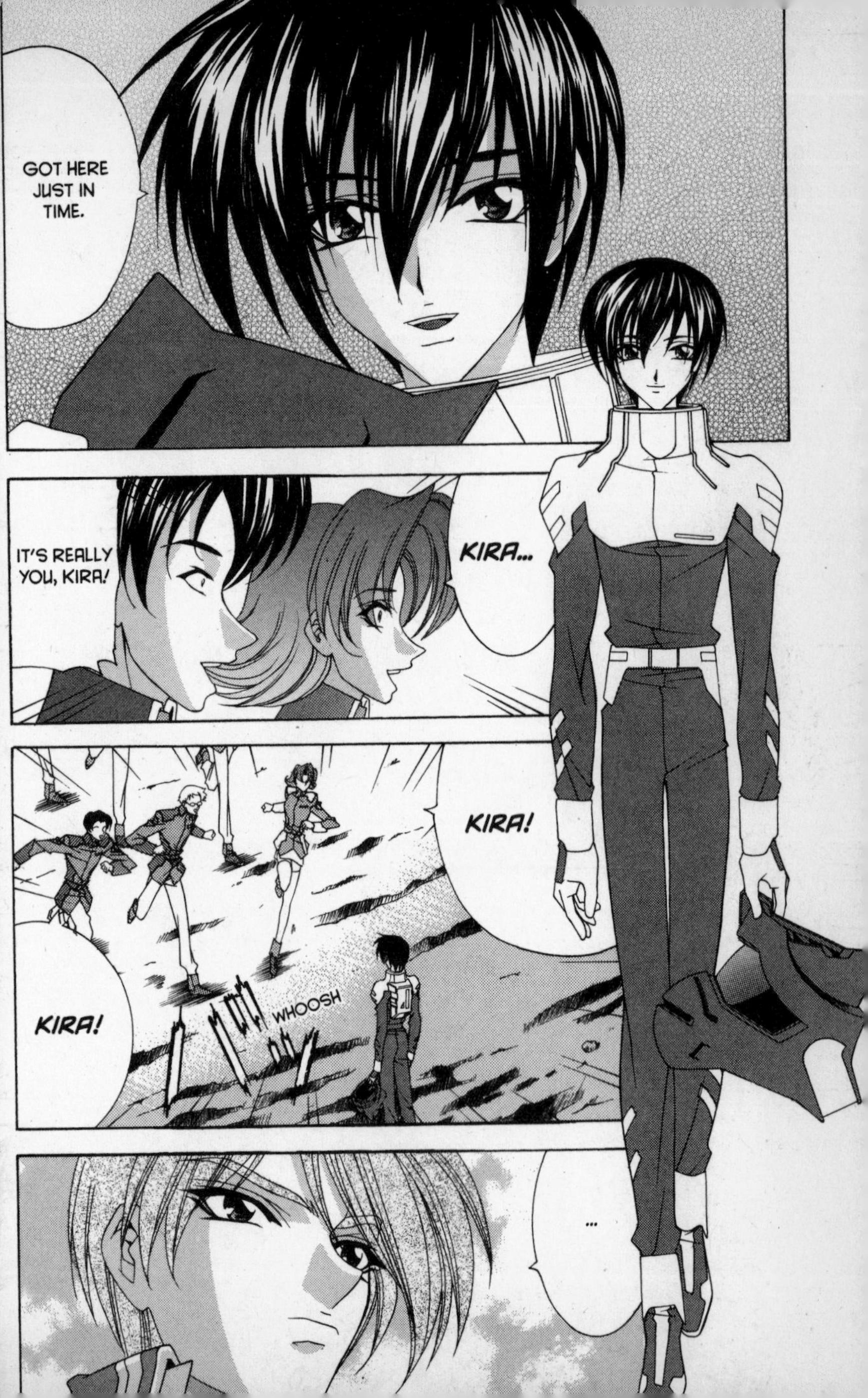
GOT HERE JUST IN TIME.
KIRA...
IT'S REALLY YOU, KIRA!
KIRA!
KIRA!
WHOOSH
...

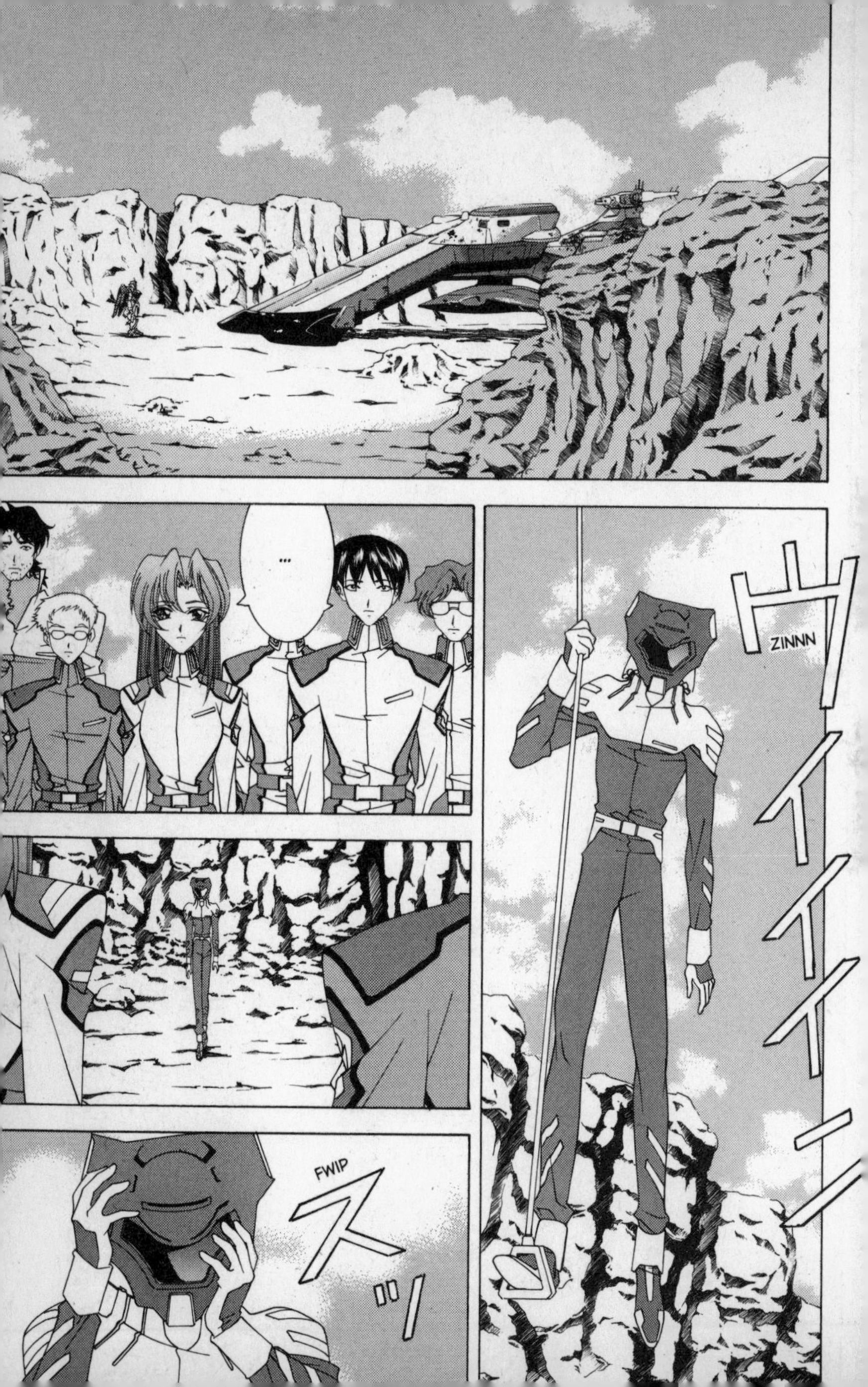
...
ZINNN
FWIP

CURSES! THEY'LL DO ANYTHING TO WIN...!

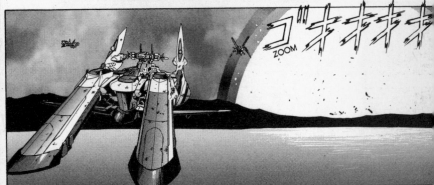

ZOOM

THE EARTH ALLIANCE...

...GOT US.

...

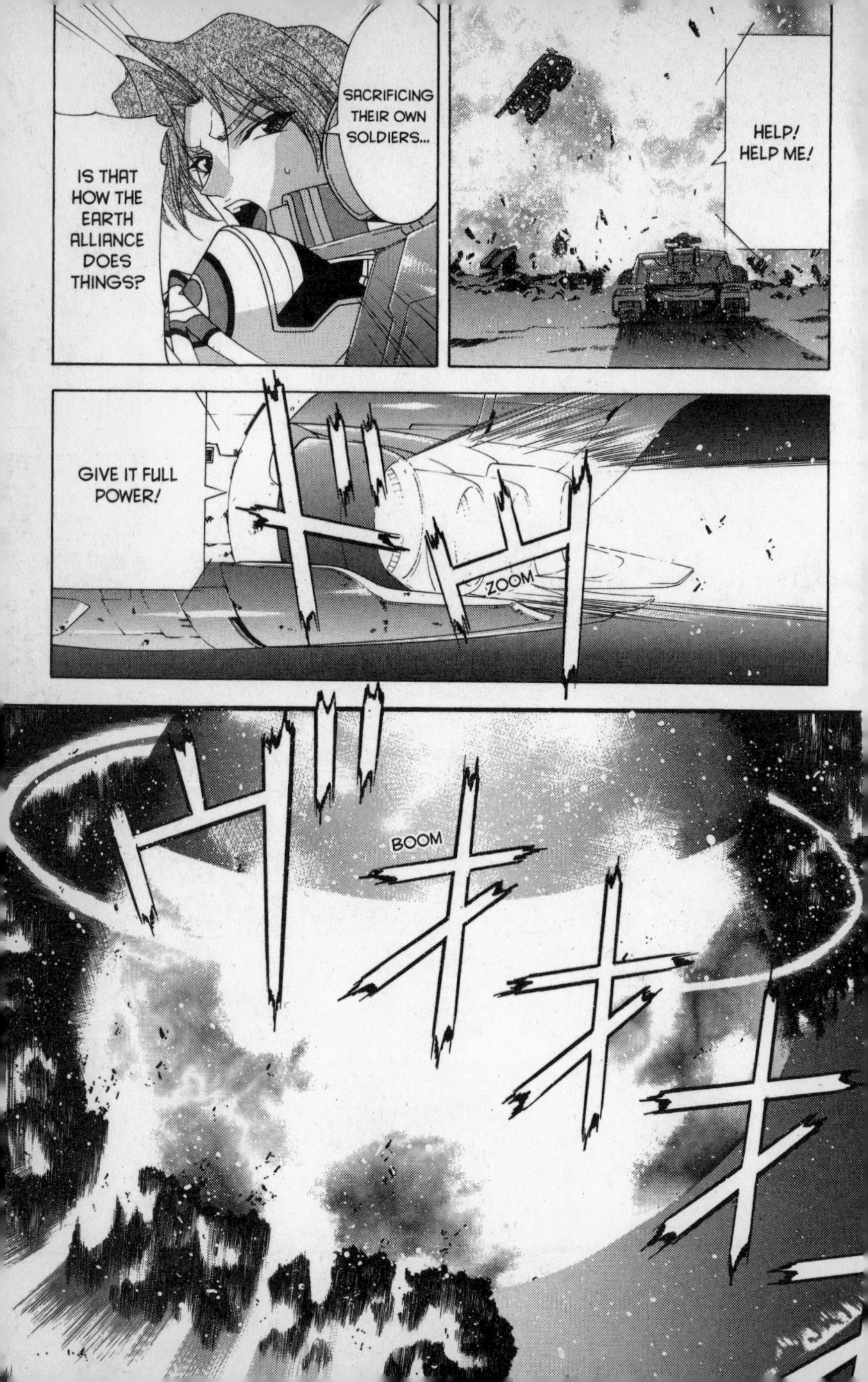
HELP! HELP ME!
SACRIFICING THEIR OWN SOLDIERS...
IS THAT HOW THE EARTH ALLIANCE DOES THINGS?
GIVE IT FULL POWER!
ZOOM
BOOM

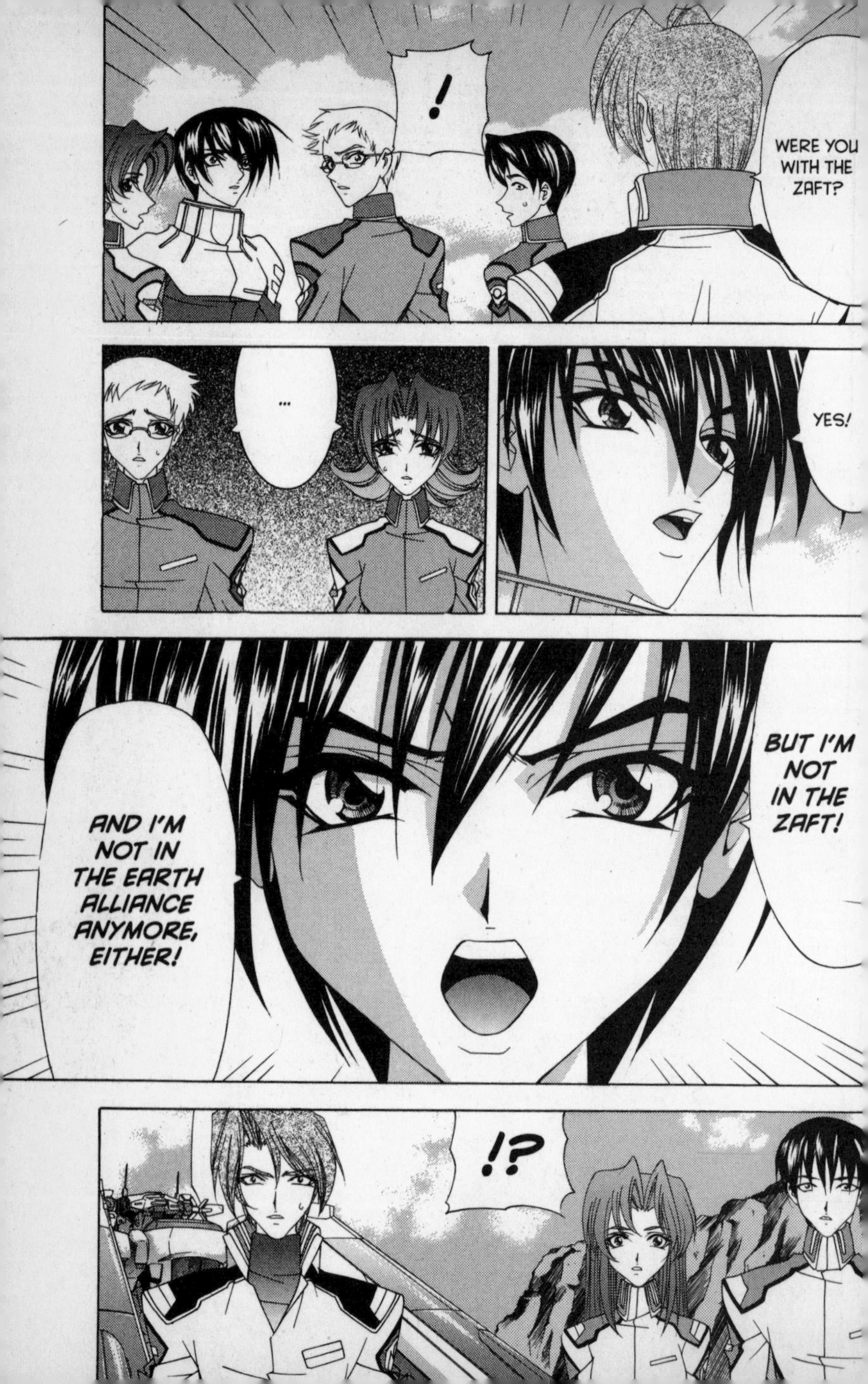
WERE YOU WITH THE ZAFT?
!
YES!
...
BUT I'M NOT IN THE ZAFT!
AND I'M NOT IN THE EARTH ALLIANCE ANYMORE, EITHER!
!?

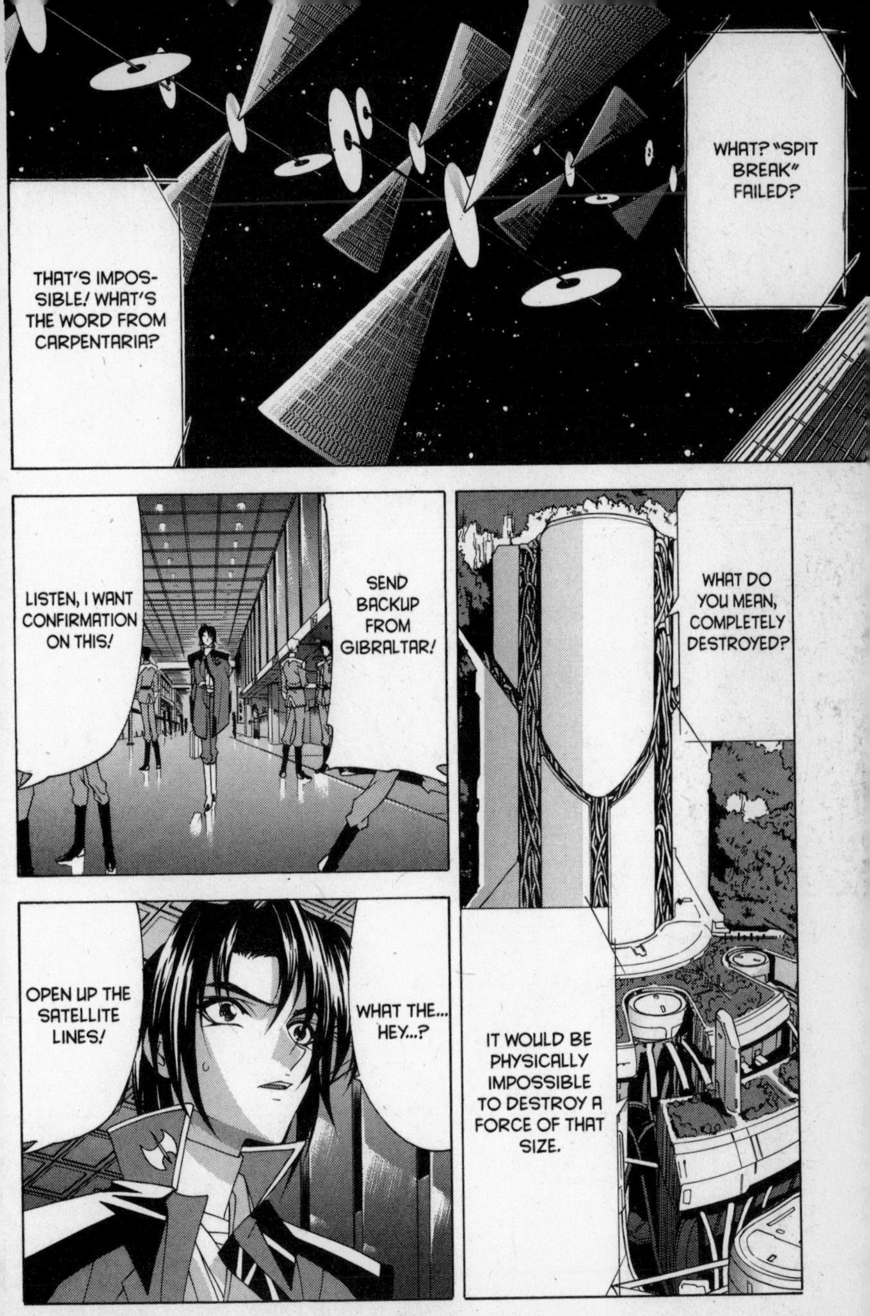
WHAT? "SPIT BREAK" FAILED?
THAT'S IMPOSSIBLE! WHAT'S THE WORD FROM CARPENTARIA?
WHAT DO YOU MEAN, COMPLETELY DESTROYED?
IT WOULD BE PHYSICALLY IMPOSSIBLE TO DESTROY A FORCE OF THAT SIZE.
SEND BACKUP FROM GIBRALTAR!
LISTEN, I WANT CONFIRMATION ON THIS!
WHAT THE... HEY...?
OPEN UP THE SATELLITE LINES!

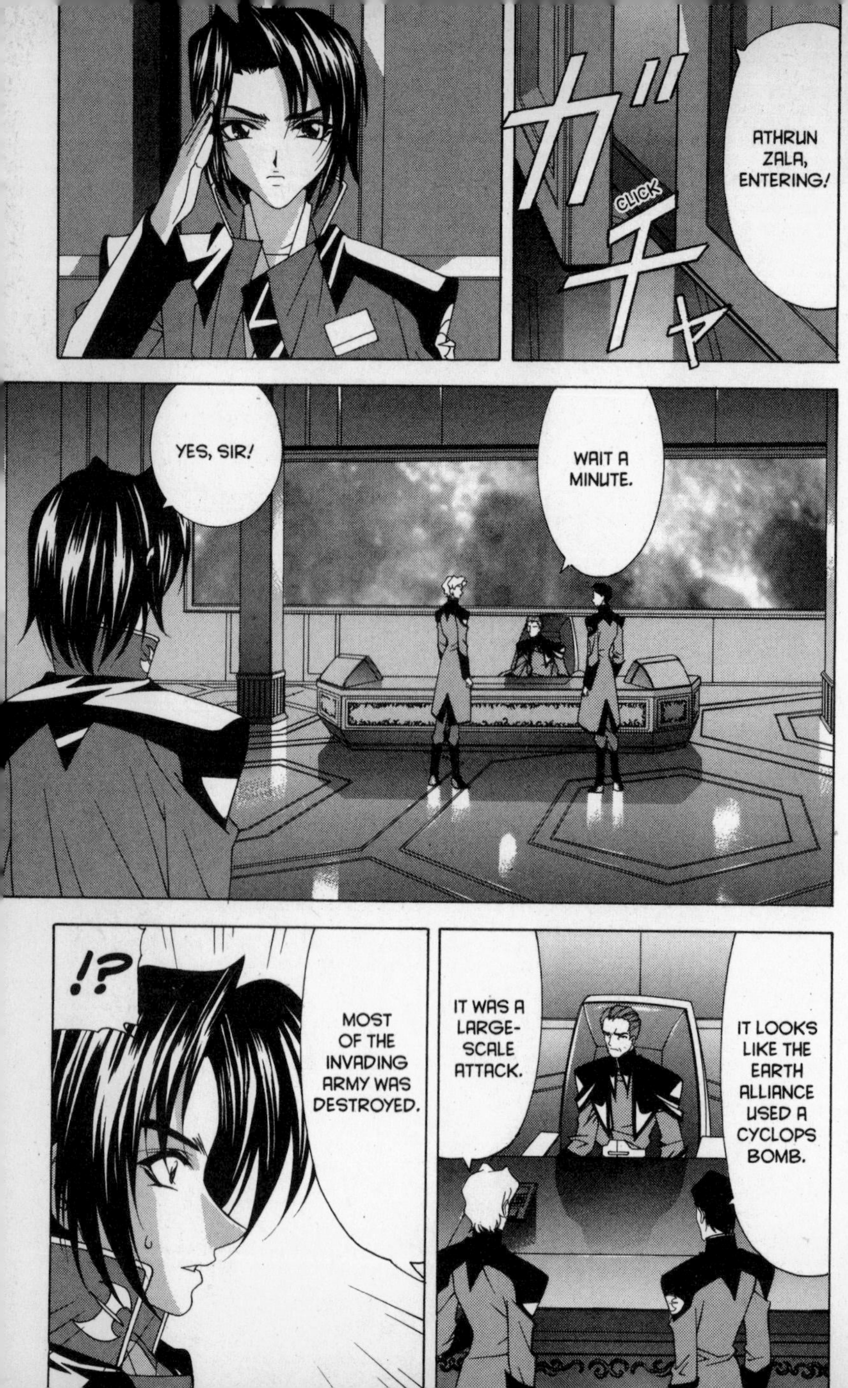

ATHRUN ZALA, ENTERING!
カチャ
CLICK
WAIT A MINUTE.
YES, SIR!
IT LOOKS LIKE THE EARTH ALLIANCE USED A CYCLOPS BOMB.
IT WAS A LARGE-SCALE ATTACK.
MOST OF THE INVADING ARMY WAS DESTROYED.
!?

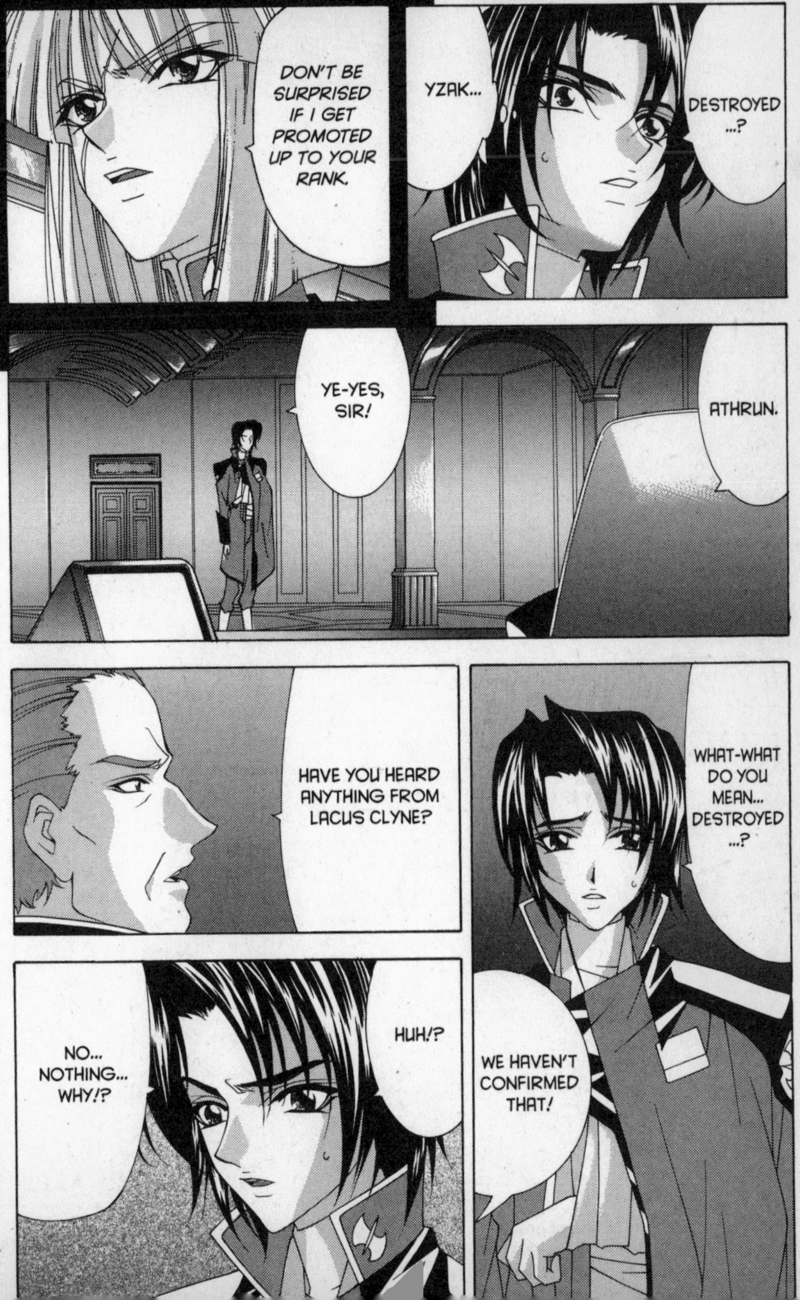
DESTROYED ...?
YZAK...
DON'T BE SURPRISED IF I GET PROMOTED UP TO YOUR RANK.
ATHRUN.
YE-YES, SIR!
WHAT-WHAT DO YOU MEAN... DESTROYED ...?
WE HAVEN'T CONFIRMED THAT!
HAVE YOU HEARD ANYTHING FROM LACUS CLYNE?
HUH!?
NO... NOTHING... WHY!?

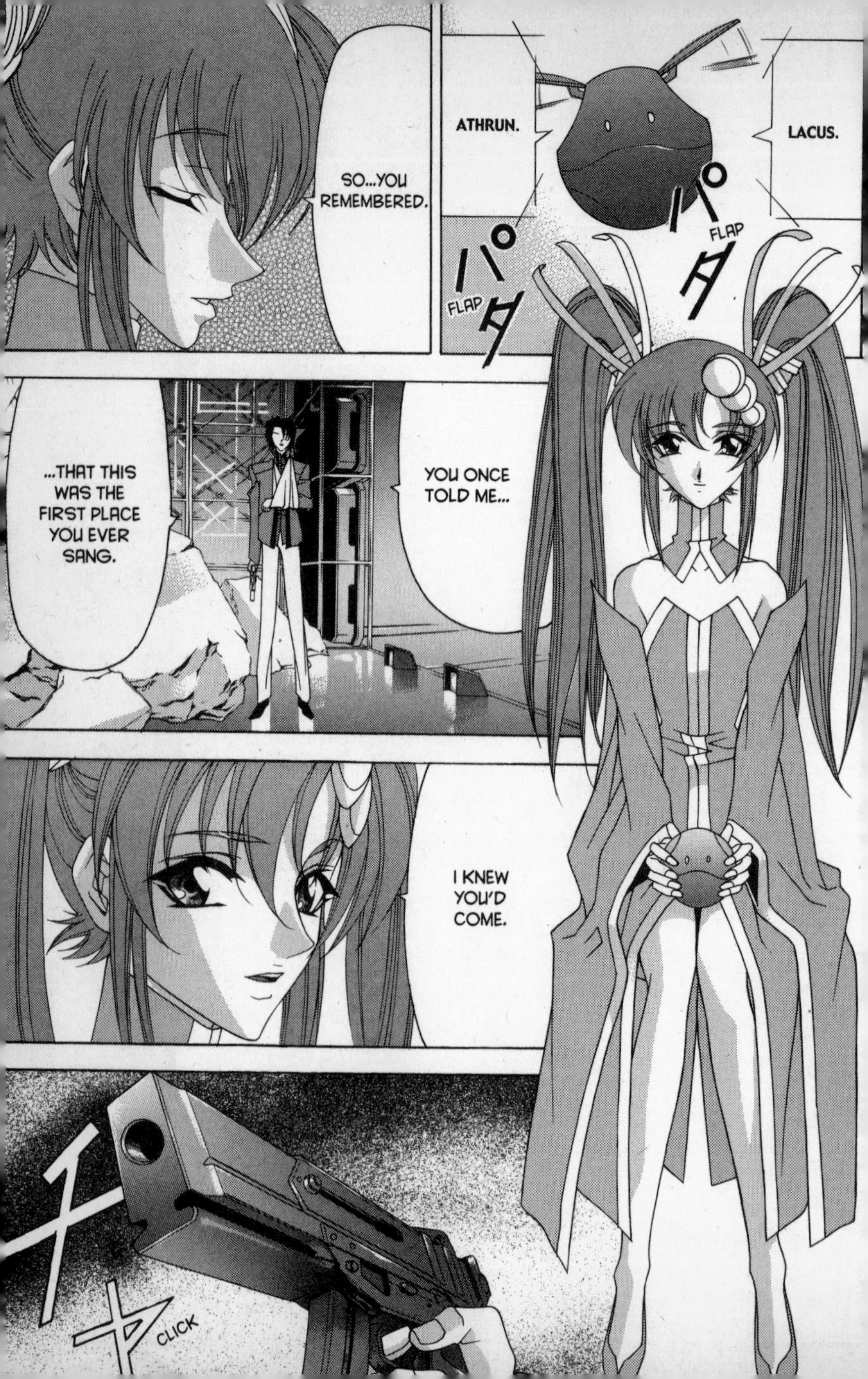
LACUS.
ATHRUN.
FLAP
FLAP
SO...YOU REMEMBERED.
YOU ONCE TOLD ME...
...THAT THIS WAS THE FIRST PLACE YOU EVER SANG.
I KNEW YOU'D COME.
CLICK

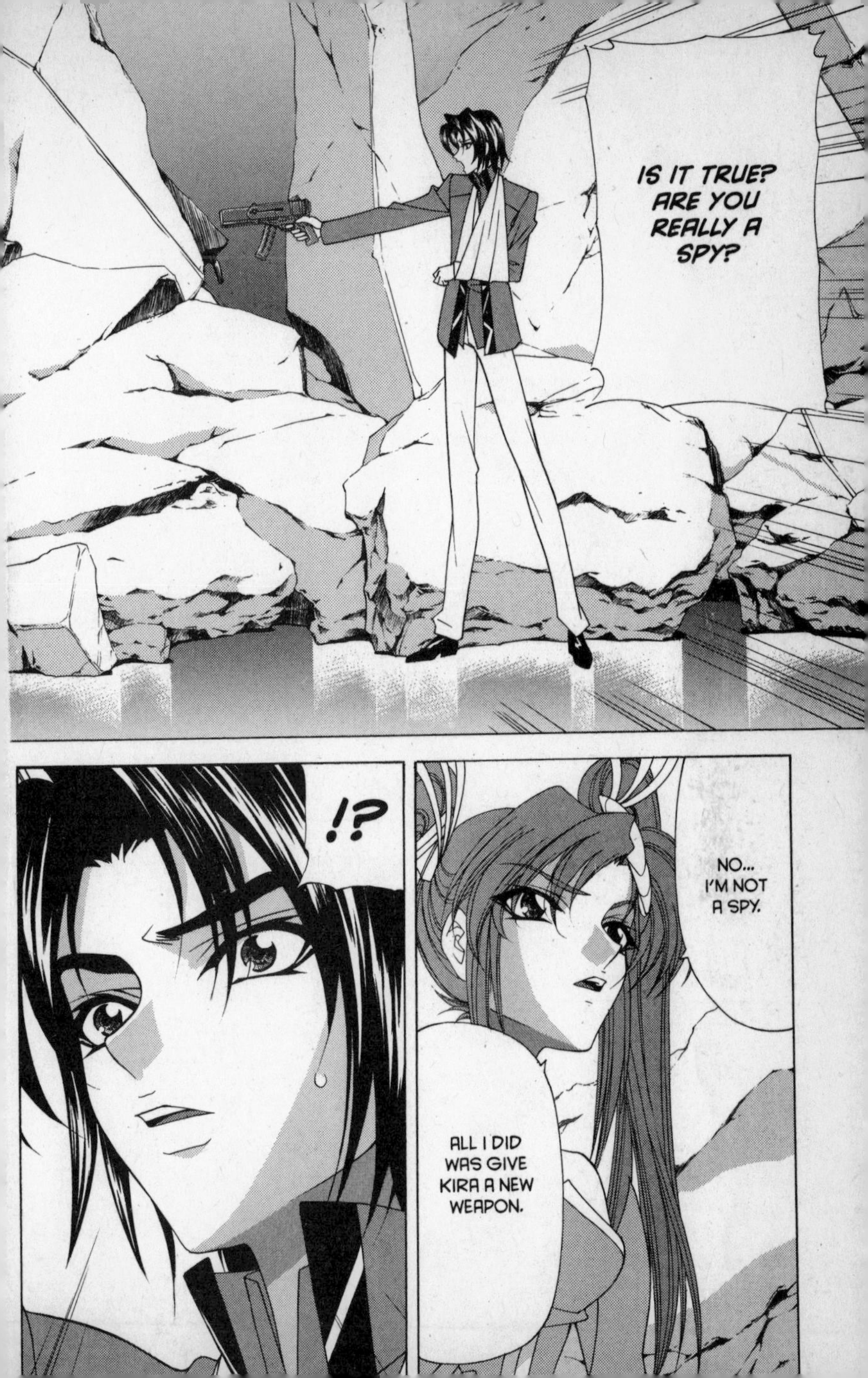
IS IT TRUE? ARE YOU REALLY A SPY?
NO... I'M NOT A SPY.
ALL I DID WAS GIVE KIRA A NEW WEAPON.
!?

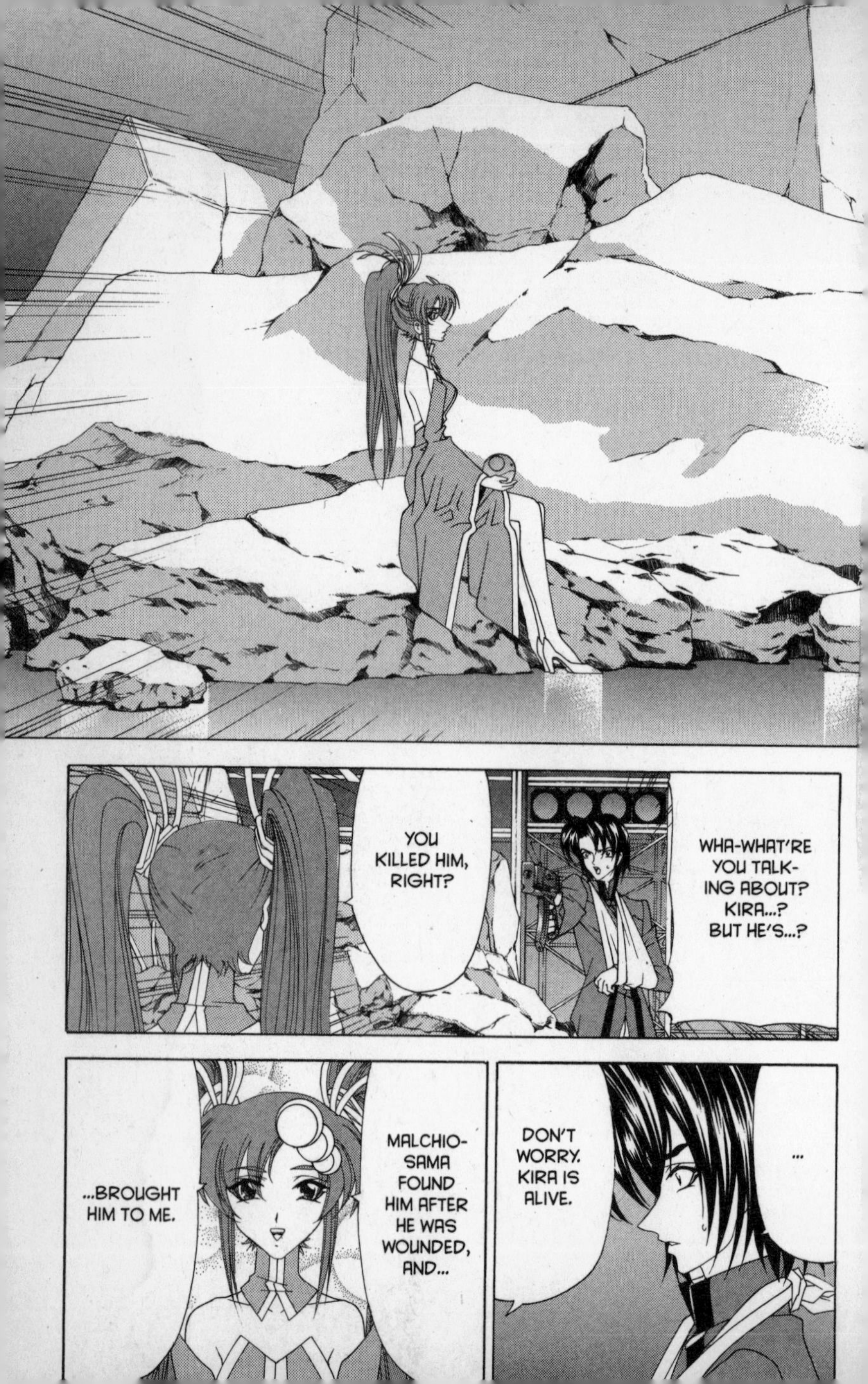
WHA-WHAT'RE YOU TALK-ING ABOUT? KIRA...? BUT HE'S...?
YOU KILLED HIM, RIGHT?
...
DON'T WORRY. KIRA IS ALIVE.
MALCHIO-SAMA FOUND HIM AFTER HE WAS WOUNDED, AND...
...BROUGHT HIM TO ME.

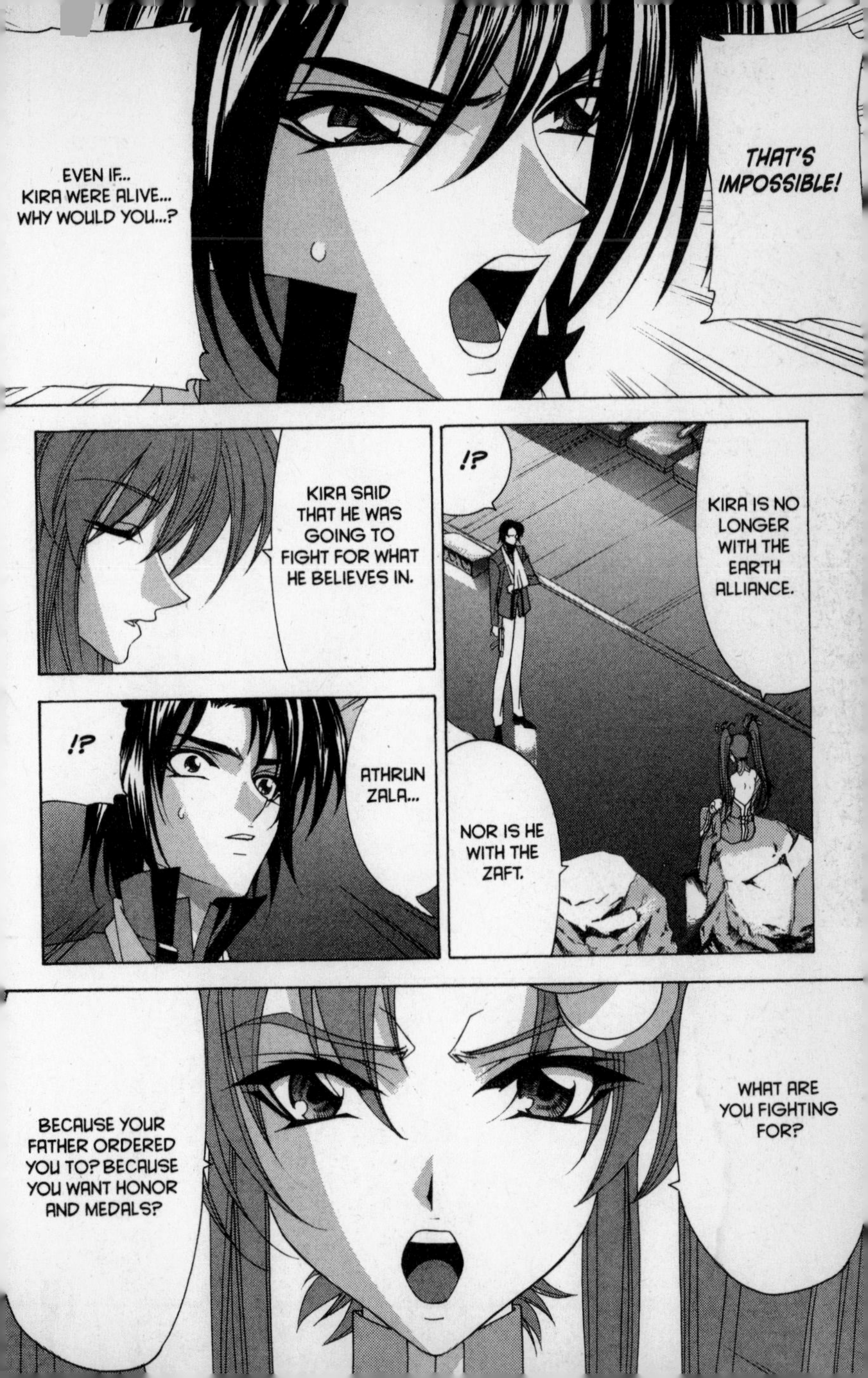
THAT'S IMPOSSIBLE!
EVEN IF... KIRA WERE ALIVE... WHY WOULD YOU...?
KIRA IS NO LONGER WITH THE EARTH ALLIANCE.
!?
NOR IS HE WITH THE ZAFT.
KIRA SAID THAT HE WAS GOING TO FIGHT FOR WHAT HE BELIEVES IN.
ATHRUN ZALA...
!?
WHAT ARE YOU FIGHTING FOR?
BECAUSE YOUR FATHER ORDERED YOU TO? BECAUSE YOU WANT HONOR AND MEDALS?

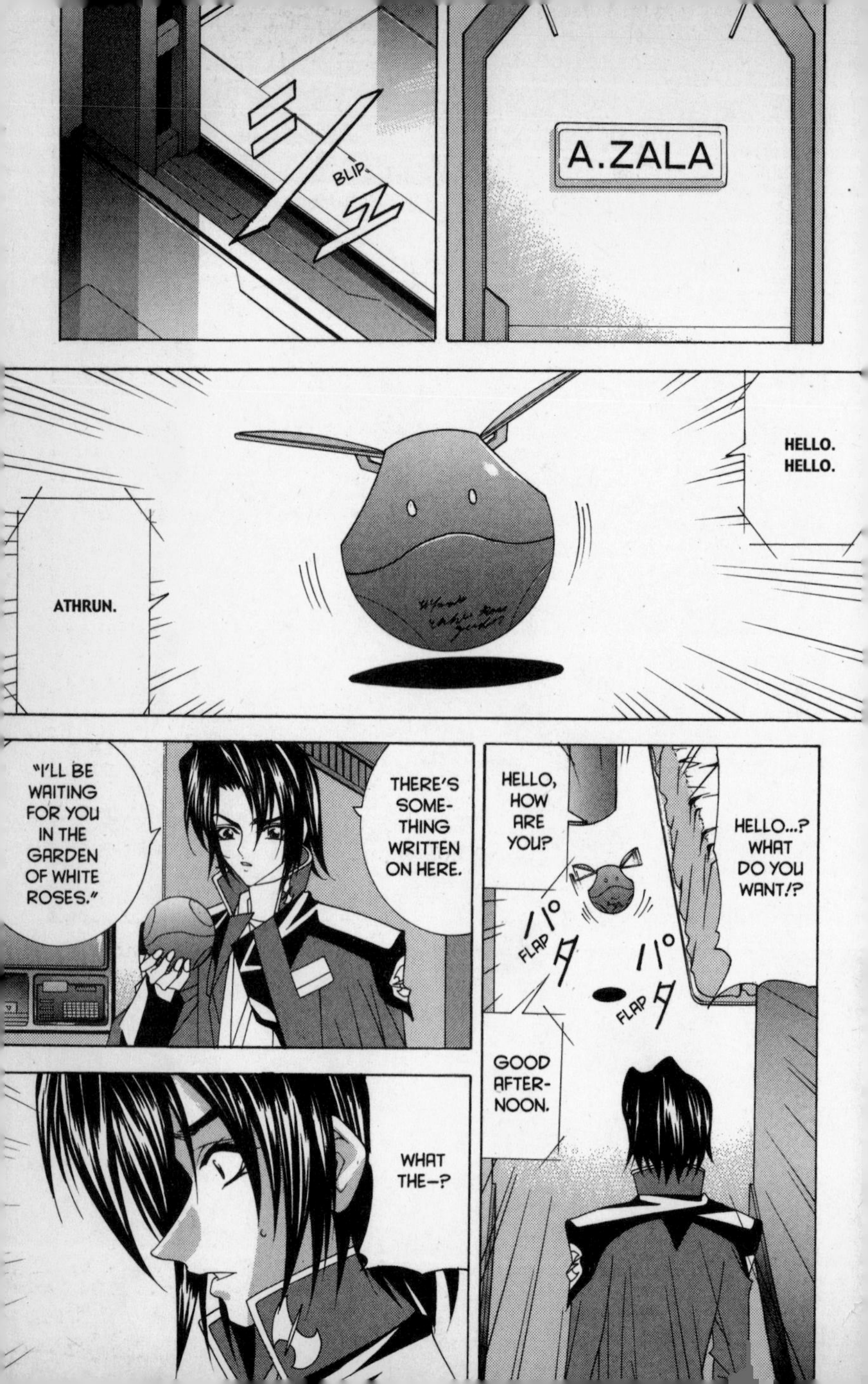
A.ZALA
BLIP
HELLO. HELLO.
ATHRUN.
HELLO...? WHAT DO YOU WANT!?
HELLO, HOW ARE YOU?
FLAP
FLAP
THERE'S SOME-THING WRITTEN ON HERE.
"I'LL BE WAITING FOR YOU IN THE GARDEN OF WHITE ROSES."
GOOD AFTER-NOON.
WHAT THE—?

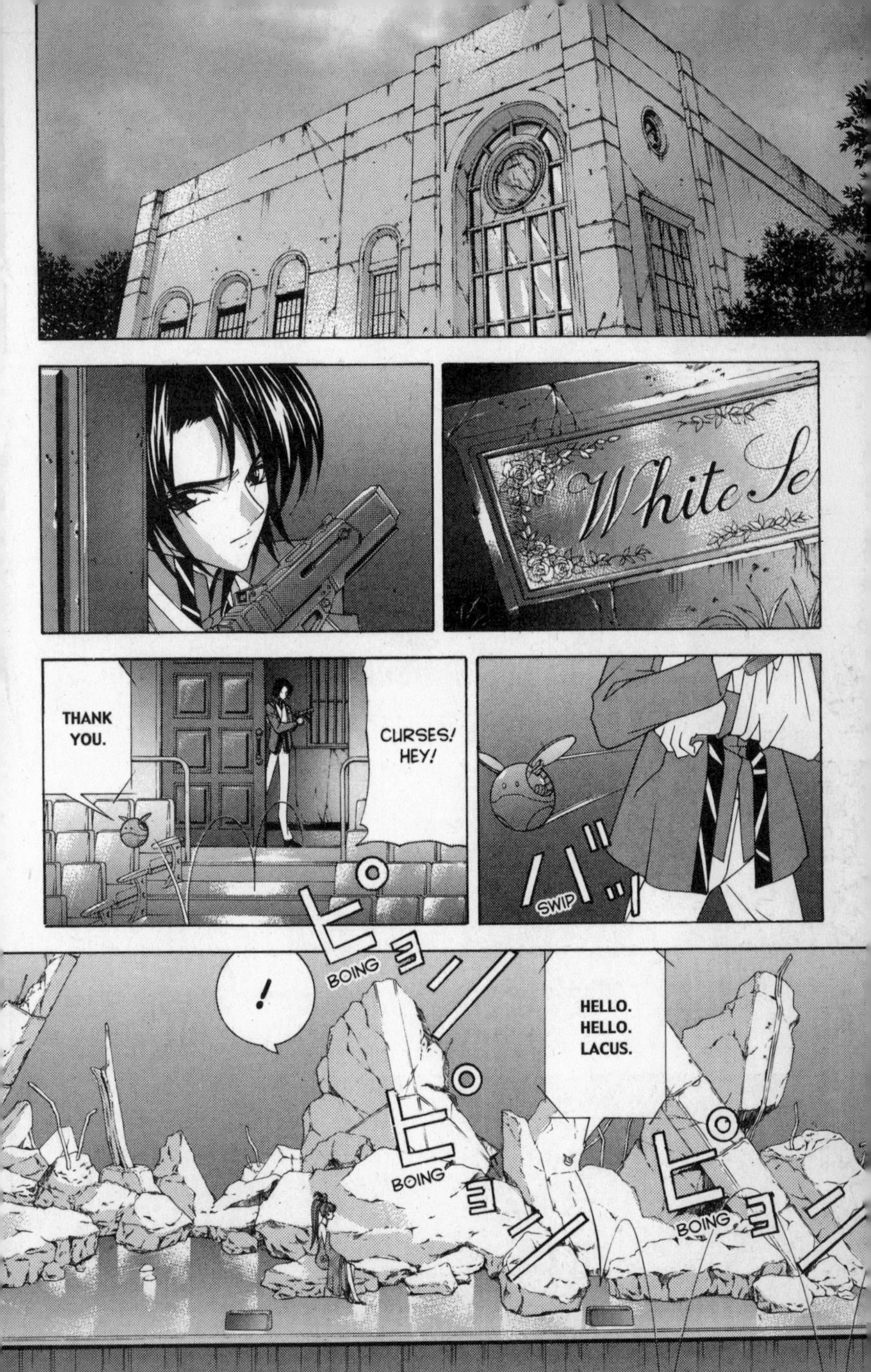

White Se
SWIP
CURSES! HEY!
THANK YOU.
HELLO. HELLO. LACUS.
!
BOING
BOING
BOING

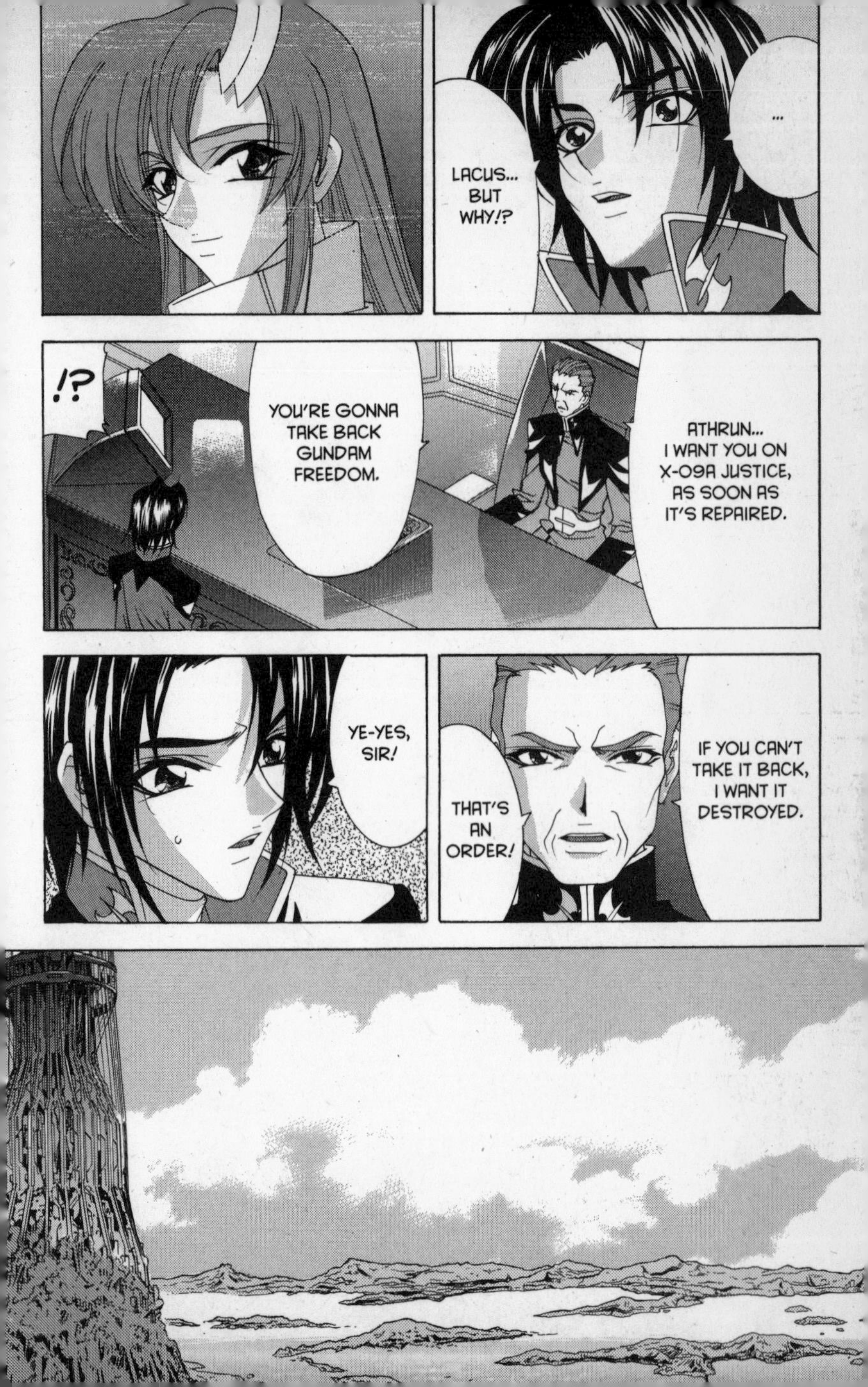
...
LACUS... BUT WHY!?
ATHRUN... I WANT YOU ON X-09A JUSTICE, AS SOON AS IT'S REPAIRED.
YOU'RE GONNA TAKE BACK GUNDAM FREEDOM.
!?
IF YOU CAN'T TAKE IT BACK, I WANT IT DESTROYED.
THAT'S AN ORDER!
YE-YES, SIR!

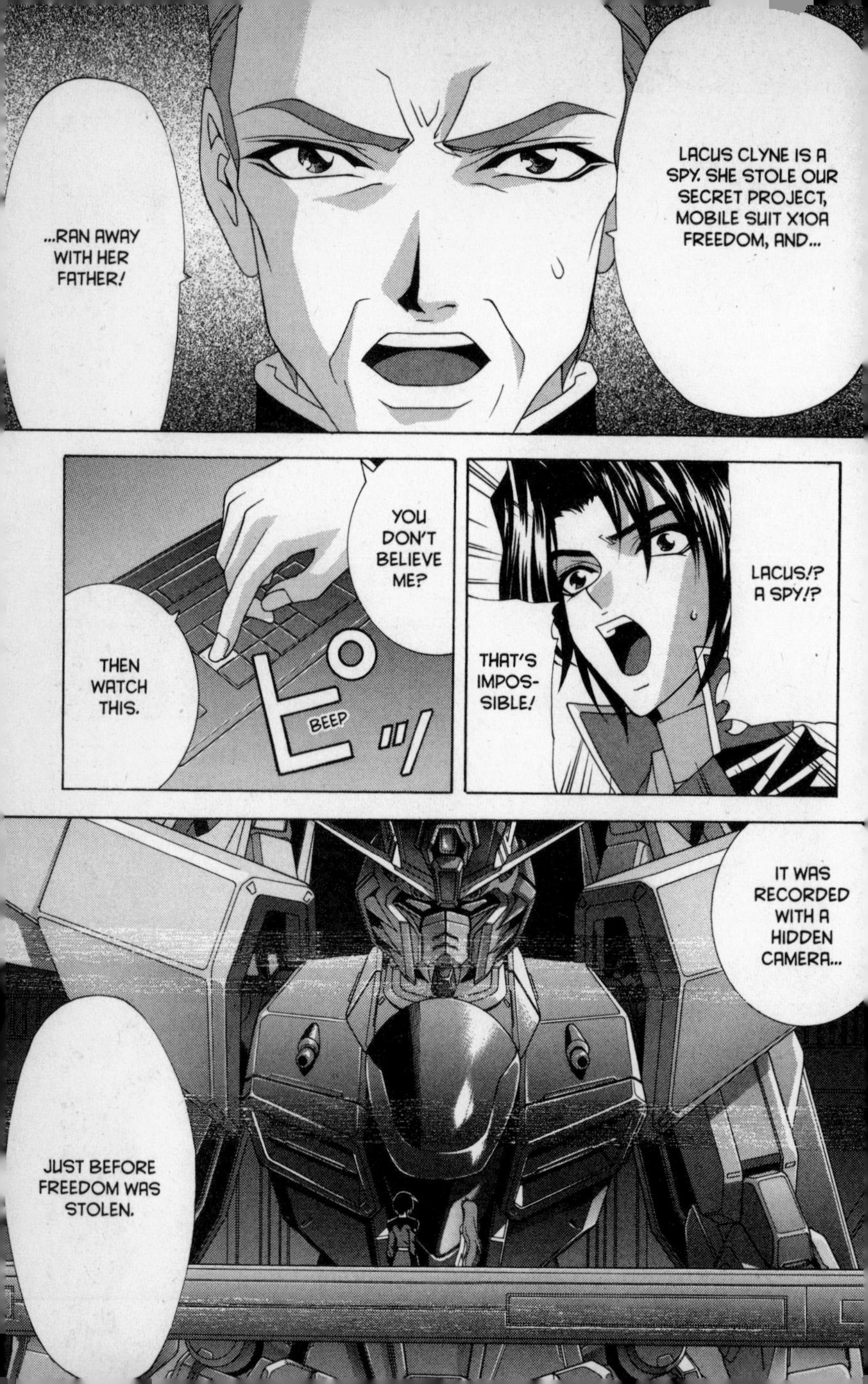
LACUS CLYNE IS A SPY. SHE STOLE OUR SECRET PROJECT, MOBILE SUIT X10A FREEDOM, AND...
...RAN AWAY WITH HER FATHER!
LACUS!? A SPY!?
THAT'S IMPOSSIBLE!
YOU DON'T BELIEVE ME?
THEN WATCH THIS.
ピッ
BEEP
IT WAS RECORDED WITH A HIDDEN CAMERA...
JUST BEFORE FREEDOM WAS STOLEN.

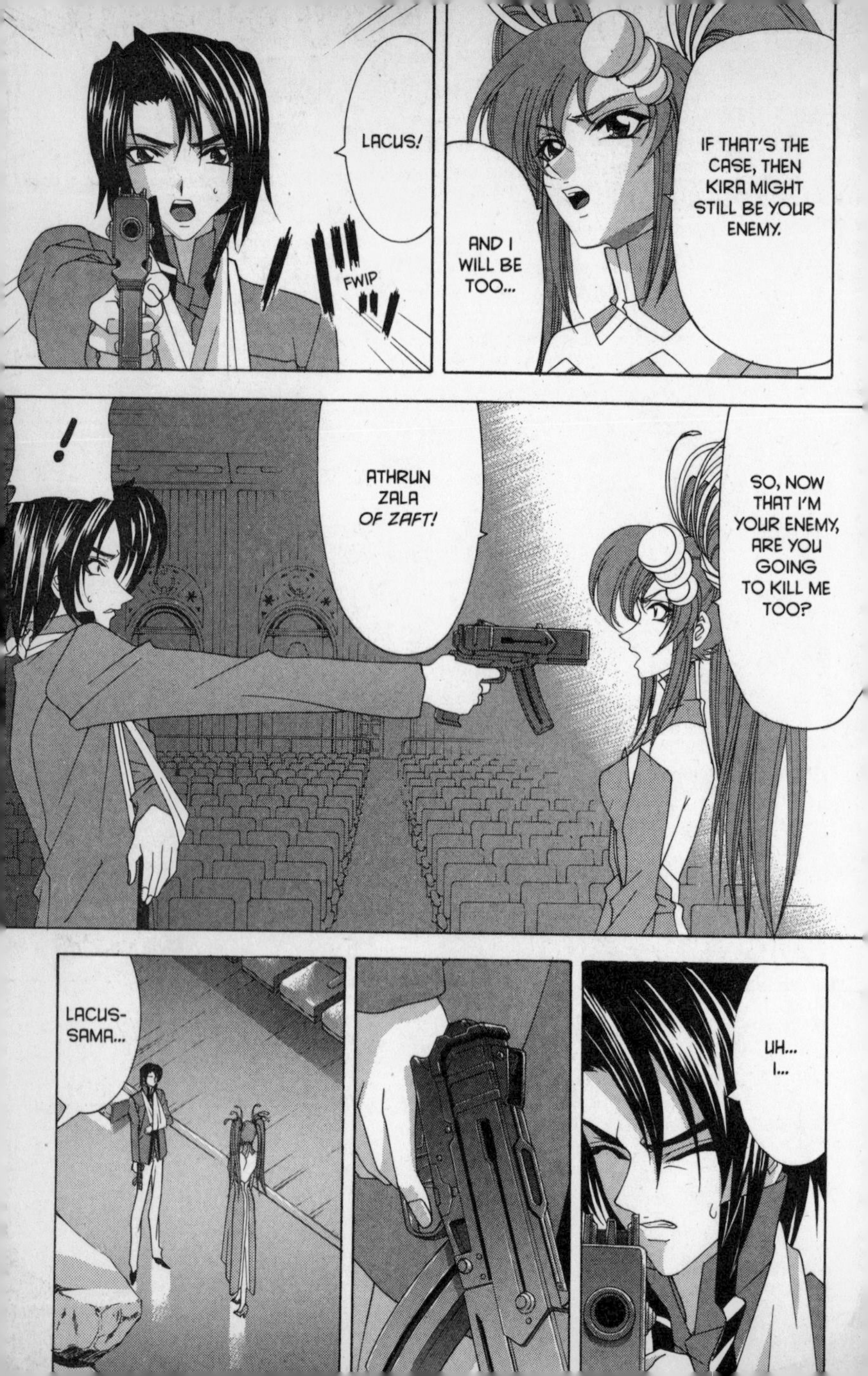
IF THAT'S THE CASE, THEN KIRA MIGHT STILL BE YOUR ENEMY.
AND I WILL BE TOO...
LACUS!
FWIP
SO, NOW THAT I'M YOUR ENEMY, ARE YOU GOING TO KILL ME TOO?
ATHRUN ZALA OF ZAFT!
!
UH... I...
LACUS-SAMA...

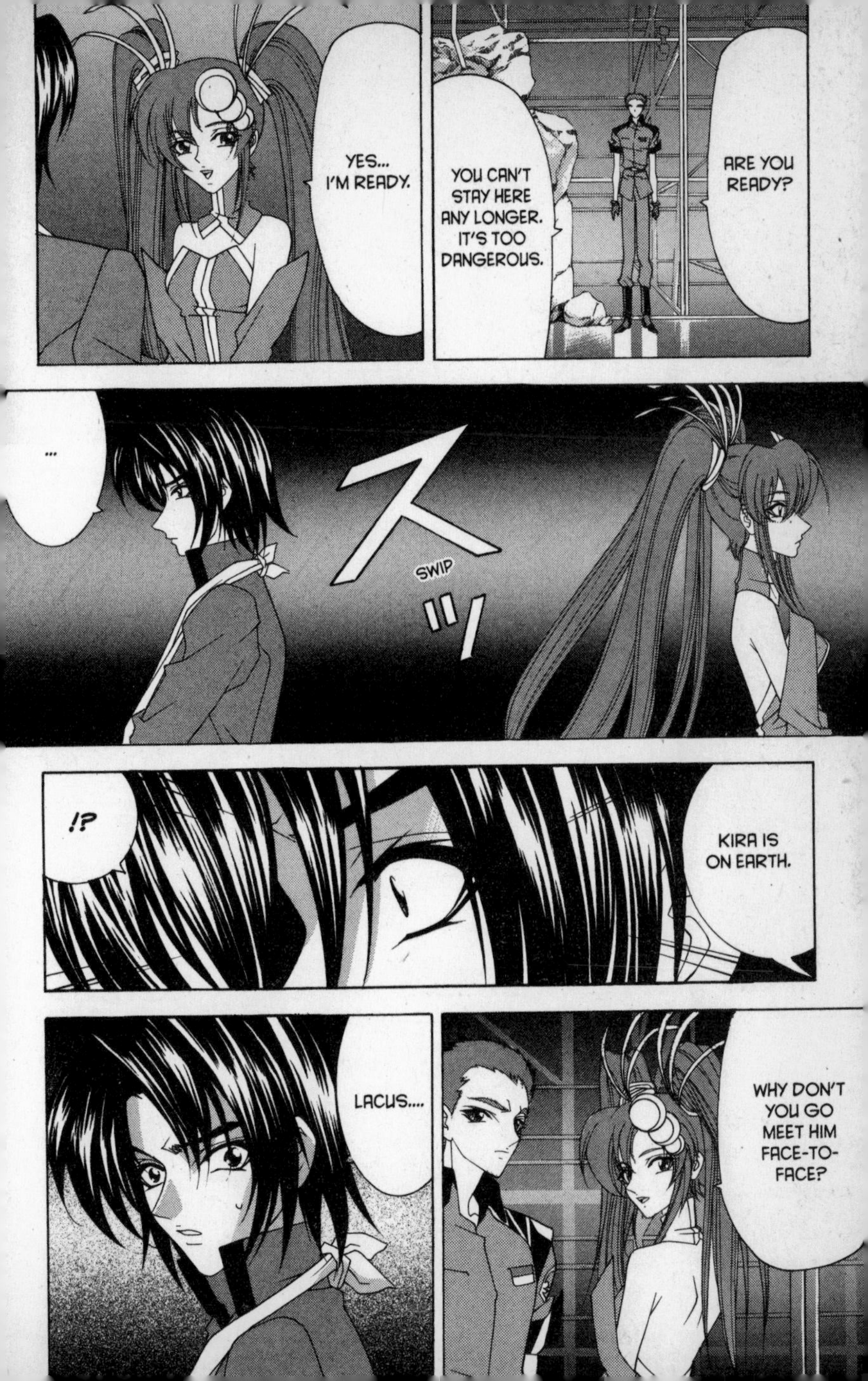
ARE YOU READY?
YOU CAN'T STAY HERE ANY LONGER. IT'S TOO DANGEROUS.
YES... I'M READY.
ス
SWIP
...
KIRA IS ON EARTH.
!?
WHY DON'T YOU GO MEET HIM FACE-TO-FACE?
LACUS....

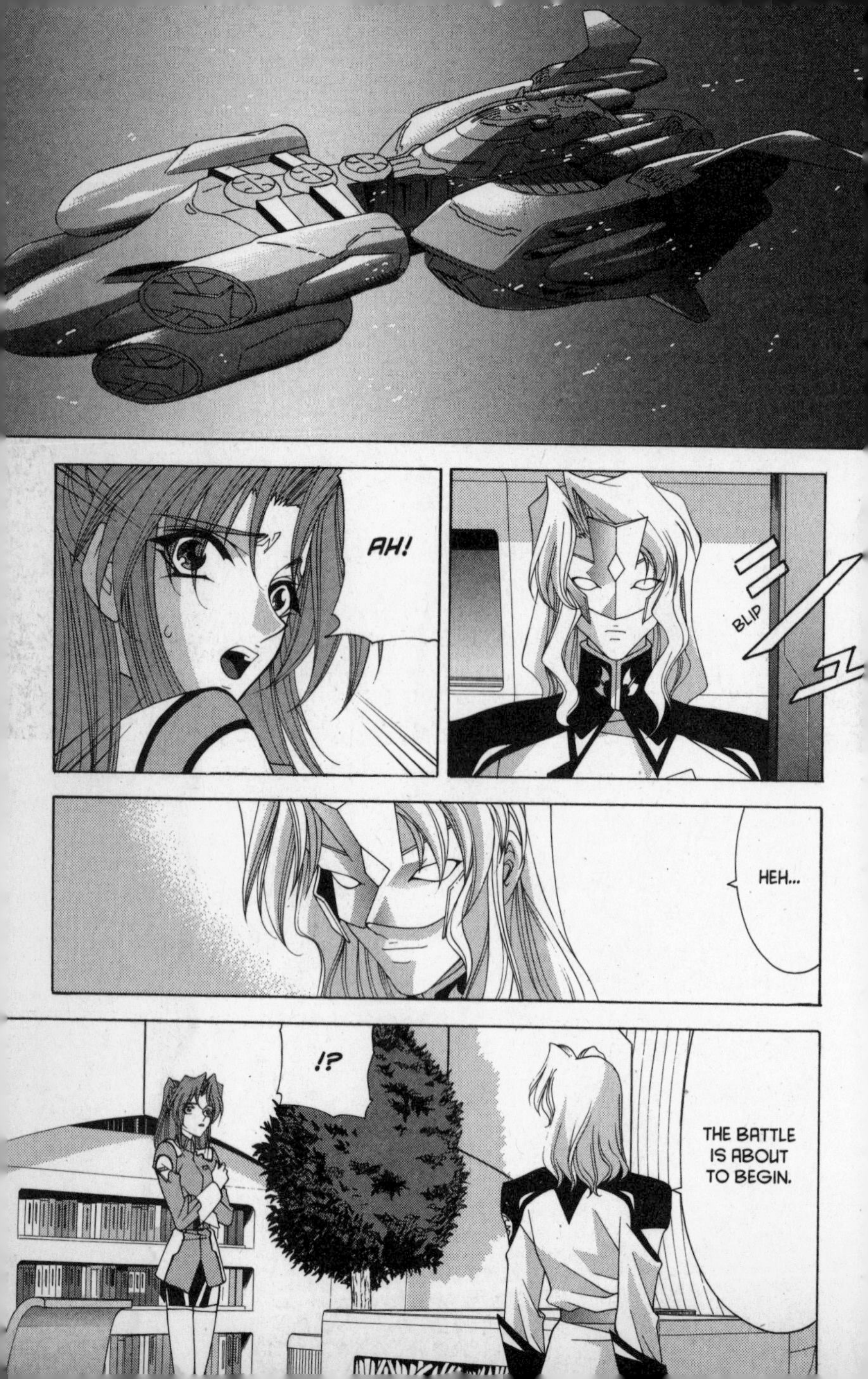
BLIP
AH!
HEH...
THE BATTLE IS ABOUT TO BEGIN.
!?

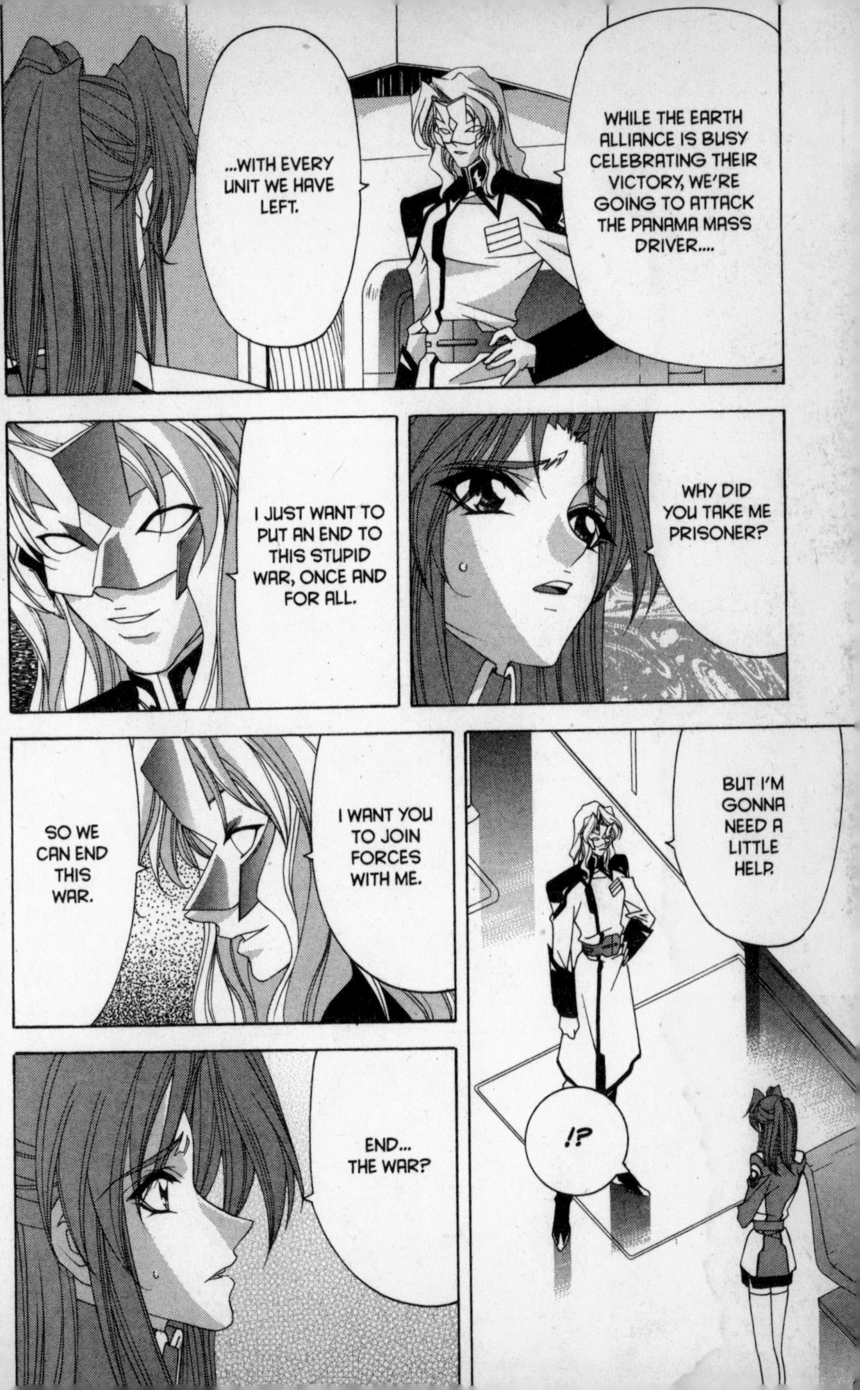
WHILE THE EARTH ALLIANCE IS BUSY CELEBRATING THEIR VICTORY, WE'RE GOING TO ATTACK THE PANAMA MASS DRIVER....
...WITH EVERY UNIT WE HAVE LEFT.
WHY DID YOU TAKE ME PRISONER?
I JUST WANT TO PUT AN END TO THIS STUPID WAR, ONCE AND FOR ALL.
BUT I'M GONNA NEED A LITTLE HELP.
!?
I WANT YOU TO JOIN FORCES WITH ME.
SO WE CAN END THIS WAR.
END... THE WAR?

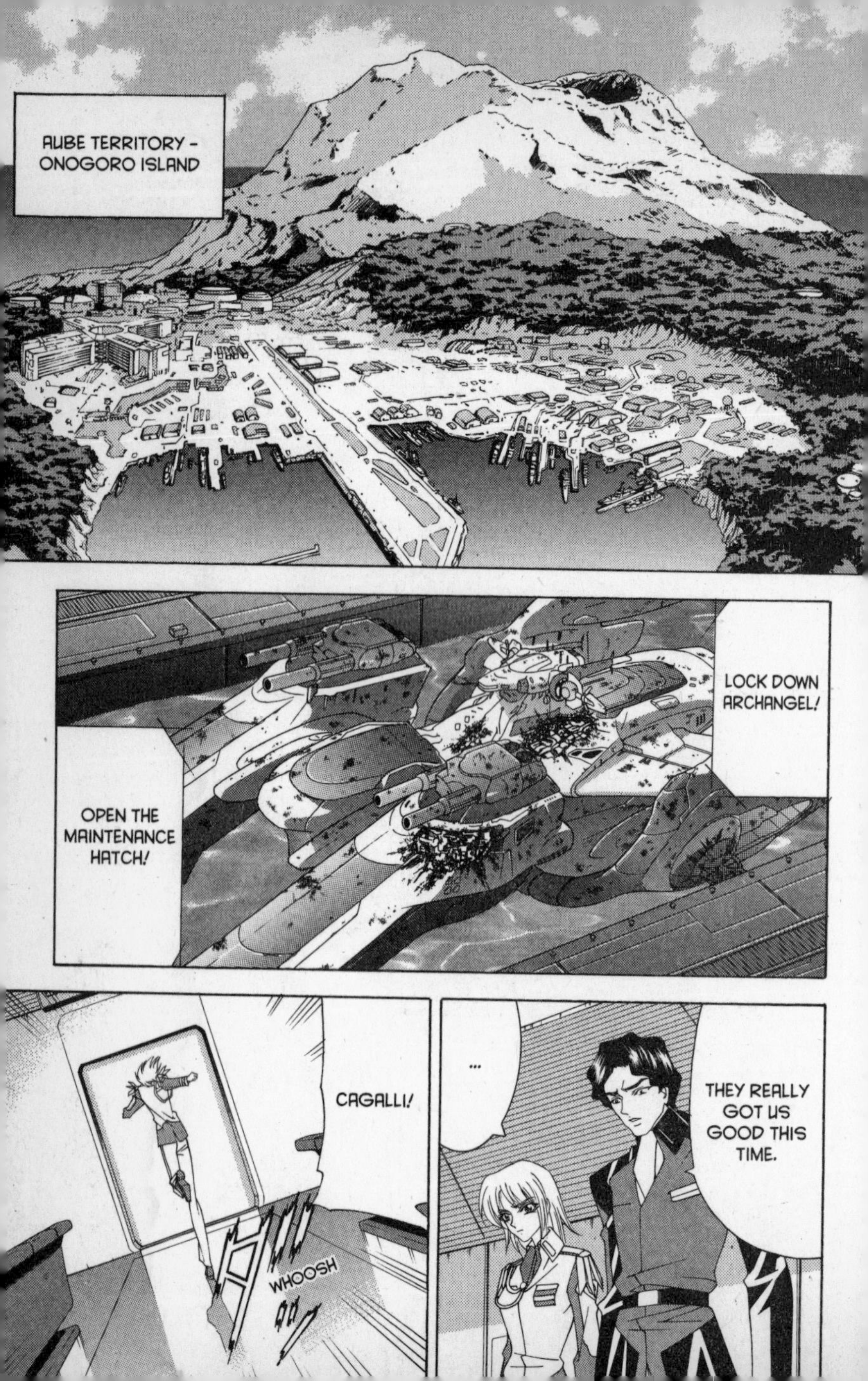
AUBE TERRITORY - ONOGORO ISLAND
LOCK DOWN ARCHANGEL!
OPEN THE MAINTENANCE HATCH!
THEY REALLY GOT US GOOD THIS TIME.
...
CAGALLI!
WHOOSH

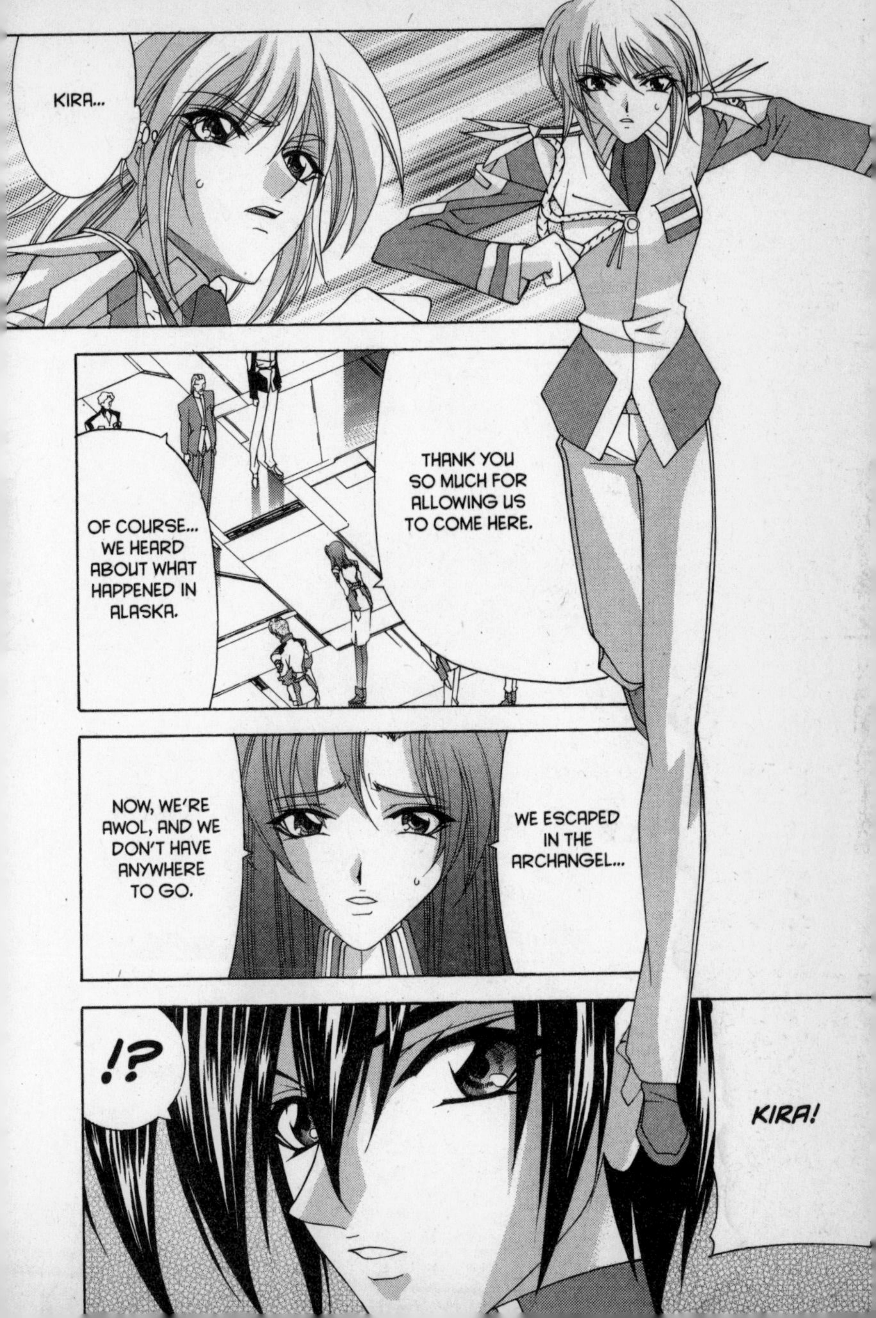
KIRA...
THANK YOU SO MUCH FOR ALLOWING US TO COME HERE.
OF COURSE... WE HEARD ABOUT WHAT HAPPENED IN ALASKA.
WE ESCAPED IN THE ARCHANGEL...
NOW, WE'RE AWOL, AND WE DON'T HAVE ANYWHERE TO GO.
KIRA!
!?

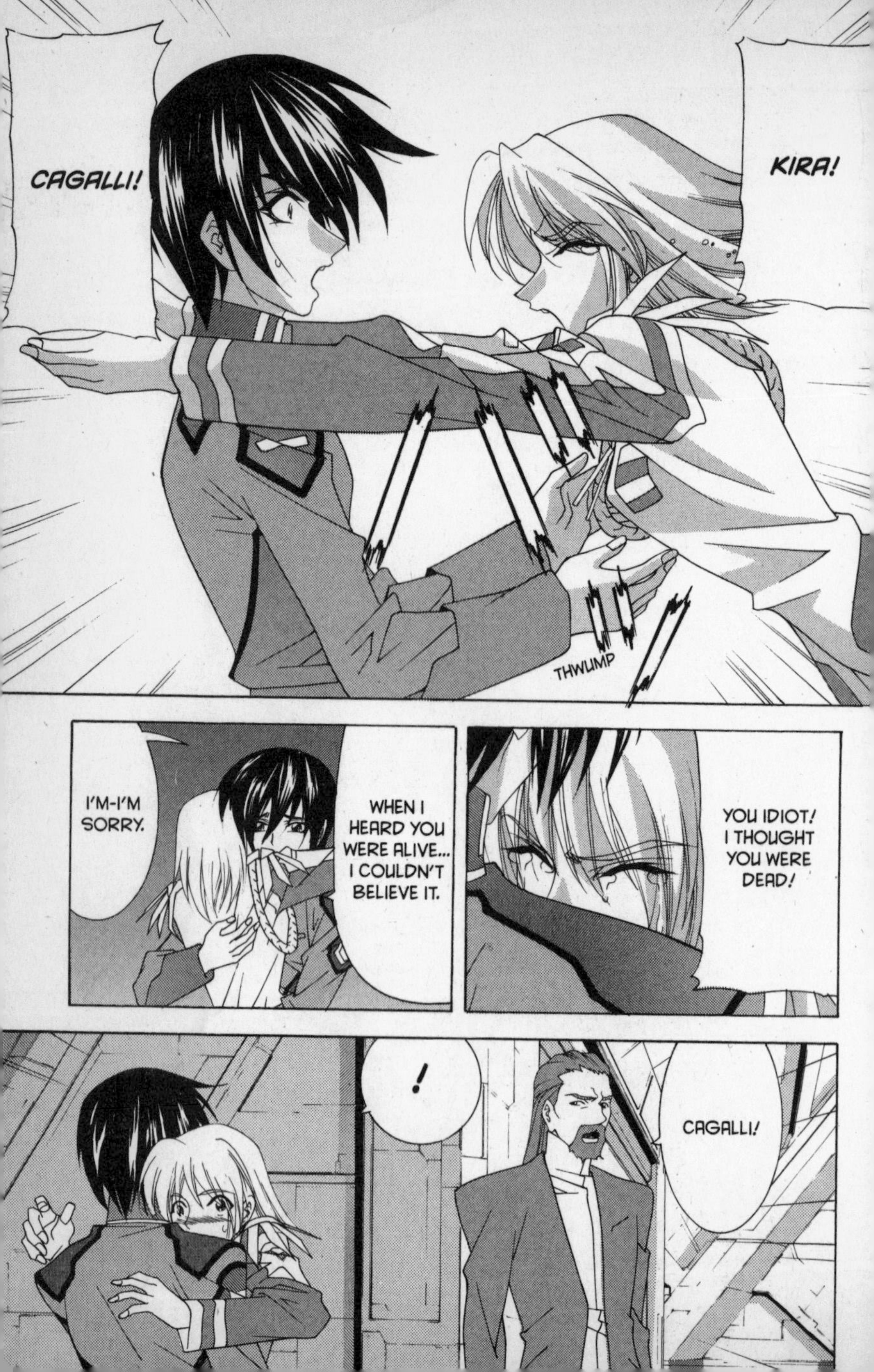
KIRA!
CAGALLI!
THWUMP
YOU IDIOT! I THOUGHT YOU WERE DEAD!
WHEN I HEARD YOU WERE ALIVE... I COULDN'T BELIEVE IT.
I'M-I'M SORRY.
CAGALLI!
!

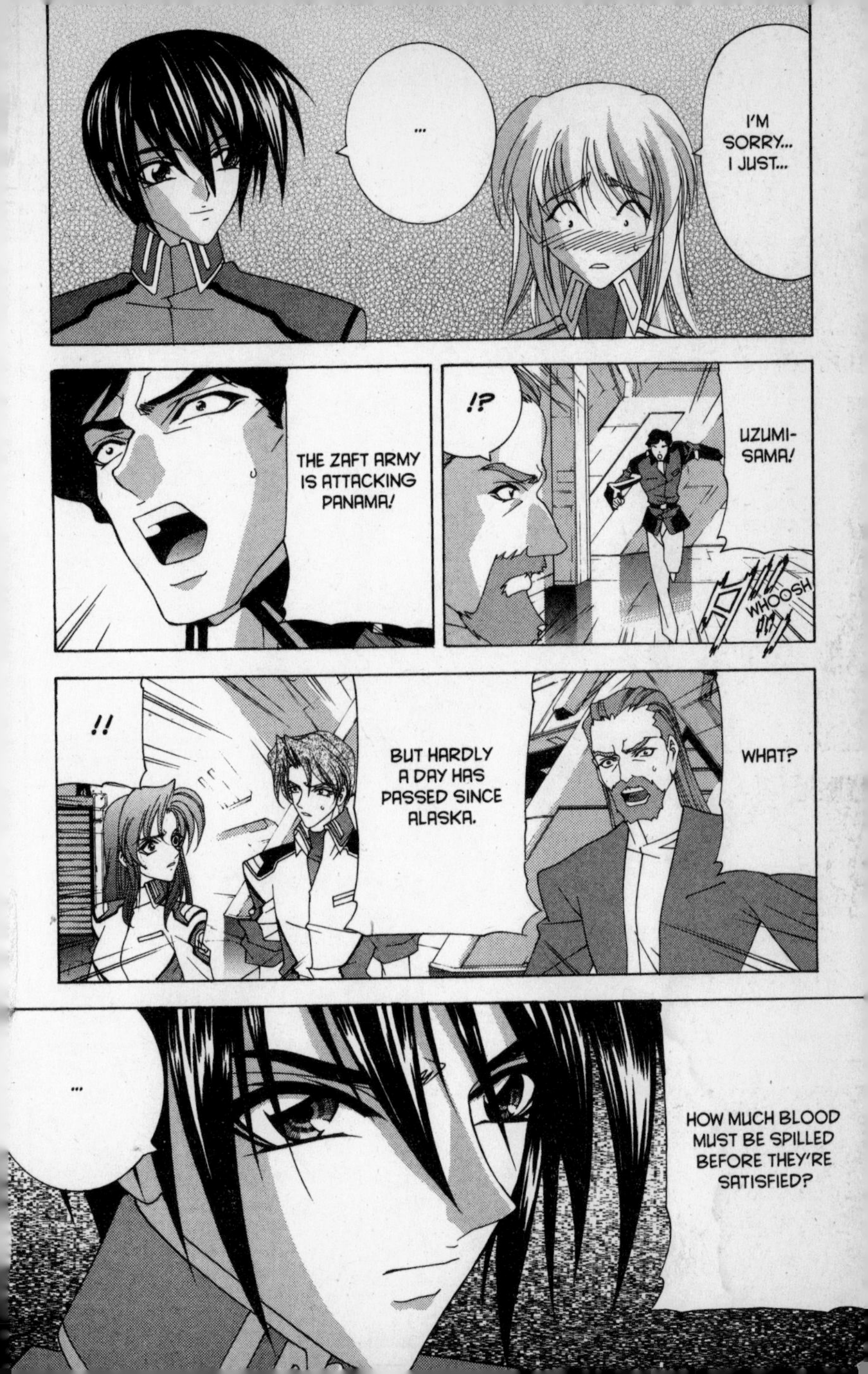

I'M SORRY... I JUST...
...
UZUMI-SAMA!
WHOOSH
!?
THE ZAFT ARMY IS ATTACKING PANAMA!
WHAT?
BUT HARDLY A DAY HAS PASSED SINCE ALASKA.
!!
HOW MUCH BLOOD MUST BE SPILLED BEFORE THEY'RE SATISFIED?
...

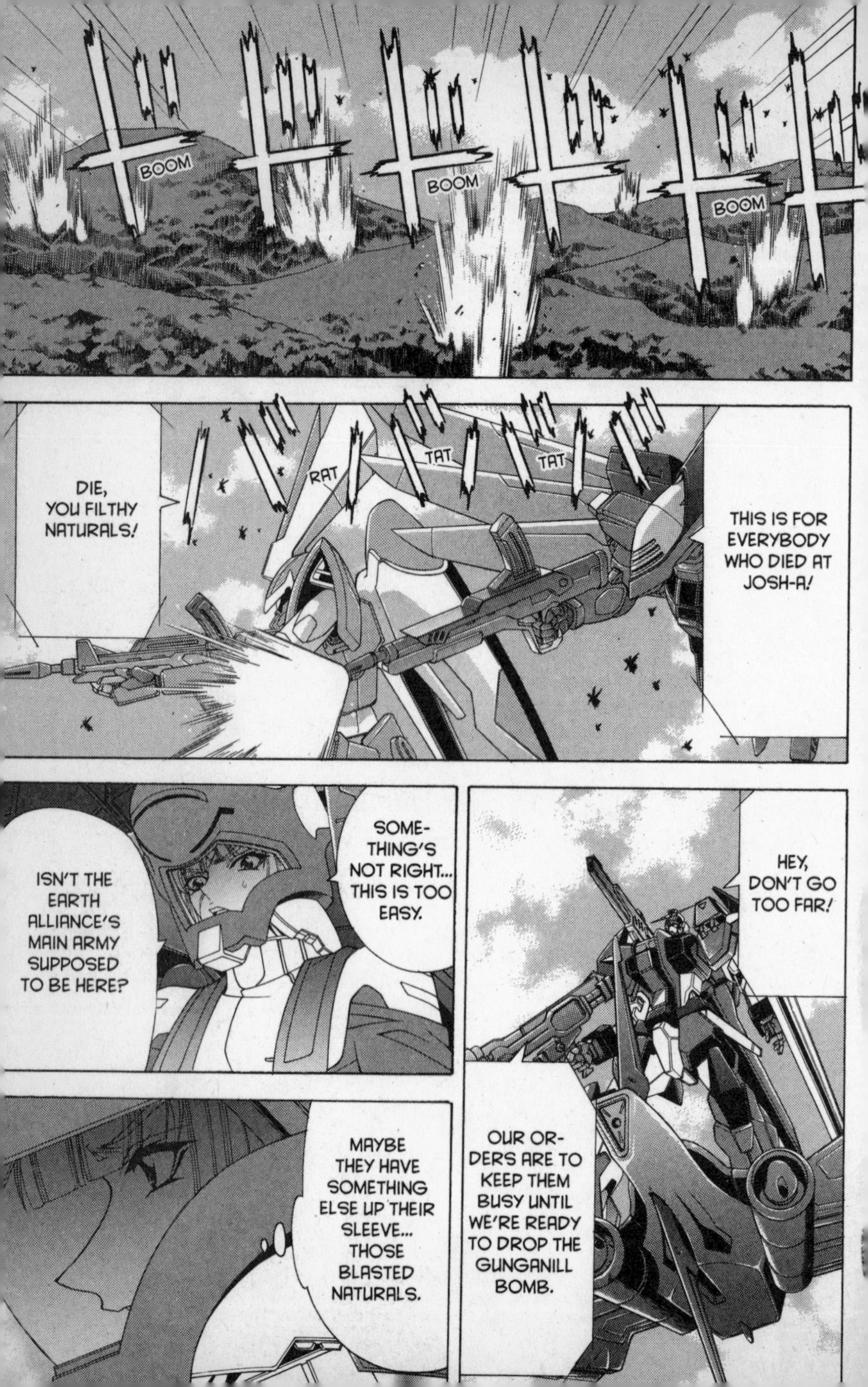
BOOM
BOOM
BOOM
THIS IS FOR EVERYBODY WHO DIED AT JOSH-A!
TAT
TAT
RAT
DIE, YOU FILTHY NATURALS!
HEY, DON'T GO TOO FAR!
OUR ORDERS ARE TO KEEP THEM BUSY UNTIL WE'RE READY TO DROP THE GUNGANILL BOMB.
SOMETHING'S NOT RIGHT... THIS IS TOO EASY.
ISN'T THE EARTH ALLIANCE'S MAIN ARMY SUPPOSED TO BE HERE?
MAYBE THEY HAVE SOMETHING ELSE UP THEIR SLEEVE... THOSE BLASTED NATURALS.

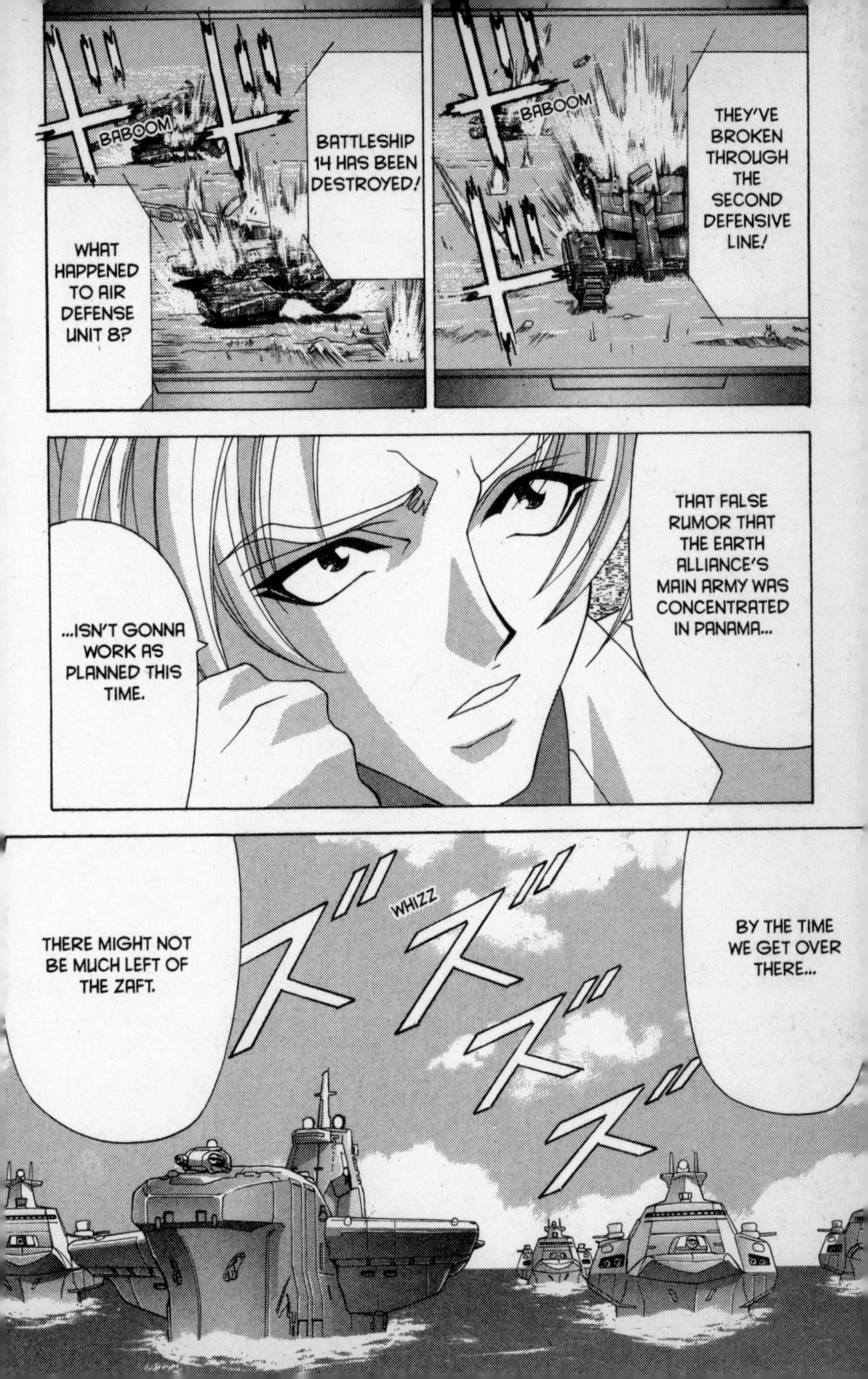
BABOOM
THEY'VE BROKEN THROUGH THE SECOND DEFENSIVE LINE!
BABOOM
BATTLESHIP 14 HAS BEEN DESTROYED!
WHAT HAPPENED TO AIR DEFENSE UNIT 8?
THAT FALSE RUMOR THAT THE EARTH ALLIANCE'S MAIN ARMY WAS CONCENTRATED IN PANAMA...
...ISN'T GONNA WORK AS PLANNED THIS TIME.
BY THE TIME WE GET OVER THERE...
WHIZZ
THERE MIGHT NOT BE MUCH LEFT OF THE ZAFT.

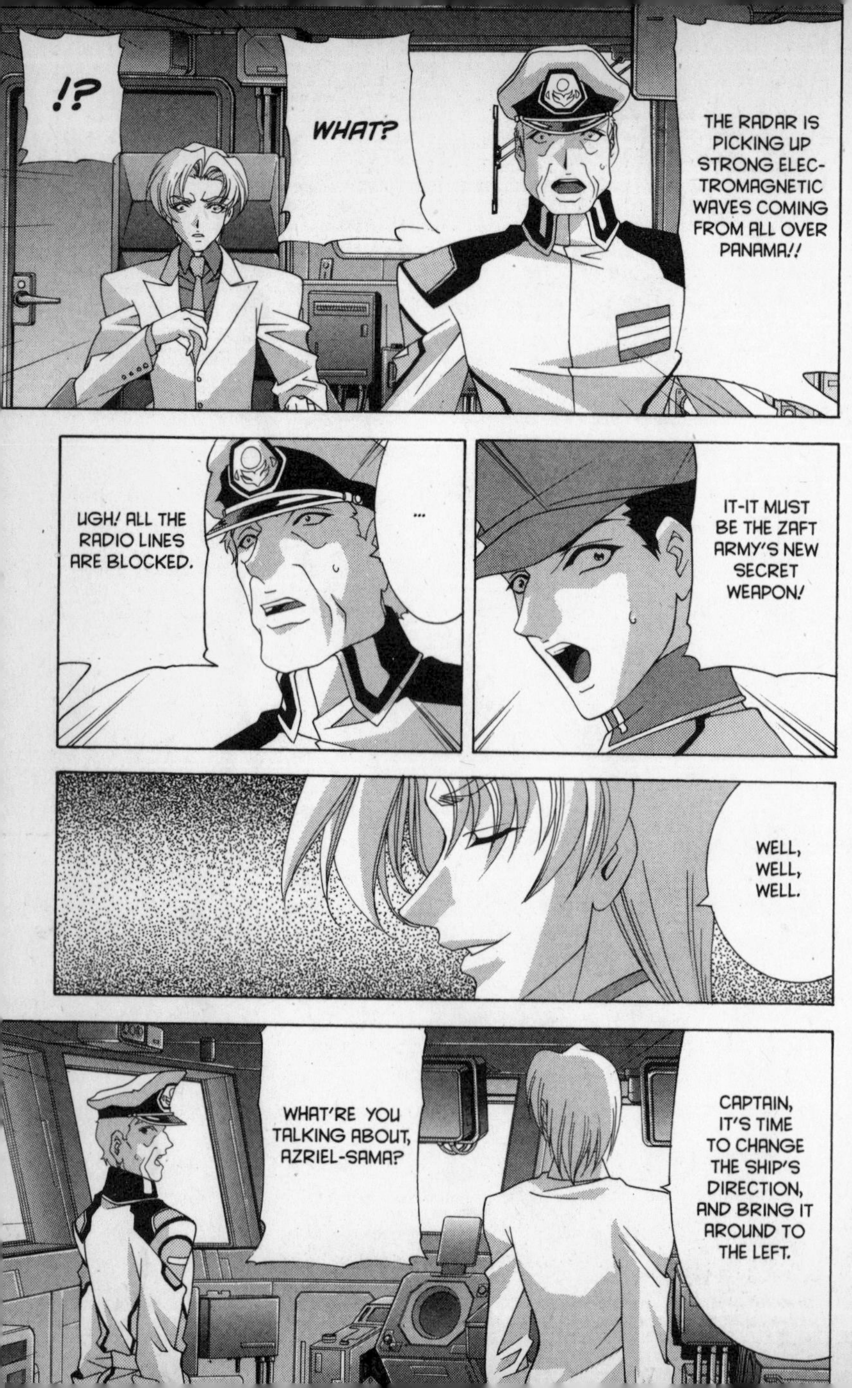
THE RADAR IS PICKING UP STRONG ELEC-TROMAGNETIC WAVES COMING FROM ALL OVER PANAMA!!
WHAT?
!?
IT-IT MUST BE THE ZAFT ARMY'S NEW SECRET WEAPON!
...
UGH! ALL THE RADIO LINES ARE BLOCKED.
WELL, WELL, WELL.
CAPTAIN, IT'S TIME TO CHANGE THE SHIP'S DIRECTION, AND BRING IT AROUND TO THE LEFT.
WHAT'RE YOU TALKING ABOUT, AZRIEL-SAMA?

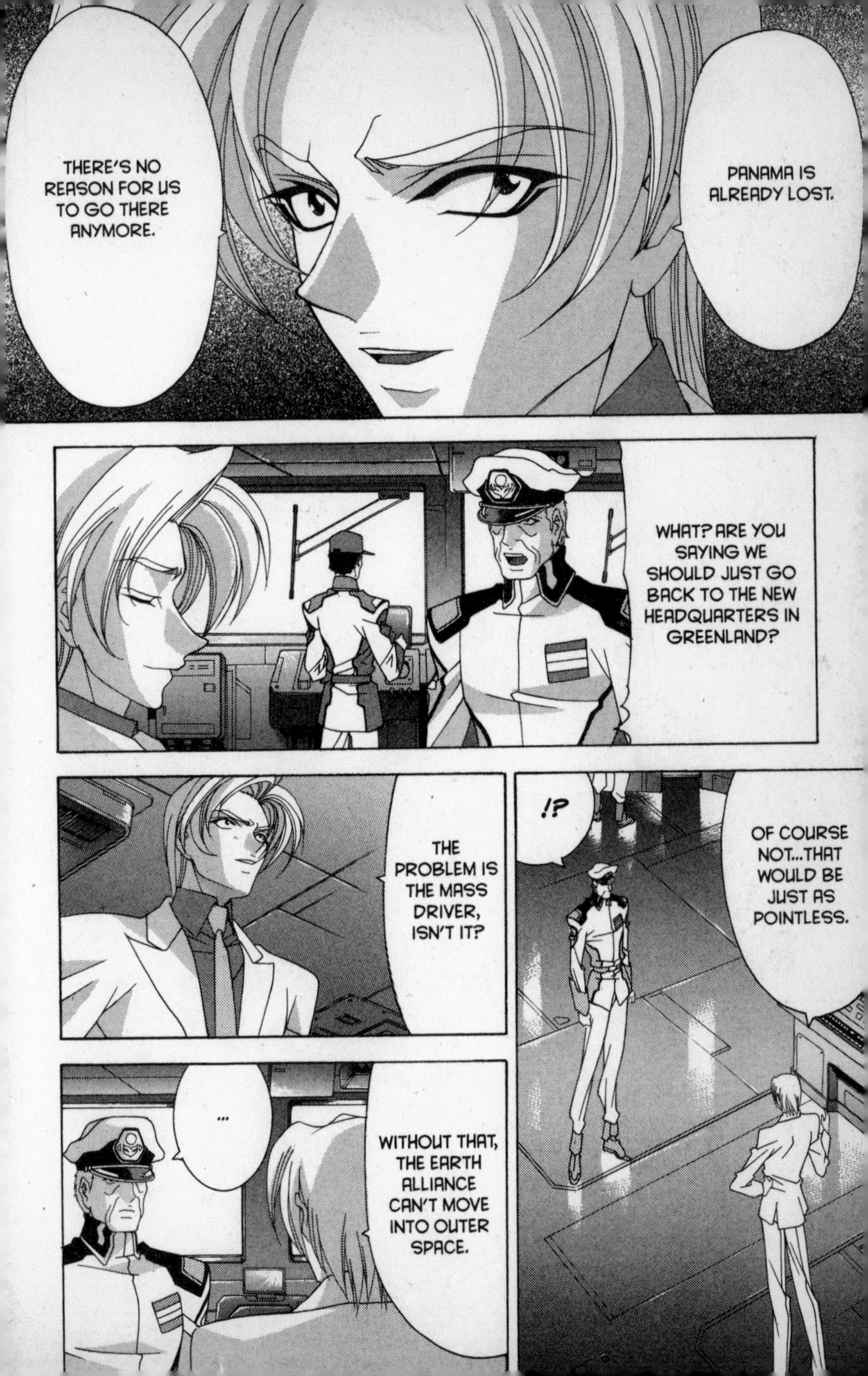
PANAMA IS ALREADY LOST.
THERE'S NO REASON FOR US TO GO THERE ANYMORE.
WHAT? ARE YOU SAYING WE SHOULD JUST GO BACK TO THE NEW HEADQUARTERS IN GREENLAND?
OF COURSE NOT...THAT WOULD BE JUST AS POINTLESS.
!?
THE PROBLEM IS THE MASS DRIVER, ISN'T IT?
WITHOUT THAT, THE EARTH ALLIANCE CAN'T MOVE INTO OUTER SPACE.
...

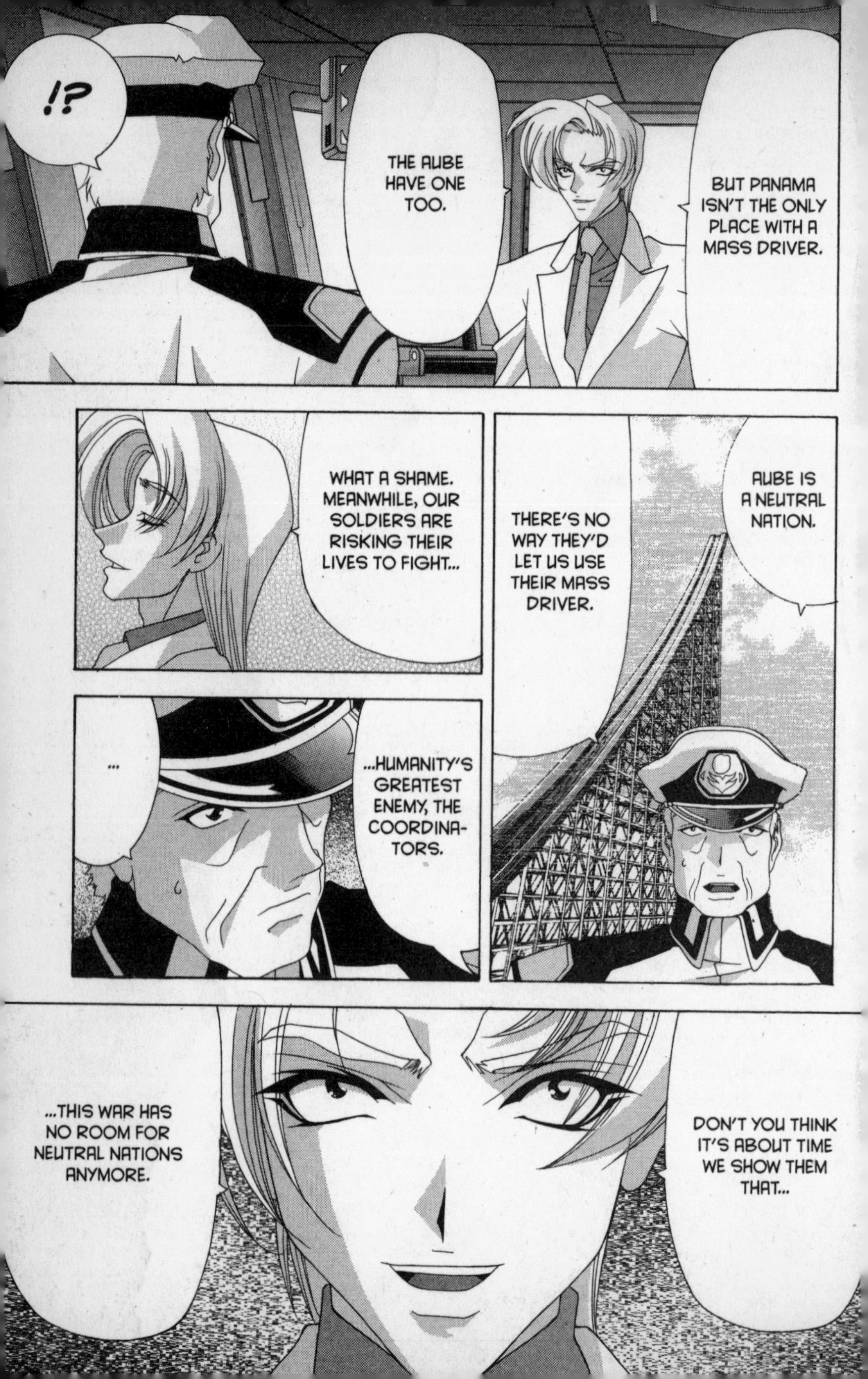
BUT PANAMA ISN'T THE ONLY PLACE WITH A MASS DRIVER.
THE AUBE HAVE ONE TOO.
!?
AUBE IS A NEUTRAL NATION.
THERE'S NO WAY THEY'D LET US USE THEIR MASS DRIVER.
WHAT A SHAME. MEANWHILE, OUR SOLDIERS ARE RISKING THEIR LIVES TO FIGHT...
...HUMANITY'S GREATEST ENEMY, THE COORDINA-TORS.
...
DON'T YOU THINK IT'S ABOUT TIME WE SHOW THEM THAT...
...THIS WAR HAS NO ROOM FOR NEUTRAL NATIONS ANYMORE.

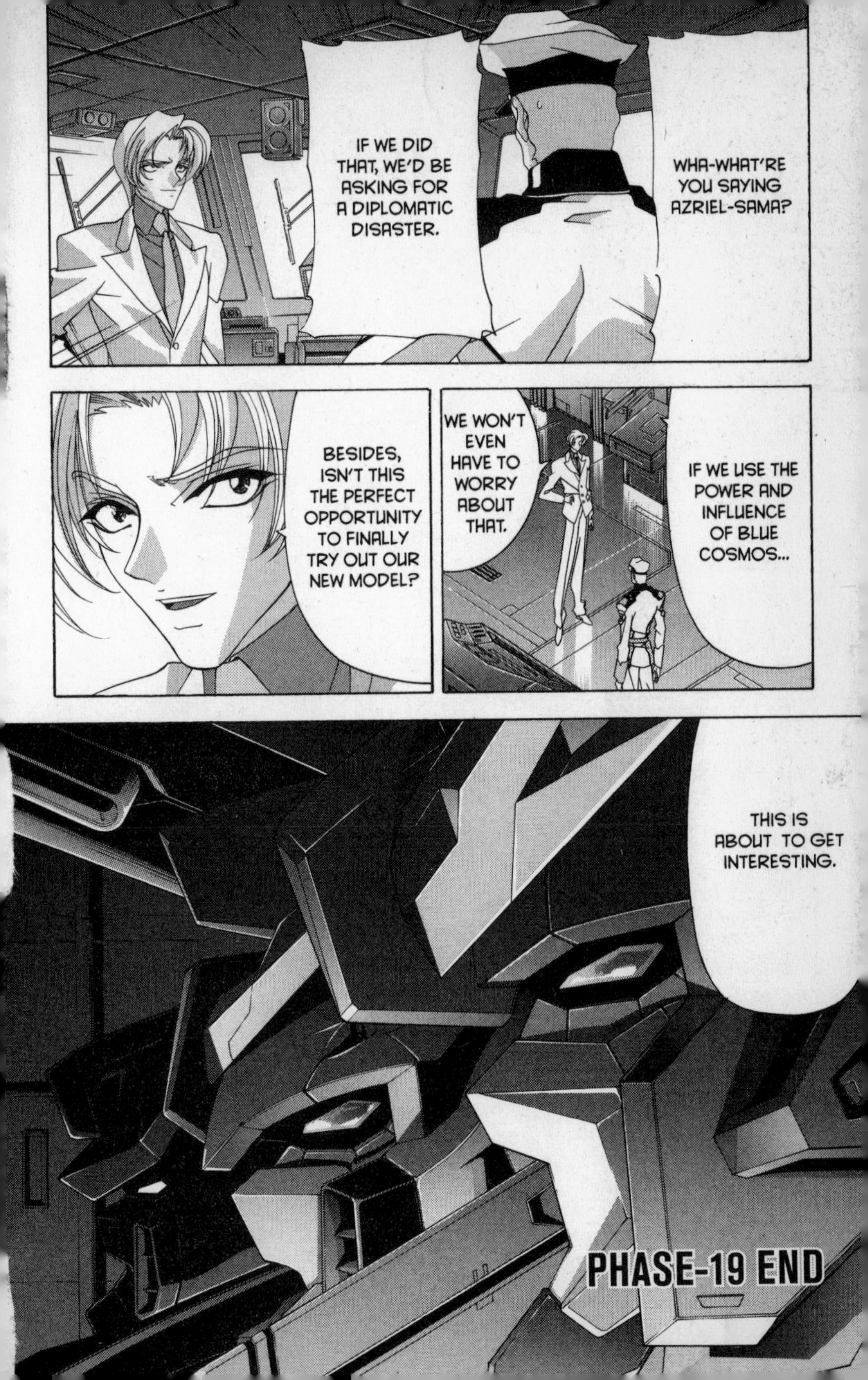
WHA-WHAT'RE YOU SAYING AZRIEL-SAMA?
IF WE DID THAT, WE'D BE ASKING FOR A DIPLOMATIC DISASTER.
IF WE USE THE POWER AND INFLUENCE OF BLUE COSMOS...
WE WON'T EVEN HAVE TO WORRY ABOUT THAT.
BESIDES, ISN'T THIS THE PERFECT OPPORTUNITY TO FINALLY TRY OUT OUR NEW MODEL?
THIS IS ABOUT TO GET INTERESTING.
PHASE-19 END

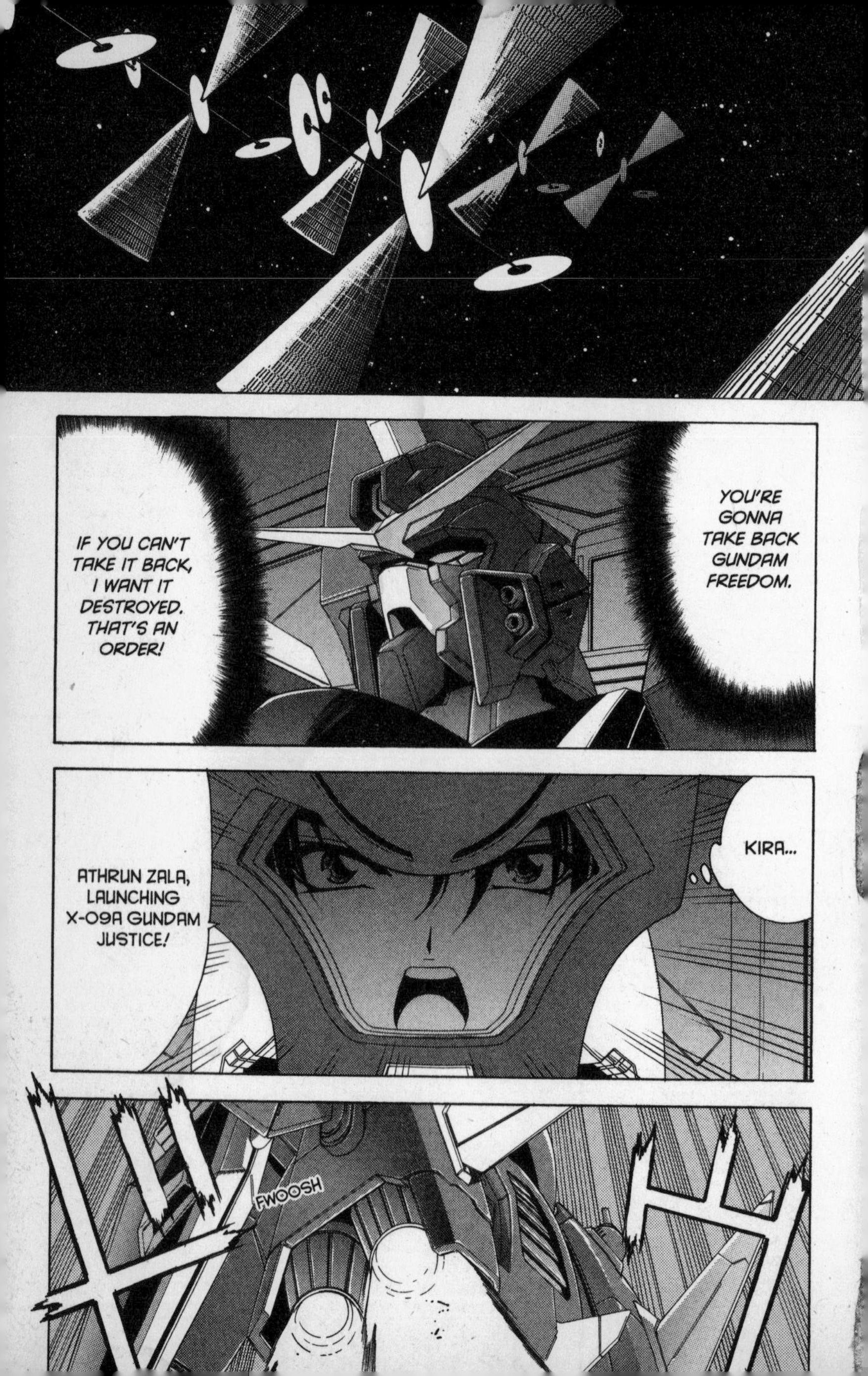
YOU'RE GONNA TAKE BACK GUNDAM FREEDOM.
IF YOU CAN'T TAKE IT BACK, I WANT IT DESTROYED. THAT'S AN ORDER!
KIRA...
ATHRUN ZALA, LAUNCHING X-09A GUNDAM JUSTICE!
FWOOSH

# PHASE-20 A DECISIVE BATTLE

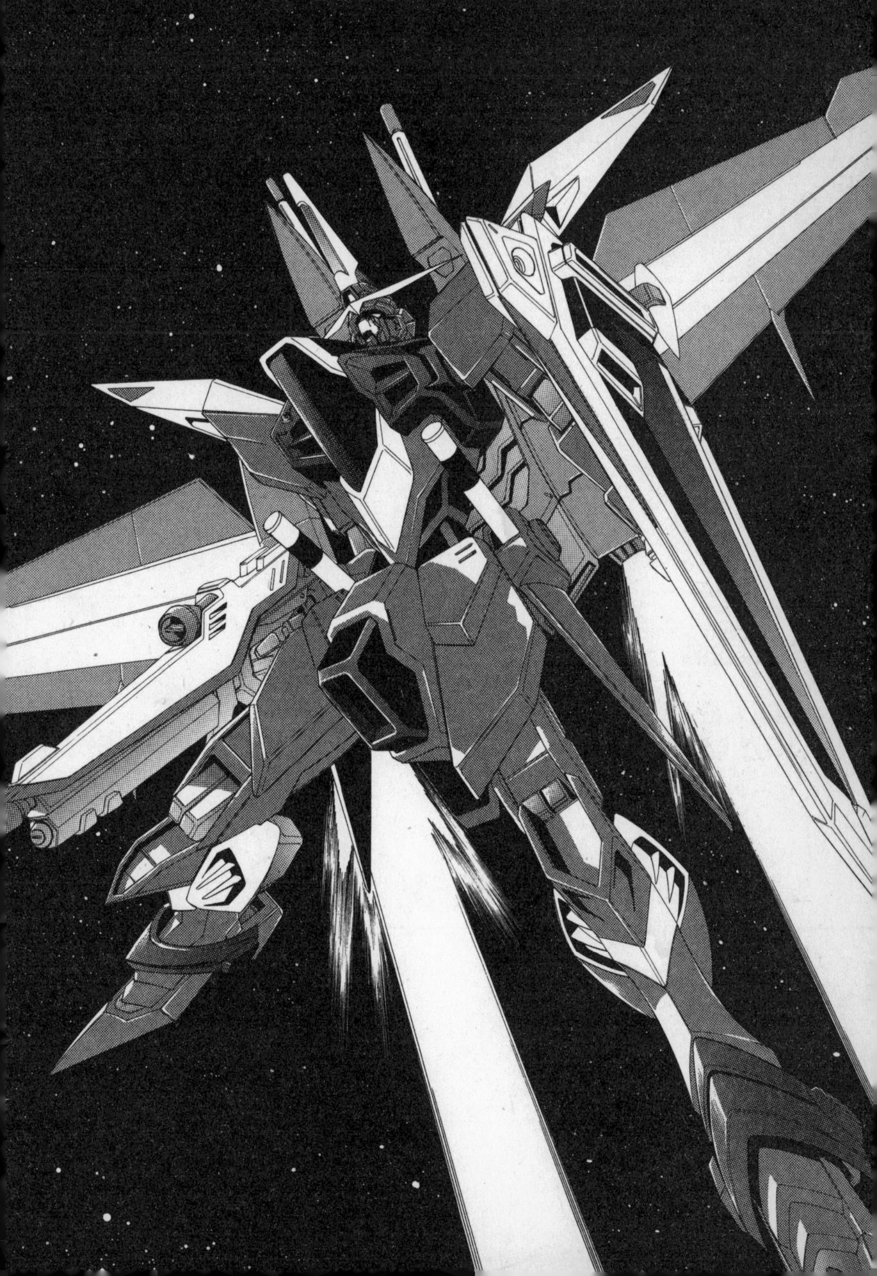

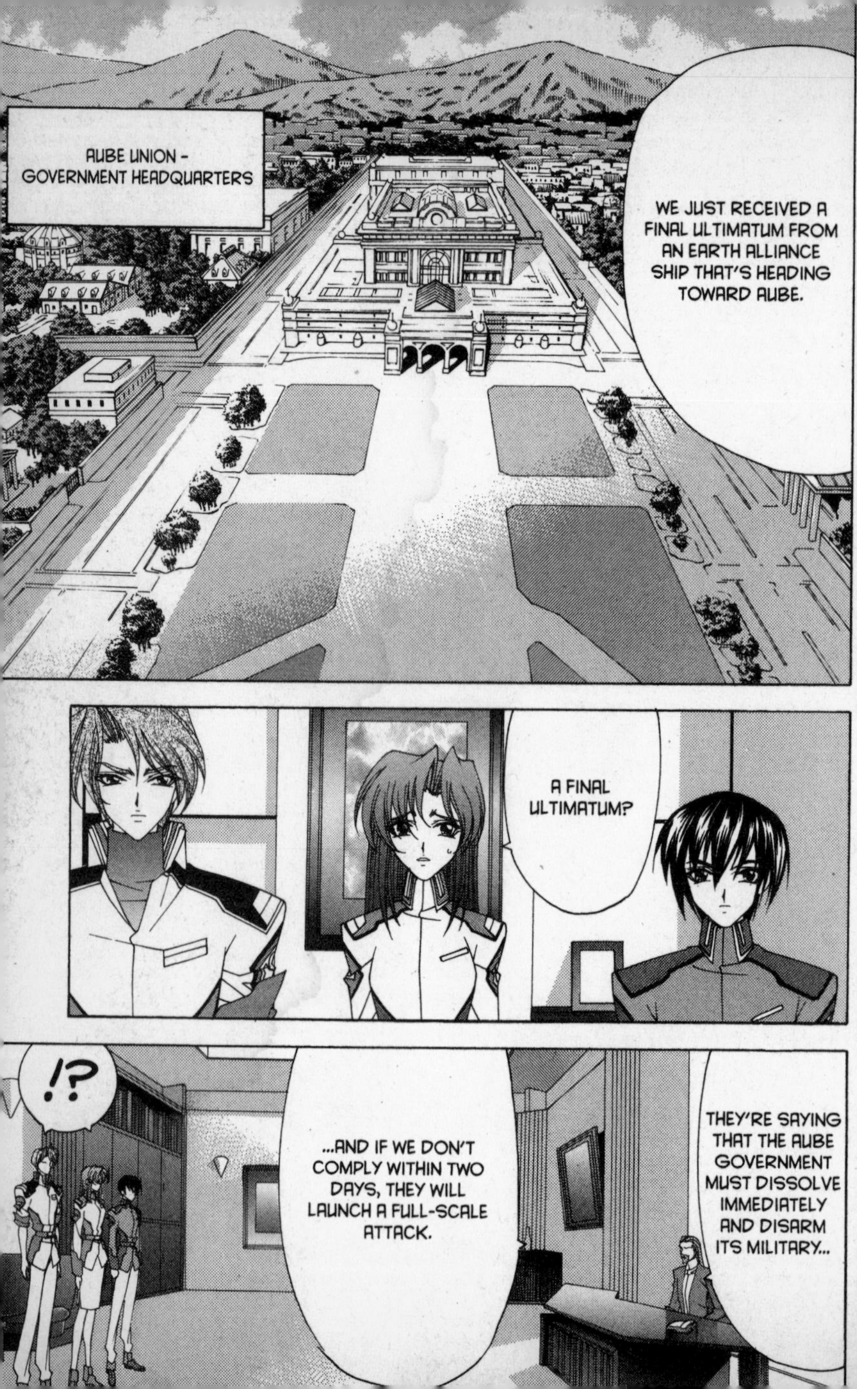
WE JUST RECEIVED A FINAL ULTIMATUM FROM AN EARTH ALLIANCE SHIP THAT'S HEADING TOWARD AUBE.
AUBE UNION - GOVERNMENT HEADQUARTERS
A FINAL ULTIMATUM?
THEY'RE SAYING THAT THE AUBE GOVERNMENT MUST DISSOLVE IMMEDIATELY AND DISARM ITS MILITARY...
...AND IF WE DON'T COMPLY WITHIN TWO DAYS, THEY WILL LAUNCH A FULL-SCALE ATTACK.
!?

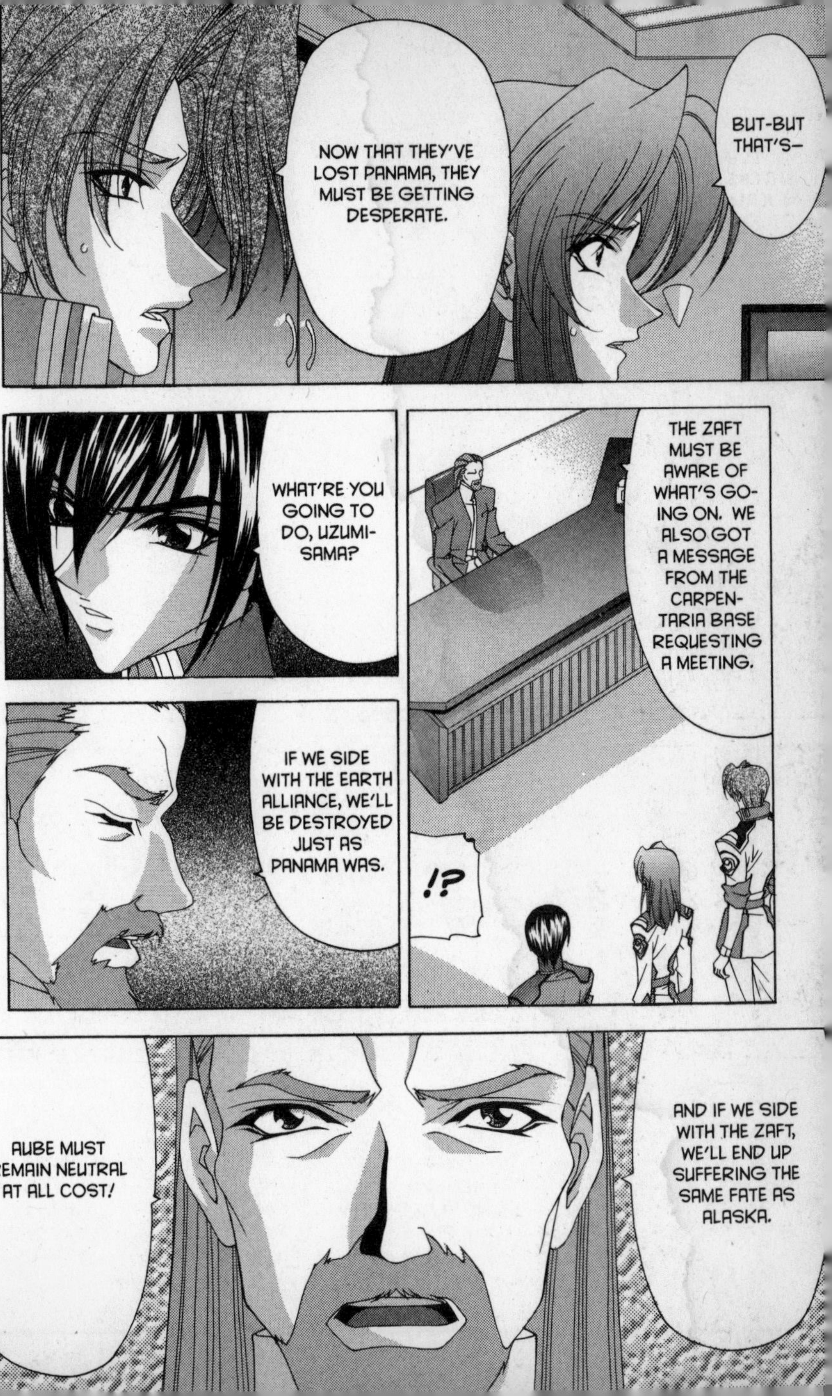
BUT-BUT THAT'S—
NOW THAT THEY'VE LOST PANAMA, THEY MUST BE GETTING DESPERATE.
THE ZAFT MUST BE AWARE OF WHAT'S GOING ON. WE ALSO GOT A MESSAGE FROM THE CARPENTARIA BASE REQUESTING A MEETING.
!?
WHAT'RE YOU GOING TO DO, UZUMI-SAMA?
IF WE SIDE WITH THE EARTH ALLIANCE, WE'LL BE DESTROYED JUST AS PANAMA WAS.
AND IF WE SIDE WITH THE ZAFT, WE'LL END UP SUFFERING THE SAME FATE AS ALASKA.
AUBE MUST REMAIN NEUTRAL AT ALL COST!

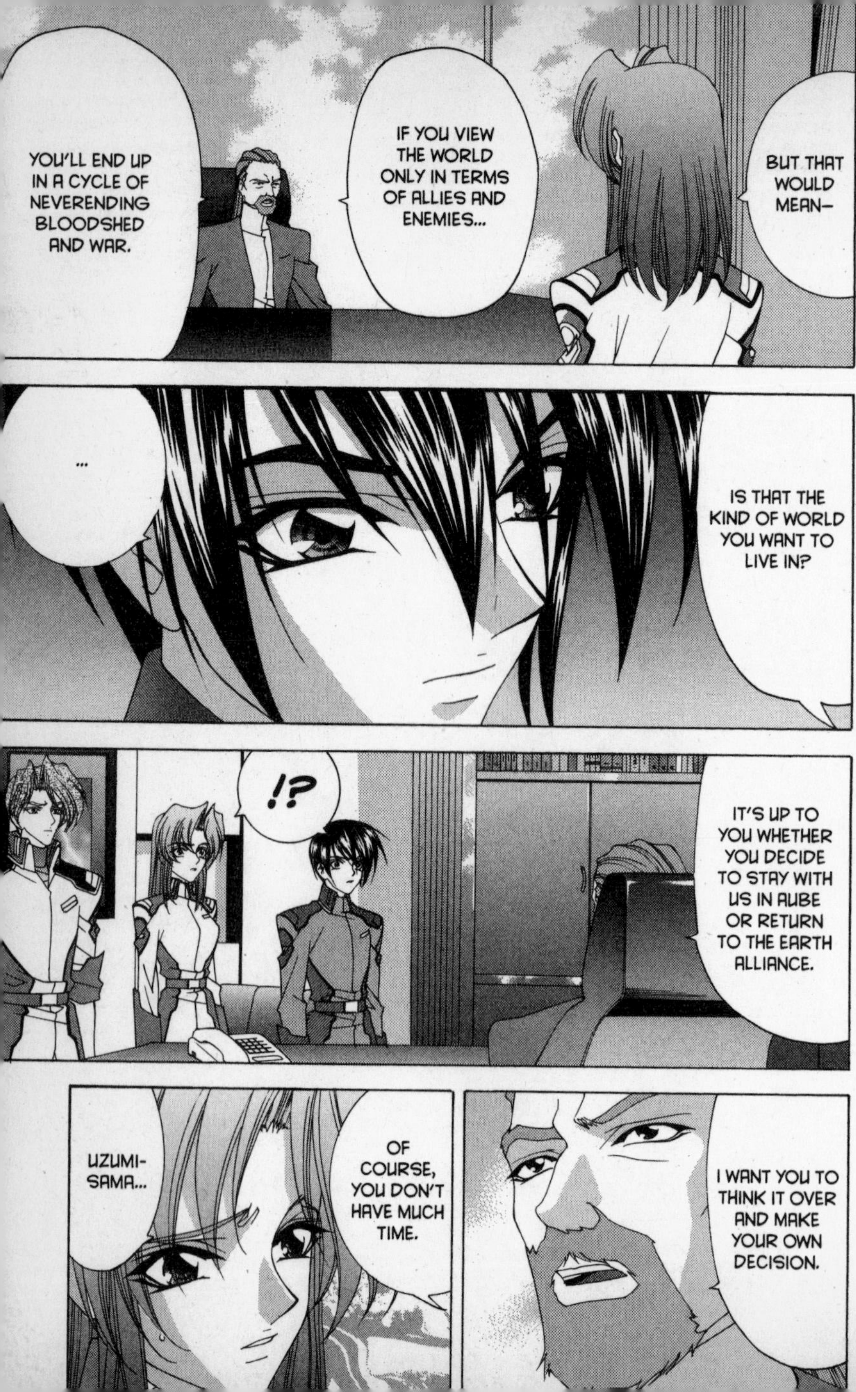
BUT THAT WOULD MEAN—
IF YOU VIEW THE WORLD ONLY IN TERMS OF ALLIES AND ENEMIES...
YOU'LL END UP IN A CYCLE OF NEVERENDING BLOODSHED AND WAR.
IS THAT THE KIND OF WORLD YOU WANT TO LIVE IN?
...
IT'S UP TO YOU WHETHER YOU DECIDE TO STAY WITH US IN AUBE OR RETURN TO THE EARTH ALLIANCE.
!?
I WANT YOU TO THINK IT OVER AND MAKE YOUR OWN DECISION.
OF COURSE, YOU DON'T HAVE MUCH TIME.
UZUMI-SAMA...

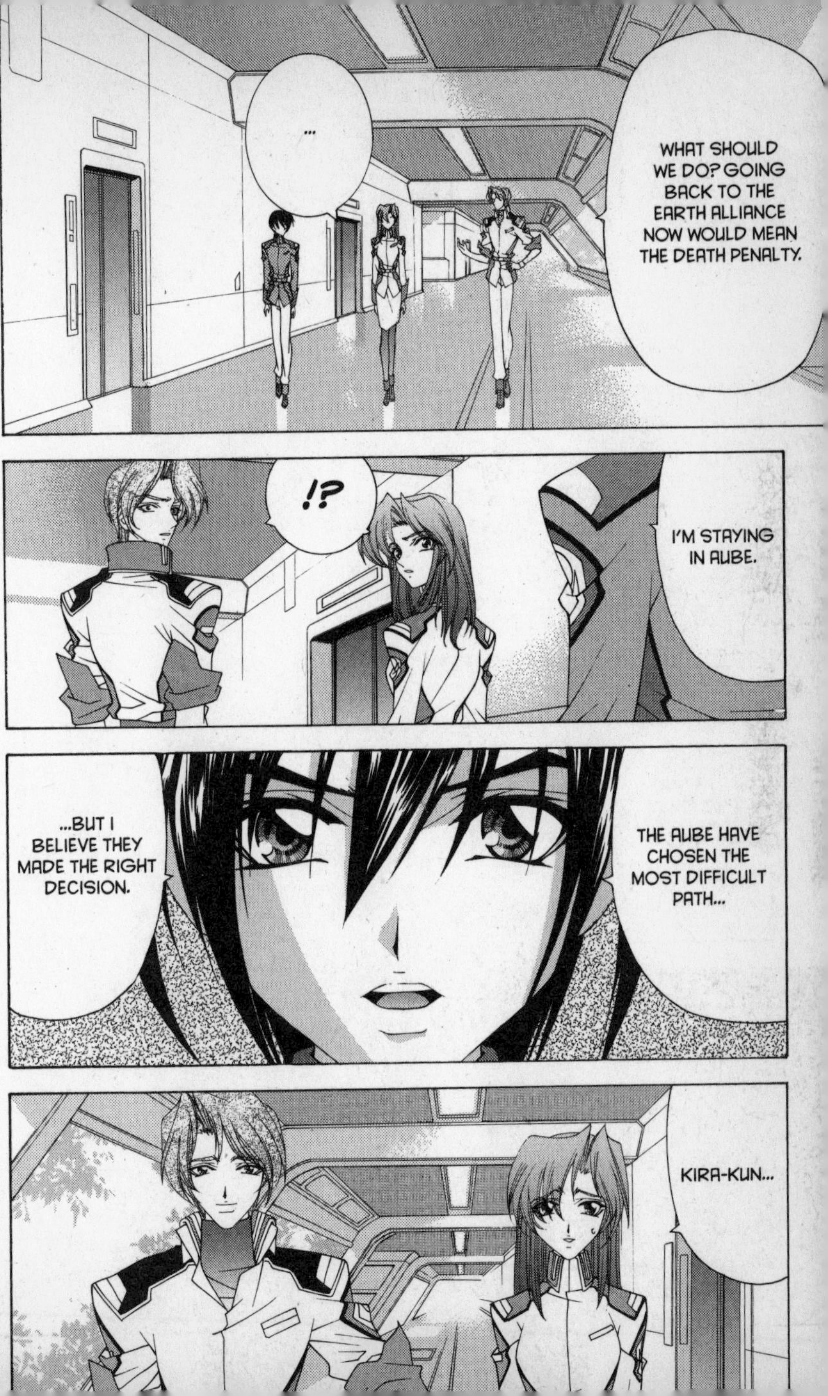
WHAT SHOULD WE DO? GOING BACK TO THE EARTH ALLIANCE NOW WOULD MEAN THE DEATH PENALTY.
...
I'M STAYING IN AUBE.
!?
THE AUBE HAVE CHOSEN THE MOST DIFFICULT PATH...
...BUT I BELIEVE THEY MADE THE RIGHT DECISION.
KIRA-KUN...

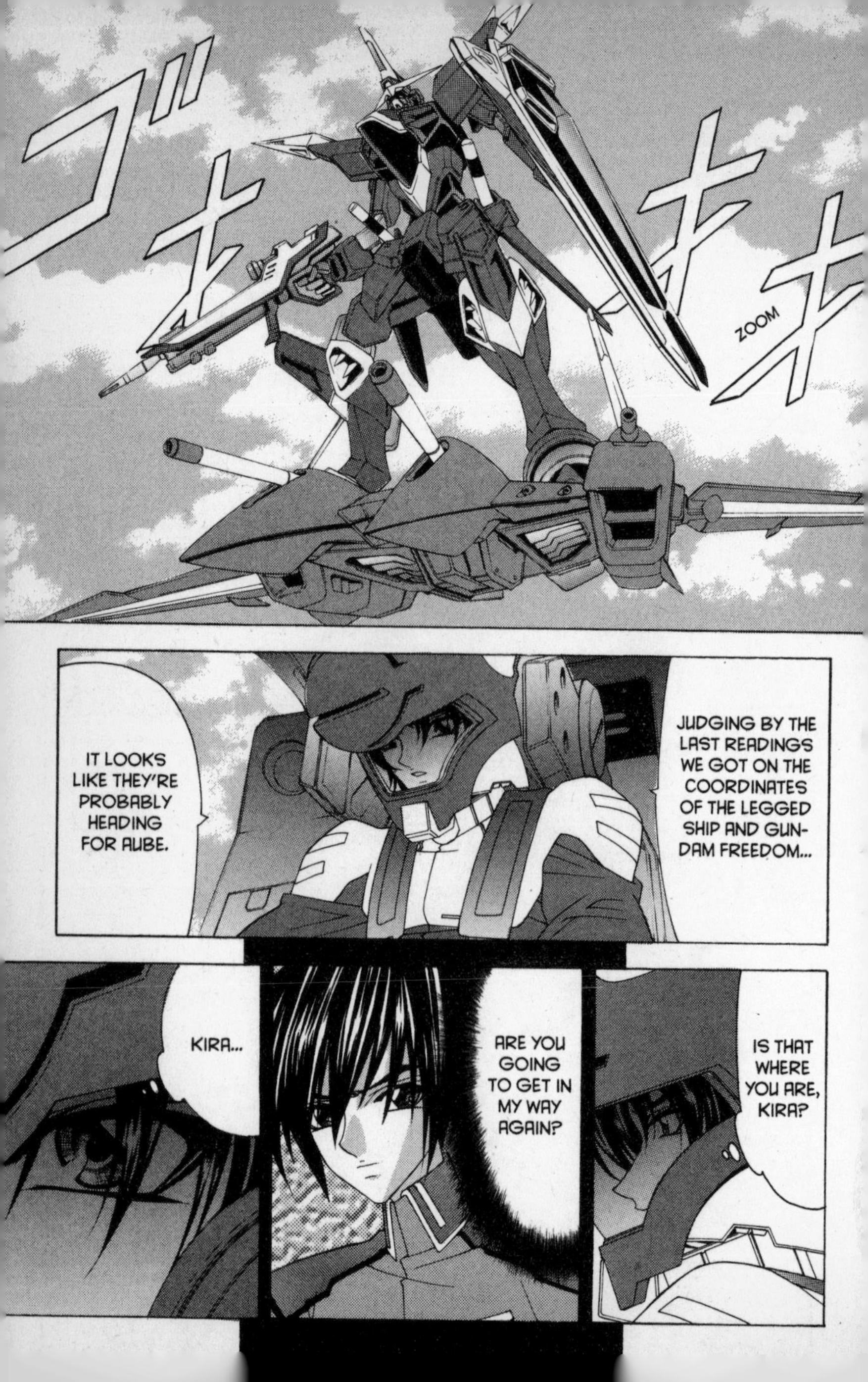
ゴォォォ
ZOOM
JUDGING BY THE LAST READINGS WE GOT ON THE COORDINATES OF THE LEGGED SHIP AND GUN-DAM FREEDOM...
IT LOOKS LIKE THEY'RE PROBABLY HEADING FOR AUBE.
IS THAT WHERE YOU ARE, KIRA?
ARE YOU GOING TO GET IN MY WAY AGAIN?
KIRA...

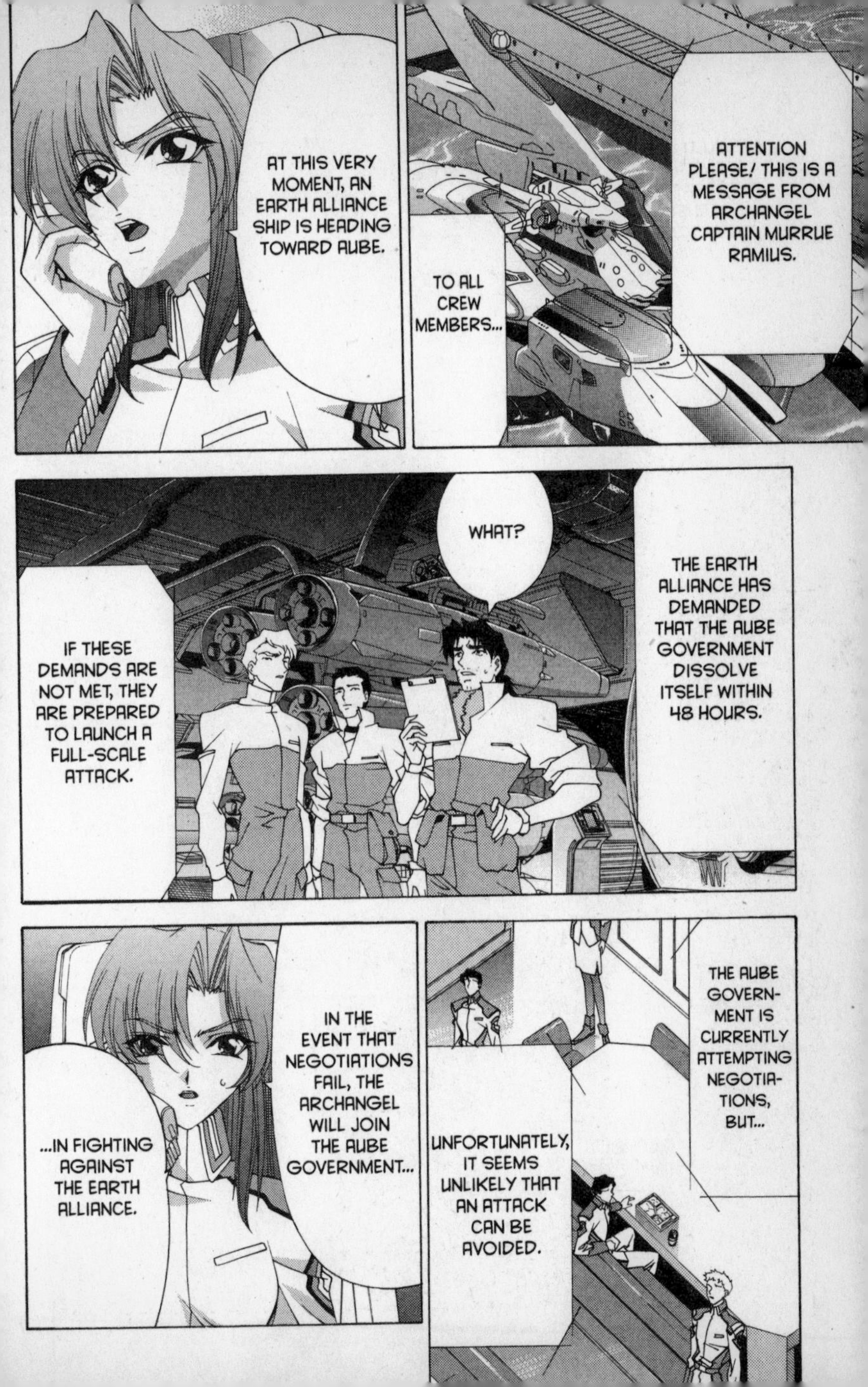
ATTENTION PLEASE! THIS IS A MESSAGE FROM ARCHANGEL CAPTAIN MURRUE RAMIUS.
TO ALL CREW MEMBERS...
AT THIS VERY MOMENT, AN EARTH ALLIANCE SHIP IS HEADING TOWARD AUBE.
THE EARTH ALLIANCE HAS DEMANDED THAT THE AUBE GOVERNMENT DISSOLVE ITSELF WITHIN 48 HOURS.
WHAT?
IF THESE DEMANDS ARE NOT MET, THEY ARE PREPARED TO LAUNCH A FULL-SCALE ATTACK.
THE AUBE GOVERN-MENT IS CURRENTLY ATTEMPTING NEGOTIA-TIONS, BUT...
UNFORTUNATELY, IT SEEMS UNLIKELY THAT AN ATTACK CAN BE AVOIDED.
IN THE EVENT THAT NEGOTIATIONS FAIL, THE ARCHANGEL WILL JOIN THE AUBE GOVERNMENT...
...IN FIGHTING AGAINST THE EARTH ALLIANCE.

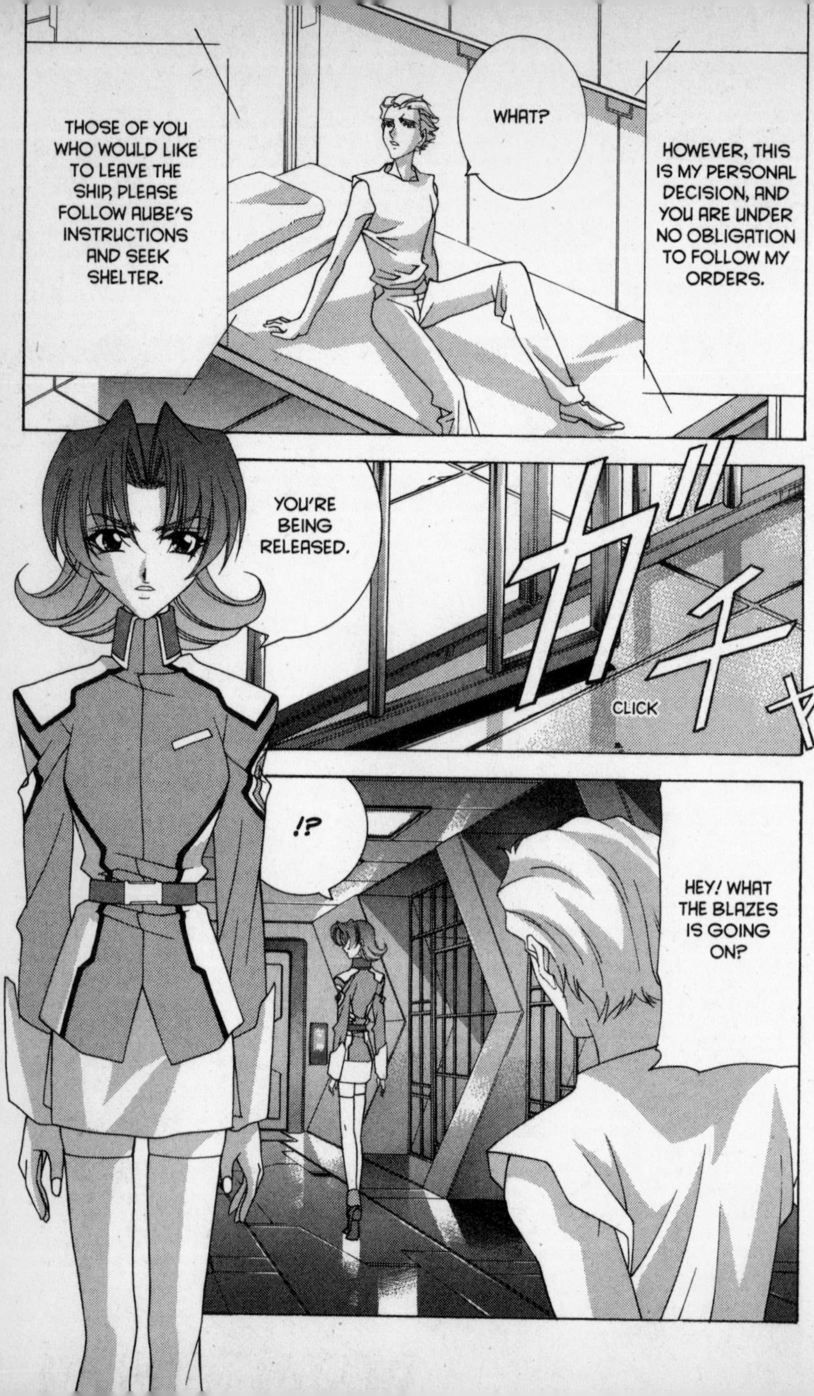
HOWEVER, THIS IS MY PERSONAL DECISION, AND YOU ARE UNDER NO OBLIGATION TO FOLLOW MY ORDERS.
WHAT?
THOSE OF YOU WHO WOULD LIKE TO LEAVE THE SHIP, PLEASE FOLLOW AUBE'S INSTRUCTIONS AND SEEK SHELTER.
ガチャ
CLICK
YOU'RE BEING RELEASED.
!?
HEY! WHAT THE BLAZES IS GOING ON?

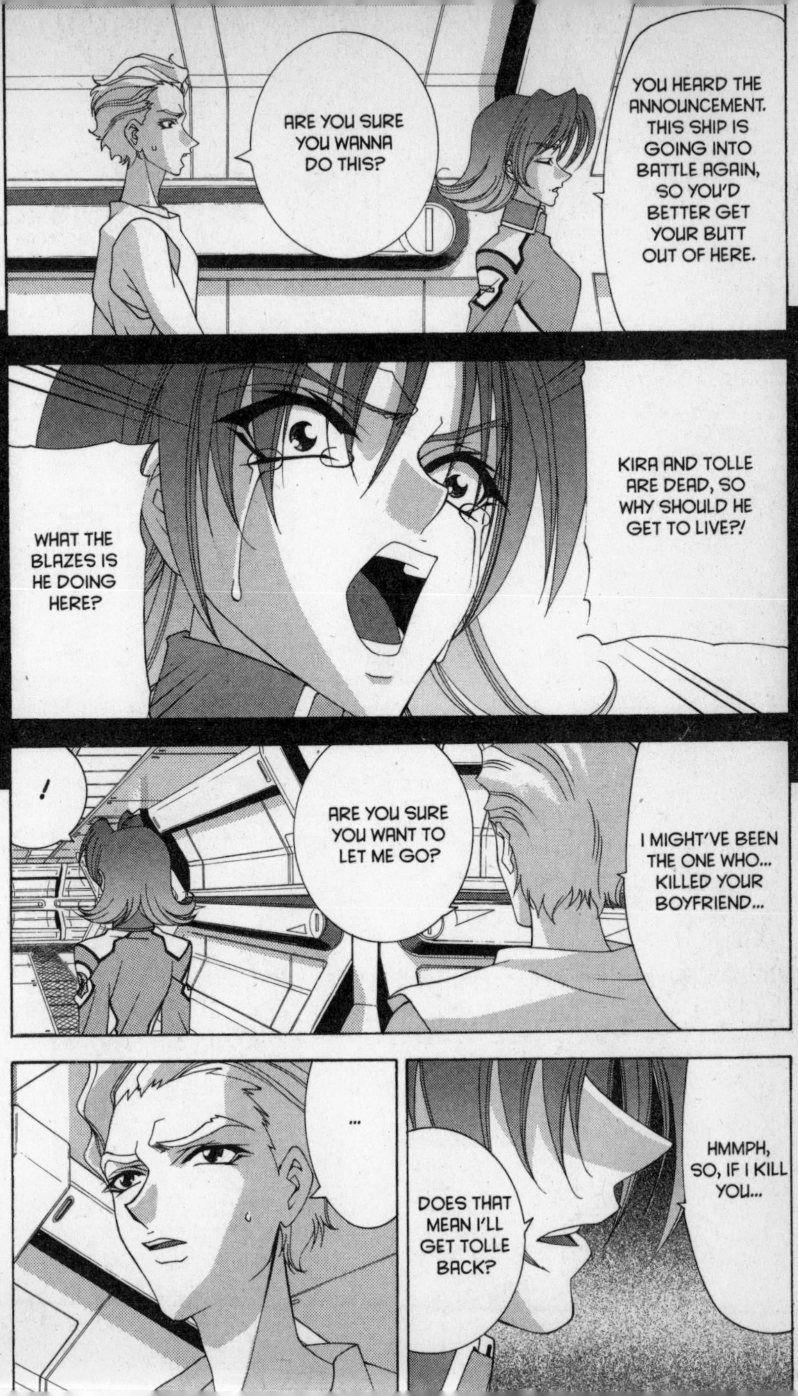
YOU HEARD THE ANNOUNCEMENT. THIS SHIP IS GOING INTO BATTLE AGAIN, SO YOU'D BETTER GET YOUR BUTT OUT OF HERE.
ARE YOU SURE YOU WANNA DO THIS?
KIRA AND TOLLE ARE DEAD, SO WHY SHOULD HE GET TO LIVE?!
WHAT THE BLAZES IS HE DOING HERE?
I MIGHT'VE BEEN THE ONE WHO... KILLED YOUR BOYFRIEND...
ARE YOU SURE YOU WANT TO LET ME GO?
!
HMMPH, SO, IF I KILL YOU...
DOES THAT MEAN I'LL GET TOLLE BACK?
...

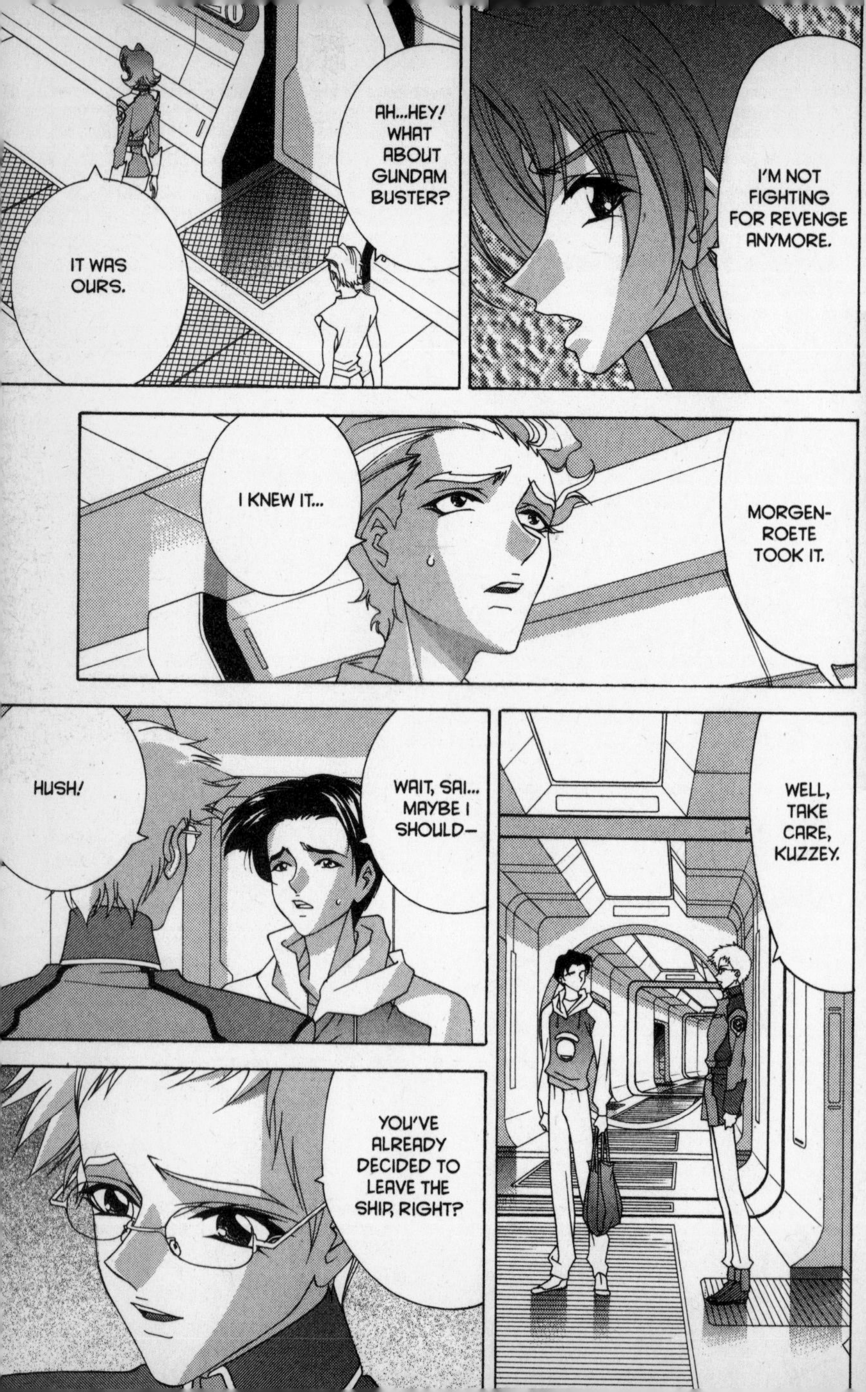
I'M NOT FIGHTING FOR REVENGE ANYMORE.
AH...HEY! WHAT ABOUT GUNDAM BUSTER?
IT WAS OURS.
MORGEN-ROETE TOOK IT.
I KNEW IT...
WELL, TAKE CARE, KUZZEY.
WAIT, SAI... MAYBE I SHOULD—
HUSH!
YOU'VE ALREADY DECIDED TO LEAVE THE SHIP, RIGHT?

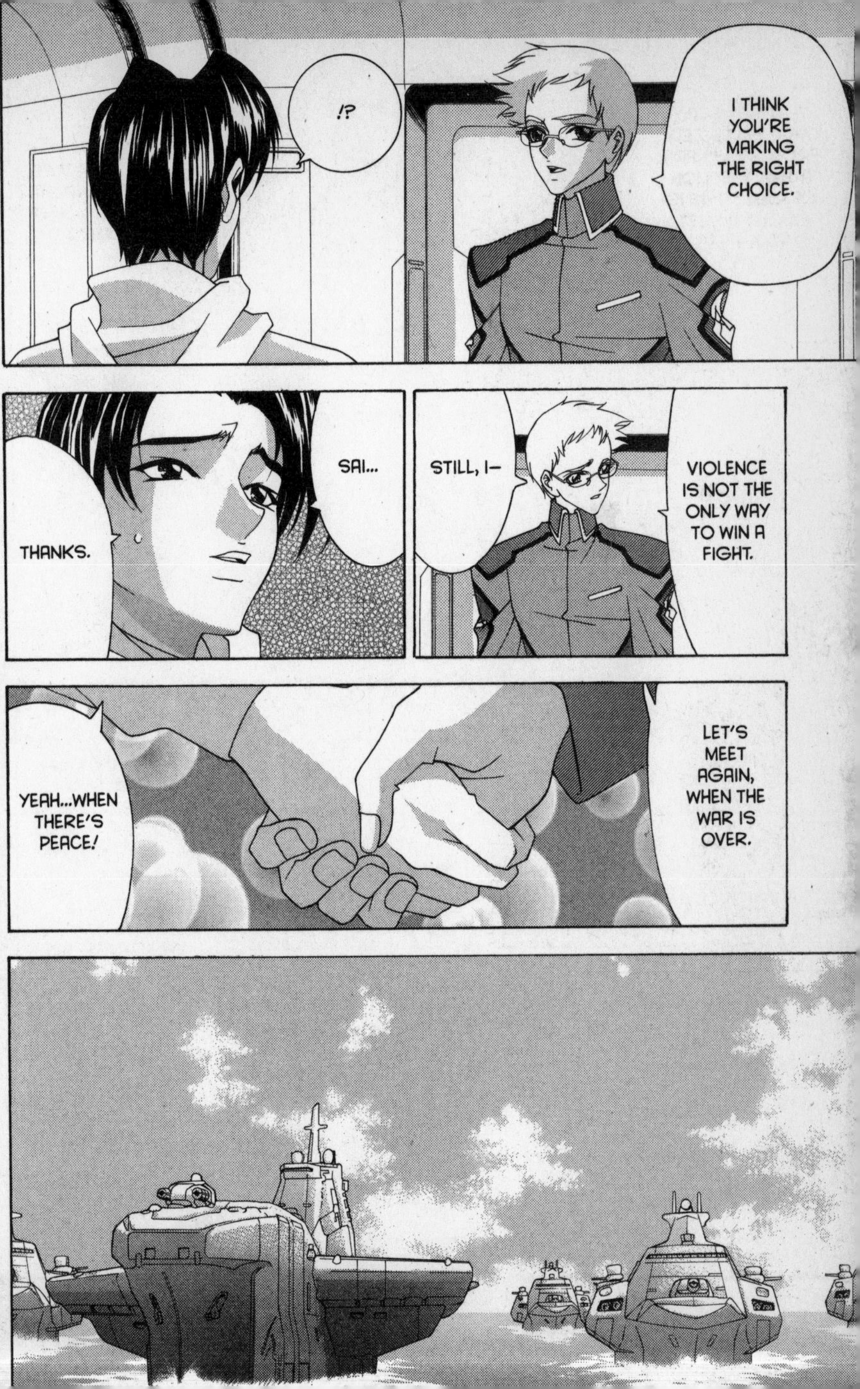
I THINK YOU'RE MAKING THE RIGHT CHOICE.
!?
VIOLENCE IS NOT THE ONLY WAY TO WIN A FIGHT.
STILL, I—
SAI...
THANKS.
LET'S MEET AGAIN, WHEN THE WAR IS OVER.
YEAH...WHEN THERE'S PEACE!

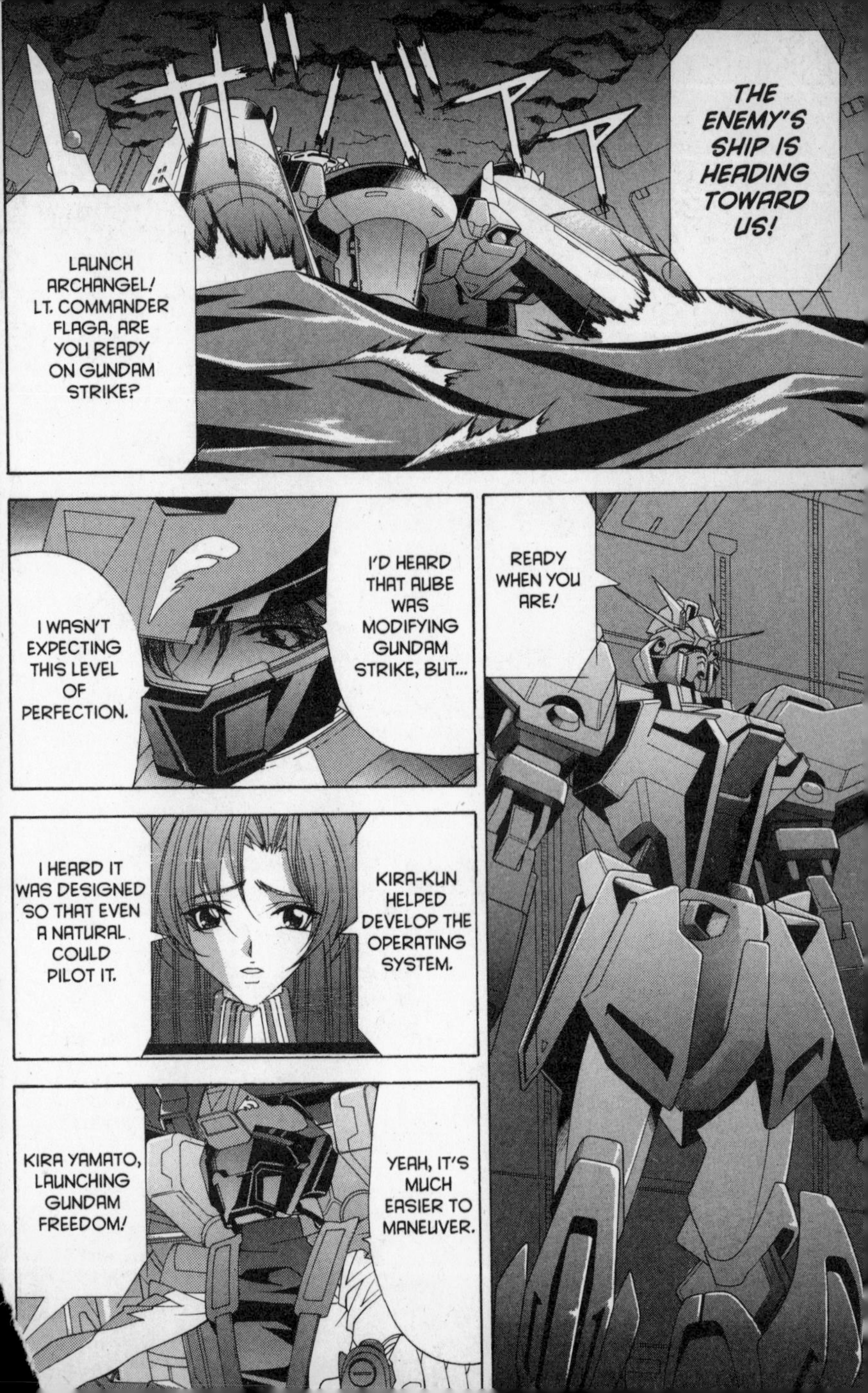
THE ENEMY'S SHIP IS HEADING TOWARD US!
LAUNCH ARCHANGEL! LT. COMMANDER FLAGA, ARE YOU READY ON GUNDAM STRIKE?
READY WHEN YOU ARE!
I'D HEARD THAT AUBE WAS MODIFYING GUNDAM STRIKE, BUT...
I WASN'T EXPECTING THIS LEVEL OF PERFECTION.
KIRA-KUN HELPED DEVELOP THE OPERATING SYSTEM.
I HEARD IT WAS DESIGNED SO THAT EVEN A NATURAL COULD PILOT IT.
YEAH, IT'S MUCH EASIER TO MANEUVER.
KIRA YAMATO, LAUNCHING GUNDAM FREEDOM!

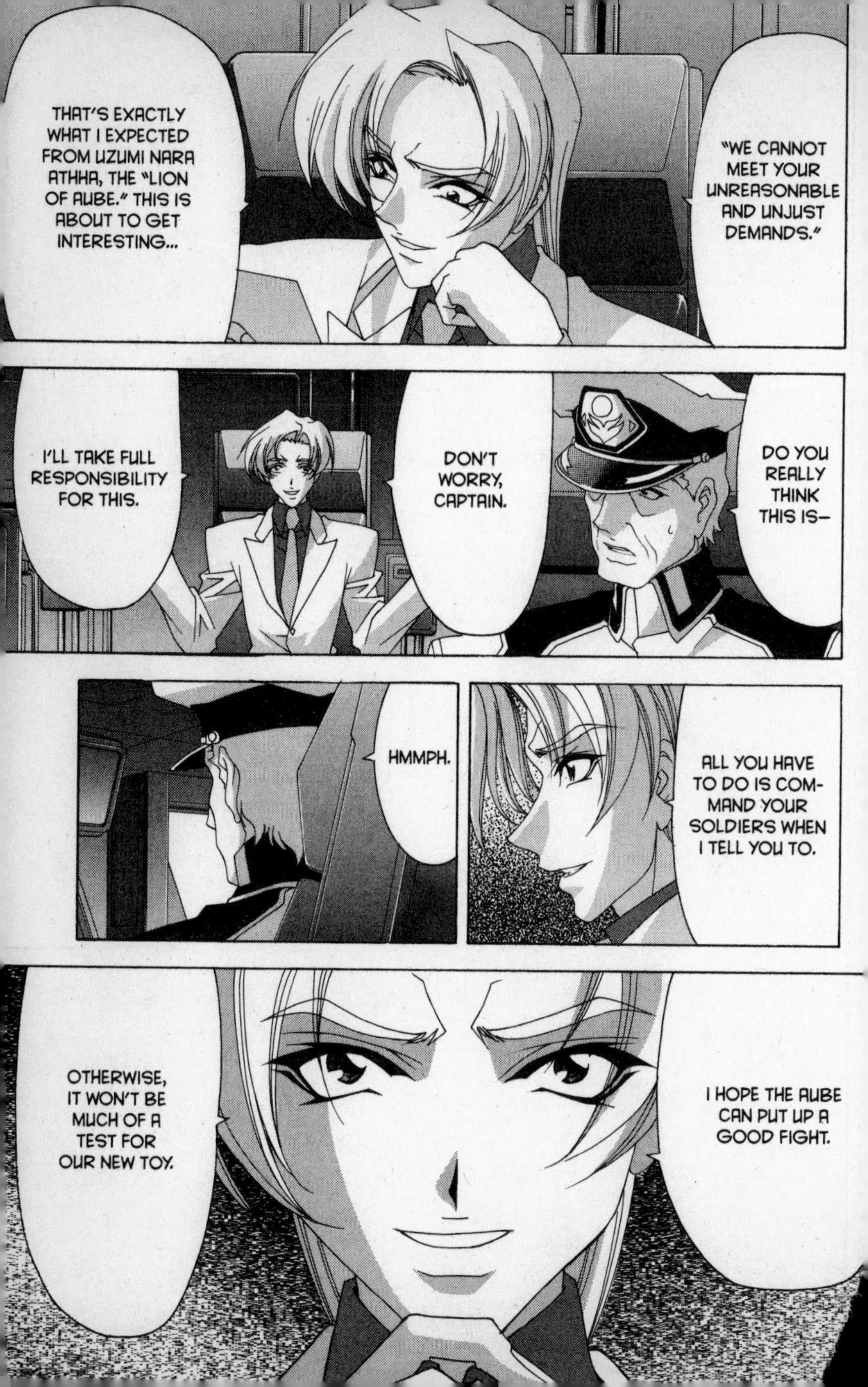
"WE CANNOT MEET YOUR UNREASONABLE AND UNJUST DEMANDS."
THAT'S EXACTLY WHAT I EXPECTED FROM UZUMI NARA ATHHA, THE "LION OF AUBE." THIS IS ABOUT TO GET INTERESTING...
DO YOU REALLY THINK THIS IS–
DON'T WORRY, CAPTAIN.
I'LL TAKE FULL RESPONSIBILITY FOR THIS.
ALL YOU HAVE TO DO IS COM-MAND YOUR SOLDIERS WHEN I TELL YOU TO.
HMMPH.
I HOPE THE AUBE CAN PUT UP A GOOD FIGHT.
OTHERWISE, IT WON'T BE MUCH OF A TEST FOR OUR NEW TOY.

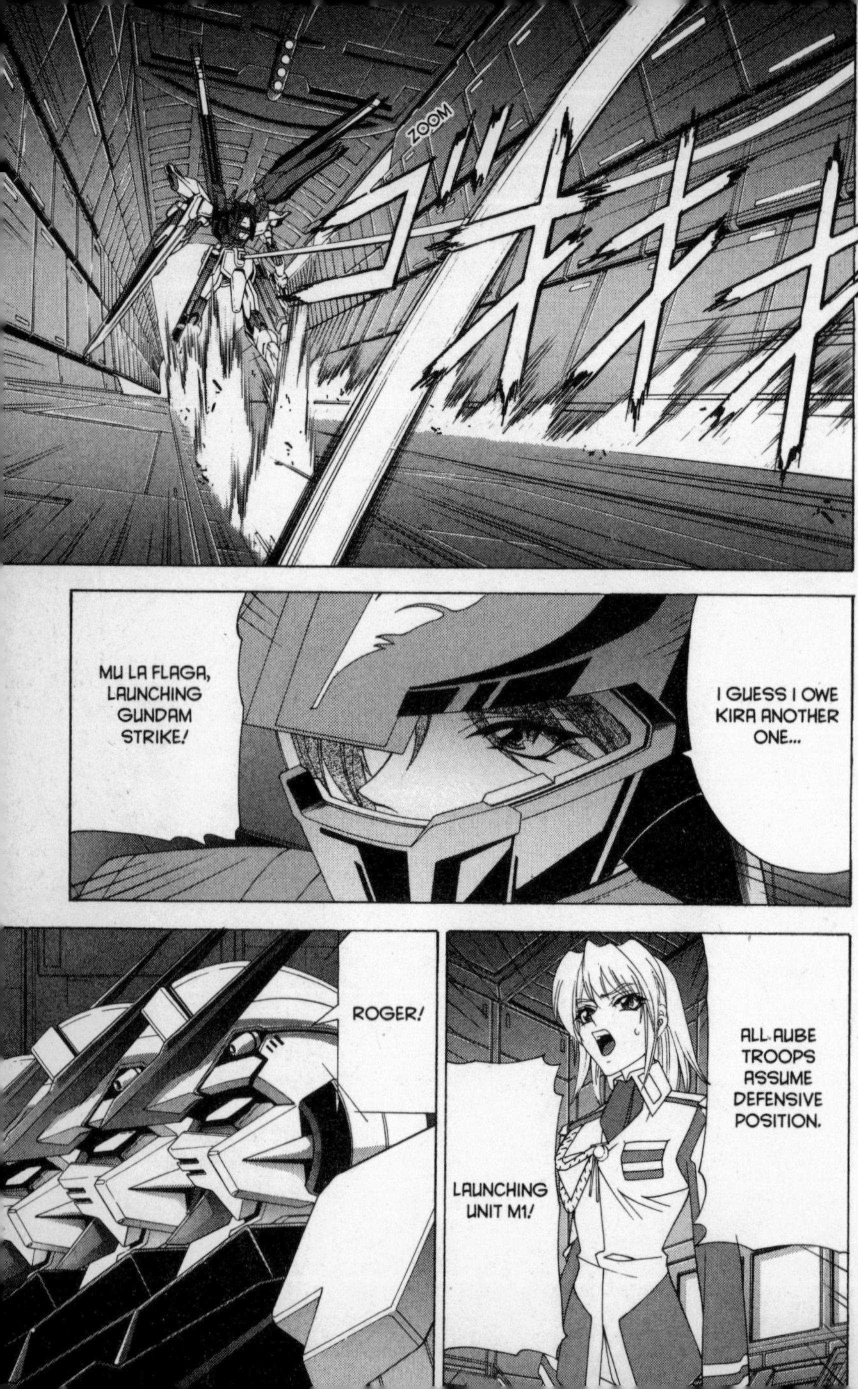
ZOOM
I GUESS I OWE KIRA ANOTHER ONE...
MU LA FLAGA, LAUNCHING GUNDAM STRIKE!
ALL AUBE TROOPS ASSUME DEFENSIVE POSITION.
LAUNCHING UNIT M1!
ROGER!

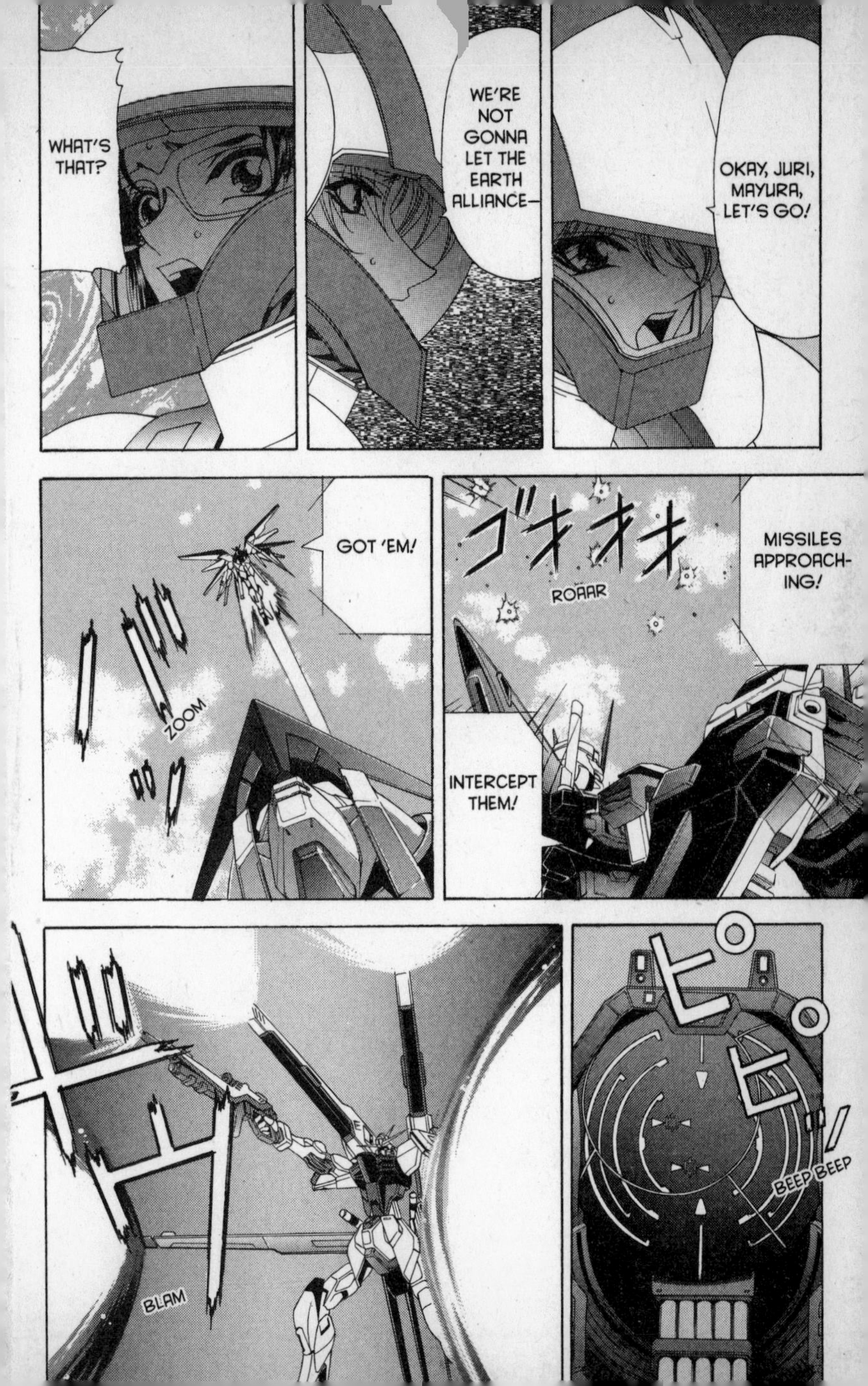
OKAY, JURI, MAYURA, LET'S GO!
WE'RE NOT GONNA LET THE EARTH ALLIANCE—
WHAT'S THAT?
MISSILES APPROACHING!
ゴオオオ
ROAAR
INTERCEPT THEM!
GOT 'EM!
ZOOM
ピッ ピッ
BEEP BEEP
BLAM

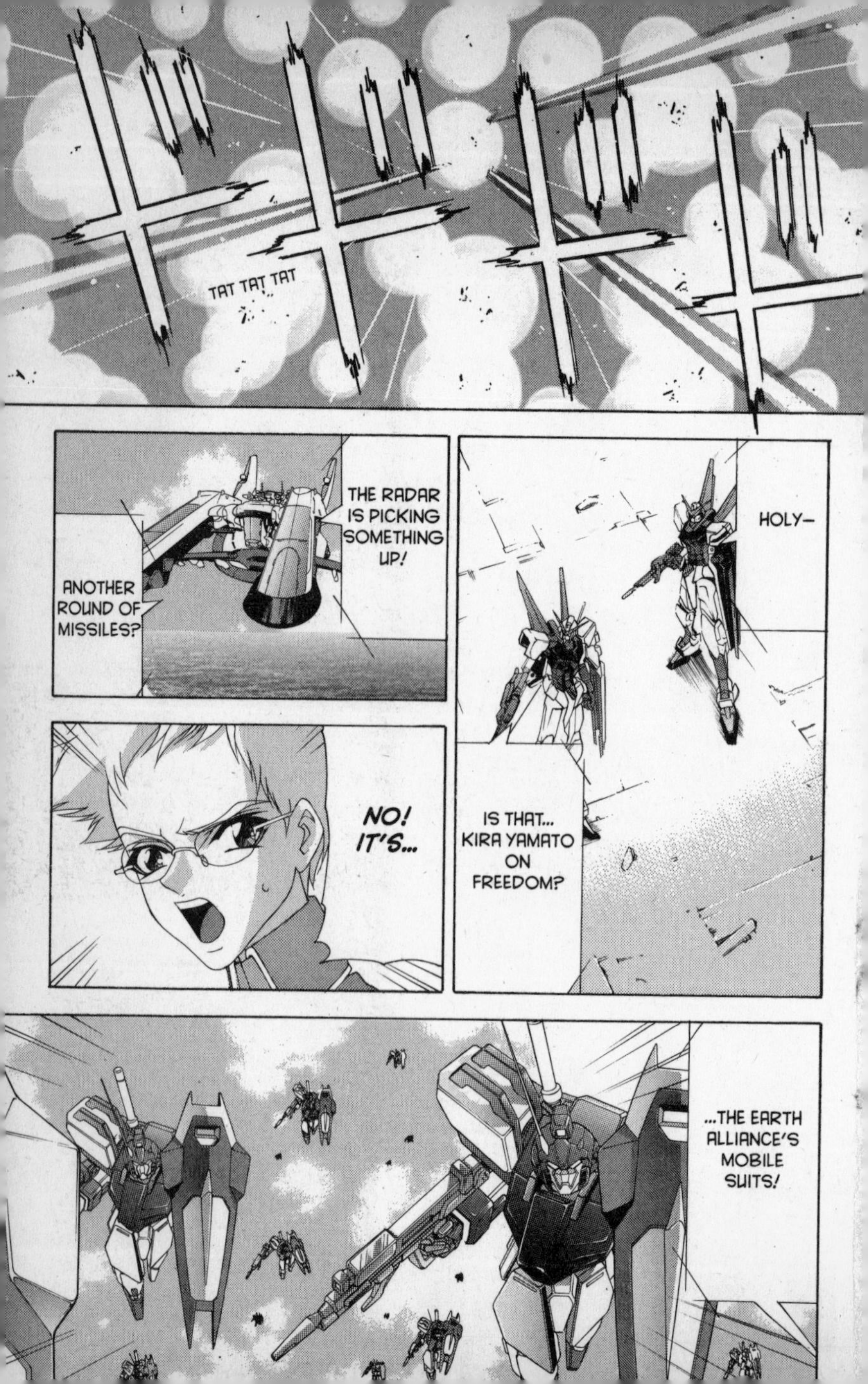
TAT TAT TAT
HOLY—
IS THAT... KIRA YAMATO ON FREEDOM?
THE RADAR IS PICKING SOMETHING UP!
ANOTHER ROUND OF MISSILES?
NO! IT'S...
...THE EARTH ALLIANCE'S MOBILE SUITS!

SO, THE EARTH ALLIANCE HAS BEEN CRANKING OUT NEW MOBILE SUITS TOO.

BUT...

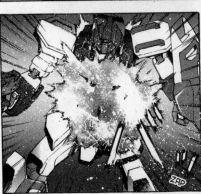

ZAP

WE'RE THE ORIGINALS!

BLAM

JURI!

ROGER THAT!

ASAGI, LET'S GIVE THE LIEUTENANT COMMANDER SOME BACKUP!

CURSE THE EARTH ALLIANCE'S MOBILE SUITS!

SCHWOOM

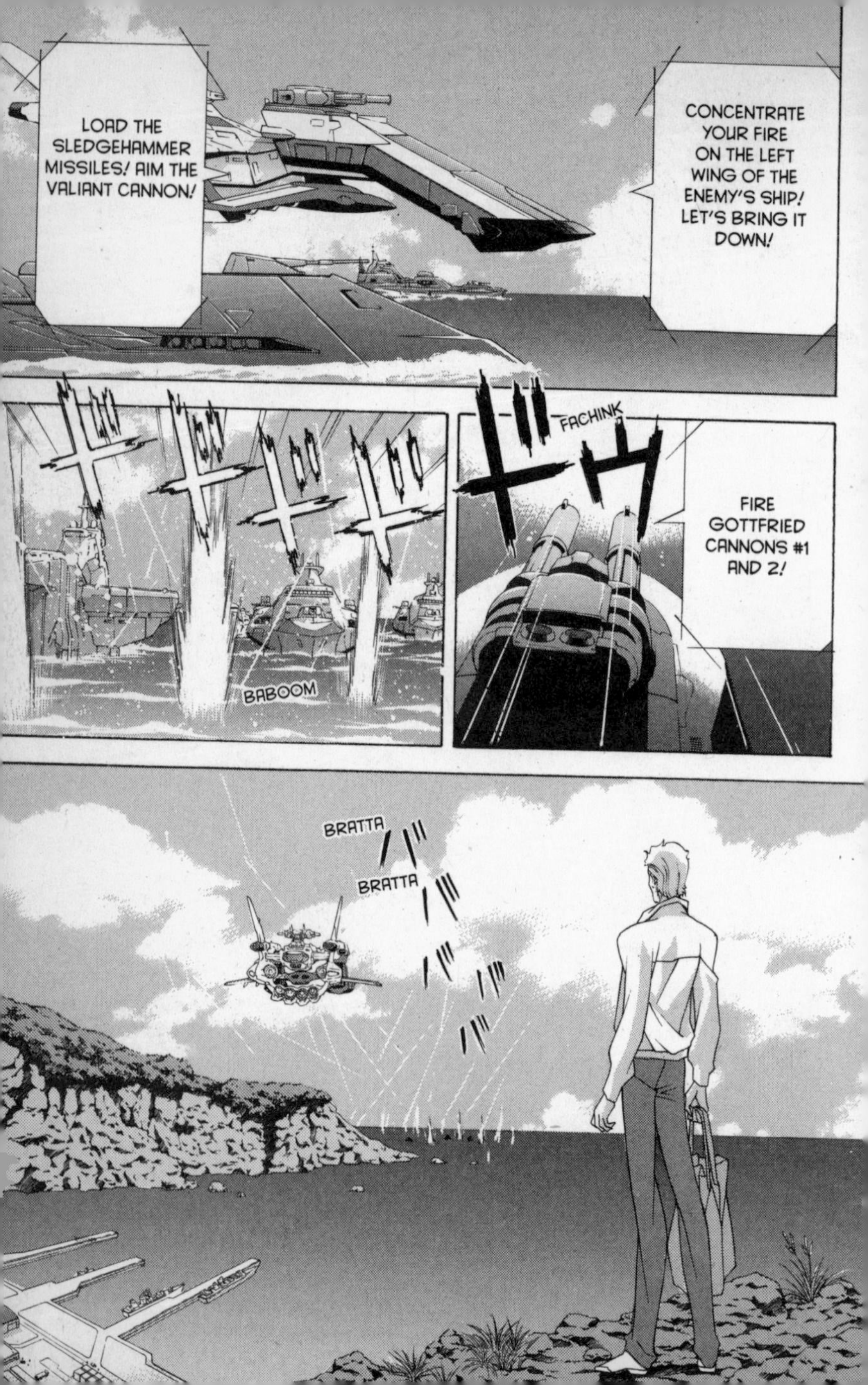
CONCENTRATE YOUR FIRE ON THE LEFT WING OF THE ENEMY'S SHIP! LET'S BRING IT DOWN!
LOAD THE SLEDGEHAMMER MISSILES! AIM THE VALIANT CANNON!
FACHINK
FIRE GOTTFRIED CANNONS #1 AND 2!
BABOOM
BRATTA
BRATTA

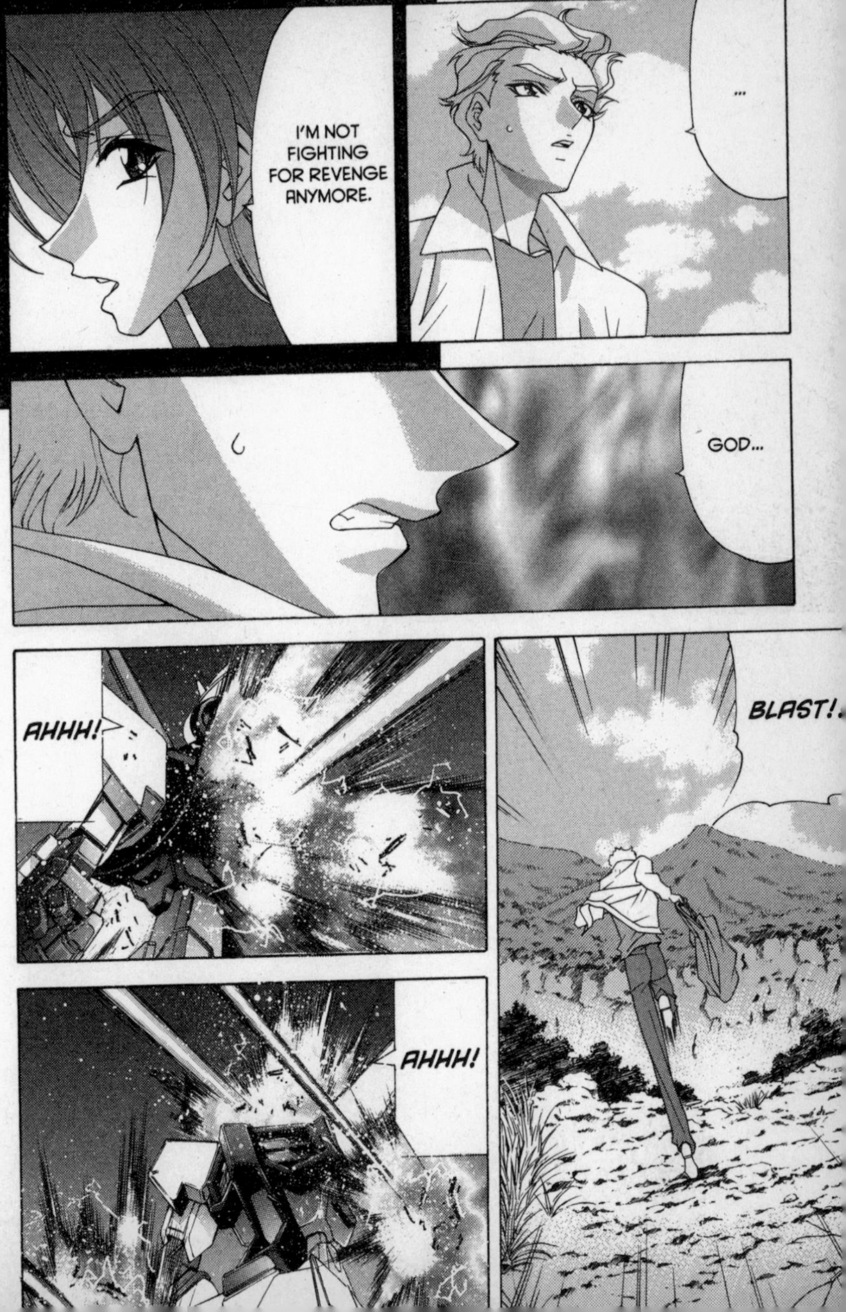
...
I'M NOT FIGHTING FOR REVENGE ANYMORE.
GOD...
BLAST!..
AHHH!
AHHH!

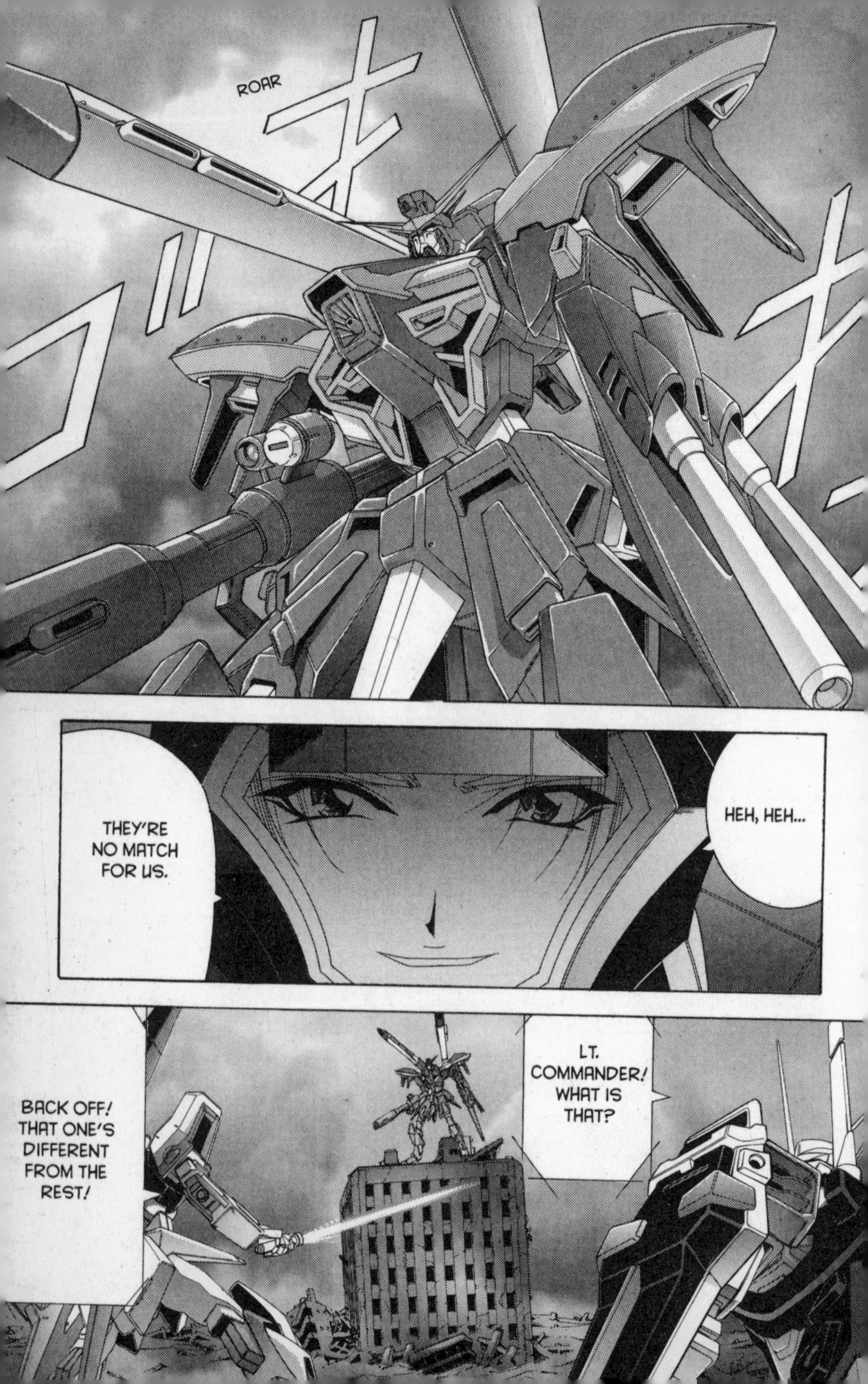
ROAR
HEH, HEH...
THEY'RE NO MATCH FOR US.
LT. COMMANDER! WHAT IS THAT?
BACK OFF! THAT ONE'S DIFFERENT FROM THE REST!

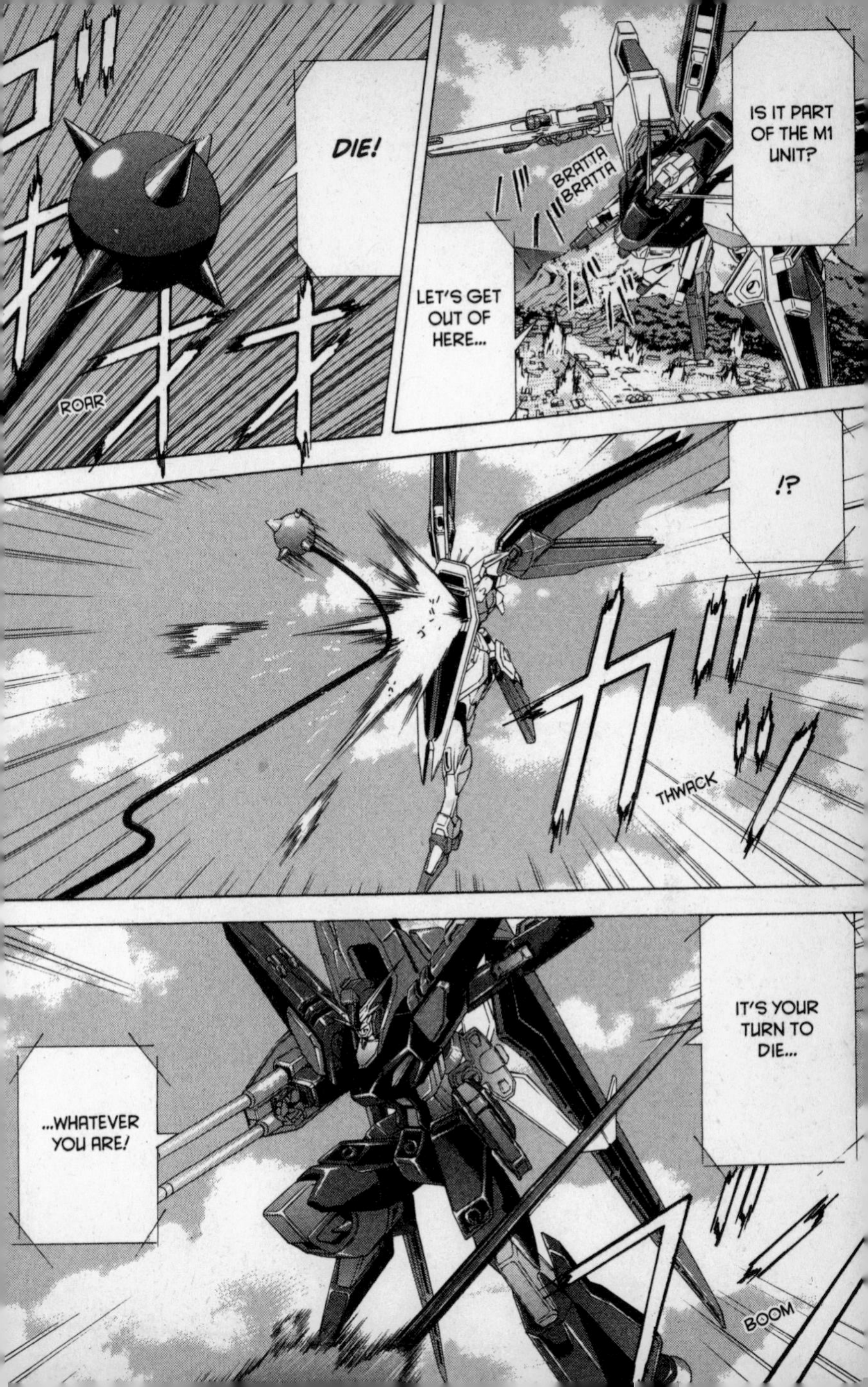
IS IT PART OF THE M1 UNIT?
BRATTA BRATTA
LET'S GET OUT OF HERE...
DIE!
ROAR
!?
THWACK
IT'S YOUR TURN TO DIE...
...WHATEVER YOU ARE!
BOOM

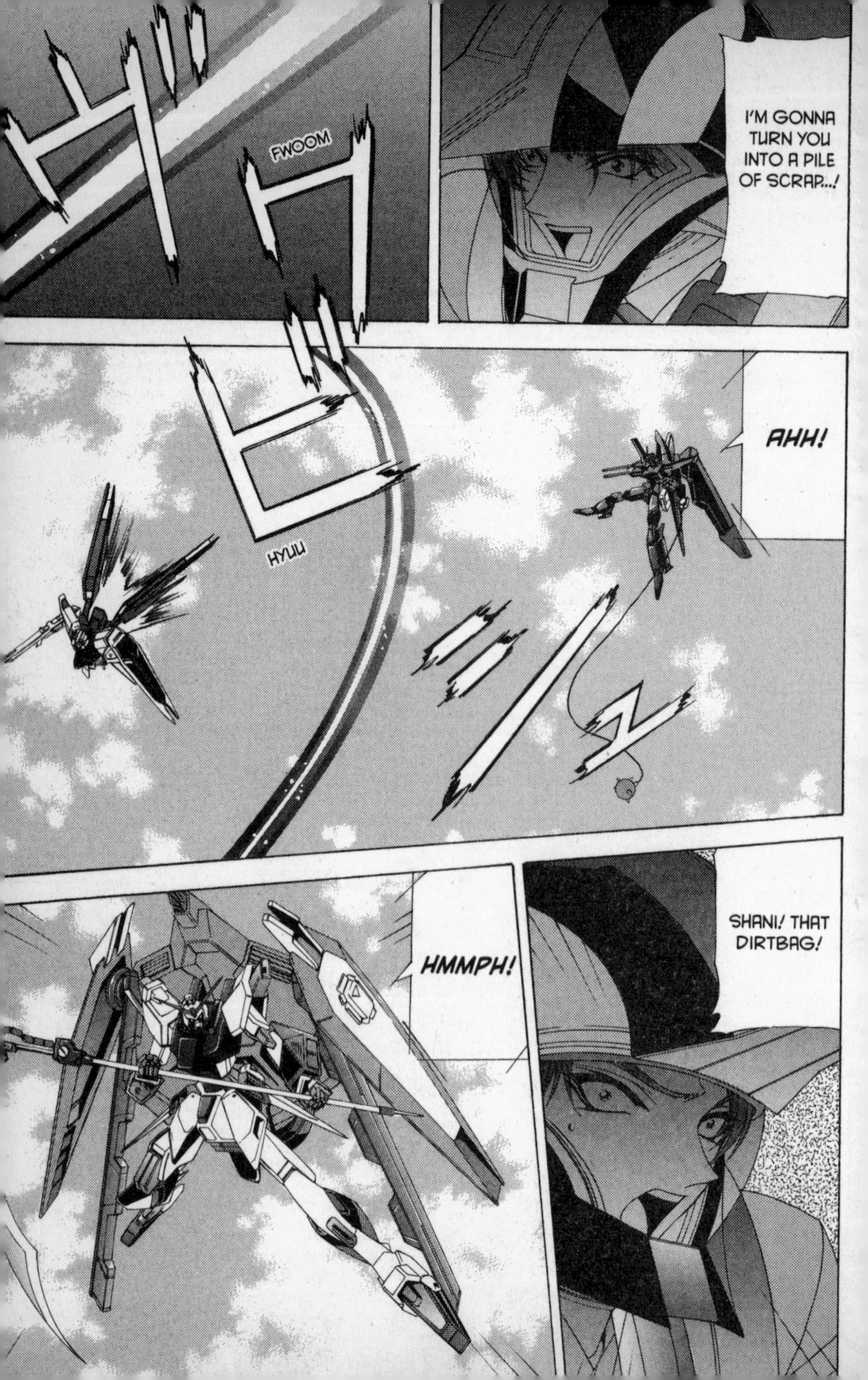
I'M GONNA TURN YOU INTO A PILE OF SCRAP...!
FWOOM
AHH!
HYUU
SHANI! THAT DIRTBAG!
HMMPH!

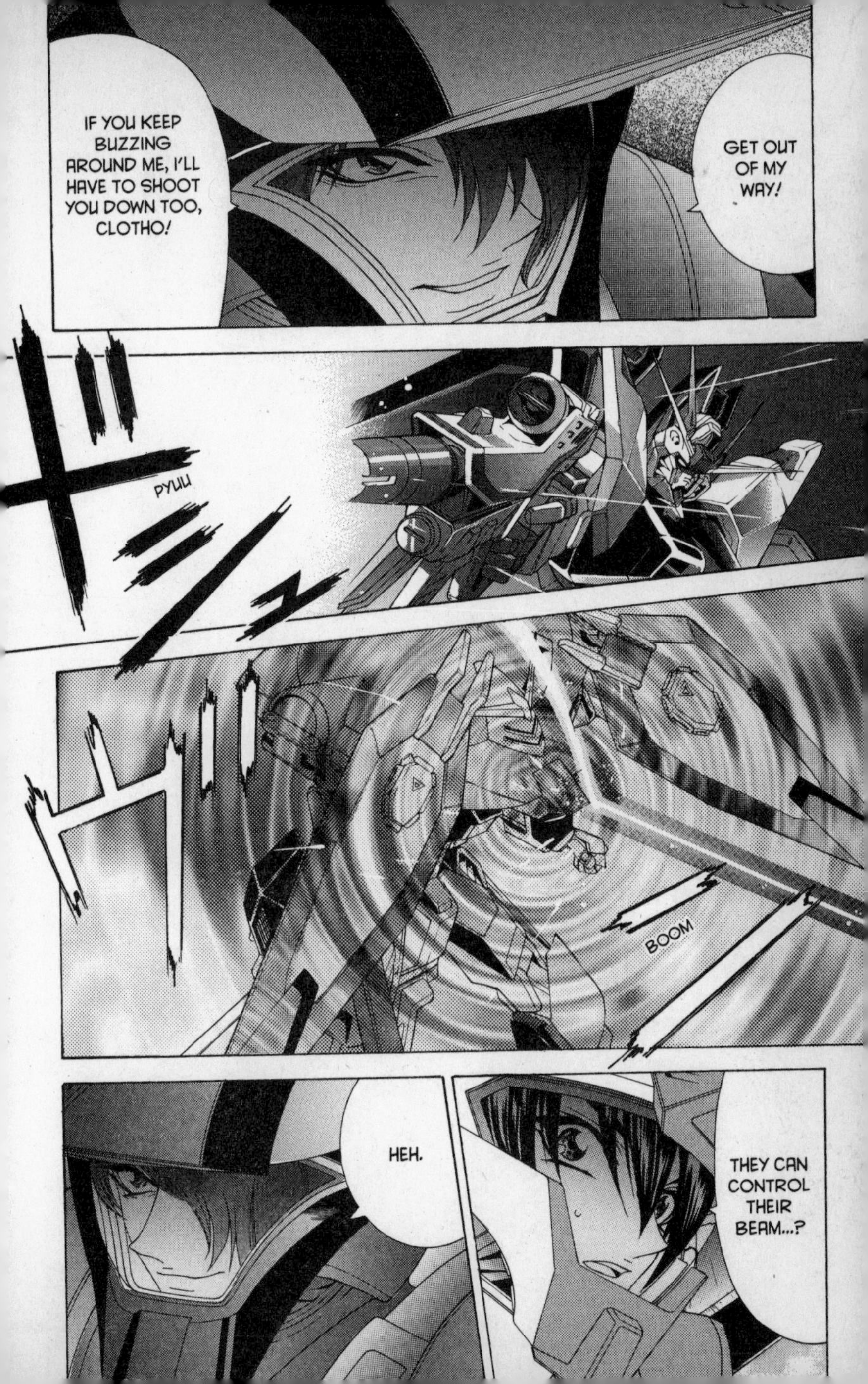
GET OUT OF MY WAY!
IF YOU KEEP BUZZING AROUND ME, I'LL HAVE TO SHOOT YOU DOWN TOO, CLOTHO!
PYUU
BOOM
THEY CAN CONTROL THEIR BEAM...?
HEH.

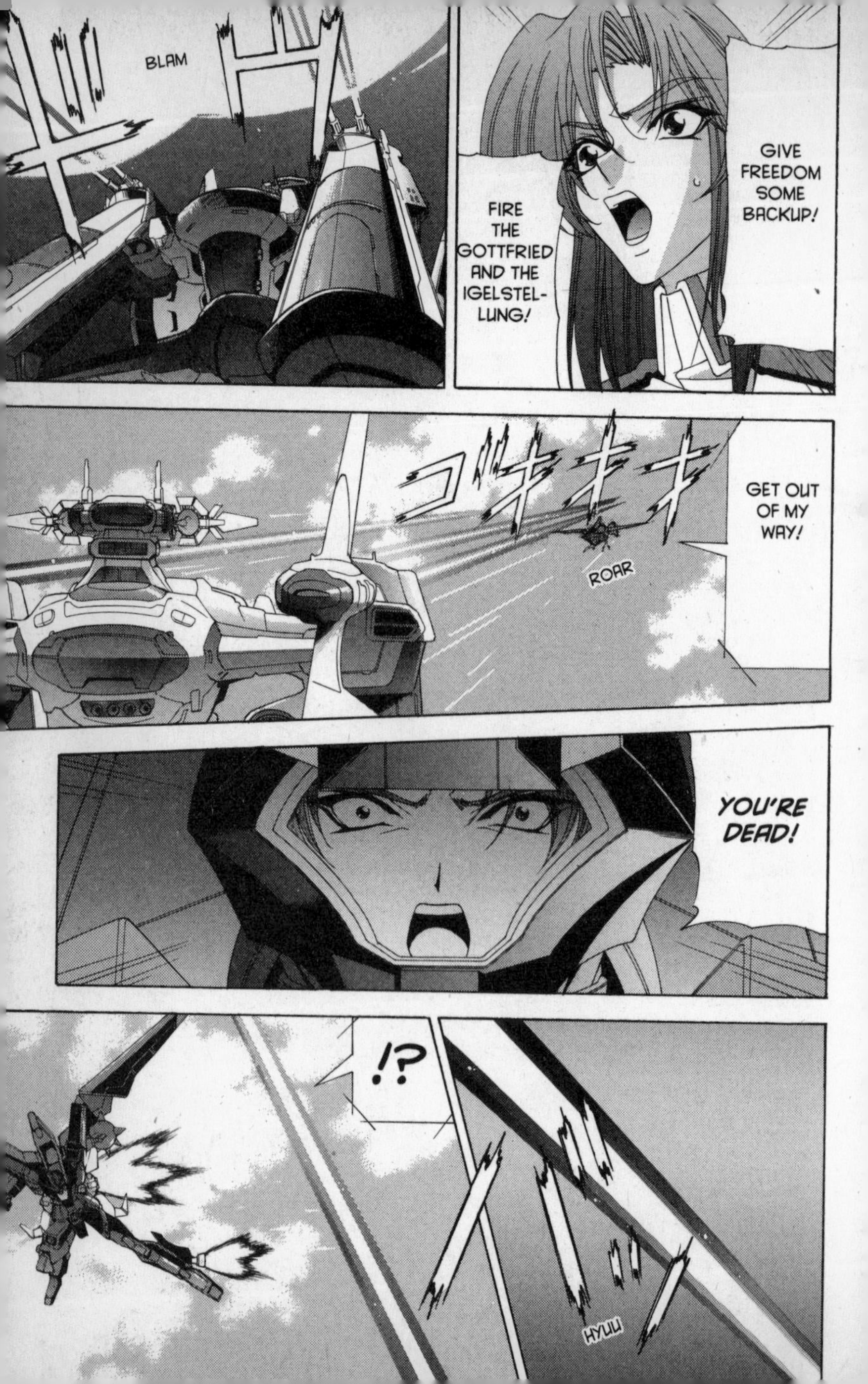
GIVE FREEDOM SOME BACKUP!
FIRE THE GOTTFRIED AND THE IGELSTEL-LUNG!
BLAM
GET OUT OF MY WAY!
ROAR
YOU'RE DEAD!
!?
HYUU

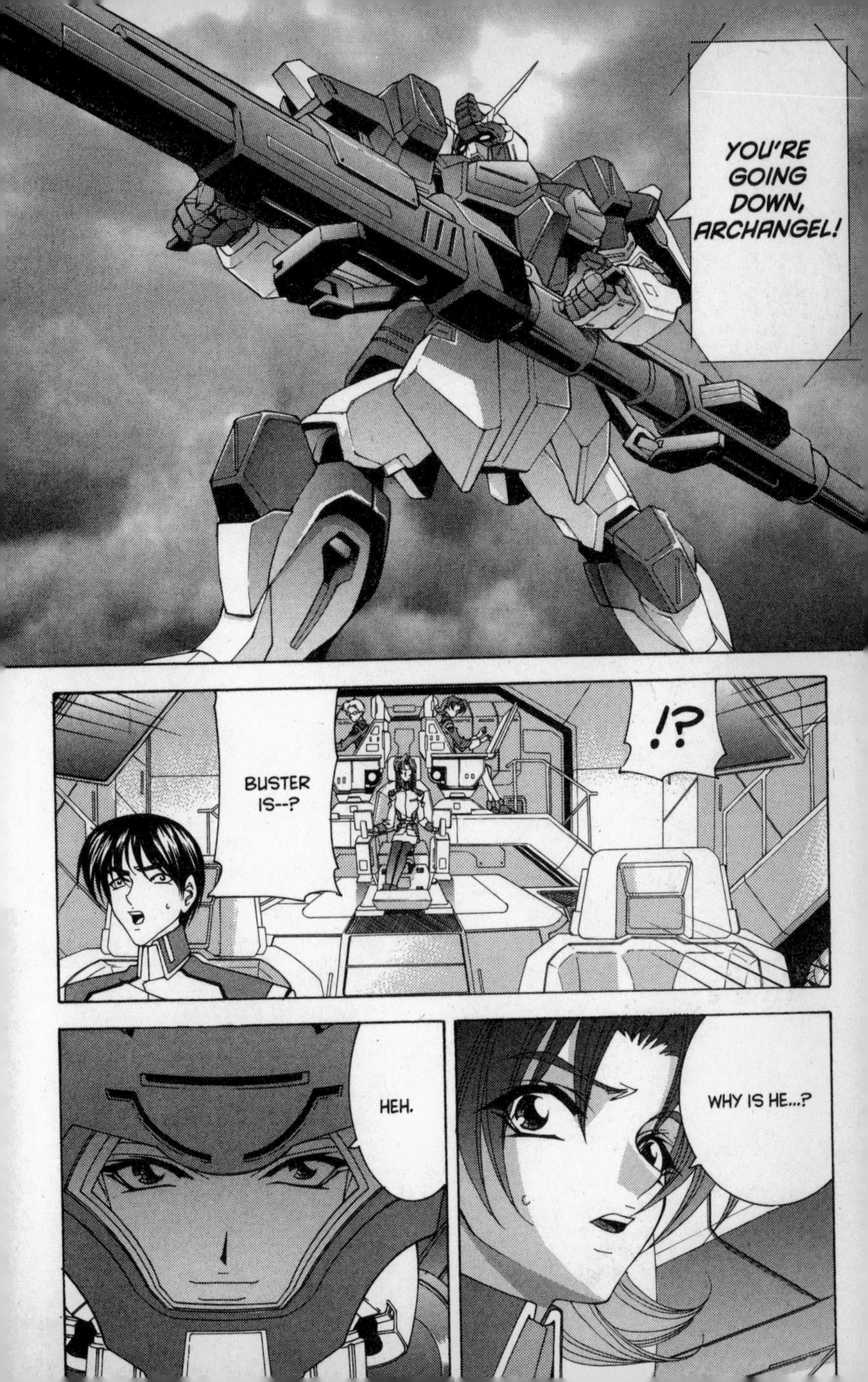
YOU'RE GOING DOWN, ARCHANGEL!
!?
BUSTER IS--?
WHY IS HE...?
HEH.

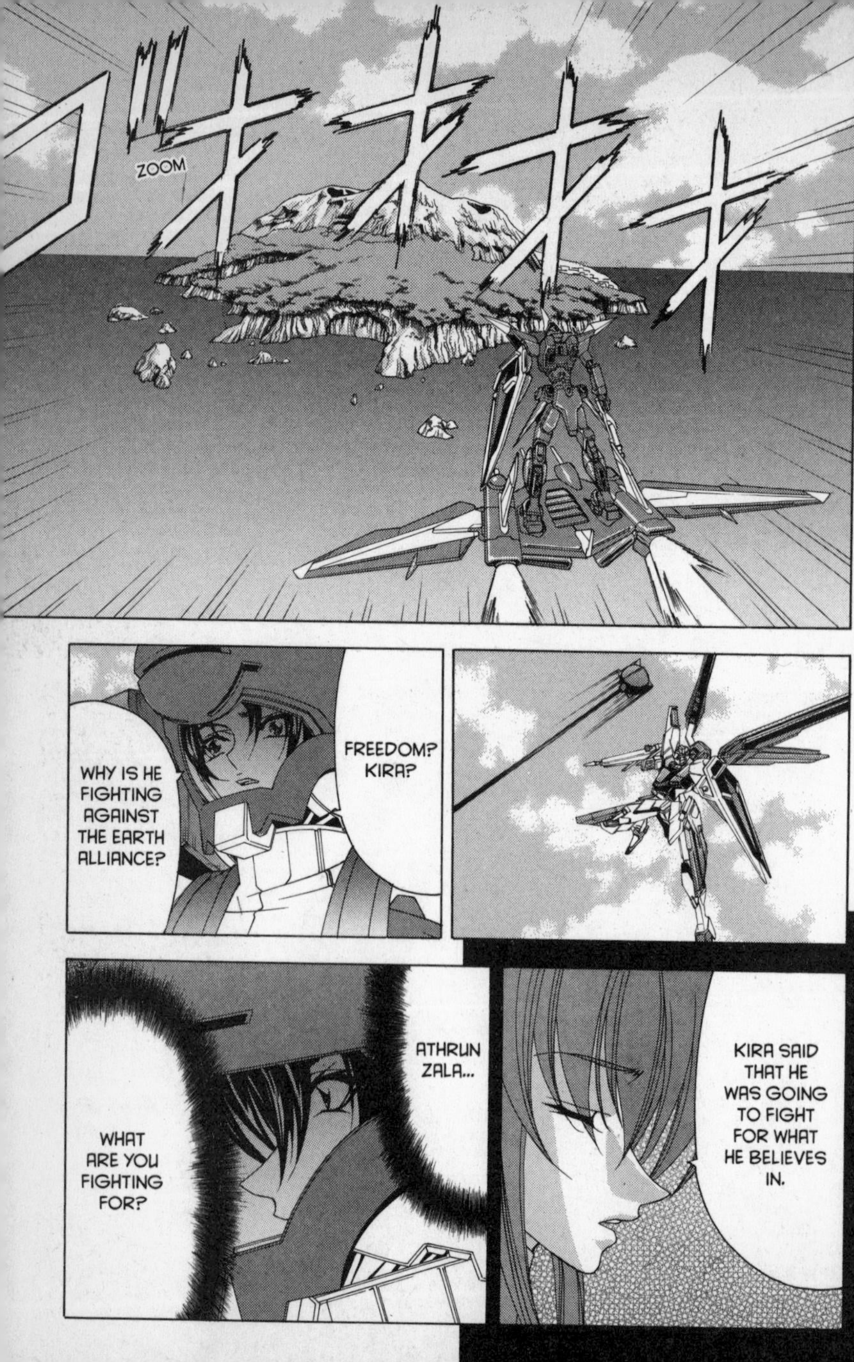
ゴオオオオ
ZOOM
FREEDOM? KIRA?
WHY IS HE FIGHTING AGAINST THE EARTH ALLIANCE?
KIRA SAID THAT HE WAS GOING TO FIGHT FOR WHAT HE BELIEVES IN.
ATHRUN ZALA...
WHAT ARE YOU FIGHTING FOR?

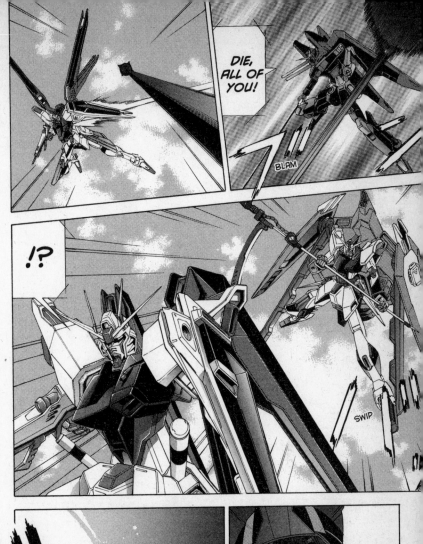

DIE, ALL OF YOU!

BLAM

!?

SWIP

CRASH

AHHHHH! IT'S ALL OVER!

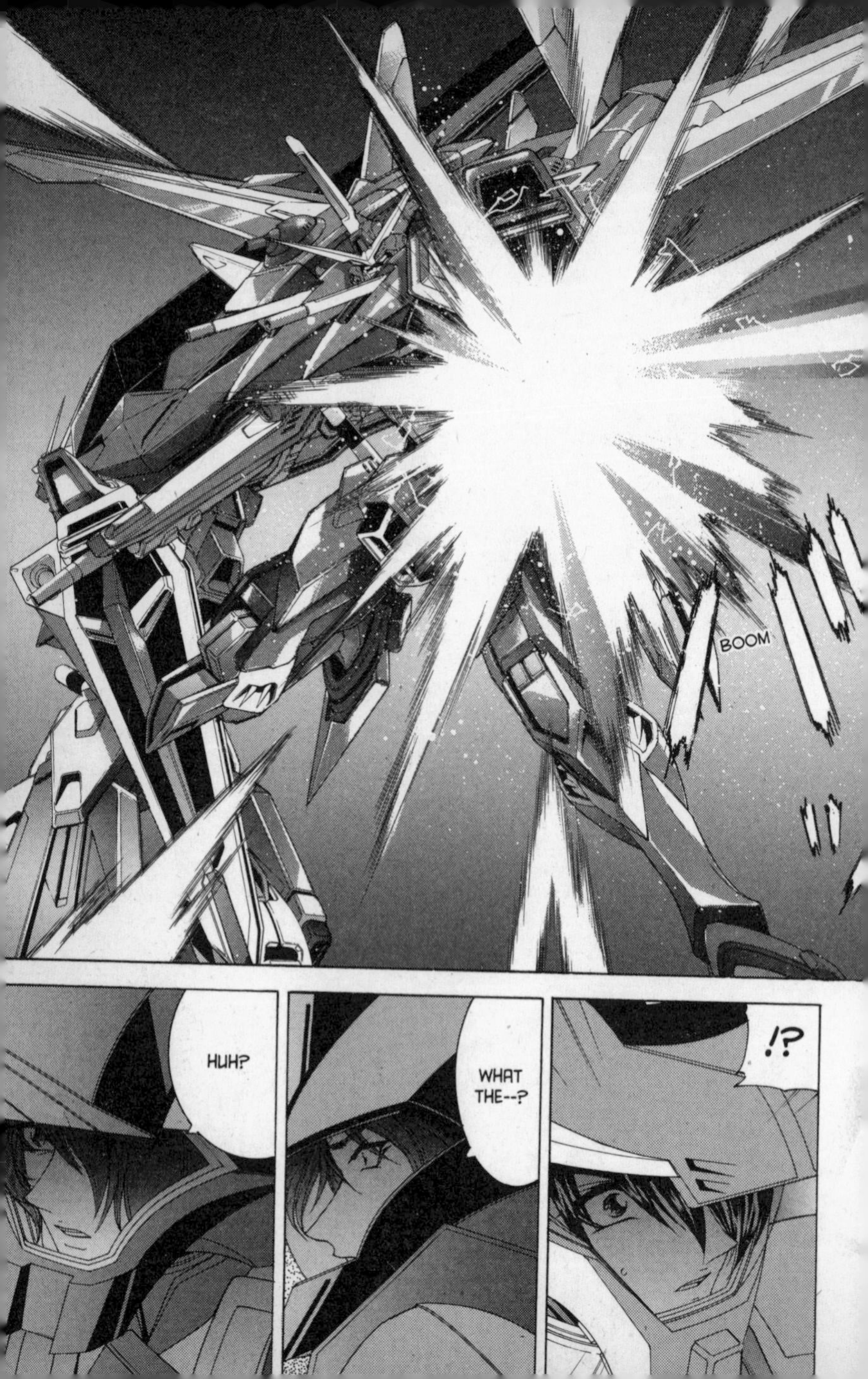
BOOM
!?
WHAT
THE--?
HUH?

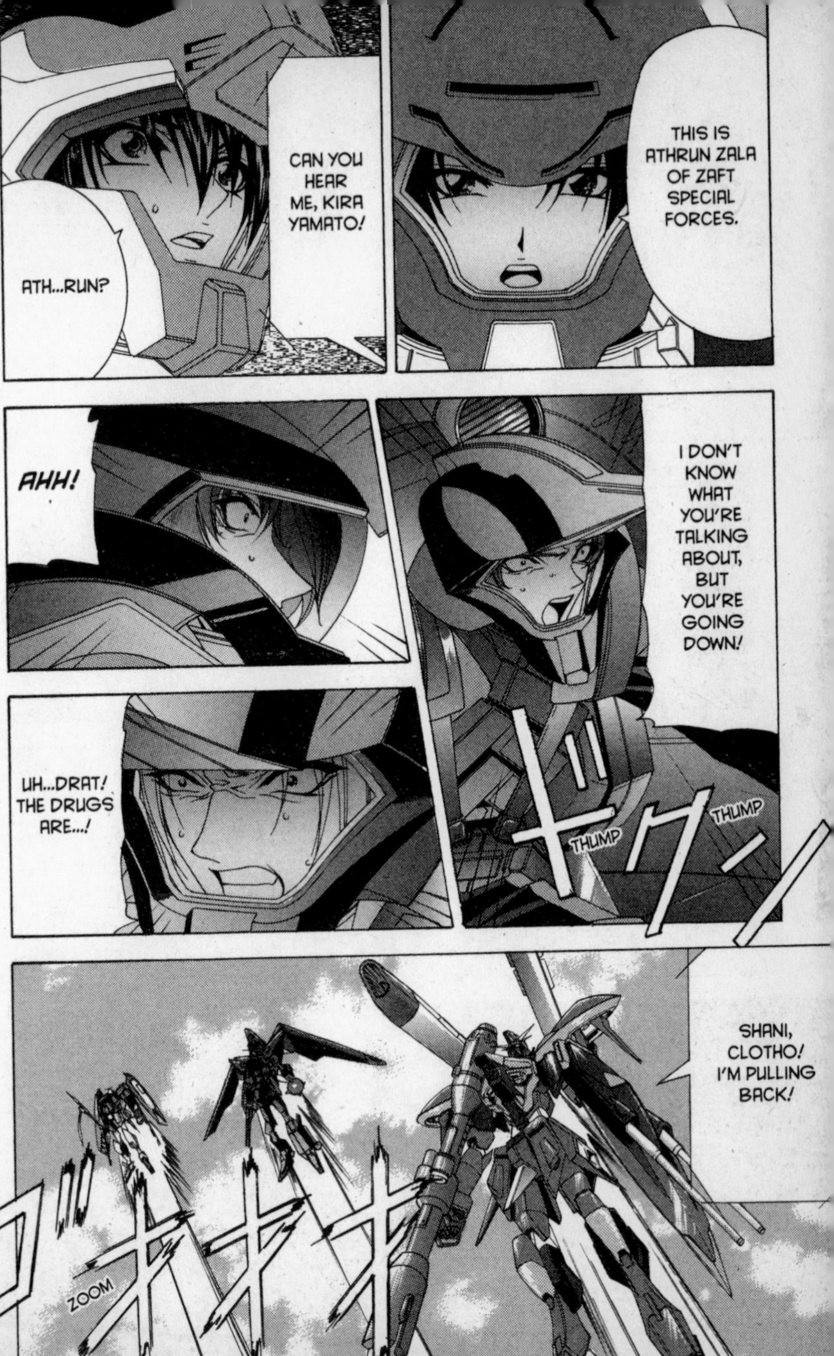
THIS IS ATHRUN ZALA OF ZAFT SPECIAL FORCES.
CAN YOU HEAR ME, KIRA YAMATO!
ATH...RUN?
I DON'T KNOW WHAT YOU'RE TALKING ABOUT, BUT YOU'RE GOING DOWN!
THUMP
THUMP
AHH!
UH...DRAT! THE DRUGS ARE...!
SHANI, CLOTHO! I'M PULLING BACK!
ZOOM

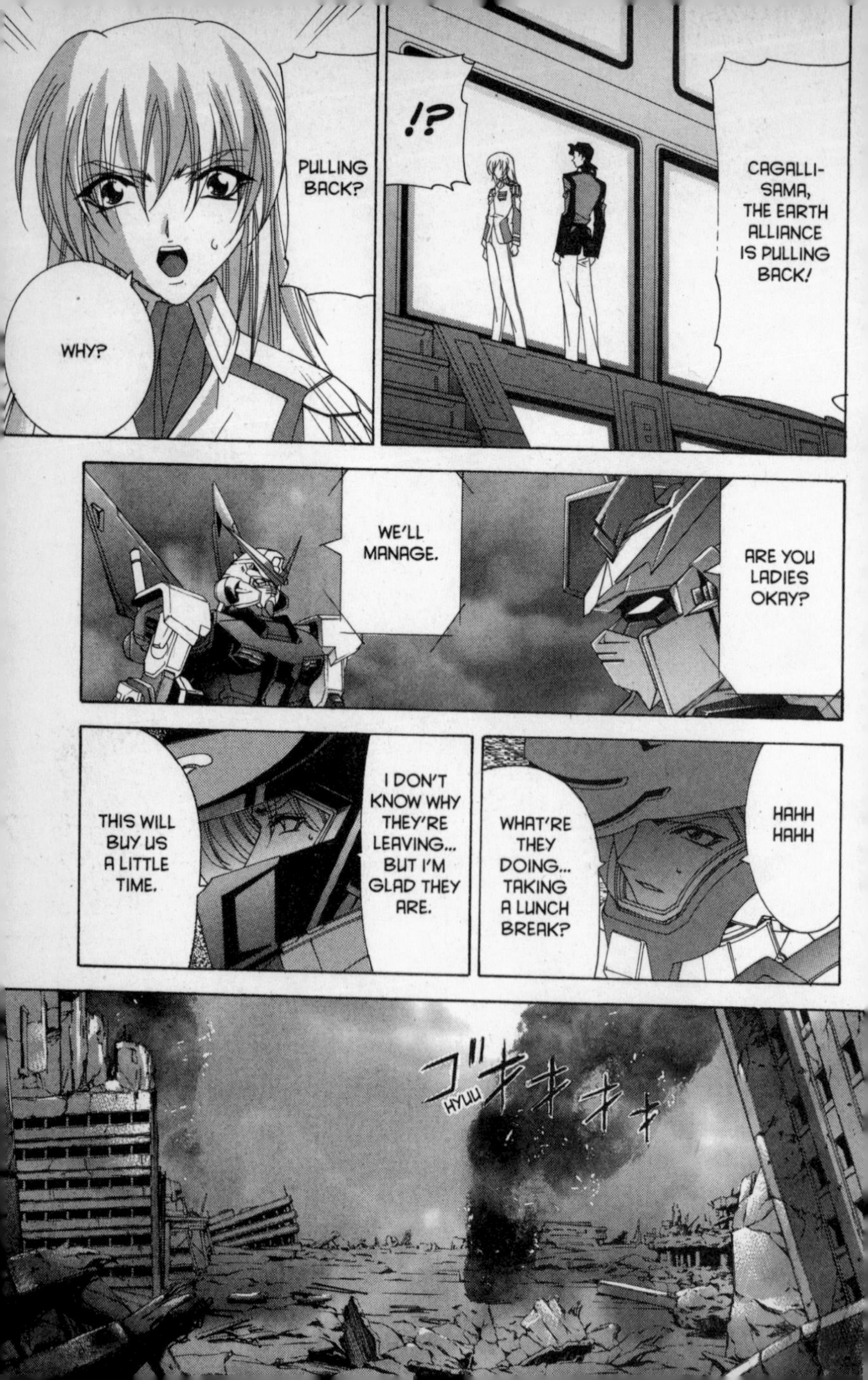
CAGALLI-SAMA, THE EARTH ALLIANCE IS PULLING BACK!
!?
PULLING BACK?
WHY?
ARE YOU LADIES OKAY?
WE'LL MANAGE.
HAHH HAHH
WHAT'RE THEY DOING... TAKING A LUNCH BREAK?
I DON'T KNOW WHY THEY'RE LEAVING... BUT I'M GLAD THEY ARE.
THIS WILL BUY US A LITTLE TIME.
HYUU

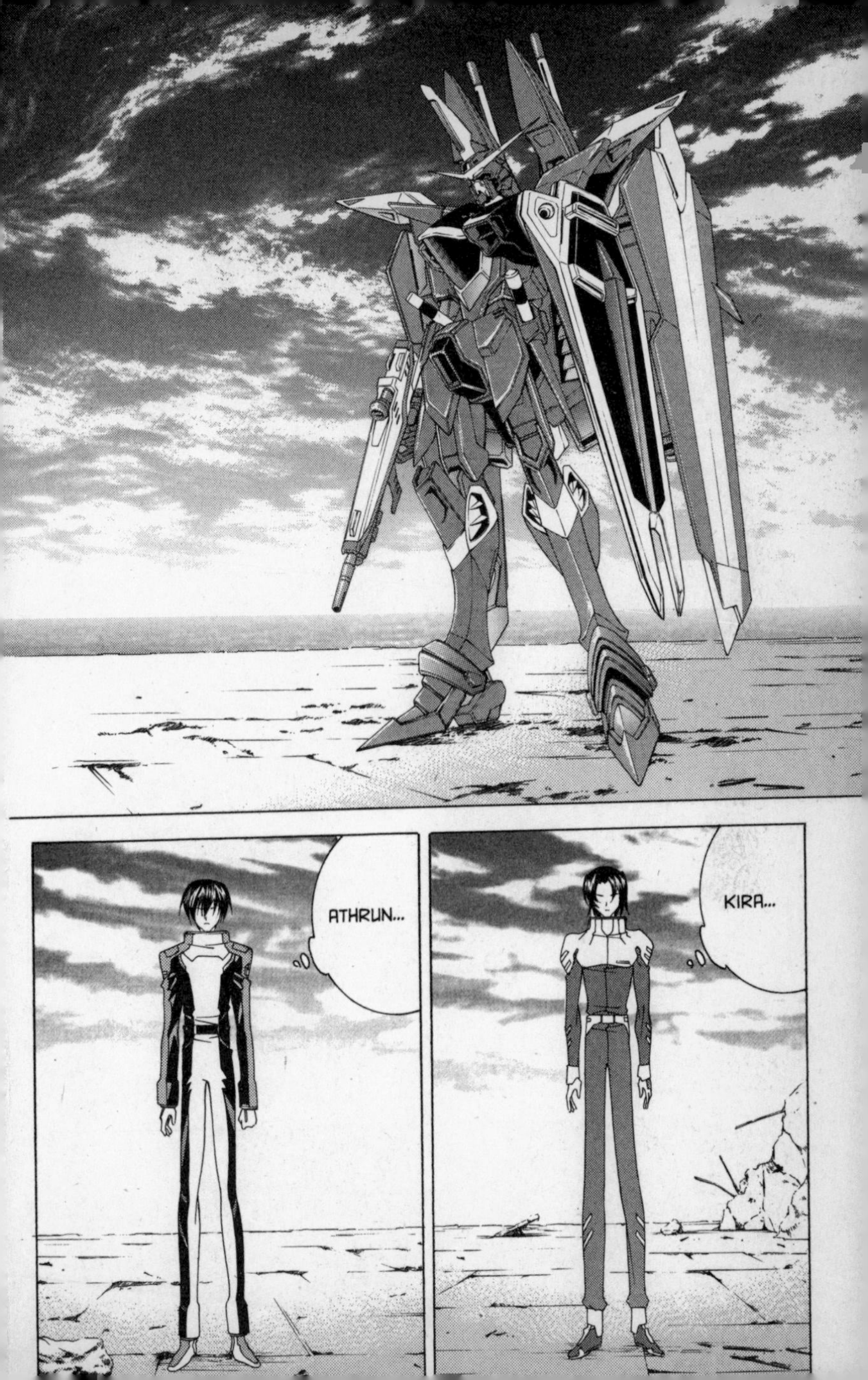
KIRA...
ATHRUN...

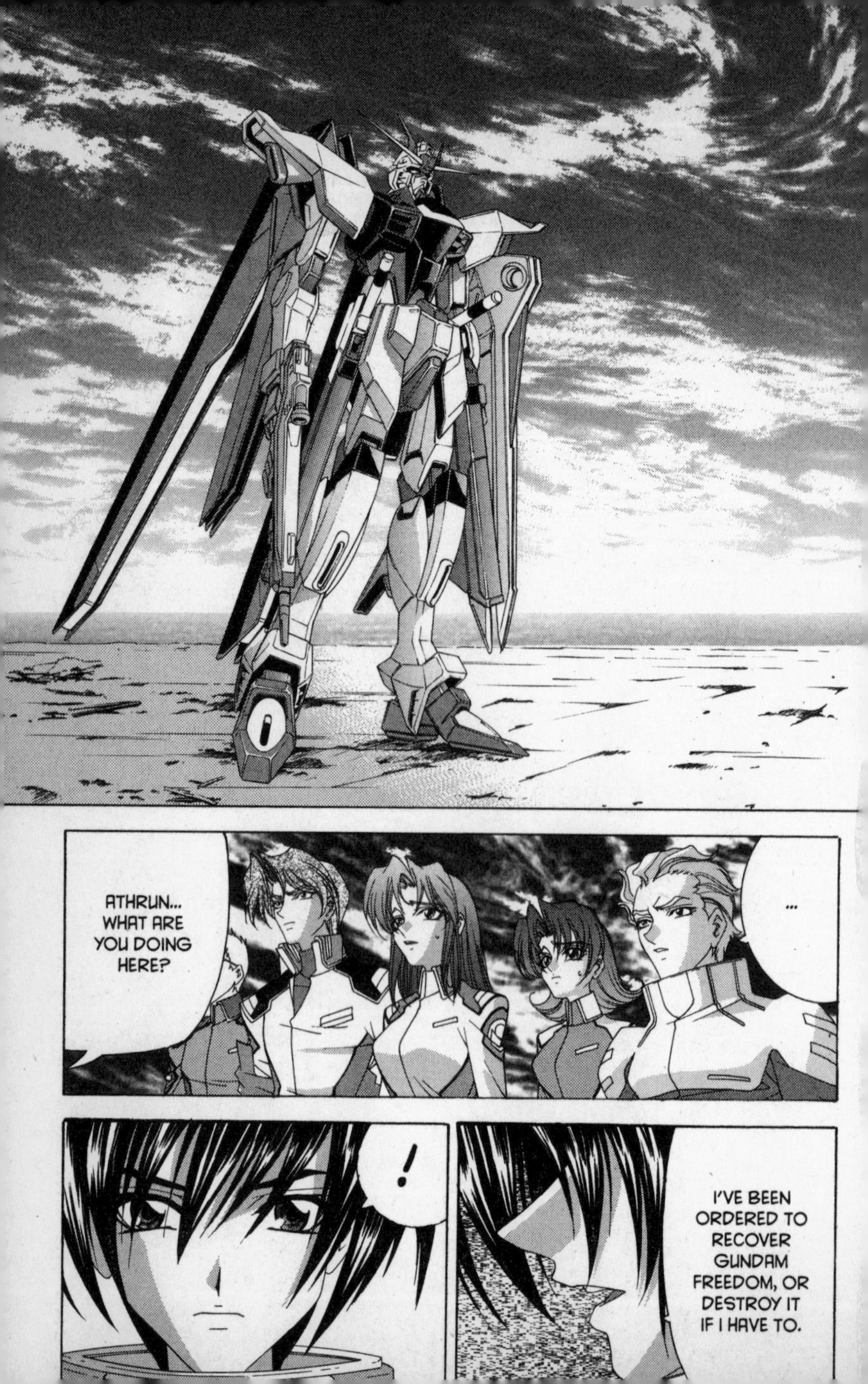
...
ATHRUN... WHAT ARE YOU DOING HERE?
I'VE BEEN ORDERED TO RECOVER GUNDAM FREEDOM, OR DESTROY IT IF I HAVE TO.
!

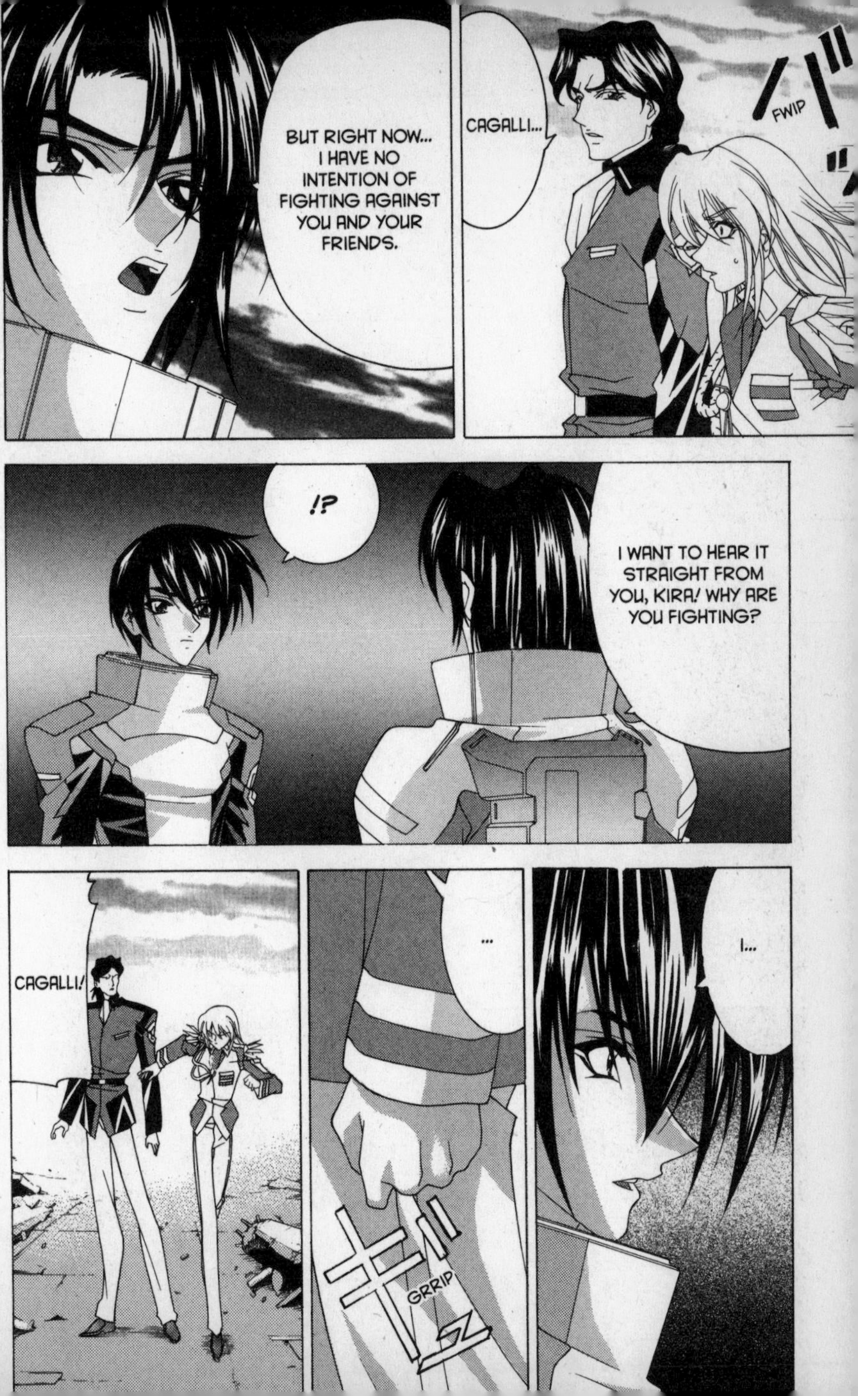
FWIP
CAGALLI...
BUT RIGHT NOW... I HAVE NO INTENTION OF FIGHTING AGAINST YOU AND YOUR FRIENDS.
I WANT TO HEAR IT STRAIGHT FROM YOU, KIRA! WHY ARE YOU FIGHTING?
!?
I...
...
GRRIP
CAGALLI!

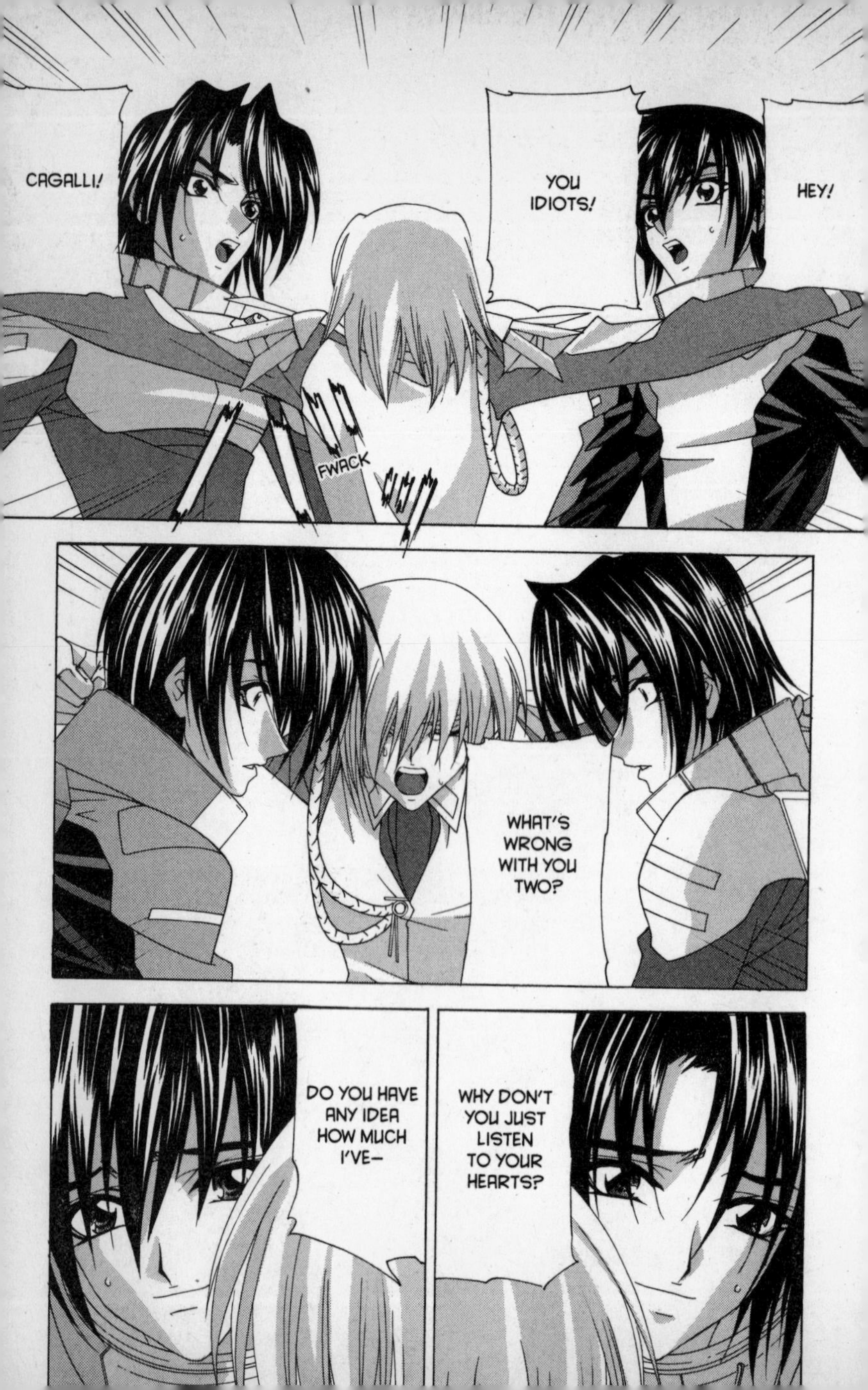
HEY!
YOU IDIOTS!
CAGALLI!
FWACK
WHAT'S WRONG WITH YOU TWO?
WHY DON'T YOU JUST LISTEN TO YOUR HEARTS?
DO YOU HAVE ANY IDEA HOW MUCH I'VE—

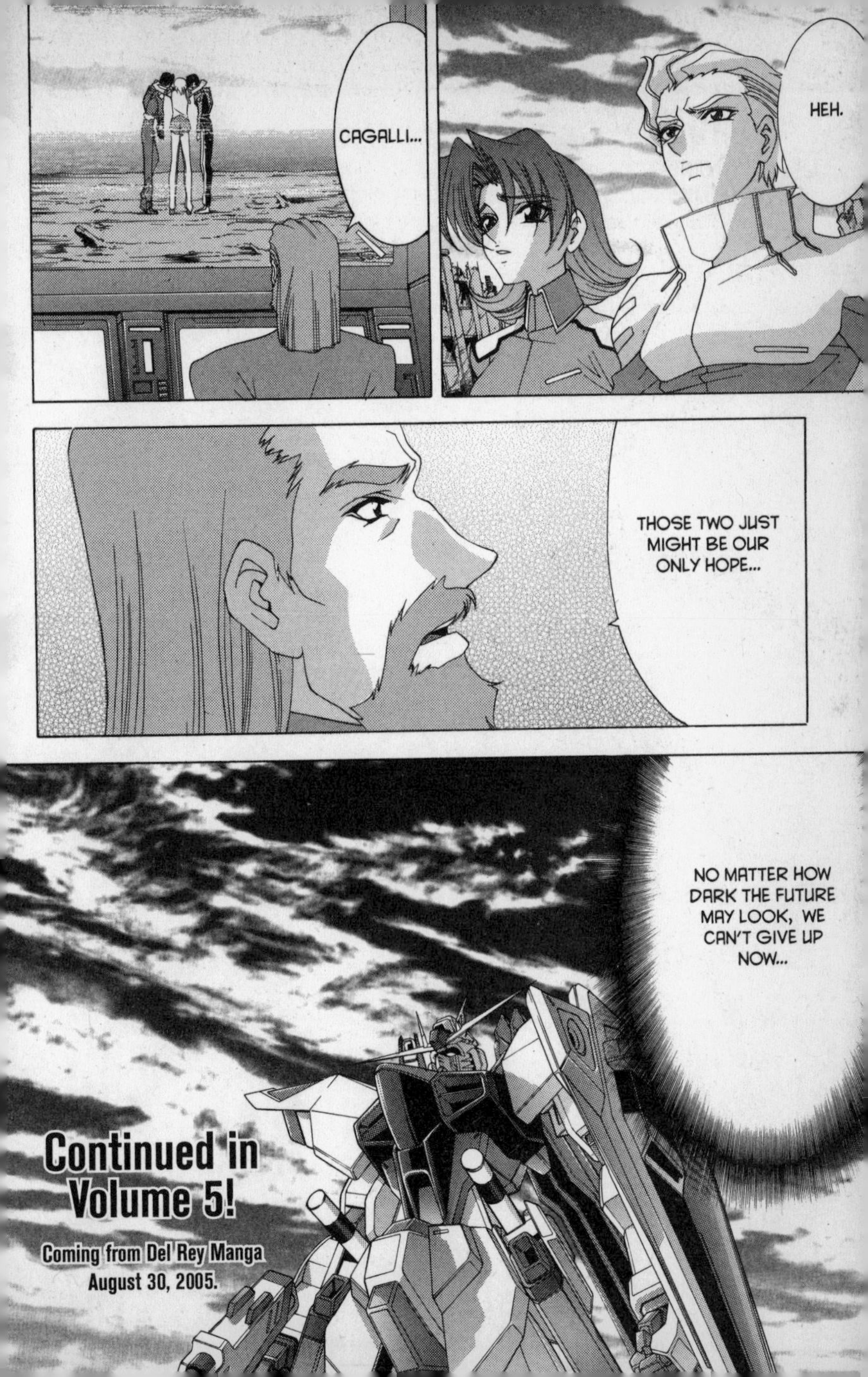
HEH.
CAGALLI...
THOSE TWO JUST MIGHT BE OUR ONLY HOPE...
NO MATTER HOW DARK THE FUTURE MAY LOOK, WE CAN'T GIVE UP NOW...
Continued in Volume 5!
Coming from Del Rey Manga August 30, 2005.

SEVERAL NEW MOBILE SUITS ARE INTRODUCED IN THIS VOLUME. HERE ARE THE DETAILS ON THE LATEST MOBILE SUITS.

# GUNDAM FREEDOM

A NEW ZAFT MOBILE SUIT THAT WAS DEVELOPED ALONG WITH GUNDAM JUSTICE. IT IMPLEMENTS THE TECHNOLOGY USED IN THE DESIGN OF THE GAT-X SERIES, WHICH WAS CAPTURED AT HELIOPOLIS. IT'S EQUIPPED WITH A NEUTRON JAMMER CANCELER, WHICH ALLOWS IT TO ENHANCE ITS POWER BY UTILIZING NUCLEAR ENERGY.

ZGMF-X10A

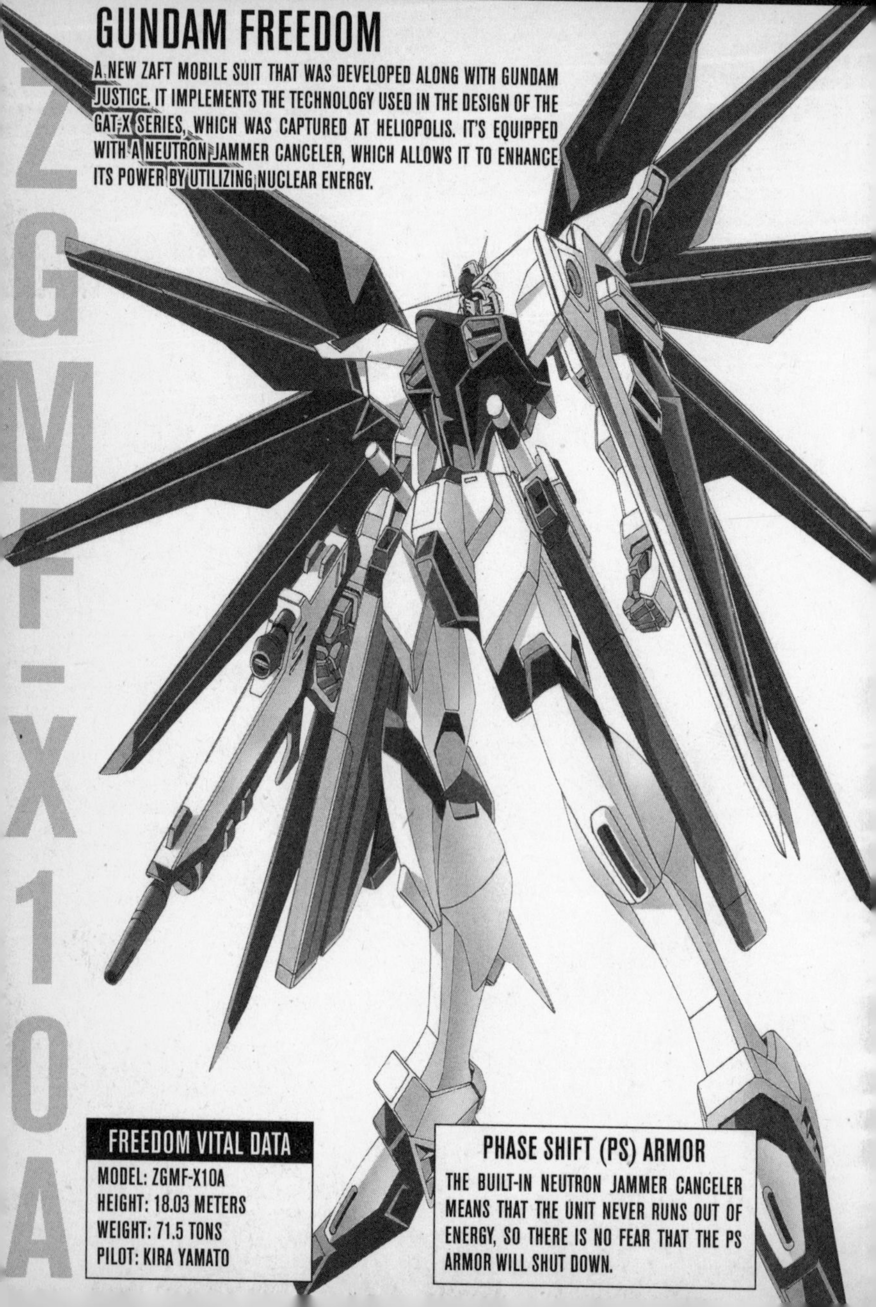

## FREEDOM VITAL DATA

MODEL: ZGMF-X10A
HEIGHT: 18.03 METERS
WEIGHT: 71.5 TONS
PILOT: KIRA YAMATO

## PHASE SHIFT (PS) ARMOR

THE BUILT-IN NEUTRON JAMMER CANCELER MEANS THAT THE UNIT NEVER RUNS OUT OF ENERGY, SO THERE IS NO FEAR THAT THE PS ARMOR WILL SHUT DOWN.

# ZGMF-X10A

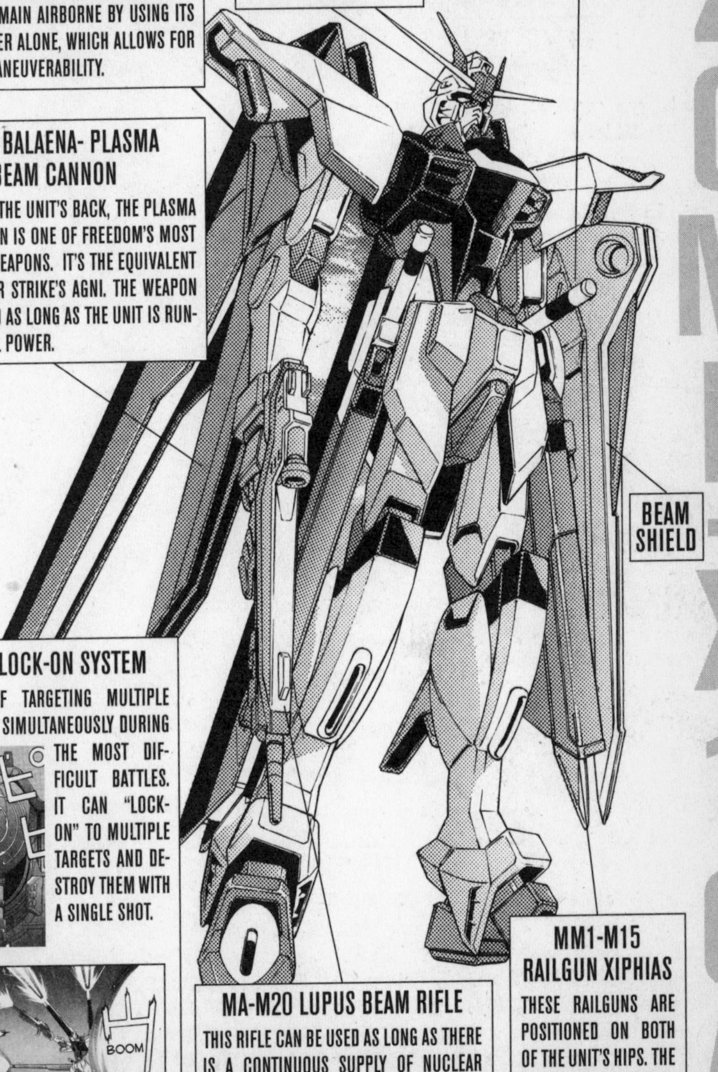

### HIGH MOBILE AERIAL TACTICS MODE (HIMAT MODE)

THE WINGS UNFOLD SO THAT THE UNIT CAN BE EASILY CONTROLLED WHILE AIRBORNE. IT CAN ALSO REMAIN AIRBORNE BY USING ITS THRUST POWER ALONE, WHICH ALLOWS FOR MAXIMUM MANEUVERABILITY.

### MM1-GAU2 PICUS76MM

SHORT-RANGE RAPID-FIRE DEFENSE MISSILES

### MA-M01 LACERTA BEAM SABER

MORE POWERFUL THAN PREVIOUS BEAM SABERS, THIS MODEL CAN HANDLE EXTENDED PERIODS OF USE.

### M100 BALAENA- PLASMA BEAM CANNON

LOCATED ON THE UNIT'S BACK, THE PLASMA BEAM CANNON IS ONE OF FREEDOM'S MOST POWERFUL WEAPONS. IT'S THE EQUIVALENT OF LAUNCHER STRIKE'S AGNI. THE WEAPON CAN BE FIRED AS LONG AS THE UNIT IS RUNNING AT FULL POWER.

### BEAM SHIELD

### MULTI LOCK-ON SYSTEM

CAPABLE OF TARGETING MULTIPLE OPPONENTS SIMULTANEOUSLY DURING THE MOST DIFFICULT BATTLES. IT CAN "LOCK-ON" TO MULTIPLE TARGETS AND DESTROY THEM WITH A SINGLE SHOT.

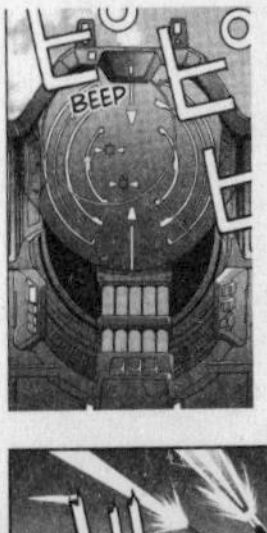
BEEP

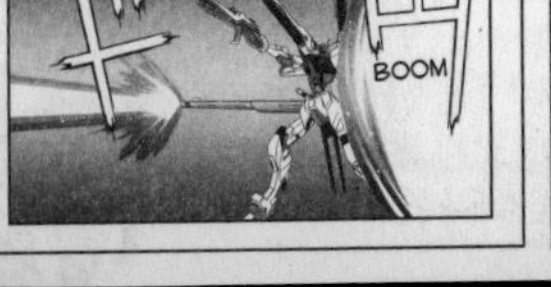
BOOM

### MA-M20 LUPUS BEAM RIFLE

THIS RIFLE CAN BE USED AS LONG AS THERE IS A CONTINUOUS SUPPLY OF NUCLEAR POWER. IT'S FAR MORE POWERFUL THAN PREVIOUS MODELS.

### MM1-M15 RAILGUN XIPHIAS

THESE RAILGUNS ARE POSITIONED ON BOTH OF THE UNIT'S HIPS. THE GUN HAS AN EXTREMELY WIDE RANGE.

# GUNDAM JUSTICE

ZGMF-X09A

THE ZAFT'S LATEST MOBILE SUIT. LIKE FREEDOM, IT WAS DESIGNED UTILIZING THE EARTH ALLIANCE'S GAT SERIES TECHNOLOGY. IT'S EQUIPPED WITH A NEUTRON JAMMER CANCELER. ITS ABILITY TO UTILIZE NUCLEAR POWER MEANS THAT IT PHASE SHIFT ARMOR NEVER SHUTS DOWN.

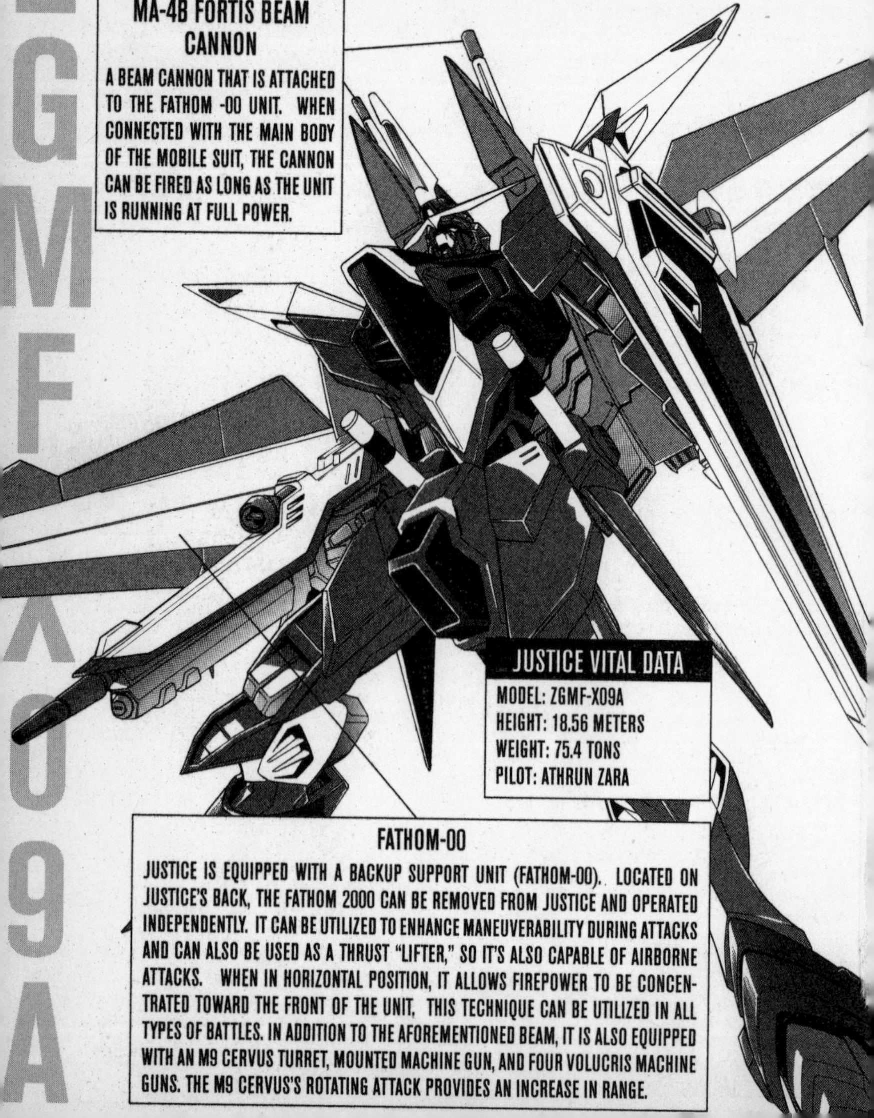

## MA-4B FORTIS BEAM CANNON

A BEAM CANNON THAT IS ATTACHED TO THE FATHOM -00 UNIT. WHEN CONNECTED WITH THE MAIN BODY OF THE MOBILE SUIT, THE CANNON CAN BE FIRED AS LONG AS THE UNIT IS RUNNING AT FULL POWER.

## JUSTICE VITAL DATA

MODEL: ZGMF-X09A
HEIGHT: 18.56 METERS
WEIGHT: 75.4 TONS
PILOT: ATHRUN ZARA

## FATHOM-00

JUSTICE IS EQUIPPED WITH A BACKUP SUPPORT UNIT (FATHOM-00). LOCATED ON JUSTICE'S BACK, THE FATHOM 2000 CAN BE REMOVED FROM JUSTICE AND OPERATED INDEPENDENTLY. IT CAN BE UTILIZED TO ENHANCE MANEUVERABILITY DURING ATTACKS AND CAN ALSO BE USED AS A THRUST "LIFTER," SO IT'S ALSO CAPABLE OF AIRBORNE ATTACKS. WHEN IN HORIZONTAL POSITION, IT ALLOWS FIREPOWER TO BE CONCENTRATED TOWARD THE FRONT OF THE UNIT, THIS TECHNIQUE CAN BE UTILIZED IN ALL TYPES OF BATTLES. IN ADDITION TO THE AFOREMENTIONED BEAM, IT IS ALSO EQUIPPED WITH AN M9 CERVUS TURRET, MOUNTED MACHINE GUN, AND FOUR VOLUCRIS MACHINE GUNS. THE M9 CERVUS'S ROTATING ATTACK PROVIDES AN INCREASE IN RANGE.

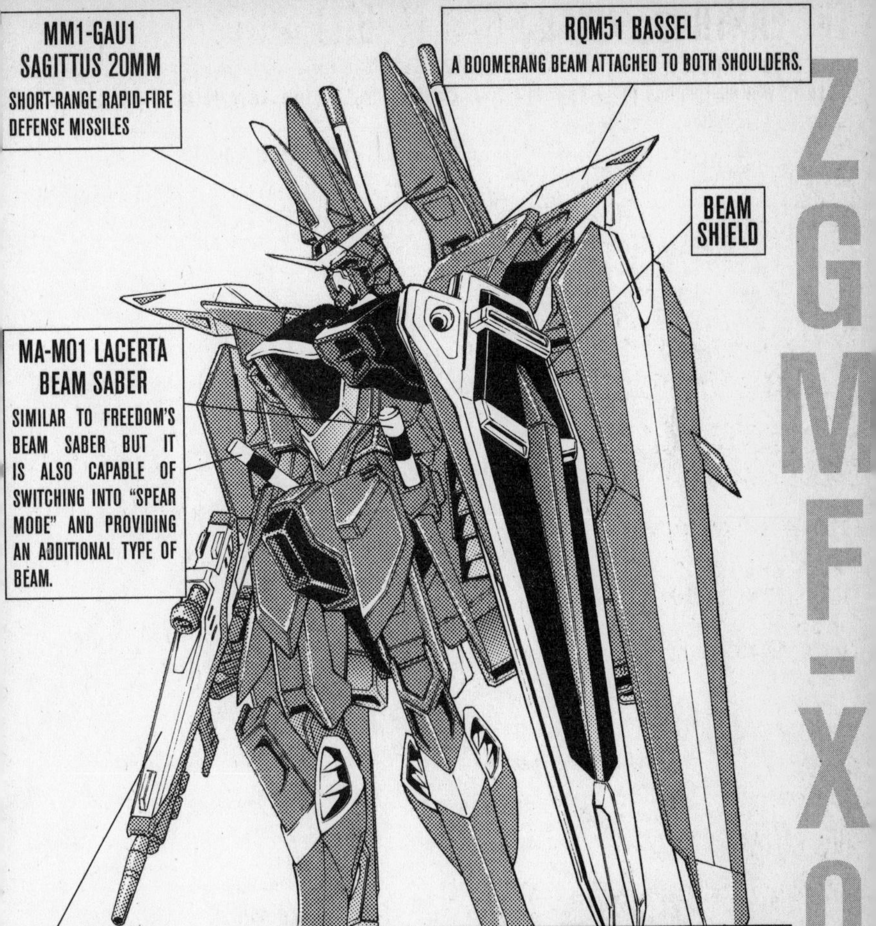
ZGMF-X09A
RQM51 BASSEL
A BOOMERANG BEAM ATTACHED TO BOTH SHOULDERS.
MM1-GAU1 SAGITTUS 20MM
SHORT-RANGE RAPID-FIRE DEFENSE MISSILES
BEAM SHIELD
MA-M01 LACERTA BEAM SABER
SIMILAR TO FREEDOM'S BEAM SABER BUT IT IS ALSO CAPABLE OF SWITCHING INTO "SPEAR MODE" AND PROVIDING AN ADDITIONAL TYPE OF BEAM.
MA-M20 BEAM RIFLE LUPUS
EQUIPPED WITH THE SAME BEAM RIFLE AS FREEDOM.

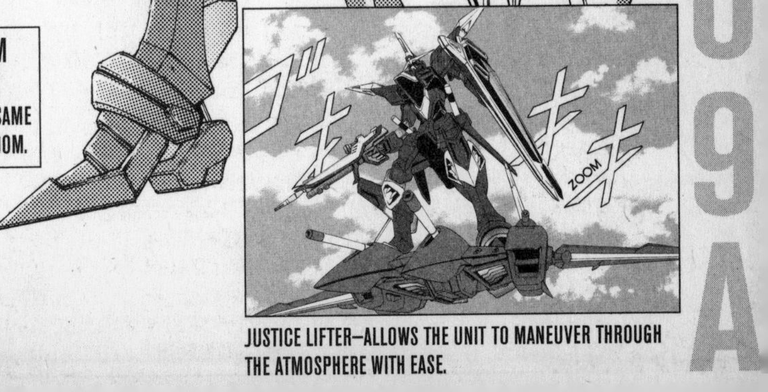
ZOOM

JUSTICE LIFTER—ALLOWS THE UNIT TO MANEUVER THROUGH THE ATMOSPHERE WITH EASE.

# THE EARTH ALLIANCE'S NEW MOBILE SUITS

THE PILOT'S OF THE EARTH ALLIANCE'S LATEST MOBILE SUITS ARE GIVEN PERFORMANCE-ENHANCING DRUGS, WHICH PROVIDE THE PILOTS WITH SUPERHUMAN REFLEXES AND TURN THEM INTO LIVING CPUS. THE NEW AND IMPROVED GAT SERIES.

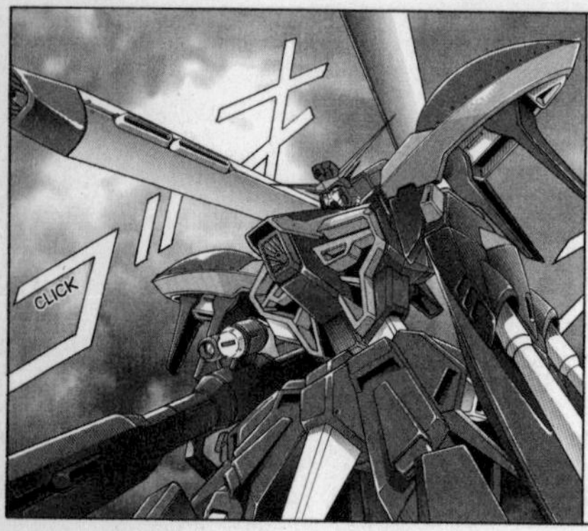
CLICK

## GAT-X131 GUNDAM CALAMITY

IT'S A NEW AND IMPROVED VERSION OF BUSTER (X-100 SERIES). A MOBILE SUIT DESIGNED FOR MAXIMUM FIREPOWER.

‹ STATS ›

HEIGHT: 18.26 METERS WEIGHT: 81.48 TONS

‹ WEAPONS ›

- 337MM PLASMA-SABOT BAZOOKA
- 580MM MULTI PHASE ENERGY CANNON (SCYLLA)
- 115MM DUAL RAM CANNON (KAEFER ZWEI)

PILOT: ORUGA SABNACK

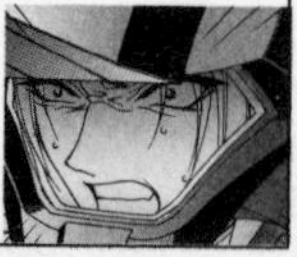

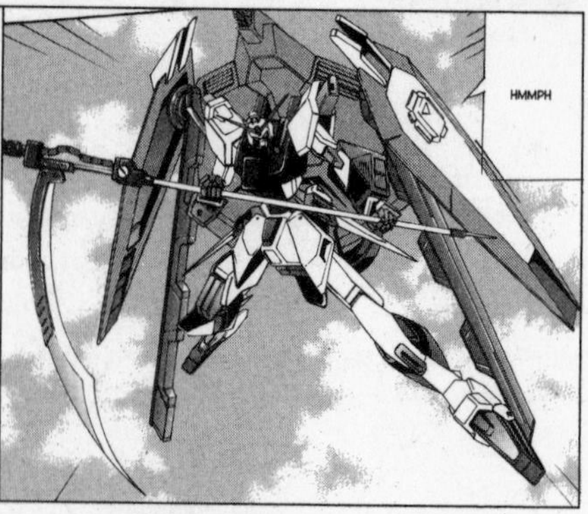
HMMPH

## GAT-X252 GUNDAM FORBIDDEN

ONE OF THE LATEST MODELS. IT WAS DEVELOPED FOR THE PURPOSE OF UTILIZING SPECIAL WEAPONRY.

‹ STATS ›

HEIGHT: 17.42 METERS WEIGHT: 85.33 TONS

‹ WEAPONS ›

- ENERGY DEFLECTION ARMOR (GESCHMEIDIG PANZER)
- HEAVY SCYTHE (NIDHOGGR)
- PLASMA INDUCTION CANNON (HRESVELGR)
- RAILGUN (ECKZAHN)

PILOT: SHANI ANDRAS

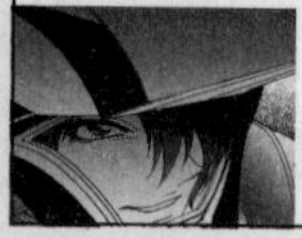

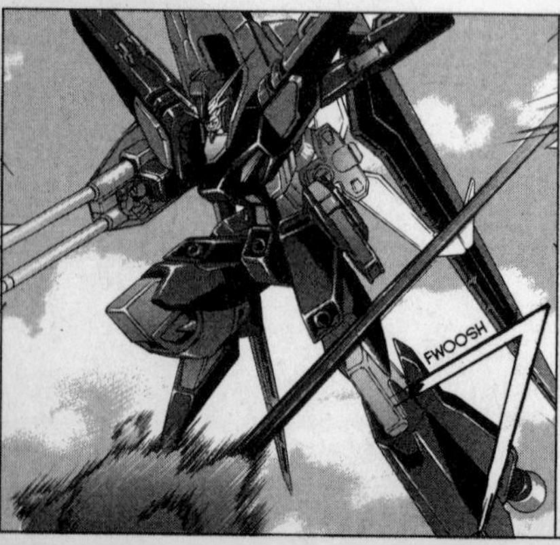
FWOOSH

## GAT-X370 GUNDAM RAIDER

BUILT WITH AN X-300 STYLE FRAME, WHICH ALLOWS IT TO TRANSFORM INTO AN MA. IT FLIES AROUND THE BATTLEFIELD, AND ATTACKS ITS ENEMIES AT CLOSE RANGE.

‹ STATS ›

HEIGHT: 17.94 METERS WEIGHT: 84.01 TONS.

‹ WEAPONS ›

- ENERGY CANNON (ZORN)
- HAMMER (MJOLLNIR)
- SHORT-RANGE PLASMA CANNON (AHURA MAZDA)
- 80MM MACHINE GUN M417

PILOT: CLOTHO BUER

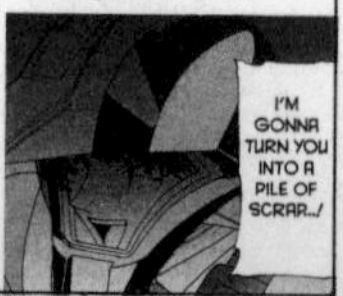
I'M GONNA TURN YOU INTO A PILE OF SCRAP..!

# About the Creators

## Yoshiyuki Tomino

Gundam was created by Yoshiyuki Tomino. Prior to Gundam, Tomino had worked on the original *Astro Boy* anime, as well as *Princess Knight* and *Brave Raideen*, among others. In 1979, he created and directed *Mobile Suit Gundam*, the very first in a long line of Gundam series. The show was not immediately popular and was forced to cut its number of episodes before going off the air, but as with the American show *Star Trek*, the fans still had something to say on the matter. By 1981, the demand for Gundam was so high that Tomino oversaw the re-release of the animation as three theatrical movies (a practice still common in Japan, and rarely if ever seen in the U.S.). It was now official: Gundam was a blockbuster.

Tomino would go on to direct many Gundam series, including *Gundam ZZ*, *Char's Counterattack*, *Gundam F91* and *Victory Gundam*, all of which contributed to the rich history of the vast Gundam universe. In addition to Gundam, Tomino created *Xabungle*, *L.Gaim*, *Dunbine*, and *Garzey's Wing*. His most recent anime is *Brain Powered*, which was released by Geneon in the United States.

## Masatsugu Iwase

Masatsugu Iwase writes and draws the manga adaptation of *Gundam SEED*. It is his first work published in the U.S. The manga creator is better known in Japan, however, for his work on *Calm Breaker*, a hilarious parody of anime, manga, and Japanese pop culture.

# On Names and Their Sources
By Mark Simmons

Freedom and Justice, Menelaos and Montgomery, Lesseps and Vesalius, Gottfried and Lohengrin; the world of *Mobile Suit Gundam SEED* is filled with allusions to human history, mythology, and philosophy. Each of the major players in *Gundam SEED*'s global conflict has its own approach to naming its weapons and warships, drawing on sources which span thousands of years of human civilization and several encyclopedia volumes.

These references aren't just there to impress the viewer, though. By exploring the real-world inspirations for the names used in this story, we can gain new insight into the ideology of the warring sides—and then impress our friends and acquaintances with our wide-ranging trivia knowledge!

## Gods, Kings, and Warriors

The Earth Alliance, creator of the Archangel and the original five Gundam prototypes, considers itself the defender of Earth's traditional civilization. Thus its space fleet includes vessels named Agamemnon, Menelaos, Seleukos, Ptolemaios, Xerxes, and Paris—all rulers of ancient kingdoms, some of whom may be familiar from the recent Hollywood epic *Troy*. The Alliance's warships also pay homage to famous military leaders, such as Argentina's Manuel Belgrano; Ramon Magsaysay of the Philippines; the American generals George Washington, Ulysses S. Grant, James Doolittle, and Colin Powell; and Britain's Winston Churchill and Bernard Law Montgomery. The Eurasian Federation, a junior partner in the Alliance, honors its Russian heritage by naming its naval vessels after medieval princes like Oleg, Yermak, Yaroslav, and Rurik.

The Alliance also invokes religion and mythology in naming its weapons. The prototype Gundams are armed with devices like the Agni and Shiva cannons, named for Hindu gods of fire and destruction; the Gleipnir grappling claw, after the magical chain of Norse mythology; and the Scylla energy cannon, whose monster namesake sank many a ship in the Greek legends. The Archangel

itself bears the name of one of the nine categories of angels recognized by medieval scholars, and its Lohengrin and Gottfried cannons pay homage to *Lohengrin,* Richard Wagner's operatic account of the search for the Holy Grail.

## Children of Science

ZAFT, whose Coordinator soldiers owe their very existence to science, uses its own vessels to honor those who have advanced human knowledge. This tradition began with the first Coordinator, the legendary George Glenn, who named his Jupiter exploration ship after rocketry pioneer Konstantin Tsiolkovsky. ZAFT's own spaceships follow suit, paying homage to the medieval anatomist Vesalius, the chemist Karl Ziegler, and the physicist George Gamow. Their terrestrial vessels, meanwhile, honor famous explorers; the land ships we see in the African desert are named after the diplomat Ferdinand de Lesseps and the Egyptologists William Flinders Petrie and Henry Carter, while the submarine carrier that becomes the mothership of ZAFT's captured Gundams is the namesake of oceanographer Jacques Cousteau.

The scientific Coordinator mindset also manifests itself in the heavy use of Latin. Even the PLANT settlements themselves are grouped into clusters named after the months of the Roman calendar—Januarius, Februarius, Martius, and so forth. Likewise, the weapons used by their mobile suits bear simple descriptive Latin names; the GINN's arsenal includes Canis (dog) and Pardus (panther) missile launchers, the Barrus (elephant) ion cannon, and the Cattus (cat) recoilless rifle, while the Freedom Gundam carries a Lupus (wolf) beam rifle, Lacerta (lizard) beam sabers, Picus (woodpecker) machine guns, Balaena (whale) plasma cannons, and Xiphias (swordfish) railguns.

## The Power of Belief

The third player in this conflict, the island kingdom of Aube, draws its inspiration from another island nation with a resolutely pacifist philosophy. Most of the technological marvels constructed by Aube bear names borrowed from Japanese mythology; the

mass driver Kaguya, which launches ships and cargo into orbit, is named after a legendary princess who ascended to the moon, and more such references will appear later in the story. Even Onogoro Island, where the Archangel finds safe harbor, has its namesake in Japanese legend. But in their religious beliefs, the people of Aube appear to favor the Hawaiian mother-goddess Haumea—perhaps understandably, since Aube relies on the geothermal energy produced by its many volcanoes, and Haumea is the mother of the volcano goddess Pele.

Where the people of Aube display a streak of mysticism, the warriors of ZAFT and the Earth Alliance seem to put their faith in scientific knowledge and the power of terrestrial civilization. But they too have their own cherished beliefs, as we see when ZAFT christens its new Gundams with the lofty names Freedom and Justice—concepts which are likely to outlive the transient fame of generals and scientists.

# Honorifics Explained

Throughout the Del Rey Manga books, you will find Japanese honorifics left intact in the translations. For those not familiar with how the Japanese use honorifics, and, more important, how they differ from American honorifics, we present this brief overview.

Politeness has always been a critical facet of Japanese culture. Ever since the feudal era, when Japan was a highly stratified society, use of honorifics—which can be defined as polite speech that indicates relationship or status—has played an essential role in the Japanese language. When addressing someone in Japanese, an honorific usually takes the form of a suffix attached to one's name (e.g. "Asuna-san"), as a title at the end of one's name, or in place of the name itself (e.g. "Negi-sensei" or simply "Sensei!").

Honorifics can be expressions of respect or endearment. In the context of manga and anime, honorifics give insight into the nature of the relationship between characters. Many translations into English leave out these important honorifics, and therefore distort the feel of the original Japanese. Because Japanese honorifics contain nuances that English honorifics lack, it is our policy at Del Rey not to translate them. Here, instead, is a guide to some of the honorifics you may encounter in Del Rey Manga.

-san:   This is the most common honorific and is equivalent to Mr., Miss, Ms., Mrs., etc. It is the all-purpose honorific and can be used in any situation where politeness is required.

-sama:  This is one level higher than -san. It is used to confer great respect.

-dono:  This comes from the word *tono*, which means *lord*. It is an even higher level than -sama and confers utmost respect.

-kun:   This suffix is used at the end of boys' names to express familiarity or endearment. It is also sometimes used by men among friends, or when addressing someone younger or of a lower station.

*-chan:*  This is used to express endearment, mostly toward girls. It is also used for little boys, pets, and between lovers. It gives a sense of childish cuteness.

*Bozu:*  This is an informal way to refer to a boy, similar to the English terms "kid" or "squirt."

*Sempai:*  This title suggests that the addressee is one's senior in a group or organization. It is most often used in a school setting, where underclassmen refer to their upperclassmen as *sempai.* It can also be used in the workplace, such as when a newer employee addresses an employee who has seniority in the company.

*Kohai:*  This is the opposite of *-sempai,* and is used toward underclassmen in school or newcomers in the workplace. It connotes that the addressee is of a lower station.

*Sensei:*  Literally meaning "one who has come before," this title is used for teachers, doctors, or masters of any profession or art.

*-[blank]:*  This is usually forgotten on these lists, but it's perhaps the most significant difference between Japanese and English. The lack of honorific means that the speaker has permission to address the person in a very intimate way. Usually, only family, spouses, or very close friends have this kind of license. Known as *yobisute,* it can be gratifying when someone who has earned the intimacy starts to call one by one's name without an honorific. But when that intimacy hasn't been earned, it can also be insulting.

# TOMARE!

## [STOP!]

You're going the wrong way!

Manga is a completely different type of reading experience.

To start at the *beginning*, go to the *end*!

That's right! Authentic manga is read the traditional Japanese way—from right to left. Exactly the *opposite* of how American books are read. It's easy to follow: Just go to the other end of the book, and read each page—and each panel—from right side to left side, starting at the top right. Now you're experiencing manga as it was meant to be.

*Gundam SEED*, Volume 4 is a work of fiction. Names, characters, places, and incidents are the products of the author's imagination or are used fictitiously. Any resemblance to actual events, locales, or persons, living or dead, is entirely coincidental.

2005 Del Rey Books Trade Paperback Edition



Published in the United States by Del Rey Books, an imprint of The Random House Publishing Group, a division of Random House, Inc., New York.

Del Rey is a registered trademark and the Del Rey colophon is a trademark of Random House, Inc.

Originally published in Japan by Kodansha Ltd., Tokyo.

Library of Congress Control Number can be obtained from the publisher upon request.

ISBN 0-345-47794-4

Printed in the United States of America

Del Rey Books website address: www.delreymanga.com

9 8 7 6 5 4 3 2 1

Lettered by Foltz Design

# MOBILE SUIT GUNDAM SEED

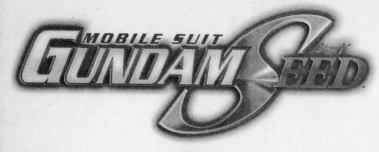

# 4

ART BY Masatsugu Iwase

ORIGINAL STORY BY
Hajime Yatate AND Yoshiyuki Tomino

TRANSLATED AND ADAPTED BY

vid Ury

TERED BY

z Design



DEL REY

BALLANTINE BOOKS • NEW YORK